D1588457

ma

Advanced Information and Knowledge Processing

Also in this series

Jason T.L. Wang, Mohammed J. Zaki,
Hannu T.T. Toivonen and Dennis Shasha (Eds)

Data Mining in Bioinformatics

With 110 Figures

 Springer

Jason T.L. Wang, PhD
New Jersey Institute of Technology, USA

Mohammed J. Zaki, PhD
Computer Science Department, Rensselaer Polytechnic Institute, USA

Hannu T.T. Toivonen, PhD
University of Helsinki and Nokia Research Center

Dennis Shasha, PhD
New York University, USA

Series Editors
Xindong Wu
Lakhmi Jain

British Library Cataloguing in Publication Data
Data mining in bioinformatics. — (Advanced information and
    knowledge processing)
    1. Data mining   2. Bioinformatics — Data processing
    I. Wang, Jason T. L.
    006.3'12
    ISBN 1852336714

Library of Congress Cataloging-in-Publication Data
A catalogue record for this book is available from the American Library of Congress.

AI&KP ISSN 1610-3947
ISBN 1-85233-671-4 Springer London Berlin Heidelberg
Springer Science+Business Media
springeronline.com

Typesetting: Electronic text files prepared by authors
Printed and bound in the United States of America
34/3830-543210   Printed on acid-free paper   SPIN 10003107

Contents

Contributors

Peter Bajcsy
Center for Supercomputing
    Applications
University of Illinois at
    Urbana-Champaign
USA

Deb Bardhan
Department of Computer Science
Rensselaer Polytechnic Institute
USA

Chris Bystroff
Department of Biology
Rensselaer Polytechnic Institute
USA

Mukund Deshpande
Oracle Corporation
USA

Cinzia Di Pietro
School of Medicine
University of Catania
Italy

Alfredo Ferro
Department of Mathematics and
    Computer Science
University of Catania
Italy

Laurie Jane Hammel
Department of Defense
USA

Jiawei Han
Department of Computer Science
University of Illinois at
    Urbana-Champaign
USA

Kai Huang
Department of Biological Sciences
Carnegie Mellon University
USA

Donald P. Huddler
Biophysics Research Division
University of Michigan
USA

George Karypis
Department of Computer Science
    and Engineering
University of Minnesota
USA

Michihiro Kuramochi
Department of Computer Science
    and Engineering
University of Minnesota
USA

Lei Liu
Center for Comparative
    and Functional Genomics
University of Illinois at
    Urbana-Champaign
USA

Heikki Mannila
Department of Computer Science
Helsinki University of Technology
Finland

Robert F. Murphy
Departments of Biological Sciences
    and Biomedical Engineering
Carnegie Mellon University
USA

Vinay Nadimpally
Department of Computer Science
Rensselaer Polytechnic Institute
USA

Päivi Onkamo
Department of Computer Science
University of Helsinki
Finland

Roderic D. M. Page
Division of Environmental
    and Evolutionary Biology
Institute of Biomedical and
    Life Sciences
University of Glasgow
United Kingdom

Jignesh M. Patel
Electrical Engineering and
    Computer Science Department
University of Michigan
USA

Giuseppe Pigola
Department of Mathematics and
    Computer Science
University of Catania
Italy

Alfredo Pulvirenti
Department of Mathematics and
    Computer Science
University of Catania
Italy

Michele Purrello
School of Medicine
University of Catania
Italy

Marco Ragusa
School of Medicine
University of Catania
Italy

Marko Salmenkivi
Department of Computer Science
University of Helsinki
Finland

Petteri Sevon
Department of Computer Science
University of Helsinki
Finland

Dennis Shasha
Courant Institute of Mathematical
    Sciences
New York University
USA

Ambuj K. Singh
Department of Computer Science
University of California at
    Santa Barbara
USA

Hannu T. T. Toivonen
Department of Computer Science
University of Helsinki
Finland

Jason T. L. Wang
Department of Computer Science
New Jersey Institute of Technology
USA

Jiong Yang
Department of Computer Science
University of Illinois at
    Urbana-Champaign
USA

Mohammed J. Zaki
Department of Computer Science
Rensselaer Polytechnic Institute
USA

Kaizhong Zhang
Department of Computer Science
University of Western Ontario
Canada

Part I

Overview

Chapter 1
Introduction to Data Mining in Bioinformatics

Jason T. L. Wang, Mohammed J. Zaki,
Hannu T. T. Toivonen, and Dennis Shasha

Summary

The aim of this book is to introduce the reader to some of the best techniques for data mining in bioinformatics in the hope that the reader will build on them to make new discoveries on his or her own. The book contains twelve chapters in four parts, namely, overview, sequence and structure alignment, biological data mining, and biological data management. This chapter provides an introduction to the field and describes how the chapters in the book relate to one another.

1.1 Background

Bioinformatics is the science of managing, mining, integrating, and interpreting information from biological data at the genomic, metabalomic, proteomic, phylogenetic, cellular, or whole organism levels. The need for bioinformatics tools and expertise has increased as genome sequencing projects have resulted in an exponential growth in complete and partial sequence databases. Even more data and complexity will result from the interaction among genes that gives rise to multiprotein functionality. Assembling the tree of life is intended to construct the phylogeny for the 1.7 million known species on earth. These and other projects require the development of new ways to interpret the flood of biological data that exists today and that is anticipated in the future.

Data mining or knowledge discovery from data (KDD), in its most fundamental form, is to extract interesting, nontrivial, implicit, previously unknown and potentially useful information from data [165]. In bioinformatics, this process could refer to finding motifs in sequences to predict folding patterns, to discover genetic mechanisms underlying a disease, to summarize clustering rules for multiple DNA or protein sequences, and so on. With the substantial growth of biological data, KDD will play a significant role in analyzing the data and in solving emerging problems.

The aim of this book is to introduce the reader to some of the best techniques for data mining in bioinformatics (BIOKDD) in the hope that the reader will build on them to make new discoveries on his or her own. This introductory chapter provides an overview of the work and how the chapters in the book relate to one another. We hope the reader finds the book and the chapters as fascinating to read as we have found them to write and edit.

1.2 Organization of the Book

This book is divided into four parts:

I. Overview
II. Sequence and Structure Alignment
III. Biological Data Mining
IV. Biological Data Management

Part I presents a primer on data mining for bioinformatics. Part II presents algorithms for sequence and structure alignment, which are crucial to effective biological data mining and information retrieval. Part III consists of chapters dedicated to biological data mining with topics ranging from genome modeling and gene mapping to protein and chemical mining. Part IV addresses closely related subjects, focusing on querying and indexing methods for biological data. Efficient indexing techniques can accelerate a mining process, thereby enhancing its overall performance. Table 1.1 summarizes the main theme of each chapter and the category it belongs to.

1.2.1 Part I: Basics

In chapter 2, Peter Bajcsy, Jiawei Han, Lei Liu, and Jiong Yang review data mining methods for biological data analysis. The authors first present methods for data cleaning, data preprocessing, and data integration. Next they show the applicability of data mining tools to the analysis of sequence, genome, structure, pathway, and microarray gene expression data. They then present techniques for the discovery of frequent sequence and structure patterns. The authors also review methods for classification and clustering in the context of microarrays and sequences and present approaches for the computational modeling of biological networks. Finally, they highlight visual data mining methods and conclude with a discussion of new research issues such as text mining and systems biology.

Table 1.1. Main theme addressed in each chapter.

Part I. Overview	
Chapter 1	Introduction
Chapter 2	Survey

Part II. Sequence and Structure Alignment	
Chapter 3	Multiple Sequence Alignment and Clustering
Chapter 4	RNA Structure Comparison

Part III. Biological Data Mining	
Chapter 5	Genome Modeling and Segmentation
Chapter 6	Gene Mapping
Chapter 7	Predicting Protein Folding Pathways
Chapter 8	Predicting Protein Subcellular Location
Chapter 9	Mining Chemical Compounds

Part IV. Biological Data Management	
Chapter 10	Phylogenetic Data Processing
Chapter 11	Protein Structure Querying
Chapter 12	Indexing Biological Data

1.2.2 Part II: Sequence and Structure Alignment

In chapter 3, by exploiting a simple and natural algorithmic technique based on randomized tournaments, C. Di Pietro and coauthors propose to use a structure they call an antipole tree to align multiple sequences in a bottom-up way along the tree structure. Their approach achieves a better running time with equivalent alignment quality when compared with the widely used multiple sequence alignment tool ClustalW. The authors conducted a case study on *Xenopus laevis* SOD2 sequences, and their experimental results indicated the excellent performance of the proposed approach. This approach could be particularly significant for large-scale clustering.

In chapter 4, Kaizhong Zhang examines algorithms for comparing RNA structures based on various models ranging from simple edit operations to their extensions with gap penalty as well as with base-pair bond breaking. Besides its major role as a template for proteins, RNA plays a significant role in regulating the functions of several viruses such as HIV. Comparing RNA structures may help one to understand their functions and hence the cause of some virus-related diseases. Other applications of the algorithms include using them to align or cluster RNA structures and to predict the secondary or tertiary structure from a given RNA sequence.

1.2.3 Part III: Biological Data Mining

In chapter 5, Marko Salmenkivi and Heikki Mannila discuss segmentation of sequential data, e.g., DNA sequences, to internally homogeneous segments. They first describe a domain-independent segmentation framework, which is based on a Bayesian model of piecewise constant functions. They then show how the posterior distributions from such models can be approximated by reversible jump Markov chain Monte Carlo methods. The authors proceed to illustrate the application of the methodology to modeling the GC content and distribution of occurrences of open reading frames (ORFs) and single-nucleotide polymorphisms (SNPs) along the human genome. Their results show how the simple models can be extended by modeling the influence of the GC content on the intensity of ORF occurrence.

In chapter 6, Petteri Sevon, Hannu Toivonen, and Paivi Onkamo present a data mining approach to gene mapping, coined haplotype pattern mining (HPM). The framework is based on finding patterns of genetic markers (e.g., single-nucleotide polymorphisms, or SNPs) that are associated with a disease and that are thus likely to occur close to the disease susceptibility gene. The authors first describe an abstract algorithm for the task. Then they show how to predict a gene location based on marker patterns and how to analyze the statistical significance of the results. Finally they present and evaluate three different instances of the algorithm for different gene mapping problems. Experimental results demonstrate the power and the flexibility of their approach.

In chapter 7, Mohammed Zaki, Vinay Nadimpally, Deb Bardhan, and Chris Bystroff present one of the first works to predict protein folding pathways. A folding pathway is the time-ordered sequence of folding events that leads from a given amino acid sequence to its given three-dimensional structure. The authors approach this problem by trying to learn how to "unfold" the protein in a time-ordered sequence of steps, using techniques borrowed from graph theory. The reversal of the obtained sequence could be a plausible protein folding pathway. Experimental results on several proteins for which there are known intermediate stages in the folding pathway demonstrate the usefulness of the proposed approach. Potential applications of this work include enhancing structure prediction methods as well as better understanding some diseases caused by protein misfolding.

In chapter 8, Kai Huang and Robert Murphy provide a comprehensive account of methods and features for the prediction of protein subcellular location. Location gives insight into protein function inside the cell. For example, a protein localized in mitochondria may mean that this protein is involved in energy metabolism. Proteins localized in the cytoskeleton are probably involved in intracellular signaling and support. The authors describe the acquisition of protein fluorescence microscope images for the study. They then discuss the construction and selection of subcellular location features and introduce different feature sets. The feature sets are then used and compared in protein classification and clustering tasks with various machine learning methods.

In chapter 9, Mukund Deshpande, Michihiro Kuramochi, and George Karypis present a structure-based approach for mining chemical compounds.

The authors tackle the problem of classifying chemical compounds by automatically mining geometric and topological substructure-based features. Once features have been found, they use feature selection and construct a classification model based on support vector machines. The key step for substructure mining relies on an efficient subgraph discovery algorithm. When compared with the well-known graph mining tool SUBDUE, the authors' technique is often faster in substructure discovery and achieves better classification performance.

1.2.4 Part IV: Biological Data Management

Querying biological databases is more than just a matter of returning a few records. The data returned must be visualized and summarized to help practicing bench biologists. In chapter 10, Roderic Page explores some of the data querying and visualization issues posted by phylogenetic databases. In particular the author discusses taxonomic names, supertrees, and navigating phylogenies and reviews several phylogenetic query languages, some of which are extensions of the relational query language SQL. The author also lists some prototypes that implemented the described ideas to some extent and indicates the need for having an integrated package suitable for the phyloinformatics community.

In chapter 11, Jignesh Patel, Donald Huddler, and Laurie Hammel propose a protein search tool based on secondary structure. The authors define an intuitive, declarative query language, which enables one to use his or her own definition of secondary structure similarity. They identify different algorithms for the efficient evaluation of the queries. They then develop a query optimization framework for their language. The techniques have been implemented in a system called Periscope, whose applications are illustrated in the chapter.

In chapter 12, Ambuj Singh presents highly scalable indexing schemes for searching biological sequences, structures, and metabolic pathways. The author first reviews the current work for sequence indexing and presents the new MAP (match table-based pruning) scheme, which achieves two orders of magnitude faster processing than BLAST while preserving the output quality. Similarly, the author gives an overview and a new indexing scheme (PSI) for searching protein structures. Finally, the author discusses in detail indexing approaches for comparative and integrative analysis of biological pathways, presenting methods for structural comparison of pathways as well as the analysis of time variant and invariant properties of pathways. While fast search mechanisms are desirable, as the author points out, the quality of search results is equally important. In-depth comparison of the results returned by the new indexing methods with those from the widely used tools such as BLAST is a main subject of future research.

1.3 Support on the Web

This book's homepage is

`http://web.njit.edu/~wangj/publications/biokdd.html`

This page provides up-to-date information and corrections of errors found in the book. It also provides links to data mining and management tools and some major biological data mining centers around the world.

Acknowledgments

This book is the result of a three-year effort. We thank the contributing authors for meeting the stringent deadlines and for helping to compile and define the terms in the glossary. Many ideas in the book benefit from discussions with speakers and attendants in BIOKDD meetings, specifically Charles Elkan, Sorin Istrail, Steven Salzberg, and Bruce Shapiro. We also thank Sen Zhang for assisting us with LaTeXsoftware and other issues in the preparation of the camera-ready copy for this book.

The U.S. National Science Foundation and other agencies have generously supported this interdisciplinary field in general and much of the work presented here in particular.

Beverley Ford at Springer-Verlag, London, was a wonderfully supportive editor, giving advice on presentation and approach. Stephen Bailey, Rosie Kemp, Tony King, Rebecca Mowat, and Mary Ondrusz gave useful suggestions at different stages of book preparation. Allan Abrams and Frank McGuckin at Springer-Verlag, New York, provided valuable guidance during the production process. Finally, a special thanks to Catherine Drury and Penelope Hull for their thoughtful comments on drafts of the book that improved its format and content. We are to blame for any remaining problems.

Chapter 2
Survey of Biodata Analysis
from a Data Mining Perspective

Peter Bajcsy, Jiawei Han, Lei Liu, and Jiong Yang

Summary

Recent progress in biology, medical science, bioinformatics, and biotechnology has led to the accumulation of tremendous amounts of biodata that demands in-depth analysis. On the other hand, recent progress in data mining research has led to the development of numerous efficient and scalable methods for mining interesting patterns in large databases. The question becomes how to bridge the two fields, *data mining* and *bioinformatics*, for successful mining of biological data. In this chapter, we present an overview of the data mining methods that help biodata analysis. Moreover, we outline some research problems that may motivate the further development of data mining tools for the analysis of various kinds of biological data.

2.1 Introduction

In the past two decades we have witnessed revolutionary changes in biomedical research and biotechnology and an explosive growth of biomedical data, ranging from those collected in pharmaceutical studies and cancer therapy investigations to those identified in genomics and proteomics research by discovering sequential patterns, gene functions, and protein-protein interactions. The rapid progress of biotechnology and biodata analysis methods has led to the emergence and fast growth of a promising new field: *bioinformatics*. On the other hand, recent progress in data mining research has led to the development of numerous efficient and scalable methods for mining interesting patterns and knowledge in large databases, ranging from efficient classification methods to clustering, outlier analysis, frequent, sequential, and structured pattern analysis methods, and visualization and spatial/temporal data analysis tools.

The question becomes how to bridge the two fields, *data mining* and *bioinformatics*, for successful data mining of biological data. In this chapter, we present a general overview of data mining methods that have been successfully applied to biodata analysis. Moreover, we analyze how data mining has helped efficient and effective biomedical data analysis and outline some research problems that may motivate the further development of powerful data mining tools in this field. Our overview is focused on three major themes: (1) data cleaning, data preprocessing, and semantic integration of heterogeneous, distributed biomedical databases, (2) exploration of existing data mining tools for biodata analysis, and (3) development of advanced, effective, and scalable data mining methods in biodata analysis.

- **Data cleaning, data preprocessing, and semantic integration of heterogeneous, distributed biomedical databases**

  Due to the highly distributed, uncontrolled generation and use of a wide variety of biomedical data, data cleaning, data preprocessing, and the semantic integration of heterogeneous and widely distributed biomedical databases, such as genome databases and proteome databases, have become important tasks for systematic and coordinated analysis of biomedical databases. This highly distributed, uncontrolled generation of data has promoted the research and development of integrated data warehouses and distributed federated databases to store and manage different forms of biomedical and genetic data. Data cleaning and data integration methods developed in data mining, such as those suggested in [92, 327], will help the integration of biomedical data and the construction of data warehouses for biomedical data analysis.

- **Exploration of existing data mining tools for biodata analysis**

  With years of research and development, there have been many data mining, machine learning, and statistics analysis systems and tools available for general data analysis. They can be used in biodata exploration and analysis. Comprehensive surveys and introduction of data mining methods have been compiled into many textbooks, such as [165, 171, 431]. Analysis principles are also introduced in many textbooks on bioinformatics, such as [28, 34, 110, 116, 248]. General data mining and data analysis systems that can be used for biodata analysis include SAS Enterprise Miner, SPSS, SPlus, IBM Intelligent Miner, Microsoft SQLServer 2000, SGI MineSet, and Inxight VizServer. There are also many biospecific data analysis software systems, such as GeneSpring, Spot Fire, and VectorNTI. These tools are rapidly evolving as well. A lot of routine data analysis work can be done using such tools. For biodata analysis, it is important to train researchers to master and explore the power of these well-tested and popular data mining tools and packages.

With sophisticated biodata analysis tasks, there is much room for research and development of advanced, effective, and scalable data mining methods in biodata analysis. Some interesting topics follow.

1. **Analysis of frequent patterns, sequential patterns and structured patterns: identification of cooccurring or correlated biosequences or biostructure patterns**

   Many studies have focused on the comparison of one gene with another. However, most diseases are not triggered by a single gene but by a combination of genes acting together. Association and correlation analysis methods can be used to help determine the kinds of genes or proteins that are likely to cooccur in target samples. Such analysis would facilitate the discovery of groups of genes or proteins and the study of interactions and relationships among them. Moreover, since biodata usually contains noise or nonperfect matches, it is important to develop effective sequential or structural pattern mining algorithms in the noisy environment [443].

2. **Effective classification and comparison of biodata**

   A critical problems in biodata analysis is to classify biosequences or structures based on their critical features and functions. For example, gene sequences isolated from diseased and healthy tissues can be compared to identify critical differences between the two classes of genes. Such features can be used for classifying biodata and predicting behaviors. A lot of methods have been developed for biodata classification [171]. For example, one can first retrieve the gene sequences from the two tissue classes and then find and compare the frequently occurring patterns of each class. Usually, sequences occurring more frequently in the diseased samples than in the healthy samples indicate the genetic factors of the disease; on the other hand, those occurring only more frequently in the healthy samples might indicate mechanisms that protect the body from the disease. Similar analysis can be performed on microarray data and protein data to identify similar and dissimilar patterns.

3. **Various kinds of cluster analysis methods**

   Most cluster analysis algorithms are based on either Euclidean distances or density [165]. However, biodata often consist of a lot of features that form a high-dimensional space. It is crucial to study differentials with scaling and shifting factors in multidimensional space, discover pairwise frequent patterns and cluster biodata based on such frequent patterns. One interesting study using microarray data as examples can be found in [421].

4. **Computational modeling of biological networks**

   While a group of genes/proteins may contribute to a disease process, different genes/proteins may become active at different stages of the disease. These genes/proteins interact in a complex network. Large amounts of data generated from microarray and proteomics studies provide rich resources for theoretic study of the complex biological system by computational modeling of biological networks. If the sequence of genetic activities across the different stages of disease development can be identified, it may be possible to develop pharmaceutical interventions that target the different stages separately, therefore achieving more effective treatment of the disease. Such path analysis is expected to play an important role in genetic studies.

5. **Data visualization and visual data mining**

   Complex structures and sequencing patterns of genes and proteins are most effectively presented in graphs, trees, cubes, and chains by various kinds of visualization tools. Visually appealing structures and patterns facilitate pattern understanding, knowledge discovery, and interactive data exploration. Visualization and visual data mining therefore play an important role in biomedical data mining.

2.2 Data Cleaning, Data Preprocessing, and Data Integration

Biomedical data are currently generated at a very high rate at multiple geographically remote locations with a variety of biomedical devices and by applying several data acquisition techniques. All bioexperiments are driven by a plethora of experimental design hypotheses to be proven or rejected based on data values stored in multiple distributed biomedical databases, for example, genome or proteome databases. To extract and analyze the data perhaps poses a much bigger challenge for researchers than to generate the data [181]. To extract and analyze information from distributed biomedical databases, distributed heterogeneous data must be gathered, characterized, and cleaned. These processing steps can be very time-consuming if they require multiple scans of large distributed databases to ensure the data quality defined by biomedical domain experts and computer scientists. From a semantic integration viewpoint, there are quite often challenges due to the heterogeneous and distributed nature of data since these preprocessing steps might require the data to be transformed (e.g., log ratio transformations), linked with distributed annotation or metadata files (e.g., microarray spots and gene descriptions), or more exactly specified using auxiliary programs running on a remote server (e.g., using one of the BLAST programs to identify a sequence match). Based on the aforementioned data quality and integration issues, the need for using automated preprocessing techniques becomes eminent. We briefly outline the strategies for taming the data by describing data cleaning using exploratory data mining (EDM), data preprocessing, and semantic integration techniques [91, 165].

2.2.1 Data Cleaning

Data cleaning is defined as a preprocessing step that ensures data quality. In general, the meaning of data quality is best described by the data interpretability. In other words, if the data do not mean what one thinks, the data quality is questionable and should be evaluated by applying data quality metrics. However, defining data quality metrics requires understanding of data gathering, delivery, storage, integration, retrieval, mining, and analysis. Data quality problems can occur in any data operation step (also denoted as a lifecycle of the data) and their corresponding data quality continuum (end-to-end data quality). Although conventional definitions of data quality would include accuracy, completeness, uniqueness, timeliness, and consistency, it is very hard to quantify data quality by using quality metrics. For example, measuring accuracy and completeness is very difficult because each datum would have to be tested for its correctness against the "true" value and all data values would have to be assessed against all relevant data values. Furthermore, data quality metrics should measure data interpretability by evaluating meanings of variables, relationships between variables, miscellaneous metadata information and consistency of data.

In the biomedical domain, the data quality continuum involves answering a few basic questions.

1. How do the data enter the system? The answers can vary a lot because new biomedical technologies introduce varying measurement errors and there are no standards for data file formats. Thus, the standardization efforts are important for data quality, for instance, the Minimum Information About a Microarray Experiment (MIAME) [51] and MicroArray and Gene Expression (MAGE) [381] standardization efforts for microarray processing, as well as, preemptive (process management) and retrospective (cleaning and diagnostic) data quality checks.
2. How are the data delivered? In the world of electronic information and wireless data transfers, data quality issues include transmission losses, buffer overflows, and inappropriate preprocessing, such as default value conversions or data aggregations. These data quality issues have to be addressed by verifying checksums or relationships between data streams and by using reliable transmission protocols.
3. Where do the data go after being received? Although physical storage may not be an issue anymore due to its low cost, data storage can encounter problems with poor accompanying metadata, missing

time stamps, or hardware and software constraints, for instance, data dissemination in Excel spread sheets stored on an Excel-unsupported platform. The solution is frequently thorough planning followed by publishing data specifications.

4. Are the data combined with other data sets? The integration of new data sets with already archived data sets is a challenge from the data quality viewpoint since the data might be heterogeneous (no common keys) with different variable definitions of data structures (e.g., legacy data and federated data) and time asynchronous. In the data mining domain, a significant number of research papers have addressed the issue of dataset integrations, and the proposed solutions involve several matching and mapping approaches. In the biomedical domain, data integration becomes essential, although very complex, for understanding a whole system. Data are generated by multiple laboratories with various devices and data acquisition techniques while investigating a broad range of hypotheses at multiple levels of system ontology.

5. How are the data retrieved? The answers to this question should be constructed with respect to the computational resources and users' needs. Retrieved data quality will be constrained by the retrieved data size, access speed, network traffic, data and database software compatibility, and the type and correctness of queries. To ensure data quality, one has to plan ahead to minimize the constraints and select appropriate tools for data browsing and exploratory data mining (EDM) [92, 327].

6. How are the data analyzed? In the final processing phase, data quality issues arise due to insufficient biomedical domain expertise, inherent data variability, and lack of algorithmic scalability for large datasets [136]. As a solution, any data mining and analysis should be an interdisciplinary effort because the computer science models and biomedical models have to come together during exploratory types of analyses [323]. Furthermore, conducting continuous analyses and cross-validation experiments will lead to confidence bounds on obtained results and should be used in a feedback loop to monitor the inherent data variability and detect related data quality problems.

The steps of microarray processing from start to finish that clearly map to the data quality continuum are outlined in [181].

2.2.2 Data Preprocessing

What can be done to ensure biomedical data quality and eliminate sources of data quality corruption for both data warehousing and data mining? In general, multidisciplinary efforts are needed, including (1) process management, (2) documentation of biomedical domain expertise, and (3) statistical and database analyses [91]. Process management in the biomedical domain should support standardization of content and format [51, 381], automation of preprocessing, e.g., microarray spot analysis [26, 28, 150], introduction of data quality incentives (correct data entries and quality feedback loops), and data publishing to obtain feedback (e.g., via MedLine and other Internet sites). Documenting biomedical domain knowledge is not a trivial task and requires establishing metadata standards (e.g., a document exchange format MAGE-ML), creating annotation files, and converting biomedical and engineering logs into metadata files that accompany every experiment and its output data set. It is also necessary to develop text-mining software to browse all documented and stored files [439]. In terms of statistical and database analyses for the biomedical domain, the focus should be on quantitative quality metrics based on analytical and statistical data descriptors and on relationships among variables.

Data preprocessing using statistical and database analyses usually includes data cleaning, integration, transformation, and reduction [165]. For example, an outcome of several spotted DNA microarray experiments might be ambiguous (e.g., a background intensity is larger than a foreground intensity) and the missing values have to be filled in or replaced by a common default value during data cleaning. The integration of multiple microarray gene experiments has to resolve inconsistent labels of genes to form a coherent data store. Mining microarray experimental data might require data normalization (transformation) with respect to the same control gene and a selection of a subset of treatments (data reduction), for instance, if the data dimensionality is prohibitive for further analyses. Every data preprocessing step should include static and dynamic constraints, such as foreign key constraints, variable bounds defined by dynamic ranges of measurement devices, or experimental data acquisition and processing workflow constraints. Due to the multifaceted nature of biomedical data measuring complex and context-dependent biomedical systems, there is no single recommended data quality metric. However, any metric should serve operational or diagnostic purpose and should change regularly with the improvement of data quality. For example, the data quality metrics for extracted spot information can be clearly defined in the case of raw DNA microarray data (images) and should depend on (a) spot to background separation and (b) spatial and topological variations of spots. Similarly, data quality metrics can be defined at other processing stages of biomedical data using outlier detection (geometric, distributional, and time series outliers), model fitting, statistical goodness of fit, database duplicate finding, and data type checks and data value constraints.

2.2.3 Semantic Integration of Heterogeneous Data

One of the many complex aspects in biomedical data mining is semantic integration. Semantic integration combines multiple sources into a coherent data store and involves finding semantically equivalent real-world entities from several biomedical sources to be matched up. The problem arises when, for instance, the same entities do not have identical labels, such as, gene_id and g_id, or are time asynchronous, as in the case of the same gene being analyzed at multiple developmental stages. There is a theoretical foundation [165] for approaching this problem by using correlation analysis in a general case. Nonetheless, semantic integration of biomedical data is still an open problem due to the complexity of the studied matter (bioontology) and the heterogeneous distributed nature of the recorded high-dimensional data.

Currently, there are in general two approaches: (1) construction of *integrated* biodata warehouses or biodatabases and (2) construction of a *federation* of heterogeneous distributed biodatabases so that query processing or search can be performed in multiple heterogeneous biodatabases. The first approach performs data integration beforehand by data cleaning, data preprocessing, and data integration, which requires common ontology and terminology and sophisticated data mapping rules to resolve semantic ambiguity or inconsistency. The integrated data warehouses or databases are often multidimensional in nature, and indexing or other data structures can be built to assist a search in multiple lower-dimensional spaces. The second approach is to build up mapping rules or semantic ambiguity resolution rules across multiple databases. A query posed at one site can then be properly mapped to another site to retrieve the data needed. The retrieved results can be appropriately mapped back to the query site so that the answer can be understood with the terminology used at the query site. Although a substantial amount of work has been done in the field of database systems [137], there are not enough studies of systems in the domain of bioinformatics, partly due to the complexity and semantic heterogeneity of biodata. We believe this is an important direction of future research.

2.3 Exploration of Existing Data Mining Tools for Biodata Analysis

With years of research and development, there have been many data mining, machine learning, and statistical analysis systems and tools available for use in biodata exploration and analysis. Comprehensive surveys and the introduction of data mining methods have been compiled into many textbooks [165, 171, 258, 281, 431]. There are also many textbooks focusing exclusively on bioinformatics [28, 34, 110, 116, 248]. Based on the theoretical descriptions of data mining methods, many general data mining and data analysis systems have been built and widely used for necessary analyses of biodata, e.g., SAS Enterprise Miner, SPSS, SPlus, IBM Intelligent Miner, Microsoft SQLServer 2000, SGI MineSet, and Inxight VizServer. In this section, we briefly summarize the different types of existing software tools developed specifically for solving the fundamental bioinformatics problems. Tables 2.1 and 2.2 provide a list of a few software tools and their Web links.

Table 2.1. Partial list of bioinformatics tools and software links. These tools were chosen based on authors' familiarity. We recognize that there are many other popular tools.

Sequence analysis
NCBI/BLAST:
http://www.ncbi.nih.gov/BLAST
ClustalW (multi-sequence alignment):
http://www.ebi.ac.uk/clustalw/
HMMER:
http://hmmer.wustl.edu/
PHYLIP:
http://evolution.genetics.washington.edu/phylip.html
MEME (motif discovery and search):
http://meme.sdsc.edu/meme/website/
TRANSFAC:
http://www.cbrc.jp/research/db/TFSEARCH.html
MDScan:
http://bioprospector.stanford.edu/MDscan/
VectorNTI:
http://www.informax.com
Sequencher:
http://www.genecodes.com/
MacVector:
http://www.accelrys.com/products/macvector/

Structure prediction and visualization
RasMol:
http://openrasmol.org/
Raster3D:
http://www.bmsc.washington.edu/raster3d/raster3d.html
Swiss-Model:
http://www.expasy.org/swissmod/
Scope:
http://scop.mrc-lmb.cam.ac.uk/scop/
MolScript:
http://www.avatar.se/molscript/
Cn3D:
http://www.ncbi.nlm.nih.gov/Structure/CN3D/cn3d.shtml

2.3.1 DNA and Protein Sequence Analysis

Sequence comparison, similarity search, and pattern finding are considered the basic approaches to protein sequence analysis in bioinformatics. The mathematical theory and basic algorithms of sequence analysis can be dated to 1960s when the pioneers of bioinformatics developed methods to predict phylogenetic relationships of the related protein sequences during evolution [281]. Since then, many statistical models, algorithms, and computation techniques have been applied to protein and DNA sequence analysis.

Table 2.2. Partial list of bioinformatics tools and software links.

Genome analysis
PHRED/PHRAP:
http://www.phrap.org/
CAP3:
http://deepc2.zool.iastate.edu/aat/cap/cap.html
Paracel GenomeAssembler:
http://www.paracel.com/products/paracel_genomeassembler.php
GenomeScan:
http://genes.mit.edu/genomescan.html
GeneMark:
http://opal.biology.gatech.edu/GeneMark/
GenScan:
http://genes.mit.edu/GENSCAN.html
X-Grail:
http://compbio.ornl.gov/Grail-1.3/
ORF Finder:
http://www.ncbi.nlm.nih.gov/gorf/gorf.html
GeneBuilder:
http://l25.itba.mi.cnr.it/ webgene/genebuilder.html

Pathway analysis and visualization
KEGG:
http://www.genome.ad.jp/kegg/
EcoCyc/MetaCyc:
http://metacyc.org/
GenMapp:
http://www.genmapp.org/

Microarray analysis
ScanAlyze/Cluster/TreeView:
http://rana.lbl.gov/EisenSoftware.htm
Scanalytics: MicroArray Suite:
http://www.scanalytics.com/product/microarray/index.shtmlExpression
Profiler (Jaak Vilo, EBI):
http://ep.ebi.ac.uk/EP/
Knowledge-based analysis of microarray gene expression data using SVM:
http://www.cse.ucsc.edu/research/compbio/genex/genex.html
Silicon Genetics - gene expression software:
http://www.sigenetics.com/cgi/SiG.cgi/index.smf

Most sequence alignment tools were based on a dynamic programming algorithm [373], including pairwise alignment tools such as the Basic Local Alignment Search Tool (BLAST) [12] and multiple sequence alignment tools such as ClustalW [176]. A series of tools was developed to construct phylogenetic trees based on various probability models and sequence alignment principles. Many of the phylogenetic tools have been packaged into software packages, such as PHYLIP and PAUP* [124]. Hidden Markov models

(HMM) is another widely used algorithm especially in (1) protein family studies, (2) identification of protein structural motifs, and (3) gene structure prediction (discussed later). HMMER, which is used to find conserved sequence domains in a set of related protein sequences and the spacer regions between them, is one of the popular HMM tools.

Other challenging search problems include promoter search and protein functional motif search. Several probability models and stochastic methods have been applied to these problems, including expectation maximization (EM) algorithms and Gibbs sampling methods [28].

2.3.2 Genome Analysis

Sequencing of a complete genome and subsequent annotation of the features in the genome pose different types of challenges. First, how is the whole genome put together from many small pieces of sequences? Second, where are the genes located on a chromosome? The first problem is related to genome mapping and sequence assembly. Researchers have developed software tools to assemble a large number of sequences using similar algorithms to the ones used in the basic sequence analysis. The widely used algorithms include PHRAP/Consed and CAP3 [188].

The other challenging problem is related to prediction of gene structures, especially in eukaryotic genomes. The simplest way to search for a DNA sequence that encodes a protein is to search for open reading frames (ORFs). Predicting genes is generally easier and more accurate in prokaryotic than eukaryotic organisms. The eukaryotic gene structure is much more complex due to the intron/exon structure. Several software tools, such as GeneMark [48] and Glimmer [343], can accurately predict genes in prokaryotic genomes using HMM and other Markov models. Similar methodologies were used to develop eukaryotic gene prediction tools such as GeneScan [58] and GRAIL [408].

2.3.3 Macromolecule Structure Analysis

Macromolecule structure analysis involves (1) prediction of secondary structure of RNA and proteins, (2) comparison of protein structures, (3) protein structure classification, and (4) visualization of protein structures. Some of the most popular software tools include DALI for structural alignment, Cn3d and Rasmol for viewing the 3D structures, and Mfold for RNA secondary structure prediction. Protein structure databases and associated tools also play an important role in structure analysis. Protein Data Bank (PDB), the classification by class, architecture, topology, and homology (CATH) database, the structural classification of proteins (SCOP) database, Molecular Modeling Database (MMDB), and Swiss-Model resource are among the best protein structure resources. Structure prediction is still an unsolved, challenging problem. With the rapid development of proteomics and high throughput structural biology, new algorithms and tools are very much needed.

2.3.4 Pathway Analysis

Biological processes in a cell form complex networks among gene products. Pathway analysis tries to build, model, and visualize these networks. Pathway tools are usually associated with a database to store the information about biochemical reactions, the molecules involved, and the genes. Several tools and databases have been developed and are widely used, including KEGG database (the largest collection of metabolic pathway graphs), EcoCyc/MetaCyc [212] (a visualization and database tool for building and viewing metabolic pathways), and GenMAPP (a pathway building tool designed especially for working with microarray data). With the latest developments in functional genomics and proteomics, pathway tools will become more and more valuable for understanding the biological processes at the system level (section 2.7).

2.3.5 Microarray Analysis

Microarray technology allows biologists to monitor genome-wide patterns of gene expression in a high-throughput fashion. Applications of microarrays have resulted in generating large volumes of gene expression data with several levels of experimental data complexity. For example, a "simple" experiment involving a 10,000-gene microarray with samples collected at five time points for five treatments with three replicates can create a data set with 0.75 million data points! Historically, hierarchical clustering [114] was the first clustering method applied to the problem of finding similar gene expression patterns in microarray data. Since then many different clustering methods have been used [323], such as k-means, a self-organizing map, a support vector machine, association rules, and neural networks. Several commercial software packages, e.g., GeneSpring or Spotfire, offer the use of these algorithms for microarray analysis.

Today, microarray analysis is far beyond clustering. By incorporating a priori biological knowledge, microarray analysis can become a powerful method for modeling a biological system at the molecular level. For example, combining sequence analysis methods, one can identify common promoter motifs from the clusters of coexpressed genes in microarray data using various clustering methods. Furthermore, any correlation among gene expression profiles can be modeled by artificial neural networks and can hopefully reverse-engineer the underlying genetic network in a cell (section 2.7).

2.4 Discovery of Frequent Sequential and Structured Patterns

Frequent pattern analysis has been a focused theme of study in data mining, and a lot of algorithms and methods have been developed for mining frequent patterns, sequential patterns, and structured patterns [6, 165, 437, 438]. However, not all the frequent pattern analysis methods can be readily adopted for the analysis of complex biodata because many frequent pattern analysis methods are trying to discover "perfect" patterns, whereas most biodata patterns contain a substantial amount of noise or faults. For example, a DNA sequential pattern usually allows a nontrivial number of insertions, deletions, and mutations. Thus our discussion here is focused on sequential and structured pattern mining potential adaptable to noisy biodata instead of a general overview of frequent pattern mining methods.

In bioinformatics, the discovery of frequent sequential patterns (such as motifs) and structured patterns (such as certain biochemical structures) could be essential to the analysis and understanding of the biological data. If a pattern occurs frequently, it ought to be important or meaningful in some way. Much work has been done on discovery of frequent patterns in both sequential data (unfolded DNA, proteins, and so on) and structured data (3D model of DNA and proteins).

2.4.1 Sequential Pattern

Frequent sequential pattern discovery has been an active research area for years. Many algorithms have been developed and deployed for this purpose. One of the most popular pattern (motif) discovery methods is BLAST [12], which is essentially a pattern matching algorithm. In nature, amino acids (in protein sequences) and nucleotides (in DNA sequences) may mutate. Some mutations may occur frequently while others may not occur at all. The *mutation scoring matrix* [110] is used to measure the likelihood of the mutations.

Figure 2.1 is one of the scoring matrices. The entry associated with row A_i and column A_j is the score for an amino acid A_i mutating to A_j. For a given protein or DNA sequence S, BLAST will find all similar sequences S' in the database such that the aggregate mutation score from S to S' is above some user-specified threshold. Since an amino acid may mutate to several others, if all combinations need to be searched, the search time may grow exponentially. To reduce the search time, BLAST partitions the query sequence into small segments (3 amino acids for a protein sequence and 11 nucleotides for DNA sequences) and searches for the exact match on the small segments and stitches the segments back up after the search. This technique can reduce the search time significantly and yield satisfactory results (close to 90% accuracy).

	A	R	N	D	C	Q	E	G	H	I	L	K	M	F	P	S	T	W	Y	V
A	5	-2	-1	-2	-1	-1	-1	0	-2	-1	-2	-1	-1	-3	-1	1	0	-3	-2	0
R	-2	7	-1	-2	-4	1	0	-3	0	-4	-3	3	-2	-3	-3	-1	-1	-3	-1	-3
N	-1	-1	7	2	-2	0	0	0	1	-3	-4	0	-2	-4	-2	1	0	-4	-2	-3
D	-2	-2	2	8	-4	0	2	-1	-1	-4	-4	-1	-4	-5	-1	0	-1	-5	-3	-4
C	-1	-4	-2	-4	13	-3	-3	-3	-3	-2	-2	-3	-2	-2	-4	-1	-1	-5	-3	-1
Q	-1	1	0	0	-3	7	2	-2	1	-3	-2	2	0	-4	-1	0	-1	-1	-1	-3
E	-1	0	0	2	-3	2	6	-3	0	-4	-3	1	-2	-3	-1	-1	-1	-3	-2	-3
G	0	-3	0	-1	-3	-2	-3	8	-2	-4	-4	-2	-3	-4	-2	0	-2	-3	-3	-4
H	-2	0	1	-1	-3	1	0	-2	10	-4	-3	0	-1	-1	-2	-1	-2	-3	2	-4
I	-1	-4	-3	-4	-2	-3	-4	-4	-4	5	2	-3	2	0	-3	-3	-1	-3	-1	4
L	-2	-3	-4	-4	-2	-2	-3	-4	-3	2	5	-3	3	1	-4	-3	-1	-2	-1	1
K	-1	3	0	-1	-3	2	1	-2	0	-3	-3	6	-2	-4	-1	0	-1	-3	-2	-3
M	-1	-2	-2	-4	-2	0	-2	-3	-1	2	3	-2	7	0	-3	-2	-1	-1	0	1
F	-3	-3	-4	-5	-2	-4	-3	-4	-1	0	1	-4	0	8	-4	-3	-2	1	4	-1
P	-1	-3	-2	-1	-4	-1	-1	-2	-2	-3	-4	-1	-3	-4	10	-1	-1	-4	-3	-3
S	1	-1	1	0	-1	0	-1	0	-1	-3	-3	0	-2	-3	-1	5	2	-4	-2	-2
T	0	-1	0	-1	-1	-1	-1	-2	-2	-1	-1	-1	-1	-2	-1	2	5	-3	-2	0
W	-3	-3	-4	-5	-5	-1	-3	-3	-3	-3	-2	-3	-1	1	-4	-4	-3	15	2	-3
Y	-2	-1	-2	-3	-3	-1	-2	-3	2	-1	-1	-2	0	4	-3	-2	-2	2	8	-1
V	0	-3	-3	-4	-1	-3	-3	-4	-4	4	1	-3	1	-1	-3	-2	0	-3	-1	5

Fig. 2.1. BLOSUM 50 mutation scoring matrix.

Tandem repeat (TR) detection is one of the active research areas. A tandem repeat is a segment that occurs more than a certain number of times within a DNA sequence. If a pattern repeats itself a significant number of times, biologists believe that it may signal some importance. Due to the presence of noise, the actual occurrences of the pattern may be different. In some occurrences the pattern may be shortened—some nucleotide is missing—while in other occurrences the pattern may be lengthened—a noise nucleotide is added. In addition, the occurrence of a pattern may not follow a fixed period. Several methods have been developed for finding tandem repeats. In [442], the authors proposed a dynamic programming algorithm to find all possible asynchronous patterns, which allows a certain type of imperfection in the pattern occurrences. The complexity of this algorithm is $O(N^2)$ where N is the length of the sequence.

The number of amino acids in a protein sequence is around several hundred. It is useful to find some segments that appear in a number of proteins. As mentioned, the amino acid may mutate without changing its biological functions. Thus, the occurrences of a pattern may be different. In [443], the authors proposed a model that takes into account the mutations of amino acids. A mutation matrix is constructed to represent the likelihood of mutation. The entry at row i and column j is the probability for amino acid i to mutate to j. For instance, assume there is a segment $ACCD$ in a protein. The probability that it is mutated from $ABCD$ is $Prob(A|A) \times Prob(C|B) \times Prob(C|C) \times Prob(D|D)$. This probability can be viewed as the expected chance of occurrences of the pattern $ABCD$ given that the protein segment $ACCD$ is observed. The mutation matrix serves as a bridge between the observations (protein sequences) and the true underlying models (frequent patterns). The overall occurrence of a pattern is the aggregated expected number of occurrences of the pattern in all sequences. A pattern is considered frequent if its aggregated expected occurrences are over a certain threshold. In addition, [443] also proposed a probabilistic algorithm that can find all frequent patterns efficiently.

2.4.2 Mining Structured Patterns in Biodata

Besides finding sequential patterns, many biodata analysis tasks need to find frequent structured patterns, such as frequent protein or chemical compound structures from large biodata sets. This promotes research into efficient mining of frequent structured patterns. Two classes of efficient methods for mining structured patterns have been developed: one is based on the apriori-like candidate generation and test approach [6], such as FSG [234], and the other is based on a frequent pattern growth approach [166] by growing frequent substructure patterns and reducing the size of the projected patterns, such as gSpan [430]. A performance study in [436] shows that a gSpan-based method is much more efficient than an FSG-based method.

Mining substructure patterns may still encounter difficulty in both the huge number of patterns generated and mining efficiency. Since a frequent large structure implies that all its substructures must be frequent as well, mining frequent large, structured patterns may lead to an exponential growth of search space because it would first find all the substructure patterns. To overcome this difficulty, a recent study in [437] proposes to mine only closed subgraph patterns rather than all subgraph patterns, where a subgraph G is *closed* if there exists no supergraph G' such as $G \subset G'$ and $support(G) = support(G')$ (i.e., they have the same occurrence frequency). The set of closed subgraph patterns has the same expressive power of the set of all subgraph patterns but is often orders of magnitude more compact than the latter in dense graphs. An efficient mining method called *CloseGraph* has been developed in [437], which also demonstrates order-of-magnitude performance gain in comparison with gSpan.

Figure 2.2 shows the discovered closed subgraph patterns for class CA compounds from the AIDS antiviral screen compound dataset of the Developmental Therapeutics Program of NCI/NIH (March 2002 release). One can see that by lowering the minimum support threshold (i.e., occurrence frequency), larger chemical compounds can be found in the dataset.

Such structured pattern mining methods can be extended to other data mining tasks, such as discovering structure patterns with angles or geometric constraints, finding interesting substructure patterns in a noisy environment, or classifying data [99]. For example, one can use the discovered structure patterns to distinguishing AIDS tissues from healthy ones.

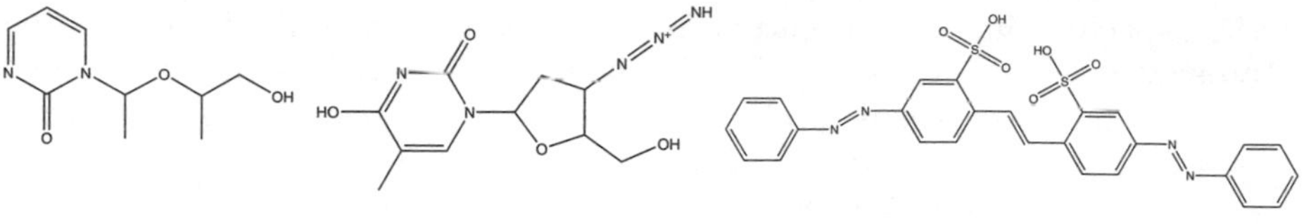

(a) min_supp = 20%   (b) min_sup = 10%   (c) min_supp = 5%

Fig. 2.2. Discovered substructures from an antiviral screen compound dataset.

2.5 Classification Methods

Each biological object may consist of multiple attributes. The relationship/
interaction among these attributes could be very complicated. In
bioinformatics, classification is one of the popular tools for understanding the
relationships among various conditions and the features of various objects.
For instance, there may be a training dataset with two classes of cells, normal
cells and cancer cells. It is very important to classify these cells so that
when a new cell is obtained, it can be automatically determined whether
it is cancerous. Classification has been an essential theme in statistics,
data mining, and machine learning, with many methods proposed and
studied [165, 171, 275, 431]. Typical methods include decision trees, Bayesian
classification, neural networks, support vector machines (SVMs), the k-
nearest neighbor (KNN) approach, associative classification, and so on. We
briefly describe three methods: SVM, decision tree induction, and KNN.

The support vector machine (SVM) [59] has been one of the most popular
classification tools in bioinformatics. The main idea behind SVM is the
following. Each object can be mapped as a point in a high-dimensional space.
It is possible that the points of the two classes cannot be separated by a
hyperplane in the original space. Thus, a transformation may be needed.
These points may be transformed to a higher dimensional space so that they
can be separated by a hyperplane. The transformation may be complicated. In
SVM, the kernel is introduced so that computing the separation hyperplane
becomes very fast. There exist many kernels, among which three are the
most popular: *linear kernel, polynomial kernel,* and *Gaussian kernel* [353].
SVM usually is considered the most accurate classification tool for many
bioinformatics applications. However, there is one drawback: the complexity
of training an SVM is $O(N^2)$ where N is the number of objects/points. There
are recent studies, such as [444], on how to scale up SVMs for large datasets.
When handling a large number of datasets, it is necessary to explore scalable
SVM algorithms for effective classification.

Another popularly used classifier is the decision-tree classifier [171, 275].
When the number of dimensions is low, i.e., when there exist only a small
number of attributes, the accuracy of the decision tree is comparable to that
of SVM. A decision tree can be built in linear time with respect to the

number of objects. In a decision tree, each internal node is labeled with a list of ranges. A range is then associated with a path to a child. If the attribute value of an object falls in the range, then the search travels down the tree via the corresponding path. Each leaf is associated with a class label. This label will be assigned to the objects that fall in the leaf node. During the decision tree construction, it is desirable to choose the most distinctive features or attributes at the high levels so that the tree can separate the two classes as early as possible. Various methods have been tested for choosing an attribute. The decision tree may not perform well with high-dimensional data.

Another method for classification is called *k-nearest neighbor* (KNN) [171]. Unlike the two preceding methods, the KNN method does not build a classifier on the training data. Instead, when a test object arrives, it searches for the k neighboring points closest to the test object and uses their labels to label the new object. If there are conflicts among the neighboring labels, a majority voting algorithm is applied. Although this method does not incur any training time, the classification time may be expensive since finding KNN in a high-dimensional space is a nontrivial task.

2.6 Cluster Analysis Methods

Clustering is a process that groups a set of objects into *clusters* so that the similarity among the objects in the same cluster is high, while that among the objects in different clusters is low. Clustering has been popular in pattern recognition, marketing, social and scientific studies, as well as in biodata analysis. Effective and efficient cluster analysis methods have also been studied extensively in statistics, machine learning, and data mining, with many approaches proposed [165, 171], including k-means, k-medoids, SOM, hierarchical clustering (such as DIANA [216], AGNES [216], BIRCH [453], and Chameleon [215]), a density-based approach (such as Optics [17]), and a model-based approach. In this section, we introduce two recently proposed approaches for clustering biodata: (1) clustering microarray data by biclustering or p-clustering, and (2) clustering biosequence data.

2.6.1 Clustering Microarray Data

Microarray has been a popular method for representing biological data. In the microarray gene expression dataset, each column represents a condition, e.g., arobetic, acid, and so on. Each row represents a gene. An entry is the expression level of the gene under the corresponding condition. The expression level of some genes is low across all the conditions while others have high expression levels. The absolute expression level may be a good indicator not of the similarity among genes but of the fluctuation of the expression levels. If the genes in a set exhibit similar fluctuation under all conditions, these genes may be coregulated. By discovering the coregulation, we may be able to refer to the gene regulative network, which may enable us to better understand how organisms develop and evolve. Row clustering [170] is proposed to cluster genes that exhibit similar behavior or fluctuation across all the conditions.

However, clustering based on the entire row is often too restricted. It may reveal the genes that are very closely coregulated. However, it cannot find the weakly regulated genes. To relax the model, the concept of *bicluster* was introduced in [74]. A *bicluster* is a subset of genes and conditions such that the subset of genes exhibits similar fluctuations under a given subset of conditions. The similarity among genes is measured as the squared mean residue error. If the similarity measure (squared mean residue error) of a matrix satisfies a certain threshold, it is a bicluster. Although this model is much more flexible than the row clusters, the computation could be costly due to the absence of pruning power in the bicluster model. It lacks the *downward closure property* typically associated with frequent patterns [165]. In other words, if a supermatrix is a bicluster, none of its submatrixes is necessarily a bicluster. As a result, one may have to consider all the combinations of columns and rows to identify all the biclusters. In [74], a nondeterministic algorithm is devised to discover one bicluster at a time. After a bicluster is discovered, its entries will be replaced by random value and a new bicluster will be searched for in the updated microarray dataset. In this scheme, it may be difficult to discover the overlapped cluster because some important value may be replaced by random value. In [441], the authors proposed a new algorithm that can discover the overlapped biclusters.

Bicluster uses squared mean residue error as the indicator of similarity among a set of genes. However, this leads to a problem: For a set of genes that are highly similar, the squared mean residue error could still be high. Even after including a new random gene in the cluster, the resulting cluster should also have high correlation; as a result, it may still qualify as a bicluster. To solve this problem, the authors of [421] proposed a new model, called *p-clusters*. In the *p*-cluster model, it is required that any 2-by-2 submatrix (two genes and two conditions) $[x_{11}, x_{12}, y_{11}, y_{12}]$ of a *p* cluster satisfies the formula $|(x_{11} - x_{12}) - (y_{11} - y_{12})| \leq \delta$ where δ is some specified threshold. This requirement is able to remove clusters that are formed by some strong coherent genes and some random genes. In addition, a novel two-way pruning algorithm is proposed, which enables the cluster discovery process be carried out in a more efficient manner on average [421].

2.6.2 Clustering Sequential Biodata

Biologists believe that the functionality of a gene depends largely on its layout or the sequential order of amino acids or nucleotides. If two genes or proteins have similar components, their functionality may be similar. Clustering the biological sequences according to their components may reveal the biological functionality among the sequences. Therefore, clustering sequential data has received a significant amount of attention recently. The foundation of any clustering algorithm is the measure of similarity between two objects (sequences). Various measurements have been proposed. One possible approach is the use of *edit distance* [160] to measure the distance between each pair of sequences. This solution is not ideal because, in addition to its inefficiency in calculation, the edit distance captures only the optimal global alignment between a pair of sequences; it ignores many other local alignments that often represent important features shared by the pair of sequences. Consider the three sequences *aaaabbb*, *bbbaaaa*, and *abcdefg*. The edit distance between *aaaabbb* and *bbbaaaa* is 6 and the edit distance between *aaaabbb* and *abcdefg* is also 6, to a certain extent contradicting the intuition that *aaaabbb* is more similar to *bbbaaaa* than to *abcdefg*. These overlooked features may be very crucial in producing meaningful clusters. Even though allowing *block operations*[1] [258, 291] may alleviate this weakness to a certain degree, the computation of edit distance with block operations is NP-hard [291]. This limitation of edit distance, in part, has motivated researchers to explore alternative solutions.

Another approach that has been widely used in document clustering is the keyword-based method. Instead of being treated as a sequence, each text document is regarded as a set of keywords or phrases and is usually represented by a weighted word vector. The similarity between two documents is measured based on keywords and phrases they share and is often defined in some form of normalized dot-product. A direct extension of this method to generic symbol sequences is to use short segments of fixed length q (generated using a sliding window through each sequence) as the set of "words" in the similarity measure. This method is also referred to in the literature [154] as the q-gram based method. While the q-gram based approach enables significant segments (i.e., keywords/phrases/q grams) to be identified and used to measure the similarity between sequences regardless of their relative positions in different sequences, valuable information may be lost as a result of ignoring sequential relationship (e.g., ordering, correlation, dependency, and so on) among these segments, which impacts the quality of clustering.

Recently statistics properties of sequence construction were used to assess the similarity among sequences in a sequence clustering system, CLUSEQ [441]. Sequences belonging to one cluster may subsume to the same probability distribution of symbols (conditioning on the preceding segment of a certain length), while different clusters may follow different underlying probability distributions. This feature, typically referred to as *short memory*, which is common to many applications, indicates that, for a certain sequence, the empirical probability distribution of the next symbol given the preceding segment can be accurately approximated by observing

---

[1] A consecutive block can be inserted/deleted/shifted/reversed in a sequence with a constant cost with regard to the edit distance.

no more than the last L symbols in that segment. Significant features of such probability distribution can be very powerful in distinguishing different clusters. By extracting and maintaining significant patterns characterizing (potential) sequence clusters, one could easily determine if a sequence should belong to a cluster by calculating the likelihood of (re)producing the sequence under the probability distribution that characterizes the given cluster. To support efficient maintenance and retrieval of the probability entries,[2] a novel variation of the suffix tree [157], namely the *probabilistic suffix tree* (PST), is proposed in [441], and it is employed as a compact representation for organizing the derived (conditional) probability distribution for a cluster of sequences. A probability vector is associated with each node to store the probability distribution of the next symbol given the label of the node as the preceding segment. These innovations enable the similarity estimation to be performed very fast, which offers many advantages over alternative methods and plays a dominant role in the overall performance of the clustering algorithm.

2.7 Computational Modeling of Biological Networks

Computational modeling of biological networks has gained much of its momentum as a result of the development of new high-throughput technologies for studying gene expressions (e.g., microarray technology) and proteomics (e.g., mass spectrometry, 2D protein gel, and protein chips). Large amounts of data generated by gene microarray and proteomics technologies provide rich resources for theoretic study of the complex biological system. Recent advances in this field have been reviewed in several books [29, 49].

2.7.1 Biological Networks

The molecular interactions in a cell can be represented using graphs of network connections similar to the network of power lines. A set of connected molecular interactions can be considered as a pathway. The cellular system involves complex interactions between proteins, DNA, RNA, and smaller molecules and can be categorized in three broad subsystem: *metabolic network or pathway*, *protein network*, and *genetic or gene regulatory network*.

Metabolic network represents the enzymatic processes within a cell, which provide energy and building blocks for the cell. It is formed by the combination of a substrate with an enzyme in a biosynthesis or degradation reaction. Typically a mathematical representation of the network is a graph with vertices being all the compounds (substrates) and the edges linking two adjacent substrates. The catalytic activity of enzymes is regulated *in vivo* by

---

[2]Even though the hidden Markov model can be used for this purpose, its computational inefficiency prevents it from being applied to a large dataset.

multiple processes including allosteric interactions, extensive feedback loops, reversible covalent modifications, and reversible peptide-bond cleavage [29]. For well-studied organisms, especially microbes such as E. coli, considerable information about metabolic reactions has been accumulated through many years and organized into large online databases, such as EcoCyc [212].

Protein network is usually meant to describe communication and signaling networks where the basic reaction is between two proteins. These protein-protein interactions are involved in signal transduction cascade such as p53 signaling pathway. Proteins are functionally connected by post-translational, allosteric interactions, or other mechanisms into biochemical circuits [29].

Genetic network or regulatory network refers to the functional inference of direct causal gene interactions. According to the Central Dogma DNA → RNA → Protein → functions, gene expression is regulated at many molecular levels. Gene products interact at different levels. The analysis of large-scale gene expression can be conceptualized as a genetic feedback network. The ultimate goal of microarray analysis is the complete reverse engineering of the genetic network. The following discussion will focus on the genetic network modeling.

2.7.2 Modeling of Networks

A systematic approach to modeling regulatory networks is essential to the understanding of their dynamics. Network modeling has been used extensively in social and economical fields for many years [377]. Recently several high-level models have been proposed for the regulatory network including Boolean networks, continuous systems of coupled differential equations, and probabilistic models. These models have been summarized by Baldi and Hartfield [29] as follows.

Boolean networks assume that a protein or a gene can be in one of two states: *active* or *inactive*, symbolically represented by 1 or 0. This binary state varies in time and depends on the state of the other genes and proteins in the network through a discrete equation:

$$X_i(t+1) = F_i[X_1(t), \ldots, X_N(t)], \tag{2.1}$$

where function F_i is a Boolean function for the update of the ith element as a function of the state of the network at time t [29]. Figure 2.3 gives a simple example. The challenge of finding a Boolean network description lies in inferring the information about network wiring and logical rules from the dynamic output (see Figure 2.3) [252].

Gene expression patterns contain much of the state information of the genetic network and can be measured experimentally. We are facing the challenge of inferring or reverse-engineering the internal structure of this genetic network from measurements of its output. Genes with similar temporal expression patterns may share common genetic control processes

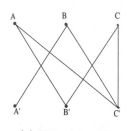

$$A' = B$$
$$B' = A \ OR \ C$$
$$C' = (A \ AND \ B)$$
$$OR \ (B \ AND \ C)$$
$$OR \ (A \ AND \ C)$$

input			output		
A	B	C	A'	B'	C'
0	0	0	0	0	0
0	0	1	0	1	0
0	1	0	1	0	0
0	1	1	1	1	1
1	0	0	0	1	0
1	0	1	0	1	1

(a) Network wiring   (b) Logical rules   (c) Dynamic output

Fig. 2.3. Target Boolean network for reverse engineering: (a) The network wiring and (b) logical rules determine (c) the dynamic output.

and may therefore be related functionally. Clustering gene expression patterns according to a similarity or distance measure is the first step toward constructing a wiring diagram for a genetic network [378].

Continuous model/Differential equations can be an alternative model to the Boolean network. In this model, the state variables X are continuous and satisfy a system of differential equations of the form

$$\frac{dX_i}{dt} = F_i[X_1(t), \dots, X_N(t), I(t)], \tag{2.2}$$

where the vector $I(t)$ represents some external input into the system. The variables X_i can be interpreted as representing concentrations of proteins or mRNAs. Such a model has been used to model biochemical reactions in the metabolic pathways and gene regulation. Most of the models do not consider spatial structure. Each element in the network is characterized by a single time-dependent concentration level. Many biological processes, however, rely heavily on spatial structure and compartmentalization. It is necessary to model the concentration in both space and time with a continuous formalism using partial differential equations [29].

Bayesian networks are provided by the theory of graphical models in statistics. The basic idea is to approximate a complex multidimensional probability distribution by a product of simpler local probability distributions. A Bayesian network model for a genetic network can be presented as a directed acyclic graph (DAG) with N nodes. The nodes may represent genes or proteins and the random variables X_i levels of activity. The parameters of the model are the local conditional distributions of each random variable given the random variables associated with the parent nodes,

$$P(X_1, \dots, X_N) = \prod_i P(X_i | X_j : j \in N^{(i)}), \tag{2.3}$$

where $N^{(i)}$ denotes all the parents of vertex i. Given a data set D representing expression levels derived using DNA microarray experiments, it is possible to use learning techniques with heuristic approximation methods to infer the network architecture and parameters. However, data from microarray experiments are still limited and insufficient to completely determine a single model, and hence people have developed heuristics for learning classes of models rather than single models, for instance, models for a set of coregulated genes [29].

2.8 Data Visualization and Visual Data Mining

The need for data visualization and visual data mining in the biomedical domain is motivated by several factors. First, it is motivated by the huge size, the great complexity and diversity of biological databases; for example, a complete genome of the yeast *Saccharomyces cerevisiae* is 12 million base pairs, of humans 3.2 billion base pairs. Second, the data-producing biotechnologies have been progressing rapidly and include spotted DNA microarrays, oligonucleotide microarrays, and serial analyses of gene expression (SAGE). Third, the demand for bioinformatics services has been dramatically increasing since the biggest scientific obstacles primarily lie in storage and analysis [181]. Finally, visualization tools are required by the necessary integration of multiple data resources and exploitation of biological knowledge to model complex biological systems. It is essential for users to visualize raw data (tables, images, point information, textual annotations, other metadata), preprocessed data (derived statistics, fused or overlaid sets), and heterogeneous, possibly distributed, resulting datasets (spatially and temporally varying data of many types).

According to [122], the types of visualization tools can be divided into (1) generic data visualization tools, (2) knowledge discovery in databases (KDD) and model visualization tools, and (3) interactive visualization environments for integrating data mining and visualization processes.

2.8.1 Data Visualization

In general, visualization utilizes the capabilities of the human visual system to aid data comprehension with the help of computer-generated representations. The number of generic visualization software products is quite large and includes AVS, IBM Visualization Data Explorer, SGI Explorer, Visage, Khoros, S-Plus, SPSS, MatLab, Mathematica, SciAn, NetMap, SAGE, SDM and MAPLE. Visualization tools are composed of (1) visualization techniques classified based on tasks, data structure, or display dimensions, (2) visual perception type, e.g., selection of graphical primitives, attributes, attribute resolution, the use of color in fusing primitives, and (3) display techniques, e.g., static or dynamic interactions; representing data as line, surface or volume geometries; showing symbolic data as pixels, icons, arrays or graphs [122]. The range of generic data visualization presentations spans line

graphs, scatter plots, 2D isosurfaces, 3D isosurfaces, rubber sheets, volume
visualizations, parallel coordinates, dimensional stacking, ribbons with twists
based on vorticity, streaklines using three time frames, combinations of
slicing and isosurface, and scalar or vector or star glyphs. Most of these
visualization forms are well suited for two-, three-, and four-dimensional
data. However, special attention should be devoted to high-dimensional
data visualization since biomedical information visualization quite often
involves displaying heterogeneous multidimensional data. The list of high-
dimensional table visualizations includes parallel coordinates, dimensional
stacking (general logic diagrams or multiple nesting of dimensions using
treemaps to display a 5D view of the DNA Exon/Intron data), multiple line
graphs, scatter plot matrices (e.g., hyperslice and hyperbox), multiple bar
charts, permutation matrices, survey "point-to-line" graphs, animations of
scatter plots (the Grand Tour or the projection pursuit techniques), "point-
to-curve" graphs (Andrew's curves), glyphs and icon-based visualization,
the display of recursive correlation between dimensions (fractal foams),
radial or grid or circular parallel coordinate visualizations (Radviz, Gridviz,
overlapping star plots), and finally clustering visualization using dendrograms
or Kohonen nets [122]. The most frequent high-dimensional biomedical
data visualization is clustering visualization because of its direct use in
studies searching for similarities and differences in biological materials.
Nonetheless, one should also mention the applications of other sophisticated
visualization systems, such as virtual reality environments for exploratory
and training purposes, collaborative visualization systems for basic research
(NCSA Biology Workbench), and telemedicine and telesurgery. In future,
collaborative visualization systems would benefit from grid computing,
scalable visualization capabilities, and integration with the tools providing
qualitative views of a dataset [267].

2.8.2 KDD and Model Visualization

Visual data mining discovers implicit and useful knowledge from large
data sets using data and/or knowledge visualization techniques [165]. It
is the human visual and brain system that gives us the power of data
model understanding and phenomenon comprehension based on visual data
mining. While KDD and data mining experts focus on the KDD process
and generate data models, researchers studying human computer interfaces,
computer graphics, multimedia systems, pattern recognition, and high-
performance computing work on effective visual data model visualizations.
The benefits of data-mining model visualization are threefold [122]. First,
anyone conducting the data analysis has to trust the developed model. In
addition to good quantitative measures of "trust," visualization can reveal
several model aspects to increase our trust. Second, good model visualization
improves understanding of the model, especially semantic understanding.

Third, several data mining techniques lead to multiple data models, and it is natural to ask questions about model comparisons.

Comparing many data models requires establishing appropriate metrics, visualizing model differences, and interpreting the differences. Thus, appropriate model visualization is critical for interpreting data. In the biomedical domain, visual data mining delivers presentations of data mining models and helps interpret them in the biological domain. For example, visualization of decision trees, clusters, and generalized or association rules does not fulfill its purpose unless an expert biologist can connect the visual data model representation with the underlying biological phenomenon. Thus, many commercial software packages support model visualization tools, for instance, software by Spotfire, InforMax, or Affymetrics. Nevertheless, there is still a need to develop a metric to evaluate effectiveness of the variety of visualization tools and to permeate the KDD process with visualization to give useful insights about data. Figure 2.4 shows how microarray processing steps can be combined with visual data mining (inspection) of spot features and labels obtained by clustering.

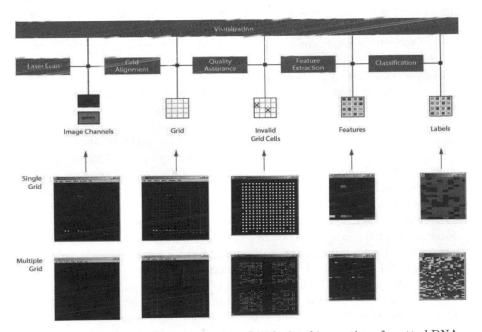

Fig. 2.4. Example of visualization combined with visual inspection of spotted DNA microarray data using I2K software developed at NCSA.

2.8.3 Integration of Data Mining and Visualization Processes

Having available all generic visualization tools and visualizations of data
models, one would like to build an environment for visualization of the
knowledge discovery in databases (KDD) process including exploratory data
mining. In the KDD process, defined as the process of discovering useful
knowledge within data [123], exploratory data mining is a class of methods
used by the KDD process to find a pattern that is valid, novel, potentially
useful, and ultimately understandable [122]. From a user viewpoint, the role
of a user can be either passive, e.g., viewing data without any significant
influence on the conducted data mining, or active, e.g., making decisions
based on presented information visualization. In addition, the integration of
data mining and visualization should be realized by various combinations
of data mining and visualization components and characterized by seamless
interface and repeatable execution at any workflow point. From a software
design viewpoint, the integration environment has to be designed (a) with
modular components performing individual workflow steps and (b) with
common data objects so that the objects can be easily passed between
processing and visualization components [122]. There are several software
integration packages, e.g., D2K by NCSA and Iris Explorer by SGI, that meet
these integration requirements by using a visual programming paradigm.

In the biomedical domain, integration challenges remain in developing
software tools and environments that can be used for solving biological
problems rather than general data mining problems. For example, there is a
need for an integrated data workflow for (a) comparative studies visualizing
comparisons of genes from different species, (b) multilevel studies visualizing
phylogenetic trees at several levels of detail, (c) interactive studies visualizing
polymer docking for drug design, and (d) mapping gene function in the
embryo [267]. Building software environments of this kind requires not only
bringing together data mining and visualization researchers but also unifying
the domain-specific languages for common elements, e.g., defining terms
for input and output data variables, intermediate data products, and user
interfaces. This type of project has been demonstrated by Variagenics, Inc.
and Small Design Firm in a nucleic acid sequence of the human genome
consisting of 3.2 billion base pairs and displayed in a coherent three-
dimensional space while preserving accurate spatial and size relationships
[3]. The last but not the least important issue is related to visualization
of the exponentially increasing volume of biological data that must utilize
distributed computational resources and interoperability of all existing tools.
This issue is being addressed by the development of (a) policies on data
sharing and standards [51, 381], (b) computational grids, and (c) visualization
techniques for large data sets [162].

2.9 Emerging Frontiers

There are many emerging technologies and research frontiers in bioinformatics. In this section, we present two emerging frontiers in bioinformatics research: text mining in bioinformatics and systems biology.

2.9.1 Text Mining in Bioinformatics

Bioinformatics and biodata analysis involve worldwide researchers and practitioners from many different fields: genetics, biochemistry, molecular biology, medical science, statistics, computer science, and so on. It becomes a challenging task to find all the related literature and publications studying the same genes and proteins from different aspects. This task is made even more demanding by the huge number of publications in electronic form that are accessible in medical literature databases on the Web.

The number of studies concerning automated mining of biochemical knowledge from digital repositories of scientific literature, such as MEDLINE and BIOSIS, has increased significantly. The techniques have progressed from simple recognition of terms to extraction of interaction relationships in complex sentences, and search objectives have broadened to a range of problems, such as improving homology search, identifying cellular location, and deriving genetic network technologies [179].

Natural language processing (NLP), also called computational linguistics or natural language understanding, attempts to process text and deduce its syntactic and semantic structure automatically. The two primary aspects of natural language are syntax and lexicon. Syntax defines structures such as the sentence made up of noun phrases and verb phrases. The smallest structural entities are words, and information about words is kept in a lexicon, which is a machine-readable dictionary that may contain a good deal of additional information about the properties of the words. Many techniques have been developed to construct lexicons and grammars automatically. For example, starting with a modest amount of manually parsed text, a parser can be "trained" by constructing rules that match the manually produced structures. This is a machine learning approach. Other kinds of analysis methods look for certain regularities in massive amounts of text. This is the statistical approach. NLP has become an important area over the last decade with the increasing availability of large, on-line corpora [23, 380].

The earliest work focused on tasks using only limited linguistic context and processing at the level of words, such as identifying protein names, or on tasks relying on word cooccurrence and pattern matching. The field now has progressed into the area of recognizing interactions between proteins and other molecules. There are two main methods in this area. The first approach is based on occurrence statistics of gene names from MEDLINE documents to predict the connections among genes [386]. The second approach uses specific linguistic structures to extract protein interaction information from MEDLINE documents [105].

Besides the recognition of protein interactions from scientific text, NLP has been applied to a broad range of information extraction problems in biology. Combining with the Unified Medical Language System (UMLS), NLP has been used for learning ontology relations in medical databases and identifying the structure of noun phrases in MEDLINE texts. Incorporating literature similarity in each iteration of PSI-BLAST search has shown that supplementing sequence similarity with information from biomedical literature search could increase the accuracy of homology search results. Methods have also been developed (a) to cluster MEDLINE abstracts into "themes" based on a statistical treatment of terms and unsupervised machine learning, and (b) to classify terms derived from standard term-weighting techniques to predict the cellular location of proteins from description abstracts [179].

2.9.2 Systems Biology

System-level understanding, the approach advocated in systems biology, requires a shift in focus from understanding genes and proteins to understanding a system's structure and dynamics [191]. A system-level understanding of a biological system can be derived from an insight into four key properties, according to the prominent systems biologist Kitano [225]:

1. *System structures.* These include the network of gene interactions and biochemical pathways, as well as the mechanisms by which such interactions modulate the physical properties of intracellular and multicellular structures.

2. *System dynamics.* The principles about how a system behaves over time under various conditions can be understood through metabolic analysis, sensitivity analysis, dynamic analysis methods such as phase portrait and bifurcation analysis, and by identifying essential mechanisms underlying specific behaviors.

3. *The control method.* The mechanisms that systematically control the state of the cell can be modulated to minimize malfunctions and provide potential therapeutic targets for treatment of disease.

4. *The design method.* Strategies to modify and construct biological systems having desired properties can be devised based on definite design principles and simulations.

Computational biology has two distinct branches: (1) knowledge discovery, or data mining, which extracts the hidden patterns from huge quantities of experimental data, forming hypotheses as a result, and (2) simulation-based analysis, which tests hypotheses with in silico experiments, providing predictions to be tested by in vitro and in vivo studies [224].

Although traditional bioinformatics has been used widely for genome analysis, simulation-based approaches have received little mainstream attention. Current experimental molecular biology is now producing the high-throughput quantitative data that is needed to support simulation-based research. At the same time, substantial advances in software and computational power have enabled the creation and analysis of reasonably realistic yet intricate biological models [224].

It is crucial for individual research groups to be able to exchange their models and create commonly accepted repositories and software environments that are available to all. Systems Biology Markup Language (SBML) [189], CellML (http://www.cellml.org/), and the Systems Biology Workbench are examples of efforts that aim to form a de facto standard and open software platform for modeling and analysis. These efforts significantly increase the value of the new generation of databases concerned with biological pathways, such as the Kyoto Encyclopedia of Genes and Genomes (KEGG), Alliance for Cellular Signaling (AfCS), and Signal Transduction Knowledge Environment (STKE), by enabling them to develop machine-executable models rather than merely human-readable forms [224].

Building a full-scale organism model or even a whole-cell or organ model is a challenging enterprise. Several groups, such as Virtual Cell [348] and E-Cell [405], have started the process. Multiple aspects of biological processes have to be integrated and the model predictions must be verified by biological and clinical data, which are at best sparse for this purpose. Integrating heterogeneous simulation models is a nontrivial research topic by itself, requiring integration of data of multiple scales, resolutions, and modalities.

2.9.3 Open Research Problems

The future of bioinformatics and data mining faces many open research problems in order to meet the requirements of high-throughput biodata analysis. One of the open problems is data quality maintenance related to (a) experimental noise, e.g., the hybridization process and microarray spot irregularities, and (b) the statistical significance of experiments, e.g., the number of experimental replicas and their variations. Other open problems include unknown model complexity and visualization difficulties with high-dimensional data related to our limited understanding of underlying phenomena. Although dimensionality reduction approaches reduce the number of data dimensions, they also introduce the problems of feature selection and feature construction. It has also become very clear over the last few years that the growing size of bioinformatics data poses new challenges on file standards, data storage, access, data mining, and information retrieval. These open research problems can be solved in future by forming interdisciplinary teams, consolidating technical terms, introducing standards, and promoting interdisciplinary education.

How to integrate biological knowledge into the designing and developing of data mining models and algorithms is an important future research direction. There exists an extensive amount of information or knowledge about the biological data. For instance, the functionality of the majority of yeast genes is captured in the gene ontology (GO). The GO is a directed acyclic graph (DAG) that illustrates the relationship (similarity) among the genes. If we can combine this information into the data mining process, e.g., in clustering algorithms, then we can produce more biologically meaningful clusters with higher efficiency. Currently, integration of biological knowledge in the data mining procedure is still a challenging problem. It is desirable to find a way to represent prior biological knowledge as a model that can be integrated into the data mining process.

Recently, many researchers have realized that although a good number of genes have been discovered and have been playing an important role in the analysis of genetic and proteomic behaviors of biological bodies, the discovered genes are only about 1% to 2% of human (or animal) genome; most of the genome belongs to so-called "dark" matter, such as introns and "junk." However, recent studies have shown that a lot of biological functions are strongly influenced or correlated with the dark part of the genome, and it is a big open problem to find the rules or regularities that may disclose the mystery of the "dark matter" of a genome. This should be an interesting research problem that data mining may contribute to as well.

2.10 Conclusions

Both data mining and bioinformatics are fast-expanding and closely related research frontiers. It is important to examine the important research issues in bioinformatics and develop new data mining methods for scalable and effective biodata analysis.

In this chapter, we have provided a short overview of biodata analysis from a data mining perspective. Although a comprehensive survey of all kinds of data mining methods and their potential or effectiveness in biodata analysis is well beyond the task of this short survey, the selective examples presented here may give readers an impression that a lot of interesting work has been done in this joint venture. We believe that active interactions and collaborations between these two fields have just started. It is a highly demanding and promising direction, and a lot of exciting results will appear in the near future.

Acknowledgments

The work was supported in part by National Science Foundation under Grants IIS-02-09199 and IIS-03-08215, National Institutes of Health under Grants No. 2 P30 AR41940-10 and PHS 2 R01 EY10457-09, the University of Illinois at Urbana-Champaign, the National Center for Supercomputing Applications (NCSA), and an IBM Faculty Award. Any opinions, findings, and conclusions or recommendations expressed in this material are those of the authors and do not necessarily reflect the views of the funding agencies.

Part II

Sequence and Structure Alignment

Chapter 3

AntiClustAl: Multiple Sequence Alignment by Antipole Clustering

Cinzia Di Pietro, Alfredo Ferro, Giuseppe Pigola,
Alfredo Pulvirenti, Michele Purrello, Marco Ragusa,
and Dennis Shasha

Summary

In this chapter, we present a new multiple sequence alignment algorithm called AntiClustAl. The method makes use of the commonly used idea of aligning homologous sequences belonging to classes generated by some clustering algorithm and then continuing the alignment process in a bottom-up way along a suitable tree structure. The final result is then read at the root of the tree. Multiple sequence alignment in each cluster makes use of progressive alignment with the 1-median (center) of the cluster. The 1-median of set S of sequences is the element of S that minimizes the average distance from any other sequence in S. Its exact computation requires quadratic time. The basic idea of our proposed algorithm is to make use of a simple and natural algorithmic technique based on randomized tournaments, an idea that has been successfully applied to large-size search problems in general metric spaces. In particular, a clustering data structure called antipole tree and an approximate linear 1-median computation are used. Our algorithm enjoys a better running time with equivalent alignment quality compared with ClustalW, a widely used tool for multiple sequence alignment. A successful biological application showing high amino acid conservation during evolution of *Xenopus laevis* SOD2 is illustrated.

3.1 Introduction

Multiple sequence alignment is the process of taking three or more input sequences and forcing them to have the same length by inserting a universal

gap symbol − in order to maximize their similarity as measured by a
scoring function. In the case of biological sequences (DNA, RNA, protein),
the resulting aligned sequences can be used for two purposes: first, to find
regions of similarity defining a conserved consensus pattern of characters
(nucleotides or amino acids) in all the sequences; second, if the alignment
is particularly strong, to use the aligned positions to infer some possible
evolutionary relationships among the sequences.

Formally, the problem is the follows: let Σ be an alphabet and $\mathcal{S} = \{S_1, \dots, S_k\}$ be a set of string defined over Σ. A *multiple sequence alignment* of $\mathcal{S}$ is a set $\mathcal{S}' = \{S_1', \dots, S_k'\}$ such that

- $S_i' \in (\Sigma \cup \{-\})^*$ for each $i = 1, \dots, k$
- S_i is obtained from S_i' by dropping all gap symbols $\{-\}$
- $|S_1'| = |S_2'| = \dots = |S_k'|$

A *scoring function* defined on the alphabet Σ is a map $\sigma : (\Sigma \cup \{-\})^k \mapsto R$. It has the following properties:

1. Reflexivity (maximum score if all the same) $\sigma(a, \dots, a) \geq \sigma(a_1, \dots, a_k)$, provided $a \neq -$.
2. Symmetry (it doesn't matter where differences are found, so the score is based on the evaluation of the multiset of characters in the argument):
$$\sigma(x_1, \dots, x_i, a, x_{i+2}, \dots, x_j, b, x_{j+2}, \dots, x_k)$$
$$= \sigma(x_1, \dots, x_i, b, x_{i+2}, \dots, x_j, a, x_{j+2}, \dots, x_k)$$
3. Triangle inequality (recall that similarity is the opposite of distance):
$$\sigma(x_1, \dots, x_i, a, x_{i+2}, \dots, x_j, b, x_{j+2}, \dots, x_k)$$
$$+\sigma(x_1, \dots, x_i, b, x_{i+2}, \dots, x_j, c, x_{j+2}, \dots, x_k)$$
$$\geq \sigma(x_1, \dots, x_i, a, x_{i+2}, \dots, x_j, c, x_{j+2}, \dots, x_k)$$

The best score $D(|S_1|, |S_2|, \dots, |S_k|)$ for aligning k sequences $S_1, S_2, \dots, S_k$ with respect to σ is the one that maximizes the sum of the σs across all positions: $\sum_{i \in 1..n} \sigma(S_1'[i], S_2'[i] \dots S_k'[i])$. If $|S_1| = |S_2| = |S_k| = n$, then the space and the time complexity of the best currently known algorithm is $\mathcal{O}(n^k)$ and $\mathcal{O}(2^k n^k) \times \mathcal{O}(\text{computation of the } \sigma \text{ function})$, respectively. Finding the optimal solution of the multiple sequence alignment therefore requires exponential space and time complexity. If only pairwise alignment is considered, then an $O(n^2/\log n))$ algorithm can be obtained [88].

The most successful solution to the problem has been provided by the program ClustalW [177]. In this chapter, we propose a new solution based on a top-down "bisector tree" [70] clustering algorithm called *antipole tree* and a linear approximate 1-median computation. Since exact 1-median computation requires a quadratic number of distance calculations and given that each of such distance computations may require quadratic time in the length of the biosequences, the use of a linear approximate 1-median computation may give a much better running time.

Both clustering and approximate 1-median computation algorithms make use of a very simple and natural technique based on randomized tournaments.

Given a set S of sequences to be aligned, we play the following tournament. At each round, the winners of the previous round are randomly partitioned into subsets of a fixed size t. Then a procedure finds each subset's 1-median and discards it. Rounds are played until fewer than $2t$ elements are left. The farthest pair of points in that remaining set is the antipole pair S_1, S_2 of elements.

If the distance (pairwise alignment) of our antipole pair lies below a given threshold, then a single new cluster is generated from all the elements and the recursion stops. Otherwise, partition the input set of elements according to their proximity to S_1, S_2. Each resulting class is then treated as a new input set and is treated recursively. The process terminates with one cluster per leaf of the generated antipole tree.

A similar randomized tournament process can be applied to each cluster to generate its approximate 1-median. Let C be such a cluster. At each round, the winners of the previous round are randomly partitioned into subsets of a fixed size t and a local optimization procedure is used to determine the winner for each subset, which is the 1-median of the subset. Rounds are played until only one element, the *final winner*, is left.

The chapter is organized as follows. Section 3.2 is a short survey of preceding work. Section 3.3 introduces the antipole tree for generic metric spaces. Section 3.4 presents the AntiClustAl alignment algorithm. Section 3.5 shows experimental results and comparison with ClustalW. Section 3.6 describes a successful biological application whose details can be found in [320]. Conclusions and future development are given in sections 3.7 and 3.8.

3.2 Related Work

To reduce the complexity of multiple sequence alignment, several approaches have been proposed. The *Carillo Lipmann method* [66] provides a heuristic to accelerate the speed of the alignment process. The exponential time is lowered by a constant factor, since, if the sequences are very similar, the optimal solution can be discovered by visiting a small neighborhood of the main diagonal of the exponential dynamic programming algorithm.

Several approximation algorithms have been proposed, including [55, 277]. Two algorithms are particularly relevant to our approach. The first one [126, 160] uses a progressive alignment strategy that consists of incrementally aligning every sequence $S_i \in \mathcal{S} - \{S_c\}$ to the centroid S_c of S. The second, called *ClustalW* [177, 178], a widely used tool for solving the multiple sequence alignment problem for biosequences, starts by building a phylogenetic (evolutionary) tree [127]. *ClustalW* consists of three main stages. First of all, the pairwise distance matrix is computed on all the pairs of sequences. Next, the algorithm uses the *neighbor-joining method* [342] to construct a phylogenetic tree. Finally, all the sequences are aligned progressively from the leaves up.

At the leaf level, the process begins by pairwise alignment of two single strings, and it proceeds by pairwise alignment of two sets of strings that are the result of previous alignments of children nodes. Each set is represented by a single vector known as a profile [156].

Let M be a multiple sequence alignment of length l defined over the alphabet Σ. A *profile* P is a $l \times |\Sigma \cup \{-\}|$ matrix, whose columns are probability vectors denoting the frequencies of each symbol in the corresponding alignment column. The profile concept is used in ClustalW as a mathematical instrument to perform either the alignment of a sequence S with a multiple sequence alignment M or the alignment of two multiple alignments M_1 and M_2. To align a profile $P = (p_{i,j})$ for $i = 1, \ldots, l$ and $j = 1, \ldots, |\Sigma| + 1$ against a sequence $S = s_1 s_2 \ldots s_n$, one can use the classical algorithm by Miller and Myers [292] appropriately modified. Let $\sigma : (\Sigma \cup \{-\}) \times (\Sigma \cup \{-\}) \mapsto \mathbb{R}$ be the scoring function defined by the rule

$$\sigma(a, b) = \begin{cases} x & a = b \\ y & \text{otherwise} \end{cases}$$

where x, y are two different real numbers. Let $\hat{\sigma} : (\Sigma \cup \{-\}) \times \{1, 2, \ldots, l\} \mapsto R$ be a new weighted average scoring function defined as follows:

$$\hat{\sigma}(b, i) = \sum_{a \in \Sigma} p_{i,a} \cdot \sigma(a, b) \tag{3.1}$$

where $p_{i,a}$ represents the frequency of the base a in the ith column of the profile P. By replacing the scoring function σ by $\hat{\sigma}$, the Miller and Myers algorithm [292] reduces the alignment-to-sequence comparison problem to a sequence-to-sequence one.

Profiles are used to align two multiple sequence alignments M_1 of length l and M_2 of length m whose profiles are, respectively, $P_1 = (p'_{i,k})$ and $P_2 = (p''_{j,k})$ with $i = 1, \ldots, l$, $j = 1, \ldots, m$, and $k = 1, \ldots, |\Sigma| + 1$. Now the new scoring function $\tilde{\sigma} : \{1, \ldots, l\} \times \{1, \ldots, m\} \mapsto \mathbb{R}$ takes as input two positions, i in the profile P_1 and j in the profile P_2, and returns the following value:

$$\tilde{\sigma}(i, j) = \sum_{k=1}^{|\Sigma|+1} f(p'_{i,k} \cdot p''_{j,k}) \tag{3.2}$$

where $f(\cdot)$ is any monotonic function.

3.3 Antipole Tree Data Structure for Clustering in Metric Spaces

Let X be a finite set of objects (for example, biosequences) and let d a distance function $dist : X \times X \mapsto \mathbb{R}$ such that the following four properties hold:

1. $dist(x, y) \geq 0 \; \forall x, y \in X$ (positiveness)
2. $dist(x, y) = dist(y, x) \; \forall x, y \in X$ (symmetry)
3. $dist(x, x) = 0 \; \forall x \in X$ (reflexivity)
4. $dist(x, y) \leq dist(x, z) + dist(z, y) \; \forall x, y, z \in X$ (triangularity)

Clustering X with a bounded diameter σ is the problem of partitioning X into few nonempty subsets (i.e., the clusters) of diameter less than σ. A centroid or the 1-median of a cluster Clu is the element C of Clu, which minimizes the following $\sum_{y \in X} d(C, y)$. The radius of a cluster Clu is the distance between the centroid C and the farthest object from C in that cluster. Assume we fix a cluster diameter σ such that sequences whose pairwise distance is greater than σ are considered to be significantly different by some application dependent criterion. The antipole clustering of bounded diameter σ [64] is performed by a top-down procedure starting from a given finite set of points (biosequences in our case) S by a splitting procedure (Figure 3.1a) which assigns each point of the splitting subset to the closest endpoint of a "pseudo-diameter" segment called *antipole*.[1]

An antipole pair of elements is generated as the final winner of a set of randomized tournaments (Figure 3.2).

The initial tournament is formed by randomly partitioning the set S into t-uples (subsets of cardinality t), locating the 1-median and then discarding it (Figure 3.2a). The winning sets (all points except the 1-median) go to the next stage of the tournament. If any of the tournaments has cardinality that is not a multiple of t, then one of the games will have at most $2t - 1$ players.

If the final winner pair has a distance (pairwise alignment) that is lower than σ, then splitting is not performed and the subset is one of the clusters (Figure 3.1b). Otherwise the cluster is split and the algorithm proceeds recursively on each of the two generated subsets. At the end of the procedure, the centroid of each cluster [63] is computed by an algorithm similar to the one to find the antipole pair (Figure 3.2b). In this case the winner of each game is the object that minimizes the sum from the other $t - 1$ elements. This procedure gives rise to a data structure called antipole tree.

---

[1]The pseudo-diameter in such a case is a pair of biosequences, the endpoints, different enough.

```
BUILD_TREE(S, σ)

 1   Q ← APPROX_ANTIPOLE(S,σ);
 2   if Q = ∅ then // splitting condition fails
 3      T.Leaf ← TRUE;
 4      T.C ← MAKE_CLUSTER(S);
 5      return T;
 6   end if;
 7   {A, B} = Q ; // A, B are the antipoles sequences
 8   T.A ← A;
 9   T.B ← B;
10   S_A ← {O ∈ S|dist(O, A) < dist(O, B)};
11   S_B ← {O ∈ S|dist(O, B) ≤ dist(O, A)};
12   T.left ← BUILD_TREE(S_A,σ);
13   T.right ← BUILD_TREE(S_B,σ);
14   return T;
15   END BUILD_TREE.
```

(a)

```
MAKE_CLUSTER(S)

 1   C.Centroid ← APPROX_1_MEDIAN(S);
 2   C.Radius ← max_{x ∈ S} dist(x, C.Centroid)
 3   C.C_{List} ← S \ {C.Centroid};
 4   return C;
 5   END MAKE_CLUSTER.
```

(b)

Fig. 3.1. (a) Antipole algorithm. (b) MakeCluster algorithm.

3.4 AntiClustAl: Multiple Sequence Alignment via Antipoles

In this section we show that replacing the phylogenetic tree with the antipole tree gives a substantial speed improvement to the ClustalW approach with as good or better quality. (The quality of our approach derives from the fact that multiple alignment of a set of sequences works better when the diameter of the set of sequences is small.) Our basic algorithm is

1. Build the antipole tree as described in section 3.3.
2. Align the sequences progressively from the leaves up, inspired by ClustalW.

Starting at the leaves, the second step aligns all the sequences of the corresponding cluster using the profile alignment technique. Figures 3.3, 3.4, and 3.5 contain the pseudocode of the multiple sequence alignment via antipole. The recursive function *AntiClustal* visits the antipole tree from the leaves up (following ClustalW's strategy of visiting the phylogenetic tree from the leaves up). It aligns all the sequences stored in the leaves (the clusters) by calling the function *AlignCluster*. Next, two aligned clusters are merged by the function *MergeAlignment*. The three mentioned procedures make use of the functions *AlignSequences*, *AlignProfileVsSequence*, and *OptimalAlignment*,

---

The approximate antipole selection algorithm

LOCAL_WINNER(T)

1 **return** $T \setminus$ 1-MEDIAN(T);
2 END LOCAL_WINNER

FIND_ANTIPOLE(T)

1 **return** P_1, $P_2 \in T$ such that
        $dist(P_1, P_2) \geq dist(x, y)\, \forall x, y \in T$;
2 END FIND_ANTIPOLE

APPROX_ANTIPOLE(S)

1 **while** $|S| >$ *threshold* **do**
2      $W \leftarrow \emptyset$;
3   **while** $S \geq 2 * t$ **do**
4   *Randomly choose a set* $T \subseteq S : |T| = t$;
5          $S \leftarrow S \setminus T$;
6          $W \leftarrow W \cup \{$LOCAL_WINNER(T)$\}$;
7   **end while**
8      $S \leftarrow W \cup \{$LOCAL_WINNER(S)$\}$;
        // (for the remaining elements of S)
9 **end while**
10 **return** FIND_ANTIPOLE(S);
11 END APPROX_ANTIPOLE

1 MEDIAN (X)

1 **for each** $x \in X$ **do**
2      $\sigma_x \leftarrow \sum_{y \in X} d(x, y)$;
3   Let $m \in X$ be an element such that
        $\sigma_m = \min_{x \in X}(\sigma_x)$;
4 **return** m
5 END 1-MEDIAN

APPROX_1_MEDIAN (S)

1 **while** $|S| >$ *Threshold* **do**
2      $W \leftarrow \emptyset$;
3   **while** $|S| \geq 2t$ **do**
4   *Randomly choose a set* $T \subseteq S : |T| = t$;
5          $S \leftarrow S \setminus T$;
6          $W \leftarrow W \cup \{$1-MEDIAN (T)$\}$;
7   **end while**;
8      $S \leftarrow W \cup \{$1-MEDIAN (S)$\}$;
        // (for the remaining elements of S)
9 **end while**;
10 **return** 1-MEDIAN (S);
11 END APPROX_1_MEDIAN

Fig. 3.2. Pseudocode of the approximate algorithms: (a) Approximate antipole search. (b) 1-median computation. The variable *threshold* is usually taken to be $(t^2 + 1)$. Indeed, this is the lowest value for which it is possible to partition the set S into subsets of size between t and $2t - 1$. In the AntiClustAl implementation, the subset size t is taken equal to three. This guarantees good performance. However it can be experimentally shown that the optimal choice of t is equal to the dimension of the underlying metric space plus one.

which, respectively, align two profiles, a profile versus a sequence and two sequences according to the Miller and Myers algorithm [292]. Finally the function *GetProfile* returns the profile of a multiple sequence alignment. Figure 3.6 shows an example of the proposed method.

```
ANTICLUSTAL(TREE T)

 1    if (!isLeaf(T)) /* if T is not a leaf */
 2        AntiClustal(T.left);
 3        AntiClustal(T.right);
 4        T ← MergeAlignment(T.left, T.right);
 5        T.leaf ← TRUE;
 6        return(T);
 7    else
 8        AlignCluster(T);
 9        return (T);
10    end if;
11    END ANTICLUSTAL
```

Fig. 3.3. Multiple sequence alignment via the antipole tree.

```
MERGEALIGNMENT(TREE A, TREE B)

 1    P₁ ← GetProfile(A);
 2    P₂ ← GetProfile(B);
 3    C ← AlignSequences(A, P₁, B, P₂);
 4    return C.
 5    END MERGEALIGNMENT
```

Fig. 3.4. How to align two clusters.

```
ALIGNCLUSTER(TREE A)

 1    if (|A.cluster| = 1)
 2        return A;
 3    else
 4        C ← OptimalAlignment(A₀, A₁);
 5        if (|A| ≥ 3)
 6            for each Aᵢ ∈ A.cluster do
 7                    P ← GetProfile(C);
 8                    C ← AlignProfileVsSequence(Aᵢ, P, C);
 9            end for
10        end if
11        return C;
12    end if;
13    END ALIGNCLUSTER
```

Fig. 3.5. How to align the sequences in a cluster.

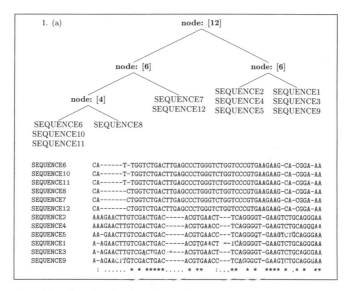

Fig. 3.6. Example of multiple sequence alignment via antipole tree using alpha-globin sequences. A portion of the aligned sequences is shown at the bottom. The symbols under the aligned sequences show the matches in concordance with the given definition.

3.5 Comparing ClustalW and AntiClustAl

In this section we experimentally compare ClustalW1.82 with AntiClustAl. The comparison is made in terms of both running time and precision. The experiments were performed on alpha globins, beta globins, and immunoglobulins downloaded from *GenBank*. Each dataset had from 10 to 200 biosequences. Each biosequence had from 120 to 100000 bases. Precision was measured by the relative match number, which is obtained by dividing the match number by the alignment length:

$$\text{Match Ratio} = 100 \cdot \frac{\text{match number}}{\text{alignment length}}$$

A biologically more significant comparison parameter is the *column blocks match*, obtained by associating an integer with each column of a multiple alignment. Call that integer *column match* and set its value to between 0 and 3 according to the following scheme.

- 3 if the ith column contains a *perfect match*, that is, every element in the ith column is the same nongap symbol
- 2 if the ith column contains a *weak match*, that is, 75% of its elements are the same nongap symbol

- 1 if the ith column contains a *trivial match*, that is, more than 50% of its elements are the same nongap symbol and the remaining elements are all *gap* symbols
- 0 otherwise. In this case we have a *mismatch*.

Figure 3.7 shows that the running time of the antipole clustering alignment is better than ClustalW because the antipole algorithm performs a linear rather than quadratic number of distance computations. The reason is that constructing an antipole tree takes only linear time. Thus the advantage increases as the number of sequences increases. As for the quality of the alignment, Figures 3.8, 3.9, and 3.10 show that antipole clustering alignment usually gives a higher quality result than ClustalW in terms of both *match ratio* and *column blocks match*.

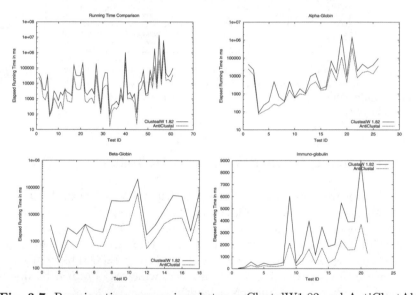

Fig. 3.7. Running time comparison between ClustalW1.82 and AntiClustAl.

AntiClustAl can also align proteins. Unlike nucleotide alignment, protein alignment uses scoring functions to reflect the functional differences among amino acids. Our implementation uses a metric version of the scoring matrix PAM [269]. We compared our method with ClustalW using the benchmark BaliBase2.0 [400]. Figure 3.11 shows the results.

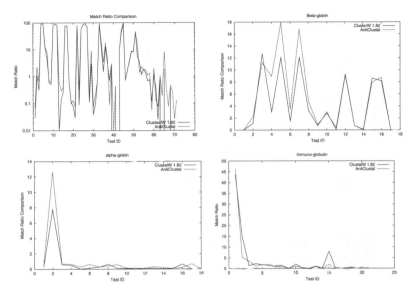

Fig. 3.8. Match comparison between ClustalW1.82 and AntiClustAl.

3.6 Case Study: In Vitro and In Silico Cloning of *Xenopus laevis* SOD2 and Its Phylogenetic Analysis with AntiClustAl

By using biological and informatic techniques (i.e., RT-PCR, cycle sequencing, and data analysis) and the data obtained through the Genome Projects, we have cloned *Xenopus laevis* SOD2 (MnSOD) cDNA and determined its nucleotide sequence. These data and the deduced primary structure of the protein were then compared with all the other SOD2 nucleotide and amino acid sequences from eukaryotes and prokaryotes published in public databases. The analysis was performed by using both ClustalW and AntiClustAl. Our results demonstrate a very high conservation of the enzyme amino acid sequence during evolution, suggesting a tight structure-function relationship. This is to be expected for very ancient molecules endowed with critical biological functions, where the functions derive from a specific structural organization.

Conservation is weaker at the nucleotide sequence level, which makes sense, given the frequency of neutral mutations. The data obtained by using AntiClustAl are of equivalent quality with those produced with ClustalW, validating this algorithm as an important new tool for biocomputational analysis. Finally, it is noteworthy that evolutionary trees, drawn by using all the available data on SOD2 amino acid and nucleotide sequences and either ClustalW or AntiClustAl, are comparable to those obtained through classical

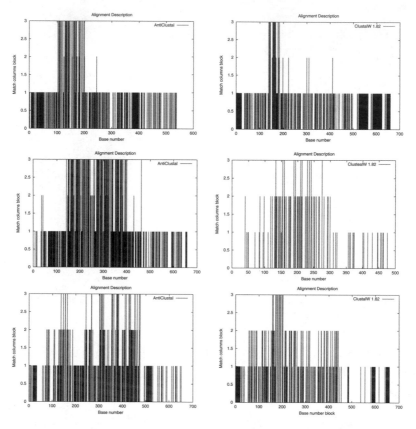

Fig. 3.9. Alignment comparison between ClustalW1.82 and AntiClustAl for alpha globins.

phylogenetic analysis (Figures 3.12B, 3.13). Biologically, it is noteworthy that *Chlamydomonas* (a chlorophyton) is an out-of-order species in both trees (Figure 3.13).

3.7 Conclusions

AntiClustAl is a new method to align a set of biosequences rapidly. AntiClustAl begins with a randomized hierarchical clustering algorithm that yields a tree whose leaf nodes consist of sequences. AntiClustAl then aligns such sequences by a post order traversal of the tree. A successful biological application concerning the enzyme *Xenopus laevis* SOD2 shows the applicability of the method. The method has a better running time than ClustalW with comparable alignment quality. The software is available on line at the following address: http://alpha.dmi.unict.it/~ctnyu/.

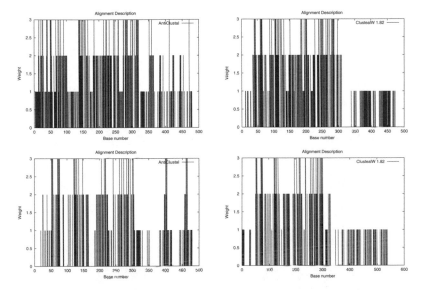

Fig. 3.10. Alignment comparison between ClustalW1.82 and AntiClustAl for immunoglobulins.

BaliBase2.0

Reference 5		
	AntiClustAl	**ClustalW**
2cba	0.704	0.717
1eft	0.278	0.0
1ivy	0.782	0.735
Kinase1	0.797	0.806
Kinase2	0.762	1
Kinase3	0.445	0.646
1pysA	0.484	0.429
1qpg	0.840	1
1thm1	0.460	0.412
1thm2	0.780	0.774
S51	0.7	0.938
S52	0.995	1

Reference 2 Long		
	AntiClustAl	**ClustalW**
1ajsA	0.724	0.324
1cpt_ref2	0.775	0.660
1enl	0.740	0.375
1idy	0.786	0.515
1lvl_ref2	0.707	0.746
1myr	0.6	0.904
1pamA_ref	0.584	0.761
1ped_ref2	0.843	0.834

Fig. 3.11. Protein alignment comparisons with ClustalW using the benchmark BaliBase2.0.

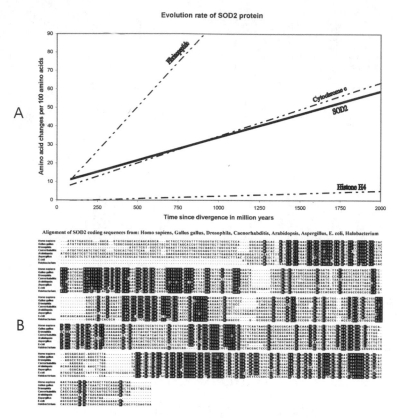

Fig. 3.12. (A) Evolution rate of SOD2 protein and its overlap with that of cytochrome C. (B) Comparison of SOD2 cDNA nucleotide sequence of *Homo sapiens, Gallus gallus, Drosophila melanogaster, Caenorhabditis elegans, Arabidopsis thaliana, Aspergillus nidulans, Escherichia coli,* and *Halobacterium salinarum.*

3.8 Future Developments and Research Problems

We believe that the randomized tournaments technique can be applied to several problems in bioinformatics. By using alternative clustering algorithms and local alignment techniques, similar to those of T-Coffee [302], we are currently studying several modifications of AntiClustAl with the aim of improving its precision. In order to afford very large multiple sequence alignments, we plan to implement a parallel version of AntiClustAl. This should be facilitated by the nice recursive top-down structure of the antipole tree clustering procedure. We plan to use these AntiClustAl extensions to analyze the evolution of the transcription apparatus as well as that of the apoptotic machinery.

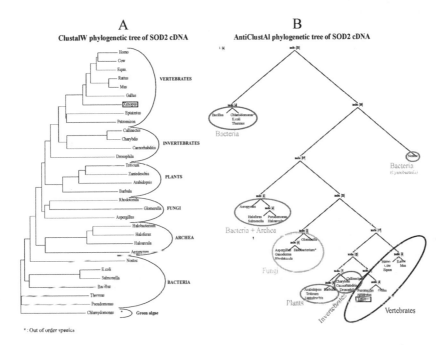

Fig. 3.13. Phylogenetic trees based on SOD2 sequence evolution, drawn by using either ClustalW (A) or AntiClustAl (B).

Chapter 4
RNA Structure Comparison and Alignment

Kaizhong Zhang

Summary

We present an RNA representation scheme in which an RNA structure is described as a sequence of units, each of which stands for either an unpaired base or a base pair in the RNA molecule. With this structural representation scheme, we give efficient algorithms for computing the distance and alignment between two RNA secondary structures based on edit operations and on the assumptions in which either no bond-breaking operation is allowed or bond-breaking activities are considered. The techniques provide a foundation for developing solutions to the hard problems concerning RNA tertiary structure comparisons. Some experimental results based on real-world RNA data are also reported.

4.1 Introduction

Ribonucleic acid (RNA) is an important molecule, which performs a wide range of functions in biological systems. In particular, it is RNA (not DNA) that contains the genetic information of viruses such as HIV and thereby regulates the functions of these viruses. RNA has recently become the center of much attention because of its catalytic properties [68], leading to an increased interest in obtaining RNA structural information.

RNA molecules have two sets of structural information. First, the *primary structure* of an RNA molecule is a single strand made of the ribonucleotides A (adenine), C (cytosine), G (guanine) and U (uracil). Second, the ribonucleotide sequences fold over onto themselves to form double-stranded regions of base pairings, yielding higher order *tertiary structures*.

It is well known that the structural features of RNAs are important
in the molecular mechanisms involving their functions. The presumption,
of course, is that, corresponding to a preserved function, there exists a
preserved molecular confirmation and therefore a preserved structure. The
RNA *secondary structure* is a restricted subset of the tertiary structure, which
plays an important role between primary structures and tertiary structures,
since the problem of comparing and aligning the tertiary structures of RNA
molecules is often intractable.   Based on a reliable secondary structure
alignment, the possible tertiary structure element alignments that are
consistent with the secondary structure alignment can then be introduced.

A coarsely grained RNA secondary structure representation that uses
the structural elements of hairpin loops, bulge loops, internal loops, and
multibranched loops is proposed in [362, 363].   It has been shown that
with this representation, a tree edit distance algorithm can be used to
compare RNA secondary structures [363]. Similar ideas have also been used
in [244, 245]. Those early works on RNA structure comparison used loops and
stacked base pairs as basic units, making it difficult to define the semantic
meaning in the process of converting one RNA structure into another. In
another line of work, RNA comparison is basically done on the primary
structures while trying to incorporate secondary structural information into
the comparison [24, 86]. More recent work also uses the notion of arc-
annotated sequences [115, 204].

In [447], edit distance, a similarity measure between two RNA secondary
structures based on edit operations on base pairs and unpaired bases is
proposed. This model has been extended from secondary structures to
tertiary structures in [259, 448]. In this model, a base pair in one structure
can be aligned only with a base pair in the other structure. Based on this
model, algorithms have been developed for global and local alignment with
affine gap penalty [72, 423]. In general, this is a reasonable model since
in RNA structures when one base of a base pair changes, we usually find
that its partner also changes so as to conserve the pairing relationship.
However, occasionally a base pair in one structure should be aligned with
unpaired bases in the other structure since a mutation of one base may forbid
the pairing. In [205, 254] a refined model, which allows base-pair breaking
(deleting the bond of the base pair) and base-pair altering (deleting one base
and therefore the bond of the base pair), is proposed. In this chapter, we
discuss these methods for comparing and aligning RNA structures.

4.2 RNA Structure Comparison and Alignment Models

In this section, we consider RNA structure comparison and alignment models.
We first consider the RNA structure comparison model based on edit
operations proposed in [259, 448] and the alignment model with gap initiation
cost based on edit operations proposed in [423]. We then extend the edit

operations with an additional operation: base-pair bond breaking. The RNA structure comparison [205, 254] and alignment models based on the extended edit operations are then considered.

An RNA structure is represented by $R(P)$, where R is a sequence of nucleotides with $r[i]$ representing the ith nucleotide, and $P \subset \{1, 2, \cdots, |R|\}^2$ is a set of pairs of which each element (i, j), $i < j$, represents a base pair $(r[i], r[j])$ in R. We use $R[i, j]$ to represent the subsequence of nucleotides from $r[i]$ to $r[j]$. We assume that base pairs in $R(P)$ do not share participating bases. Formally, for any (i_1, j_1) and (i_2, j_2) in P, $j_1 \neq i_2$, $i_1 \neq j_2$, and $i_1 = i_2$ if and only if $j_1 = j_2$.

Let $s = r[k]$ be an unpaired base and $p = (r[i], r[j])$ be a base pair in $R(P)$. We define the relation between s and p as follows. We say s is *before* p if $k < i$. We say s is *inside* p if $i < k < j$. We say s is *after* p if $j < k$.

Let $s = (r[i], r[j])$ and $t = (r[k], r[l])$ be two base pairs in $R(P)$. We define the relation between s and t as follows. We say s is *before* t if $j < k$. We say s is *inside* t if $k < i$ and $j < l$. We say s and t are *crossing* if $i < k < j < l$ or $k < i < l < j$.

For an RNA structure $R(P)$, if any two of its base pairs are noncrossing, then we say $R(P)$ is a secondary structure. Otherwise, we say $R(P)$ is a tertiary structure.

For an RNA structure $R(P)$, we define $p_r( )$ as follows.

$$p_r(i) = \begin{cases} i & \text{if } r[i] \text{ is an unpaired base} \\ j & \text{if } (r[i], r[j]) \text{ or } (r[j], r[i]) \text{ is a base pair in } P \end{cases}$$

By this definition $p_r(i) \neq i$ if and only if $r[i]$ is a base in a base pair of $R(P)$ and $p_r(i) = i$ if and only if $r[i]$ is an unpaired base of $R(P)$. If $p_r(i) \neq i$, then $p_r(i)$ is the base paired with base i. When there is no confusion we use R instead of $R(P)$ to represent an RNA structure assuming that there is an associated function $p_r( )$.

4.2.1 RNA Structure Comparison and Alignment Based on Edit Operations

Following the tradition in sequence comparison [296, 373], we define three edit operations, substitute, delete, and insert, on RNA structures. For a given RNA structure R, each operation can be applied to either a base pair or an unpaired base. To substitute a base pair is to replace one base pair with another. This means that at the sequence level, two bases may be changed at the same time. To delete a base pair is to delete the two bases of the base pair. At the sequence level, this means to delete two bases at the same time. To insert a base pair is to insert a new base pair. At the sequence level, this means to insert two bases at the same time. To relabel an unpaired base is to replace it with another unpaired base. To delete an unpaired base is to delete the base from the sequence. To insert an unpaired base is to insert a new base into the sequence as an unpaired base. Note that there is no substitute operation that can change a base pair to an unpaired base or vice versa. Figure 4.1 shows edit operations on RNA structures.

Fig. 4.1. RNA structure edit operations. Base-pair substitution is shown at the left and base-pair deletion is shown at the right.

In this model, a base pair can be matched only with a base pair. In general, this is a reasonable model since in RNA structures when one base of a base pair changes, its partner usually also changes to conserve that pairing relationship.

We represent an edit operation as $a \to b$, where a and b are λ, the null label, labels of base pairs from $\{A, C, G, U\} \times \{A, C, G, U\}$, or unpaired bases from $\{A, C, G, U\}$. We call $a \to b$ a substitute operation if $a \neq \lambda$ and $b \neq \lambda$, a delete operation if $b = \lambda$, and an insert operation if $a = \lambda$. Let Γ be a cost function that assigns to each edit operation $a \to b$ a nonnegative real number $\Gamma(a \to b)$. We constrain Γ to be a distance metric. That is, (1) $\Gamma(a \to b) \geq 0$, $\Gamma(a \to a) = 0$, (2) $\Gamma(a \to b) = \Gamma(b \to a)$, and (3) $\Gamma(a \to c) \leq \Gamma(a \to b) + \Gamma(b \to c)$. We extend Γ to a sequence of edit operations $S = s_1, s_2, \ldots s_n$ by letting $\Gamma(S) = \sum_{i=1}^{n} \Gamma(s_i)$.

The edit distance between two RNA structures R_1 and R_2 is defined by considering the minimum-cost edit operation sequence that transforms R_1 to R_2. Formally, the edit distance between R_1 and R_2 is defined as

$$D(R_1, R_2) = \min_{S} \{\Gamma(S) \mid S \text{ is an edit operation sequence taking } R_1 \text{ to } R_2\}.$$

In the computation of the edit distance, the goal is to find the minimum-cost edit sequence that can change one structure to the other. A similarity (maximization) version can also be considered, where the goal is to find the maximum-scoring edit sequence that can change one structure to the other. We will refer to the edit distance, $D(R_1, R_2)$, as the RNA structure comparison model based on edit operations.

RNA structure distance/similarity can also be represented by an alignment of two RNA structures. In the alignment representation, the gap initiation cost can be considered. Formally, given two RNA structures R_1 and R_2, a structural alignment of R_1 and R_2 is represented by (R'_1, R'_2) satisfying the following conditions.

(1) R_1' is R_1 with some new $'-'$'s inserted and R_2' is R_2 with some new $'-'$'s inserted such that $|R_1'| = |R_2'|$.

(2) If $r_1'[i]$ is an unpaired base in R_1', then either $r_2'[i]$ is an unpaired base in R_2' or $r_2'[i] = '-'$. If $r_2'[i]$ is an unpaired base in R_2', then either $r_1'[i]$ is an unpaired base in R_1' or $r_1'[i] = '-'$.

(3) If $(r_1'[i], r_1'[j])$ is a base pair in R_1', then either $(r_2'[i], r_2'[j])$ is a base pair in R_2' or $r_2'[i] = r_2'[j] = '-'$. If $(r_2'[i], r_2'[j])$ is a base pair in R_2', then either $(r_1'[i], r_1'[j])$ is a base pair in R_1' or $r_1'[i] = r_1'[j] = '-'$.

From this definition, it is clear that an alignment preserves the order of unpaired bases and the topological relationship between base pairs. Since the alignment specifies how base pairs are aligned and preserves the relationship between the base pairs, it is in fact a structural alignment. Figure 4.2 gives a simple illustration of this alignment.

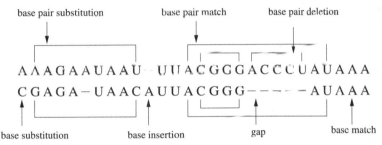

Fig. 4.2. RNA structure alignment with edit operations.

A gap in an alignment (R_1', R_2') is a consecutive subsequence of $'-'$'s in either R_1' or R_2' with maximal length. More formally, $[i \cdots j]$ is a gap in (R_1', R_2') if either $r_1'[k] = '-'$ for $i \leq k \leq j$, $r_1'[i-1] \neq '-'$, $r_1'[j+1] \neq '-'$, or $r_2'[k] = '-'$ for $i \leq k \leq j$, $r_2'[i-1] \neq '-'$, $r_2'[j+1] \neq '-'$. For each gap in an alignment, in addition to the insertion/deletion costs, we will assign a constant, *gap_cost*, as the gap initiation cost. This means that longer gaps are preferred since for a longer gap the additional cost distributed to each base is relatively small. This kind of affine gap penalty has long been used in sequence alignment [152]. In biological alignment, whenever possible, longer gaps are preferred since it is difficult to delete the first element, but after that, continuing to delete subsequent elements is much easier.

Given an alignment (R_1', R_2'), we define an unpaired base match set SM, an unpaired base deletion set SD, an unpaired base insertion set SI, a base-pair match set PM, a base-pair deletion set PD, and a base-pair insertion set PI as follows.

$SM = \{\ i\ |\ r_1'[i]\ \text{and}\ r_2'[i]\ \text{are unpaired bases in}\ R_1\ \text{and}\ R_2\}.$
$SD = \{\ i\ |\ r_1'[i]\ \text{is an unpaired base in}\ R_1\ \text{and}\ r_2'[i] = {'-'}\}.$
$SI\ = \{\ i\ |\ r_2'[i]\ \text{is an unpaired base in}\ R_2\ \text{and}\ r_1'[i] = {'-'}\}.$
$PM = \{\ (i,j)\ |\ (r_1'[i], r_1'[j])\ \text{and}\ (r_2'[i], r_2'[j])\ \text{are base pairs in}\ R_1\ \text{and}\ R_2\}.$
$PD = \{\ (i,j)\ |\ (r_1'[i], r_1'[j])\ \text{is a base pair in}\ R_1\ \text{and}\ r_2'[i] = r_2'[j] = {'-'}\}.$
$PI\ = \{\ (i,j)\ |\ (r_2'[i], r_2'[j])\ \text{is a base pair in}\ R_2\ \text{and}\ r_1'[i] = r_1'[j] = {'-'}\}.$

The cost of an alignment (R_1', R_2') is defined as follows, where $\#gap$ is the number of gaps in (R_1', R_2').

$$cost((R_1', R_2')) = gap\_cost \times \#gap$$
$$+ \sum_{i \in SM} \Gamma(r_1'[i] \to r_2'[i]) + \sum_{i \in SD} \Gamma(r_1'[i] \to \lambda) + \sum_{i \in SI} \Gamma(\lambda \to r_2'[i])$$
$$+ \sum_{(i,j) \in PM} \Gamma((r_1'[i], r_1'[j]) \to (r_2'[i], r_2'[j])) + \sum_{(i,j) \in PD} \Gamma((r_1'[i], r_1'[j]) \to \lambda)$$
$$+ \sum_{(i,j) \in PI} \Gamma(\lambda \to (r_2'[i], r_2'[j]))$$

Given two RNA structures R_1 and R_2, the edit alignment between them is defined as

$$A(R_1, R_2) = \min_{(R_1', R_2')} \{cost((R_1', R_2'))\}.$$

We will refer to the edit alignment, $A(R_1, R_2)$, as the RNA structure alignment model based on edit operations. When $gap\_cost = 0$, it is easy to see that $D(R_1, R_2) = A(R_1, R_2)$ [259, 448].

4.2.2 RNA Structure Comparison and Alignment Based on Extended Edit Operations

Although the alignment based on edit operations is of good quality, sometimes one may have to consider alignments where a base pair of one RNA structure is aligned with two unpaired bases in the other RNA structure. Suppose that the base pair involved in the former RNA structure is (A, U) and the two unpaired bases in the latter RNA structure are U and U. Then with the edit operations, this alignment would be interpreted as deleting the base pair followed by inserting the two unpaired bases. A more realistic interpretation is that base A in the base pair (A, U) mutates into U, and this mutation causes the bond between the two bases to break. Therefore in this subsection, we will consider the situation where the bond between the two bases of a base pair is allowed to break.

In addition to the edit operations of insertion, deletion, and substitution, we now consider one more operation: base-pair bond breaking. This operation can be applied to a base pair, causing the bond between the two bases of the pair to break and the base pair to become two unpaired bases. Figure 4.3 illustrates the base-pair bond-breaking operation. We will refer to edit operations with the base-pair bond-breaking operation as extended edit operations.

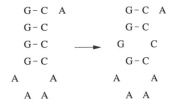

Fig. 4.3. Base-pair bond-breaking operation.

For this model, we will not consider an explicit base-pair altering operation [205, 254] since that operation is replaced by a base-pair bond-breaking operation and then an unpaired base deletion operation. With the base-pair bond-breaking operation, we do not have to explicitly define a base-pair deletion operation. Instead, we can use a base-pair bond-breaking operation followed by two unpaired base deletion operations to replace a base-pair deletion operation. The reason follows.

Let the cost of a base-pair bond-breaking operation, a base-pair deletion operation, an unpaired base deletion operation, and an unpaired base substitution operation be W_b, W_p, W_d, and W_s, respectively. By triangle inequality, we have $W_p \leq W_b + 2W_d$. On the other hand, by inspecting the two alignments in Figure 4.4, it is clear that the alignment on the left is better than the alignment on the right. Therefore we have $W_b + 2W_s \leq W_p + 2W_d$, which means that $W_b + 2(W_s - W_d) \leq W_p$. Since W_s can be as large as $2W_d$, by triangle inequality, it is reasonable to choose $W_b + 2W_d \leq W_p$. These two inequalities show that the cost of a base-pair deletion should be the same as the cost of one base-pair bond breaking plus the cost of two unpaired base deletions. Figure 4.5 shows some examples of extended edit operations.

Fig. 4.4. Two alignments.

Alternatively, suppose a base-pair deletion operation is defined and its cost W_p is smaller than $W_b + 2W_d$. Then, since $W_p = W_b + 2((W_p - W_b)/2)$, we can consider that, after a base-pair bond-breaking operation, deleting a base from a base pair will have a cost of $(W_p - W_b)/2$.

Similar to the edit distance of two RNA structures R_1 and R_2, the extended edit distance between R_1 and R_2 is defined as

$$D_b(R_1, R_2) =$$
$$\min_{S}\{\Gamma(S) \mid S \text{ is an extended edit operation sequence taking } R_1 \text{ to } R_2\}.$$

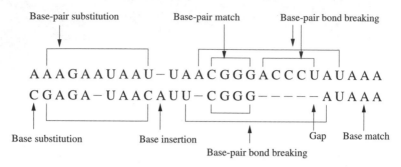

Fig. 4.5. RNA structure alignment with extended edit operations.

We refer to the extended edit distance, $D_b(R_1, R_2)$, as the RNA structure comparison model based on extended edit operations. Based on the extended edit operations, RNA structure alignment can also be considered. Figure 4.5 gives a simple illustration of this alignment. Given two RNA structures R_1 and R_2, a structural alignment of R_1 and R_2 is represented by (R_1', R_2') satisfying the following condition.

- R_1' is R_1 with some new $'-'$s inserted and R_2' is R_2 with some new $'-'$s inserted such that $|R_1'| = |R_2'|$.

The cost of the alignment (R_1', R_2') can be determined in two steps. In the first step, we consider the base pairs in R_1 and R_2. Suppose that $(r_1[i_1], r_1[i_2])$ is a base pair in R_1 and $(r_2[j_1], r_2[j_2])$ is a base pair in R_2 and in the alignment (R_1', R_2') $r_1[i_1]$ is aligned with $r_2[j_1]$ and $r_1[i_2]$ is aligned with $r_2[j_2]$. Then this is either a base-pair match or a base-pair substitution with cost $\Gamma((r_1[i_1], r_1[i_2]) \to (r_2[j_1], r_2[j_2]))$. For all the other base pairs, the bonds are broken with a cost of Γ_b for each of those base pairs. In the second step, after base-pair substitution and base-pair bond breaking, we consider all the bases that are not involved in either base-pair matches or base-pair substitutions. If $r_1[i]$ is aligned with $r_2[j]$, then we have a base match or a base substitution with a cost of $\Gamma(r_1[i] \to r_2[j])$. If a base is aligned with a space, then we have a base deletion (or insertion) with a cost of $\Gamma(r_1[i] \to '-')$ (or $\Gamma('-' \to r_2[j])$). Note that the bases we consider in the second step may not necessarily be unpaired bases. They might be bases in the base pairs that have undergone base-pair bond breakings.

Given two RNA structures R_1 and R_2, the extended edit alignment between them is defined as

$$A_b(R_1, R_2) = \min_{(R_1', R_2')} \{cost((R_1', R_2'))\}.$$

We refer to the extended edit alignment, $A_b(R_1, R_2)$, as the RNA structure alignment model based on extended edit operations. When $gap\_cost = 0$, it is easy to see that $D_b(R_1, R_2) = A_b(R_1, R_2)$.

4.3 Hardness Results

In this section, we consider the problem of alignment between RNA structures where both structures are tertiary structures. In general, this problem is Max SNP-hard.

When the gap cost is zero, there are two results from [259].

1. The problem of computing the edit distance between two RNA tertiary structures is Max SNP-hard.

This means that there is no polynomial time approximation scheme (PTAS) for this problem unless $P = NP$ [311].

A maximization (similarity) version can also be considered, where the goal is to find a maximal-scoring edit sequence that can change one structure to the other. For the maximization version, the result is stronger than that for the minimization version.

2. For any $\delta < 1$, the maximization version of the problem cannot be approximated within ratio $2^{\log^{\delta} n}$ in polynomial time unless $NP \in DTIME[2^{poly \log n}]$.

When the gap cost is greater than zero, there is a result from [423].

3. The problem of computing the edit alignment based on the edit operations with an arbitrary nontrivial affine score scheme is Max SNP-hard.

These results can be extended to the model with base-pair bond breakings. Therefore the problems of computing the extended edit distance and extended edit alignment between two RNA tertiary structures are Max SNP-hard. Note that these results are for the theoretical case where the tertiary structures can be arbitrarily complex. In reality, however, the number of tertiary-structure base pairs is relatively small compared with the number of secondary-structure base pairs. Therefore successful heuristic methods have been developed for the alignment between RNA tertiary structures [80].

4.4 Algorithms for RNA Secondary Structure Comparison

In this section, we consider the problem of computing the edit distance and extended edit distance between two RNA secondary structures. Since an RNA secondary structure appears as a treelike structure (Figure 4.6), there are algorithms for RNA structure comparison using tree comparison [244, 363, 392, 447, 449]. This is indeed true for computing the edit distance and extended edit distance of two RNA secondary structures if suitable tree (sometimes forest) representations are used.

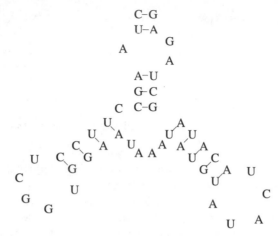

Fig. 4.6. RNA secondary structure.

4.4.1 Edit Distance

Recall that a secondary structure is represented by a set S of noncrossing base pairs that form bonds. For $(i,j) \in S$, h is accessible from (i,j) if $i < h < j$ and there is no pair $(k,l) \in S$ such that $i < k < h < l < j$. Define (i,j) as the parent of $(k,l) \in S$ if k,l are accessible from (i,j). Define (i,j) as the parent of $h \notin S$ if h is accessible from (i,j). Note that each base pair $(i,j) \in S$ and each unpaired base h has at most one parent, implying a tree (sometimes forest) on the elements of a secondary structure. The definitions of "child," "sibling," and "leaf" follow naturally. The order imposed based on the 5' to 3' nature of an RNA molecule makes the tree an ordered tree (Figure 4.7). In this representation, internal nodes represent base pairs and leaves represent unpaired bases.

Following [392, 449], let us consider tree edit operations. Relabeling a node means changing the label of the node. Deleting a node n means making the children of n become the children of the parent of n and then removing n. Inserting is the complement of deleting. Examining each of the edit operations defined on RNA secondary structures, we can see that they are exactly the same as the tree edit operations defined on the tree representation.

Conversely, the edit operations defined on this tree representation are meaningful operations on RNA secondary structures. Theoretically there could be operations that do not result in a valid secondary structure (e.g. inserting an unpaired base as an internal node), but we can show that the minimum-cost sequence of tree edit operations that transforms one tree into another will not use this kind of operations. Therefore we can use tree edit algorithms on this tree representation to compare two RNA secondary structures.

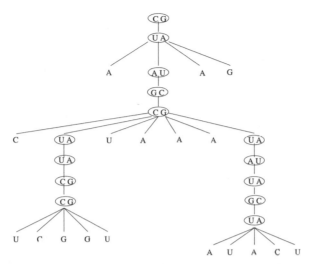

Fig. 4.7. Tree representation of the RNA structure in Figure 4.6.

The ordered tree edit distance algorithm [449] has a time complexity of $O(|T_1||T_2| \min(depth(T_1), leaves(T_1)) \min(depth(T_2), leaves(T_2)))$ and space complexity of $O(|T_1||T_2|)$ where $|T_i|$ is the size of the tree T_i. The depth is really the collapsed depth, where nodes with degree one are ignored when counting the depth.

Using the tree representation for RNA secondary structures, the size of the tree, denoted by R^T, is the total number of unpaired bases plus the total number of base pairs, which is actually smaller than the length of the corresponding primary structure. The collapsed depth here, denoted by dp, is really the maximum number of loops on a path from the root to a leaf. Here the loops are bulge loops, internal loops, multibranched loops, and hairpin loops. Taking the loops into account, the resulting algorithm for computing the edit distance between two RNA secondary structures has a time complexity of $O(R_1^T R_2^T dp_1 dp_2)$.

4.4.2 Extended Edit Distance

Since there is no tree edit operation corresponding to base-pair bond breakings, we cannot directly use tree edit distance algorithms here. However with an extended tree representation and a small modification of the tree edit distance algorithms, an algorithm for computing the extended edit distance between RNA secondary structures can easily be developed. This extended tree representation is shown in Figure 4.8. In this representation, each internal node represents the bond between the two bases of a base pair, the leftmost and the rightmost leaves of an internal node represent the two bases of a base pair, and all the other leaves represent unpaired bases.

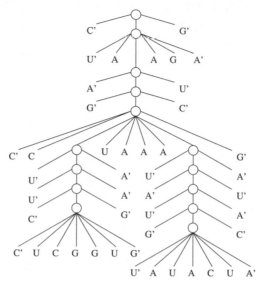

Fig. 4.8. Extended tree representation of the RNA structure in Figure 4.6.

With this extended tree representation, unpaired base substitution, insertion, and deletion correspond to tree leaf substitution, insertion, and deletion and a base-pair bond breaking corresponds to an internal node insertion or deletion. The only problem is concerned with the base-pair substitution operation since a base pair now is represented by three nodes: an internal node and its leftmost and rightmost leaves. This means that if we want to use the tree edit distance algorithms, some modifications are necessary.

In fact, we need only a very small modification. When applying the tree edit distance algorithms to this extended tree representation, whenever we match an internal node of one tree T to an internal node in the other tree T', we have to make sure that, simultaneously, the leftmost leaf of the internal node in tree T is matched with the leftmost leaf of the internal node in tree T' and the rightmost leaf of the internal node in tree T is matched with the rightmost leaf of the internal node in tree T'.

Using the extended tree representation, the size of the tree is larger than the length of the corresponding primary structure. The collapsed depth here is the same as the depth of the tree. Therefore the real running time of this modified algorithm using the extended tree representation in Figure 4.8 would be slower than the running time of the algorithm using the tree representation in Figure 4.7. Since the tree size is actually larger than the length of the corresponding primary structure, in the actual implementation one may avoid using the explicit tree representation [205, 423].

4.5 Algorithms for RNA Structure Alignment

In this section, we consider the problem of computing the edit alignment and extended edit alignment between two RNA structures R_1 and R_2. Since computing the structure alignment for RNA tertiary structures is Max SNP-hard, we cannot expect to find the optimal solution in polynomial time. However we will present algorithms that will find the optimal solution when at least one of the RNA structures is a secondary structure and good solutions when both RNA structures are tertiary structures. Therefore, we do not assume that the input RNA structures are secondary structures and will not use any tree representation.

4.5.1 Edit Alignment

Since aligning crossing base pairs is difficult, we add one more condition in defining a structural alignment (R'_1, R'_2) of R_1 and R_2.

(4) If $(r'_1[i], r'_1[j])$ and $(r'_1[k], r'_1[l])$ are base pairs in R'_1 and $(r'_2[i], r'_2[j])$ and $(r'_2[k], r'_2[l])$ are base pairs in R'_2, then $(r'_1[i], r'_1[j])$ and $(r'_1[k], r'_1[l])$ are noncrossing in R'_1 and $(r'_2[i], r'_2[j])$ and $(r'_2[k], r'_2[l])$ are noncrossing in R'_2.

Therefore, even though the input RNA structures may have crossing base pairs, the aligned base pairs in them are noncrossing. We present an algorithm that computes the optimal alignment of two RNA structures based on this new alignment definition. We will show that our algorithm can be used for aligning tertiary structures in practical applications, though the alignment may not be the optimal one according to the original definition.

In extending techniques of Gotoh [152] to handle gap initiation costs from sequence alignment to structure alignment, the main difficulty is that, with the deletion of a base pair, two gaps might be created simultaneously. We deal with this problem by considering the deletion of a base pair as two separate deletions of its two bases, each with a cost of half of the base-pair deletion cost. We will use a bottom up dynamic programming algorithm to find the optimal alignment between R_1 and R_2. That is, we consider the smaller substructures in R_1 and R_2 first and eventually consider the whole structures of R_1 and R_2.

Property of optimal alignments. Consider two RNA structures R_1 and R_2. Let $\gamma_g = gap\_cost$. We use $\Gamma( )$ to define $\gamma(i,j)$ for $0 \leq i \leq |R_1|$ and $0 \leq j \leq |R_2|$.

$$\gamma(i,0) = \Gamma(r_1[i] \rightarrow \lambda) \qquad\qquad\qquad \text{if } i = p_{r_1}(i)$$
$$\gamma(0,i) = \Gamma(\lambda \rightarrow r_2[i]) \qquad\qquad\qquad \text{if } i = p_{r_2}(i)$$
$$\gamma(i,j) = \Gamma(r_1[i] \rightarrow r_2[j]) \qquad\qquad \text{if } i = p_{r_1}(i) \text{ and } j = p_{r_2}(j)$$
$$\gamma(i,0) = \gamma(j,0) = \Gamma((r_1[i],r_1[j]) \rightarrow \lambda)/2 \quad \text{if } i = p_{r_1}(j) < j$$
$$\gamma(0,i) = \gamma(0,j) = \Gamma(\lambda \rightarrow (r_2[i],r_2[j]))/2 \quad \text{if } i = p_{r_2}(j) < j$$
$$\gamma(i,j) = \Gamma((r_1[i_1],r_1[i]) \rightarrow (r_2[j_1],r_2[j])) \quad \text{if } i_1 = p_{r_1}(i) < i$$
$$\text{and } j_1 = p_{r_2}(j) < j$$

From this definition, if $r_1[i]$ is a single base, then $\gamma(i,0)$ is the cost of deleting this base, and if $r_1[i]$ is a base of a base pair, then $\gamma(i,0)$ is half of the cost of deleting the base pair. Therefore we distribute evenly the deletion cost of a base pair to its two bases. The meaning of $\gamma(0,i)$ is similar. When $i > 0$ and $j > 0$, $\gamma(i,j)$ is the cost of aligning base pairs $(r_1[i_1],r_1[i])$ and $(r_2[j_1],r_2[j])$.

We now consider the optimal alignment between $R_1[i_1,i_2]$ and $R_2[j_1,j_2]$. We use $A(i_1,i_2 \; ; \; j_1,j_2)$ to represent the optimal alignment cost between $R_1[i_1,i_2]$ and $R_2[j_1,j_2]$. We use $D(i_1,i_2 \; ; \; j_1,j_2)$ to represent the optimal alignment cost such that $r_1[i_2]$ is aligned to $'-'$. If $i_1 \leq p_{r_1}(i_2) < i_2$, then by the definition of alignment, in the optimal alignment of $D(i_1,i_2 \; ; \; j_1,j_2)$, $r_1[p_{r_1}(i_2)]$ has to be aligned to $'-'$. We use $I(i_1,i_2 \; ; \; j_1,j_2)$ to represent the optimal alignment cost such that $r_2[j_2]$ is aligned to $'-'$. If $j_1 \leq p_{r_2}(j_2) < j_2$, then in the optimal alignment of $I(i_1,i_2 \; ; \; j_1,j_2)$, $r_2[p_{r_2}(j_2)]$ has to be aligned to $'-'$.

In computing $A(i_1,i_2 \; ; \; j_1,j_2)$, $D(i_1,i_2 \; ; \; j_1,j_2)$ and $I(i_1,i_2 \; ; \; j_1,j_2)$ for any $i_1 \leq i \leq i_2$, if $p_{r_1}(i) < i_1$ or $i_2 < p_{r_1}(i)$, then $r_1[i]$ will be forced to be aligned to $'-'$; for any $j_1 \leq j \leq j_2$, if $p_{r_2}(j) < j_1$ or $j_2 < p_{r_2}(j)$, then $r_2[j]$ will be forced to be aligned to $'-'$. It will be clear from Lemmas 4.5.3, 4.5.4, and 4.5.5 that this proposition is used to deal with two situations: aligning one base pair among crossing base pairs and deleting a base pair.

We can now consider how to compute the optimal alignment between $R_1[i_1,i_2]$ and $R_2[j_1,j_2]$. The first two lemmas are trivial, so we omit their proofs.

Lemma 4.5.1.

$$A(\emptyset \; ; \; \emptyset) = 0$$
$$D(\emptyset \; ; \; \emptyset) = \gamma_g$$
$$I(\emptyset \; ; \; \emptyset) = \gamma_g$$

Lemma 4.5.2. *For $i_1 \leq i \leq i_2$ and $j_1 \leq j \leq j_2$,*

$$D(i_1,i \; ; \; \emptyset) = D(i_1,i-1 \; ; \; \emptyset) \qquad I(\emptyset \; ; \; j_1,j) = I(\emptyset \; ; \; j_1,j-1)$$
$$\qquad\qquad\qquad + \gamma(i,0) \qquad\qquad\qquad\qquad\qquad + \gamma(0,j)$$
$$A(i_1,i \; ; \; \emptyset) = D(i_1,i \; ; \; \emptyset) \qquad\quad A(\emptyset \; ; \; j_1,j) = I(\emptyset \; ; \; j_1,j)$$
$$I(i_1,i \; ; \; \emptyset) = D(i_1,i \; ; \; \emptyset) + \gamma_g \quad D(\emptyset \; ; \; j_1,j) = I(\emptyset \; ; \; j_1,j) + \gamma_g$$

Lemma 4.5.3. *For $i_1 \leq i \leq i_2$ and $j_1 \leq j \leq j_2$,*

$$D(i_1, i \; ; \; j_1, j) = \min \begin{cases} D(i_1, i-1 \; ; \; j_1, j) + \gamma(i, 0) \\ A(i_1, i-1 \; ; \; j_1, j) + \gamma(i, 0) + \gamma_g \end{cases}$$

Proof. If $D(i_1, i \; ; \; j_1, j)$ is from $D(i_1, i-1 \; ; \; j_1, j)$, then aligning $r_1[i]$ with $'-'$ does not open a gap. Therefore there is no gap penalty. If $D(i_1, i \; ; \; j_1, j)$ is from either $A(i_1, i-1 \; ; \; j_1, j)$ or an alignment where $r_1[i-1]$ is aligned to $r_2[j]$, then aligning $r_1[i]$ to $'-'$ opens a gap. Therefore there is a gap penalty.

Notice that if $i_1 \leq p_{r_1}(i) < i$, then aligning $r_1[i]$ to $'-'$ means aligning $r_1[p_{r_1}(i)]$ to $'-'$. Therefore with the deletion of a base pair, two gaps may be opened. However aligning $r_1[p_{r_1}(i)]$ to $'-'$ is indeed true in both $D(i_1, i-1 \; ; \; j_1, j)$ and $A(i_1, i-1 \; ; \; j_1, j)$. The reason for this is that for base pair $(r_1[p_{r_1}(i)], r_1[i])$, one base, $r_1[p_{r_1}(i)]$, is inside the interval $[i_1, i-1]$, and one base, $r_1[i]$, is outside the interval $[i_1, i-1]$. This means that $r_1[p_{r_1}(i)]$ is forced to be aligned to $'-'$. $\qquad\square$

Lemma 4.5.4. *For $i_1 \leq i \leq i_2$ and $j_1 \leq j \leq j_2$,*

$$I(i_1, i \; ; \; j_1, j) = \min \begin{cases} I(i_1, i \; ; \; j_1, j-1) + \gamma(0, j) \\ A(i_1, i \; ; \; j_1, j-1) + \gamma(0, j) + \gamma_g \end{cases}$$

Proof. Similar to Lemma 4.5.3. $\qquad\square$

Lemma 4.5.5. *For $i_1 \leq i \leq i_2$ and $j_1 \leq j \leq j_2$,*

if $i = p_{r_1}(i)$ and $j = p_{r_2}(j)$, then

$$A(i_1, i \; ; \; j_1, j) = \min \begin{cases} D(i_1, i \; ; \; j_1, j) \\ I(i_1, i \; ; \; j_1, j) \\ A(i_1, i-1 \; ; \; j_1, j-1) + \gamma(i, j) \end{cases}$$

if $i_1 \leq p_{r_1}(i) < i$ and $j_1 \leq p_{r_2}(j) < j$, then

$$A(i_1, i \; ; \; j_1, j) = \min \begin{cases} D(i_1, i \; ; \; j_1, j) \\ I(i_1, i \; ; \; j_1, j) \\ A(i_1, p_{r_1}(i) - 1 \; ; \; j_1, p_{r_2}(j) - 1) + \\ \quad + A(p_{r_1}(i) + 1, i-1 \; ; \; p_{r_2}(j) + 1, j-1) + \gamma(i, j) \end{cases}$$

otherwise,

$$A(i_1, i \; ; \; j_1, j) = \min \begin{cases} D(i_1, i \; ; \; j_1, j) \\ I(i_1, i \; ; \; j_1, j) \end{cases}$$

Proof. Consider the optimal alignment between $R_1[i_1, i]$ and $R_2[j_1, j]$. There are three cases: (1) $i = p_{r_1}(i)$ and $j = p_{r_2}(j)$, (2) $i_1 \leq p_{r_1}(i) < i$ and $j_1 \leq p_{r_2}(j) < j$, and (3) all the other cases.

For case 1, since $i = p_{r_1}(i)$ and $j = p_{r_2}(j)$, both $r_1[i]$ and $r_2[j]$ are unpaired bases. In the optimal alignment, $r_1[i]$ may be aligned to $'-'$, $r_2[j]$ may be aligned to $'-'$, or $r_1[i]$ may be aligned to $r_2[j]$. Therefore we take the minimum of the three cases.

For case 2, since $i_1 \leq p_{r_1}(i) < i$ and $j_1 \leq p_{r_2}(j) < j$, both $(r_1[p_{r_1}(i)], r_1[i])$ and $(r_2[p_{r_2}(j)], r_2[j])$ are base pairs. In the optimal alignment, $(r_1[p_{r_1}(i)], r_1[i])$ may be aligned to $('-', '-')$, $(r_2[p_{r_2}(j)], r_2[j])$ may be aligned to $('-', '-')$, or $(r_1[p_{r_1}(i)], r_1[i])$ may be aligned to $(r_2[p_{r_2}(j)], r_2[j])$.

If $(r_1[p_{r_1}(i)], r_1[i])$ is aligned to $('-', '-')$, then $A(i_1, i ; j_1, j) = D(i_1, i ; j_1, j)$. If $(r_2[p_{r_2}(j)], r_2[j])$ is aligned to $('-', '-')$ then $A(i_1, i ; j_1, j) = I(i_1, i ; j_1, j)$.

If $(r_1[p_{r_1}(i)], r_1[i])$ is aligned to $(r_2[p_{r_2}(j)], r_2[j])$, then the optimal alignment between $R_1[i_1, i]$ and $R_2[j_1, j]$ is divided into three parts: (1) the optimal alignment between $R_1[i_1, p_{r_1}(i) - 1]$ and $R_2[j_1, p_{r_2}(j) - 1]$, (2) the optimal alignment between $R_1[p_{r_1}(i) + 1, i - 1]$ and $R_2[p_{r_2}(j) + 1, j - 1]$, and (3) the alignment of $(r_1[p_{r_1}(i)], r_1[i])$ to $(r_2[p_{r_2}(j)], r_2[j])$. This is true since any base pair across $(r_1[p_{r_1}(i)], r_1[i])$ or $(r_2[p_{r_2}(j)], r_2[j])$ should be aligned to $'-'$ and the cost of such an alignment has already been included in part 1 and part 2. Hence we have $A(i_1, i ; j_1, j) = A(i_1, p_{r_1}(i) - 1 ; j_1, p_{r_2}(j) - 1) + A(p_{r_1}(i) + 1, i - 1 ; p_{r_2}(j) + 1, j - 1) + \gamma(i, j)$.

In case 3, we consider all the other possibilities in which we cannot align $r_1[i]$ to $r_2[j]$. We examine several subcases involving base pairs.

- Subcase 1: $p_{r_1}(i) > i$. This means that $r_1[p_{r_1}(i)]$ is outside the interval $[i_1, i]$ and we have to align $r_1[i]$ to $'-'$.
- Subcase 2: $p_{r_2}(j) > j$. This is similar to subcase 1. Together with subcase 1, this implies that when $p_{r_1}(i) > i$ and $p_{r_2}(j) > j$, even if $r_1[i] = r_2[j]$, we cannot align them to each other.
- Subcase 3: $p_{r_1}(i) < i_1$. This is similar to subcase 1. Together with subcase 1, we know that if a base pair is across an aligned base pair, then it has to be aligned to $'-'$.
- Subcase 4: $p_{r_2}(j) < j_1$. This is similar to subcase 3.   □

Basic algorithm. From Lemmas 4.5.1 to 4.5.5, we can compute $A(R_1, R_2) = A(1, |R_1| ; 1, |R_2|)$ using a bottom-up approach. Moreover, it is clear that we do not need to compute all $A(i_1, i_2 ; j_1, j_2)$. From Lemma 4.5.5, we need to compute only the $A(i_1, i_2 ; j_1, j_2)$ such that $(r_1[i_1 - 1], r_1[i_2 + 1])$ is a base pair in R_1 and $(r_2[j_1 - 1], r_2[j_2 + 1])$ is a base pair in R_2.

Given R_1 and R_2, we can first compute sorted base-pair lists L_1 for R_1 and L_2 for R_2. This sorted order is in fact a bottom-up order since, for two base pairs s and t in R_1, if s is before or inside t, then s is before t in the sorted list L_1. For each pair of base pairs $L_1[i] = (i_1, i_2)$ and $L_2[j] = (j_1, j_2)$, we use Lemma 4.5.1 to Lemma 4.5.5 to compute $A(i_1 + 1, i_2 - 1 ; j_1 + 1, j_2 - 1)$. We use the procedure in Figure 4.9 to compute $A(R_1[i_1, i_2], R_2[j_1, j_2])$. Figure 4.10 shows the algorithm.

Let R_1 and R_2 be the two given RNA structures and P_1 and P_2 be the number of base pairs in R_1 and R_2, respectively. The time to compute $A(i_1, i_2 ; j_1, j_2)$ is $O((i_2 - i_1)(j_2 - j_1))$, which is bounded by $O(|R_1| \times |R_2|)$. The time complexity of the algorithm in the worst case is $O(P_1 P_2 |R_1| |R_2|)$. We can

To compute $A(R_1[i_1, i_2], R_2[j_1, j_2])$

compute $A(0,0)$, $D(0,0)$, and $I(0,0)$ as in Lemma 4.5.1;

for $i := i_1$ **to** i_2
    compute $A(i,0)$, $D(i,0)$, and $I(i,0)$ as in Lemma 4.5.2;

for $j := j_1$ **to** j_2
    compute $A(0,j)$, $D(0,j)$, and $I(0,j)$ as in Lemma 4.5.2;

for $i := i_1$ **to** i_2
    for $j := j_1$ **to** j_2
        compute $A(i,j)$, $D(i,j)$, and $I(i,j)$ as in Lemma 4.5.3,
        Lemma 4.5.4, and Lemma 4.5.5.

Fig. 4.9. Procedure for computing $A(R_1[i_1, i_2], R_2[j_1, j_2])$.

Input: $R_1[1..m]$ and $R_2[1..n]$

compute a sorted (by $3'$ end) base pair list L_1 for R_1;
compute a sorted (by $3'$ end) base pair list L_2 for R_2;

for $i := 1$ **to** $|L_1|$
    for $j := 1$ **to** $|L_2|$
        let $L_1[i] = (r_1[i_1], r_1[i_2])$;
        let $L_1[j] = (r_2[j_1], r_2[j_2])$;
        compute $A(R_1[i_1 + 1, i_2 - 1], R_2[j_1 + 1, j_2 - 1])$;

compute $A(R_1[1, m], R_2[2, n])$;

trace back to find the optimal alignment between R_1 and R_2.

Fig. 4.10. Algorithm for computing $A(R_1, R_2)$.

improve our algorithm so that the worst case running time is $O(S_1 S_2 |R_1||R_2|)$ where S_1 and S_2 are the number of stems, i.e., stacked pairs of maximal length, in R_1 and R_2, respectively. The space complexity of the algorithm is $O(|R_1||R_2|)$.

Notice that when one of the input RNA structures is a secondary structure, this algorithm computes the optimal solution of the problem. Also, since the number of tertiary interactions is relatively small compared with the number of secondary interactions, we can use this algorithm to compute the alignment between two RNA tertiary structures. Essentially the algorithm tries to find the best sets of noncrossing base pairs to align and delete tertiary interactions. Although this is not an optimal solution, in practice it would produce a reasonable result by aligning most of the base pairs in the two RNA tertiary structures.

4.5.2 Extended Edit Alignment

From the algorithm for computing the edit alignment of two RNA structures, it is easy to develop an algorithm for computing the extended edit alignment between the RNA structures. To begin with, we make the following modifications. A base in a base pair can be deleted, inserted, or aligned with another base. In these situations, the bond between the two bases in the base pair is broken, and therefore there is a base-pair bond-breaking cost. The simplest way is to evenly distribute this cost to the two bases of the base pair.

Let Γ_g be the cost of a base-pair bond-breaking operation. Suppose that $r_1[i]$ is a base in R_1 and $r_2[j]$ is a base in R_2. Then the cost of deleting $r_1[i]$ is $\Gamma(r_1[i] \to \lambda)$ if $r_1[i]$ is an unpaired base in R_1 and $\Gamma(r_1[i] \to \lambda) + \Gamma_g/2$ if $r_1[i]$ is a base in a base pair in R_1; the cost of inserting $r_2[j]$ is $\Gamma(\lambda \to r_2[j])$ if $r_2[j]$ is an unpaired base in R_2 and $\Gamma(\lambda \to r_2[j]) + \Gamma_g/2$ if $r_2[j]$ is a base in a base pair in R_2; the cost of aligning $r_1[i]$ to $r_2[j]$ is $\Gamma(r_1[i] \to r_2[j])$ if both $r_1[i]$ and $r_2[j]$ are unpaired bases, $\Gamma(r_1[i] \to r_2[j]) + \Gamma_g/2$ if exactly one of $r_1[i]$ and $r_2[j]$ is an unpaired base, $\Gamma(r_1[i] \to r_2[j]) + \Gamma_g$ if both $r_1[i]$ and $r_2[j]$ are a base in a base pair.

After performing these changes, Lemmas 4.5.1 to 4.5.4 remain the same as before and Lemma 4.5.5 needs to be changed so that $r_1[i]$ can be aligned with $r_2[j]$ regardless of whether or not they are unpaired bases.

4.6 Some Experimental Results

In our experiments, we compute alignments between RNA tertiary structures. Figures 4.11 and 4.12 show the 2D drawings of two RNA structures where secondary bondings are represented by a dash or a dot between two bases and tertiary bondings are represented by a solid line between distant bases. Figure 4.13 shows another representation of these two RNA structures where nested parentheses, (and), represent secondary base pairs and square brackets, [and], represent tertiary base pairs.

These RNA structures are taken from the RNase P database [54]. Ribonuclease P is the ribonucleoprotein endonuclease that cleaves transfer RNA precursors, removing 5′ precursor sequences and generating the mature 5′ terminus of the tRNA. *Alcaligenes eutrophus* is from the beta purple bacteria group and *Anacystis nidulans* is from the Cyanobacterial group. Notice that both RNA structures are tertiary structures.

We deal with these tertiary structures in the following way. Given two RNA tertiary structures, we first apply the alignment algorithm to produce

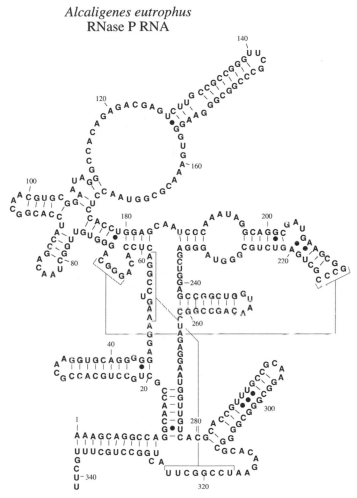

Fig. 4.11. *Alcaligenes eutrophus* from the RNase P database. This image is taken from http://www.mbio.ncsu.edu/RNaseP/.

an alignment where aligned base pairs are noncrossing, and then, using a constrained alignment algorithm, we align tertiary base pairs if they are not in conflict with the base pairs already aligned. The reason for this two-step procedure is that in real RNA data, the number of tertiary base pairs is relatively small compared with the number of secondary base pairs. Therefore the first step will handle the majority secondary base pairs and the second step will handle the minority tertiary base pairs.

Figures 4.14 to 4.17 show four alignment results where the cost of an unpaired base deletion or insertion is 1, the cost of an unpaired base substitution is 1, the cost of a base-pair deletion or insertion is 2, and the

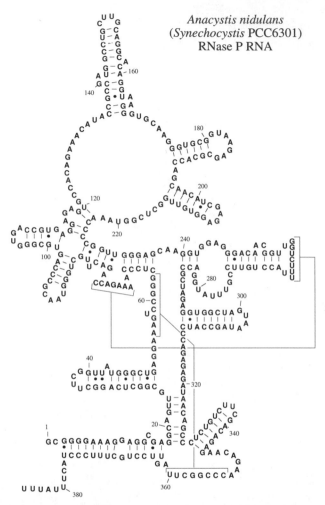

Fig. 4.12. *Anacystis nidulans* from the RNase P database. This image is taken from http://www.mbio.ncsu.edu/RNaseP/.

cost of a base-pair substitution is 1. The first and the second alignments are an edit alignment and an extended edit alignment where *gap_cost* is zero. The third and the fourth alignments are an edit alignment and an extended edit alignment where *gap_cost* is nonzero. Since *gap_cost* is zero for the first and the second alignments, the alignments in fact correspond to computing the edit distance and extended edit distance of those RNA structures.

It is clear that the extended edit distance in Figure 4.15 [205, 254] and the edit alignment in Figure 4.16 [72, 423] are better than the edit distance in Figure 4.14 [259, 448]. The extended edit alignment in Figure 4.17 is better

Alcaligenes eutrophus:

```
     (((((((((((((((((( (( (((((((((      )))))))) ))    [[[ [[[[[[((((   [[[[ ((((( ((((
  1  AAAGCAGGCCAGGCAACCGCUGCCUGCACCGCAAGGUGCAGGGGGAGGAAAGUCCGGACUCCACAGGGCAGGGUGUUGGC

        )))) (((((   )))) )((   ((                  (((( ((((((((   )))))))) ))))
 81  UAACAGCCAUCCACGGCAACGUGCGGAAUAGGGCCACAGAGACGAGUCUUGCCGCCGGGUUCGCCCGGCGGGAAGGGUGA

              )))))))))))))  ((((       ((((((   ((((( ]]]])))))))))))   ))))
161  AACGCGGUAACCUCCACCUGGAGCAAUCCCAAAUAGGCAGGCGAUGAAGCGGCCCGCUGAGUCUGCGGGUAGGGAGCUGG

     ((((((((   ))))))))        ))))))) (( (((((((((   )))))))) ))       ]]]]
241  AGCCGGCUGGUAACAGCCGGCCUAGAGGAAUGGUUGUCACGCACCGUUUGCCGCAAGGCGGGCGGGGCGCACAGAAUCCG

     ]]]] ) )))))))))))
321  GCUUAUCGGCCUGCUUUGCUU
```

Anacystis nidulans:

```
     (((((((( ((( ((((( ((( (((((((((((    ))) ))))))))    [[[ [[[[[((((( [[[[[[[ (((
  1  GCGGGGAAAGGAGGCGAGGCAGUUGCGGCUCAGGCUUCGGUUAUGGGCUGAGGAAAGUCCGGGCUCCCAAAAGACCAGAC

     (((((((       ))))))(((((      )))) )((   ((               (((( (((((((   )))) ))
 81  UUGCUGGGUAACGCCCAGUGCGGGUGACCGUGAGGAUAGUGCCACAGAAACAUACCGCCGAUGGCCUGCUUGCAGGCACA

     ))) )) ((((((       ))))))  (((((((   ))))))))       ))))))))))))))   (
161  GGUAAGGGUGCAAGGGUGCGGUAAGAGCGCACCAGCAACAUCGAGACGGUGUUGGCUCGGUAAACCCCGGUUGGGGAGCAAG

     ((   ((((( ((( ]]]]]]] ))))))))         )))    ((((((((   ))))))))
241  GUGGAGGGACAACGGUUGGUCUUUUACCUGUUCCGUUUAUGGACCGCUACGAGGUGGCUAGUAAUAGCCAUCCCAGAGAGA

     ))) )))((((((   )))))))    ]]]]]]]] ) )))) ))))))))
321  UAACAGCCCUGUGUCUUCGACACAGAACAGAACGGGCUUAUGUCCUGCUUUUCCCUACUUUAUUU
```

Fig. 4.13. Two RNA structures from the RNase P database.

than the extended edit distance in Figure 4.15 and the edit alignment in Figure 4.16.

From the implementation point of view, the programs for computing the edit distance and the edit alignment are much faster than those for computing the extended edit distance and the extended edit alignment. The improvements from the edit distance case to the extended edit distance case or from the edit alignment case to the extended edit alignment case are relatively small. Consequently, in applications where only a distance value rather than an actual alignment is needed, perhaps faster programs for computing the edit distance and edit alignment could be used.

Acknowledgments

This work was supported in part by the Natural Sciences and Engineering Research Council of Canada under research grant no. OGP0046373 and a Sharcnet research fellowship. I would like to thank my coauthors for their work on several projects discussed in this chapter: S. Y. Chen, G. Collins, S. Y. Le, T. Jiang, G. H. Lin, B. Ma, L. S. Wang and Z. Z. Wang.

```
Alcaligenes-eutrophus-pb-b
Anacystis-nidulans-cb: gap = 0, score = 197.000000

--((((((-(--((-(((((-(((( (( ((((((((( -   )))-))))) ))    [[[ [[[[[[(((- --- [[
  (((((((( ((( ((((( -((( ((-((((((((    -))) )))))-))    [[[ [[[[[[((((( [[[--[[
--AAAGCA-G--GC-CAGGC-AACCGCUGCCUGCACCG-CAAGGU-GCAGGGGGAGGAAAGUCCGGACUCC-A---CAGG
GCGGGGAAAGGAGGCGAGGCA-GUUGCG-GCUCAGGCUUCG-GUUAUGGGC-UGAGGAAAGUCCGGGCUCCCAAAA--GA

[[ (((-((- ((((    ))))- ((((( )))) )((  ((        -  (((( (--(((((((-
[[ ((( (((-(((( )))))-((((( )))) )((  ((        -((((-( ((((((
GCAGGG-UG-UUUGGCUAACAGCCA-UCCACGGCAACGUGCGGAAUAGGGCCACAGAGACG-AGUCUUGC--CGCCGGG-U
CCAGACUUGC-UGGGUAACGCCCAG-UGCGGGUGACCGUGAGGAGAGUGCCACAGAAACAUA-CCGC-CGAUGGCCUGCU

    )))))-))) ))--))    -  --------  -------------------------- --       ))))))
    - ))))) )))-)) ))   ((((((       )))))) ((((((( )))))))            ))))))
UCGCCCGG-CGGGAA--GGGUG-AA---------ACG------------------------------C--GGUAACCUCCA
U-GCAGGCACAG-GUAAGGGUGCAAGGGUGCGGUAAGAGCGCACCAGCAACAUCGAGAGGUGUUGGCUCGGUAAACCCCG

)))-)))  ((((    (((((  (((( ]]]----)))))))))))  - ---))))     (((((
)))))))) -(((  -- (((((-- --((( ]]]]]]] )))---)))))            )))-    (((((
CCU-GGAGCAAUCCCAAAUAGGCAGGCGAUGAAGCGGCCC----GCUGAGUCUGCGGGU-A---GGGAGCUGGAGCCGGC
GUUGGGAGCAA-GGUGGA--GGGACA--AC--GGUUGGUCUUUUACC---UGUUCCGUUUAUGGACC-GCUAGAGGUGGC

((   )))))))))       -   )))-)))) (( ((((((((( -  ))))))))) ))       ]]]]]]]]
((   )))))))))       - ))) -)))---(-(((---((( --)))---)))-)- -      ]]]]]]]]
UGGUAACAGCCGGCCUAGAG-GAAUGGU-UGUCACGCACCGUUUGCCG-CAAGGCGGGCGGGGCGCACAGAAUCCGGCUU
UAGUAAUAGCCAUCCCAGAGAGA-UAACA-GCC---C-UCU---GUCUUC--GAC---AGA-G-A-ACAGAACCCGGCUU

) )))--)-)))))       -----
) )))) ))))))))
AUCGGC--C-UGCUUUGCUU-----
AUGUCCUGCUUUCCCUACUUUAUUU
```

Fig. 4.14. Edit distance.

```
Alcaligenes-eutrophus-pb-b
Anacystis-nidulans-cb: gap = 0, break = 1,  score = 188.000000

------((((((((((((((((((( (( ((((((((( -   )))-))))) ))    [[[ [[[[[[(((-   [[[[-
  (((((((( ((( ((((( ((( ((-((((((((    -))) )))))-))    [[[ [[[[[[((((( [[[[[[
------AAAGCAGGCCAGGCAACCGCUGCCUGCACCG-CAAGGU-GCAGGGGGAGGAAAGUCCGGACUCC-ACAGGGC-A
GCGGGGAAAGGAGGCGAGGCAGUUGCG-GCUCAGGCUUCG-GUUAUGGGC-UGAGGAAAGUCCGGGCUCCCAAAAGACCA

(((-(( ((((    )))) ((((( )))) )((  ((        -  (((((- -(((((((( )))
((( (((((((    ))))))((((( )))) )((  ((        -((((( ((((((( - -))
GGG-UGUUGGCUAACAGCCAUCCACGGCAACGUGCGGAAUAGGGCCACAGAGACG-AGUCUU-G-CCGCCGGGUUCGCCC
GACUUGCUGGGUAACGCCCAGUGCGGGUGACCGUGAGGAGAGUGCCACAGAAACAUA-CCGCCGAUGGCCUGCUU-G-CA

)))-)) ))--))    -  ---------  ----  ------  ------------------ --       )))))))))-))
))) )))))  ))   ((((((       )))))) ((((((( )))))))            ))))))))))))
GGC-GGGAA--GGGUG-AA---------A----C------G----------------------C--GGUAACCACCU-GG
GGCACAGGUAAGGGUGCAAGGGUGCGGUAAGAGCGCACCAGCAACAUCGAGAGGUGUUGGCUCGGUAAACCCCGGUUGGG

))  ((((      (((((  (((((- ]]]]---)))))))))))  - -)-)))     (((((((( )
))  (((-   -- (((((-- --((( ]]]]]]] )))---)))))            )))     (((((((( )
AGCAAUCCCAAAUAGGCAGGCGAUGAAGC-GGCCC---GCUGAGUCUGCGGGU-A-G-GGAGCUGGAGCCGGCUGGUAAC
AGCAAGGU-GGA--GGGACA--AC--GGUUGGUCUUUUACC---UGUUCCGUUUAUGGACCGCUAGAGGUGGCUAGUAAU

)))))))       -   )))))))) (( ((((((((( -  ))))))))) ))       ]]]]]]]] ) )))))
)))))))       - ))) )))---(-(((---((( --)))---)))-)- -      ]]]]]]]] ) )-)))
AGCCGGCCUAGAG-GAAUGGUUGUCACGCACCGUUUGCCG-CAAGGCGGGCGGGGCGCACAGAAUCCGGCUUAUCGGCCU
AGCCAUCCCAGAGAGA-UAACAGCC---C-UCU---GUCUUC--GAC---AGA-G-A-ACAGAACCCGGCUUAUGU-CCU

)))))----    -----
))))))))
GCUUU----GCUU-----
GCUUUCCCUACUUUAUUU
```

Fig. 4.15. Extended edit distance.

```
Alcaligenes-eutrophus-pb-b
Anacystis-nidulans-cb: gap = 3, score = 311.000000

--(((((((((---(-((((((-((( (( ((((((((    )))-))))) ))    [[[ [[[[[((((----    [[
   ((((((((( ((( ((-((( ((( ((-(((((((    ))) )))))-))    [[[ [[[[[((((( [[[---[[
--AAAGCAGG---C-CAGGCA-ACCGCUGCCUGCACCGCAAGGU-GCAGGGGGAGGAAAGUCCGGACUCC-----ACAGG
GCGGGGAAAGGAGGCGA-GGCAGUUGCG-GCUCAGGCUUCGGUUAUGGGC-UGAGGAAAGUCCGGGCUCCCAAAA---GA

[[ (((-((- ((((    ))))- ((((( )))) )(( ((            (((( (--(((((((
[[ ((( ((-((((    )))))-((((( )))) )(( ((            (((( ((-((( (((((((
GCAGGG-UG-UUGGCUAACAGCCA-UCCACGGCAACGUGCGGAAUAGGGCCACAGAGACGAGUCUUGC--CGCCGGGUUC
CCAGACUUGC-UGGGUAACGCCCAG-UGCGGGUGACCGUGAGGAGAGUGCCACAGAAACAUACCGC-CGAUGGCCUGCUU

)))))-))) ))--))    ------------------------------------    )))))))))
))))) )))-)) ))    ((((((    )))))) ((((((( )))))))    ))))))))
GCCCGG-CGGGAA--GGGUGAAA------------------------------------CGCGGUAACCUCCACC
GCAGGCACAG-GUAAGGGUGCAAGGGUGCGGUAAGAGCGCACCAGCAACAUCGAGAGGUGUUGGCUCGGUAAACCCCGGU

)-)))) ((((    (((((( ((((( ]]]----)))))))))    ----))))    (((((((((
))))))  (((--- (((((-- --((( ]]]]]]] )))---)))))    -)))    ((((((((
U-GGAGCAAUCCCAAAUAGGCAGGCGAUGAAGCGGCCC----GCUGAGUCUGCGGGUA----GGGAGCUGGAGCCGGCUG
UGGGAGCAAGGU---GGAGGGACA--AC--GGUUGGUCUUUUACC---UGUUCCGUUUAUGG-ACCGCUAGAGGUGGCUA

)))))))))            )))-)))) (( (((((((((    ))))))))) ))    ]]]]]]]] ) )
))))))))            ))) )))--------((((((( -)))))))------    ]]]]]]] ) )
GUAACAGCCGGCCUAGAGGAAUGGU-UGUCACGCACCGUUUGCCGCAAGGCGGGCGGGGCGCACAGAAUCCGGCUUAUCG
GUAAUAGCCAUCCCAGAGAGAUAACAGCC--------CUCUGUCUUC-GACAGAG------AACAGAACCCGGCUUAUGU

)---))))))))    -----
))) ))))))))
G---CCUGCUUUGCUU-----
CCUGCUUUCCCUACUUUUAUUU
```

Fig. 4.16. Edit alignment.

```
Alcaligenes-eutrophus-pb-b
Anacystis-nidulans-cb: gap = 3, break = 1, score = 254.500000

------(((((((((((((((((( (( ((((((((    ))))))) ))    [[[ [[[[[((((-- [[[[ ((
   ((((((((( ((( ((((( ((( ((((((-(((    ))) )))))))    [[[ [[[[[((((( [[[[[[ ((
------AAAGCAGGCCAGGCAACCGCUGCCUGCACCGCAAGGUGCAGGGGGAGGAAAGUCCGGACUCC--ACAGGGCAGG
GCGGGGAAAGGAGGCGAGGCAGUUGCGGCUCA-GGCUUCGGUUAUGGGCUGAGGAAAGUCCGGGCUCCCAAAAGACCAGA

(-(( ((((    )))) (((((    )))) )(( ((            ((((-- (((((((    ))))))
( (((((((    )))))((((    )))) ((-((( ((            (((((  ((-((( (    )))))
G-UGUUGGCUAACAGCCAUCCACGGCAACGUGCGGAAUAGGGCCACAGAGACGAGUCUU--GCCGCCGGGUUCGCCCGGC
CUUGCUGGGUAACGCCCAGUGCGGGUGACCGUGAGGAGAGUGCCACAGAAACAUACCGCGAUG-GCCUGCUUGCAGGCA

)) ))--))    ------------------------------------    )))))))))-))))
))))) ))    ((((((    )))))) ((((((( )))))))    )))))))))))))
GGGAA--GGGUGAAA------------------------------------CGCGGUAACCUCCACCU-GGAGCA
CAGGUAAGGGUGCAAGGGUGCGGUAAGAGCGCACCAGCAACAUCGAGAGGUGUUGGCUCGGUAAACCCCGGUUGGGAGCA

((((    (((((( ((--((( ]]]----)))))))))))    ))))    ((((((( )))))
(((    ------(((---(( ((( ]]]]]]] ))))))))    )))    ((((((( )))))
AUCCCAAAUAGGCAGGCGAUGA--AGCGGCCC----GCUGAGUCUGCGGGUAGGGAGCUGGAGCCGGCUGGUAACAGCCG
AGGUGGAG------GGA---CAACGGUUGGUCUUUUACCUGUUCCGUUUAUGGACCGCUAGAGGUGGCUAGUAAUAGCCA

))            )))))) (( (((((((((    ))))))))) ))    ]]]]]]]] ) )))))))))
))            ))) )))))------(((((((( ---))))))) ))    ]]]]]]]] ) )-))) )))))
GCCUAGAGGAAUGGUUGUCACGCACCGUUUGCCGCAAGGCGGGCGGGGCGCACAGAAUCCGGCUUAUCGGCCUGCUUUGC
UCCCAGAGAGAUAACAGCC------CUCUGUCUUC---GACAGAG-----AACAGAACCCGGCUUAUGU-CCUGCUUUCC

---------
))
---------UU
CUACUUUAUUU
```

Fig. 4.17. Extended edit alignment.

Part III

Biological Data Mining

Chapter 5

Piecewise Constant Modeling of Sequential Data Using Reversible Jump Markov Chain Monte Carlo

Marko Salmenkivi and Heikki Mannila

Summary

We describe the use of reversible jump Markov chain Monte Carlo (RJMCMC) methods for finding piecewise constant descriptions of sequential data. The method provides posterior distributions on the number of segments in the data and thus gives a much broader view on the potential data than do methods (such as dynamic programming) that aim only at finding a single optimal solution. On the other hand, MCMC methods can be more difficult to implement than discrete optimization techniques, and monitoring convergence of the simulations is not trivial. We illustrate the methods by modeling the GC content and distribution of occurrences of ORFs and SNPs along the human genomes. We show how the simple models can be extended by modeling the influence of GC content on the intensity of ORF occurrence.

5.1 Introduction

Sequential data occur frequently in biological applications. At least three different types of sequential data can be distinguished: strings, sequences of events, and time series. A string is simply a sequence of symbols from some alphabet Σ (typically Σ is assumed to be finite). In genomic applications, the alphabet is typically the four-letter DNA alphabet. A sequence of events over alphabet Σ is a collection of pairs (e, t), where $e \in \Sigma$ is the event and t is the occurrence time (or position) of the event. As an example, if we are interested in the occurrences of certain specific words $w_1, \ldots, w_k$ in the genome, we can model the occurrences as a sequence of events consisting of pairs (w_i, t), where t is the position in the sequence of w_i. A time series consists also of pairs (e, t), where t is the occurrence, or measurement time,

but e is a possibly many-dimensional value. For example, we can consider
the frequency of all two-letter words in overlapping windows of some length
in the genome to obtain a time series with dimension 16.

The process that creates the sequential data can often be assumed to
have several hidden states. For example, a genomic sequence could contain
segments stemming from different sources. This leads to the question of
verifying whether there are different segments, and if there are, finding the
change points between the segments.

A natural way of modeling the sources and transitions between them is
to use *piecewise constant functions*. Change points of a piecewise constant
function can be interpreted as modeling the transitions between hidden
sources. Function values in each piece correspond to the relatively stable
behavior between the transitions.

In the case of time series data, a common choice for modeling is to use
some function $\alpha(t)$, which determines the value of the time series at time t,
except for random error. The error is assumed to be normally distributed
with zero mean, which leads to the loglikelihood being proportional to the
sum of squared distances between the observations and the model predictions.
In piecewise representations of $\alpha(t)$, we obtain the total loglikelihood as the
sum of the loglikelihoods in each piece.

As we use piecewise constant functions, the function $\alpha(t)$ has the following
form:

$$
\alpha(t) = \begin{cases}
\alpha_1 \text{ if } S_s \leq t < c_1 \\
\alpha_2 \text{ if } c_1 \leq t < c_2 \\
\vdots \quad \vdots \\
\alpha_i \text{ if } c_{i-1} \leq t \leq S_e \\
0 \quad \text{elsewhere}
\end{cases}
$$

Here $\{S_s, S_e\} \in \mathbf{R}$ are the start and end points of the sequence, the values
$\{\alpha_1, ..., \alpha_i\} \in \mathbf{R}^+$ are the function values in i pieces, and
$\{c_1, ..., c_{i-1}\} \in [S_s, S_e]$ are the *change points* of the function.

Figure 5.1 shows an example of a piecewise constant description $\alpha(t)$ of a
time series. Measurements are indicated by the values at positions $t_1, \ldots t_7$,
and they are illustrated by the filled bars.

Dynamic programming methods can be used to find the best-fitting
piecewise constant function in time $\mathcal{O}(n^2 k)$, for n observations and k segments
[36, 268]. The problem with the dynamic programming methods is that, as
maximum likelihood methods, they always provide a segmentation with a
given number of segments, whether the data support one or not. This can lead
to spurious or downright misleading results, unless care is taken to control
carefully for the significance of the output.

In this chapter we give an introduction to Bayesian modeling of
sequential data and the reversible jump Markov chain Monte Carlo

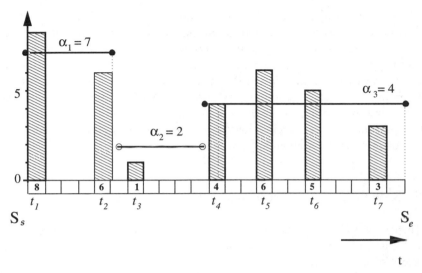

Fig. 5.1. A piecewise constant description $\alpha(t)$ of a time series, with the observations illustrated by the filled bars. The observation range is $[S_s, S_e]$. The loglikelihood of the time series given $\alpha(t)$ may, for example, be proportional to $\Sigma_j(\alpha(t_j) - y(t_j))^2$, where $y(t_j)$ is the observation at t_j.

(RJMCMC) simulation methods for finding posterior distributions of the model parameters. We use piecewise constant functions in the models, but the number of pieces is not fixed. Consequently, the methods produce the posterior distribution of the number of segments as a marginal distribution. The posterior description of the data, whether time series or event sequence, is a continuous function, though originally represented by piecewise constant functions.

The running time of the algorithm is $\mathcal{O}(n + I)$, where n is the number of measurements/occurrences and I is the size of the sample generated from the posterior distribution. That is, each sample can be generated in constant time with respect to the amount of data, given linear preprocessing. Typically, I is quite large.

We illustrate the method by modeling the GC content and distribution of occurrences of ORFs and SNPs along the human genomes. The methods can, however, be applied to any time series or set of discrete events along the genome, e.g., recombinations, transcription factors, and so on.

The rest of the chapter is organized as follows. At the end of this section we take a look at related work. Section 5.2 provides basics of the Bayesian modeling approach and gives an introduction to the reversible jump Markov chain Monte Carlo simulation methods. Examples of applying the methods are given in section 5.3. Section 5.4 is a short conclusion.

The Bayesian approach to segmentation has been used before; see, e.g.,
[47]. A general Bayesian approach to finding change points of the distribution
of letters along a sequence with multinomial likelihood is described in [256].
Dynamic programming approaches are utilized to speed up the Bayesian
analysis. A further application of Bayesian techniques for DNA segmentation
is given in [328]. Computationally, we apply the MCMC approach to estimate
the posterior probabilities on the whole space of segmentations. The use of
RJMCMC methods is especially useful for studying segmentations containing
different numbers of segments.

5.2 Bayesian Approach and MCMC Methods

In this section we briefly describe the Bayesian modeling approach and apply
it to finding piecewise constant models for sequential data. For more detailed
descriptions, see, e.g., [40, 140].

Bayesian data analysis sets up a model that determines a joint distribution
for all the quantities of the problem, that is, model parameters θ and data
Y. Bayes rule is obtained by conditioning the joint distribution on the known
data:

$$P(\theta|Y) = \frac{P(\theta)P(Y|\theta)}{P(Y)}.$$

The conditional distribution $P(\theta|Y)$ is the *posterior distribution* of the
model parameters, and $P(Y|\theta)$ is the likelihood of data given the parameters.
Assuming that the data are known, the computational part of Bayesian data
analysis is to update the *prior distribution* $P(\theta)$ to the posterior distribution
according to Bayes rule. The probability of the data $P(Y)$ is independent of
θ. Thus, the posterior distribution is proportional to the product of the prior
distribution and the likelihood.

Integration of the posterior distribution analytically or even by numerical
methods is seldom possible. Monte Carlo integration could be used for
approximate integration if only random samples could be drawn from the
distribution. Markov chain Monte Carlo (MCMC) methods enable sampling
from complex distributions. A sequence of samples generated by MCMC
methods is a realization of a Markov chain that has the desired distribution
f as the stationary distribution.

A simple condition can be utilized to guarantee that the values of a
sequence of samples follow f. Denote by $T(\theta, \theta')$ the probability of choosing
θ' to be the next sample, given that the last chosen is θ. The reversibility
condition holds if for all pairs of values θ and θ' we have

$$f(\theta)T(\theta, \theta') = f(\theta')T(\theta', \theta). \tag{5.1}$$

The reversibility condition and the technical conditions of aperiodicity and irreducibility are sufficient to guarantee that the Markov chain has f as the stationary distribution, that is, the distribution of states converges to f [163, 402].

The Metropolis-Hastings algorithm solves the problem of finding a suitable function T as follows [172, 273]. A distribution $q(\theta, \theta')$ is used to draw a candidate for the next sample. The candidate is accepted with probability

$$\alpha(\theta, \theta') = \min(1, \frac{f(\theta') \, q(\theta', \theta)}{f(\theta) \, q(\theta, \theta')}).$$

In the case of Bayesian posterior distribution, as we only need to know $f(\theta')/f(\theta)$ to apply the Metropolis-Hastings algorithm, the probabilities $P(Y)$ of Bayes rule cancel. Hence, as long as $P(\theta)P(Y|\theta)$ can be calculated, the MCMC methods can be used to integrate the posterior approximately.

Theoretically, a Markov chain with a stationary distribution converges to the distribution from any initial state. However, there are usually remarkable differences between initial states in how long the chain has to be run before reaching the stationary distribution. When using the Metropolis-Hastings algorithm, a *burn-in* period must be run without storing the parameter values. Finding the sufficient length of the burn-in is not always easy. There are many heuristic methods for solving the problem in practical situations (see, e.g., [52, 53]).

5.2.1 Finding Piecewise Constant Functions with RJMCMC Methods

We are interested in piecewise constant models with the number of pieces as a model parameter. That is, we want to consider models with different numbers of parameters. In a Bayesian framework this can be done by specifying a hierarchical model, which assigns a prior distribution to the number of pieces. Figure 5.2 displays a graphical representation of two models: a piecewise constant model with a fixed number of pieces and its extension to variable dimensions, with the number of pieces m as a hyperparameter of the model.

To exploit the MCMC methods in the extended model, we should be able to move from a state to another state with a different number of dimensions. In the following we present the reversible jump MCMC (RJMCMC) algorithm, which is a generalization of the Metropolis-Hastings algorithm to state spaces of variable dimensions. The form of the presentation is easily applicable for our purposes, modeling sequential data by utilizing piecewise constant presentations. For more general conditions and a detailed theoretical description of variable-dimension MCMC, see [155]. The main sources of the presentation are [419] and [155].

To use RJMCMC simulation, we need to specify proposal distributions that update the existing parameter vector. The updates are divided into

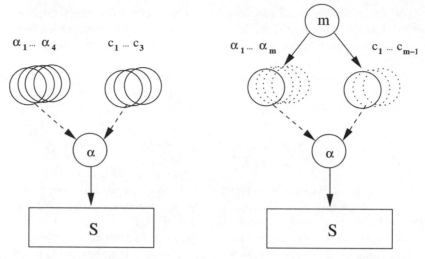

Fig. 5.2. Graphical representation of (left) a model with a fixed number of pieces, here $m = 4$, and (right) a model with the number of pieces not fixed. S is sequential data.

two groups: those that maintain the dimension and those that do not. The proposal distributions that maintain the dimension can change the function value in one segment and modify the start or end point of a segment. The operations that modify the dimension can create a new segment by splitting an existing one or merge two adjacent segments into one.

Let us divide the parameter vector into two components $\theta = (m, z)$, where $m \in \{1, 2, \ldots, K\}$ determines the dimension of the model $n_m \geq 1$ and z is the vector of the other parameters of the model, possibly of varying length. Given m, z can take only values in $E^{n_m} \subseteq R^{n_m}$. To enable the use of reversibility, the following condition has to be met for all pairs z, z':

$$n_m + n_{mm'} = n_{m'} + n_{m'm}, \tag{5.2}$$

where $n_{mm'}$ is the dimension of the vector of random numbers used in determining the candidate state z' in state z and $n_{m'm}$ is the dimension of the vector of random numbers used in the reverse operation. This condition is to ensure that both sides of the reversibility equation have densities on spaces of equal dimension:

$$f(z \mid m) \, q_{mm'}(z, z') \; = \; f(z' \mid m') \, q_{m'm}(z', z). \tag{5.3}$$

Here $f(z|m)$ is the density of z in the target distribution, given the dimension n_m, and $q_{mm'}(z, z')$ is the proposal density of proposing z' in z, given that a move is proposed from the model dimension n_m to $n_{m'}$.

For our purposes it is enough to consider the situation where $n_{mm'} > 0$ and $n_{m'm} = 0$, when $m' > m$. That is, we use a stochastic proposal only when moving to a state with higher dimension. In the reverse operation a deterministic proposal is used instead; thus $n_{m'm} = 0$.

Piecewise constant model. Consider a model consisting of a single piecewise constant function. Using the notation discussed, denote the number of the pieces of the piecewise constant function by m; then the other parameters are $c_1, \ldots, c_{m-1}, \alpha_1, \ldots, \alpha_m$, where $c_1, \ldots, c_{m-1}$ are the change points of the function and $\alpha_1, \ldots, \alpha_m$ are the function levels. The dimension of the model is $n_m = 2m - 1$.

We update each change point and each level componentwise. These updates do not change the dimension of the model. For the number of pieces we first choose between increasing or decreasing the value with some probabilities q_{add} and $q_{del} = 1 - q_{add}$, and then propose to insert or delete one piece at a time. Thus,

$$q(m, m') = \begin{cases} q_{add} & \text{if } m' = m + 1 \\ 1 - q_{add} & \text{if } m' = m - 1 \\ 0 & \text{otherwise} \end{cases} \qquad (5.4)$$

Inserting a piece means adding one change point, which splits one of the pieces into two. In addition to the location of the new change point, the function levels around the change point must be determined. We employ a strategy introduced by Green [155], which maintains the integral of the piecewise constant function in the adding and removing processes. This property of the proposal distribution is often useful for achieving good convergence and for covering the target distribution exhaustively in feasible time.

Denote the function value in the piece to be split by α_0, the candidate for the new change point by c', the candidate for the function value to the left from c' by α'_l, and the candidate for the function value to the right from c' by α'_r (Figure 5.3). We should define how the parameters of the new state $(c', \alpha'_l, \alpha'_r)$ are determined from the current state (α_0) and a vector of random numbers.

We use two random numbers, $u = (u_1, u_2)$, in constructing the new state; thus, $n_{mm'} = 2$. We draw u_1 uniformly from range $]S_s, S_e[$ and set $c' = u_1$. For the function values, we draw u_2 from the normal distribution $N(0, \sigma \cdot \alpha_0)$, where σ is a constant that controls how close the new function values are to the original value.

Accordingly, we have the following function g for determining the new state:

$$g(\alpha_0, u_1, u_2) = (g_1(\alpha_0, u_1, u_2), g_2(\alpha_0, u_1, u_2), g_3(\alpha_0, u_1, u_2)),$$

where

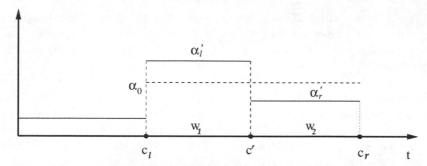

Fig. 5.3. Changing the number of pieces of a piecewise constant function. When adding a piece, the new change point c' is inserted between the existing change points c_l and c_r; w_1 and w_2 are the distances of c' from c_l and c_r, respectively. The function value before the operation is α_0. The new levels α'_l and α'_r are determined according to Equation 5.5. The remove operation is carried out similarly in reverse order.

$$
\begin{aligned}
g_1(\alpha_0, u_1, u_2) &= \alpha_0 + u_2/w_1 = \alpha'_l, \\
g_2(\alpha_0, u_1, u_2) &= \alpha_0 - u_2/w_2 = \alpha'_r, \\
g_3(\alpha_0, u_1, u_2) &= u_1 \qquad\quad = c',
\end{aligned}
\tag{5.5}
$$

and

$$
\begin{aligned}
u_1 &\sim U(S_s, S_e), \\
u_2 &\sim N(0, \sigma \cdot \alpha_0).
\end{aligned}
\tag{5.6}
$$

Here w_1 is the distance of the new change point c' from the previous change point c_l (or the start point of the observation period if there is no change point before c'), and w_2 is the distance of the new change point from the next change point c_r (or the end point of the observation period, if there is no change point after c'). Thus $w_1 = c' - c_l$ and $w_2 = c_r - c'$.

Reversibility condition. Now we can write the reversibility condition more explicitly. For the transition into a higher dimension, the following conditions should be met:

1. $m' = m + 1$ is proposed.
2. given the proposal of m', $z' = g(z, u)$ is proposed.
3. (m', z') is accepted.

Hence, we can write the reversibility condition as follows:

$$
\int_{A_m} \int I_{mm'} p(m) f(z|m) \; q_{add} \; a[(m, z), (m', z')] \; q_{mm'}(z, u) dz du
$$

$$
= \int_{B_{m'}} I_{m'm} p(m') f(z'|m') \; q_{del} \; a[(m', z'), (m, z)] \; dz',
$$

where $A_m \subseteq E^{n_m}, B_{m'} \subseteq E^{n_{m'}}$, $p(m)$ is the probability of m and $I_{mm'}$ and $I_{m'm}$ are the indicator functions $I_{mm'} = 1(z \in A_m, g(z, u) \in B_{m'})$, $I_{m'm} = 1(g^{-1}(z') \in A_m)$.

Now we want to present the right-hand side in terms of variables z and u instead of z'. Since the function g of the Equation 5.5 is a differentiable bijection, we can substitute the variables $z = (\alpha_0)$ and $u = (u_1, u_2)$ for $z' = (\alpha_l', \alpha_r')$ (for the transformation of random variables, see, e.g. [161]):

$$\int_{A_m} \int I_{mm'} p(m) \; f(z|m) \; q_{add} \; a[(m, z), (m', g(z, u))] \; q_{mm'}(z, u) \; dz du$$

$$= \int \int p(m') f(g(z, u)|m') \; q_{del} \; a[(m', g(z, u)), (m, z)] \mid J \mid dz du,$$

where the Jacobian $|J|$ of the transformation is

$$| J | = \left| \frac{\partial(q(z, u))}{\partial z \partial u} \right| = \begin{vmatrix} \frac{\partial \alpha_l'}{\partial \alpha_0} & \frac{\partial \alpha_l'}{\partial u_1} & \frac{\partial \alpha_l'}{\partial u_2} \\ \frac{\partial \alpha_r'}{\partial \alpha_0} & \frac{\partial \alpha_r'}{\partial u_1} & \frac{\partial \alpha_r'}{\partial u_2} \\ \frac{\partial \partial}{\partial \alpha_0} & \frac{\partial}{\partial u_1} & \frac{\partial}{\partial u_2} \end{vmatrix} = \begin{vmatrix} 1 & 0 & \frac{1}{w_1} \\ 1 & 0 & -\frac{1}{w_2} \\ 0 & 1 & 0 \end{vmatrix} = \frac{1}{w_1} + \frac{1}{w_2} = \frac{w_1 + w_2}{w_1 w_2}.$$

The reversibility condition is met if

$$p(m) f(z \mid m) \; q_{add} \; a[(m, z), (m', g(z, u))] \; q_{mm'}(z, u)$$

$$= p(m') f(g(z, u) \mid m') \; q_{del} \; a[(m', g(z, u)), (m, z)] \mid J \mid.$$

Hence the acceptance ratio for inserting a piece is

$$a[(m, z), (m', z')] = \min \left(1, \frac{p(m') f(z' \mid m') q_{del}}{p(m) f(z \mid m) q_{add} \, q_{mm'}(z, u)} \left| \frac{\partial(g(z, u))}{\partial z \, \partial u} \right| \right)$$

$$= \min \left(1, \frac{Pr(m+1)}{Pr(m)} \frac{Pr(c_1', \dots, c_m')}{Pr(c_1, \dots, c_{m-1})} \frac{Pr(\alpha_l') Pr(\alpha_r')}{Pr(\alpha_0)} \times \frac{L(z')}{L(z)} \times \right.$$

$$\left. \frac{q_{del}}{q_{add}} \frac{1}{m+1} \frac{1}{(S_e - S_s) \cdot y} \times \frac{w_1 + w_2}{w_1 w_2} \right).$$

Here $Pr(m)$ is the prior probability of m being the number of pieces, $Pr(c_1, \dots, c_{m-1})$ is the prior density of the change points $c_1, \dots, c_{m-1}$, and

$Pr(\alpha_0)$ is the prior density of function value α_0. Further, $L(z')$ and $L(z)$ are the likelihoods in the candidate state and current state, respectively, and q_{add} and q_{del} are the probabilities of proposing to insert a new segment and delete an existing one. The probability of removing a specific piece is $1/(m+1)$, and the density of inserting a specific piece is $1/(S_e - S_s) \cdot y$, where $y \sim N(0, \sigma \cdot \alpha_0)$. Finally, $(w_1 + w_2)/w_1 w_2$ is the Jacobian of the deterministic transformation of the random variables when changing the dimension of the model. Notice also the exception of the potential initial state where the denominator is zero; then the acceptance rate is 1.

The acceptance probability for the reverse remove operation yields reversibly $a[(m', z'), (m, z)] = \min(1, 1/a[(m, z), (m', z')])$.

5.3 Examples

In this section we give some simple examples of applying the framework to biological data. Our focus is on describing the applicability of the method, not on interpretation of the results.

5.3.1 Segmenting GC Content

We illustrate applying the reversible jump MCMC methods to time series data by modeling GC content in human chromosome 10 with a variable-dimension piecewise constant model. The graphical representation of the model was shown at the right in Figure 5.2. We computed the GC content by taking the proportion of bases C and G in the window of 250 kbp around every 50,000th base in the DNA sequence. This resulted a time series of 2688 observations.

The joint probability distribution $M(\theta, S)$ of time series data S and model parameters $\theta = (m, \alpha_1, \ldots, \alpha_m, c_1, \ldots, c_{m-1})$ is

$$M(\theta, S) = P(m)P(\alpha_i, c_i | m)P(S | \alpha_i, c_i).$$

The levels of the function α_i, the change times c_i, and the number of pieces m are random variables. We assign the following prior distributions to them:

$$
\begin{aligned}
\text{number of pieces } m &\sim \text{Geom}(\gamma), \\
\text{levels } \alpha_i &\sim \text{Norm}(\mu, \sigma^2), \\
\text{change points } c_i &\sim \text{Unif}(S_s, S_e).
\end{aligned}
\tag{5.7}
$$

We choose fairly noninformative priors by setting $\mu = 50$, and $\sigma^2 = 225$. S_s and S_e are the start and end points of the DNA sequence in the chromosome. In the first trial we set $\gamma = 0.5$, in the second one $\gamma = 0.9999$.

Thus in the second trial the prior strongly supports smaller numbers of segments.

We assume the likelihood being of the form described, that is,

$$\log L(S) \propto \sum_{j=1}^{n}(\alpha(t_j) - y(t_j))^2,$$

where $y(t_j)$ is the observation at position t_j and n is the number of observations.

The simulation was run with 1,000,000 burn-in iterations and 10,000,000 actual iterations. Every 10th parameter value was picked up, and consequently the sample size $k = 1,000,000$.

The results are shown in Figures 5.4 and 5.5. The left graph in Figure 5.4 shows the marginal distribution of the number of segments in case of $\gamma = 0.5$. We see that the number of segments is fairly strongly concentrated around 350. After setting $\gamma = 0.9999$ the mode of the distribution shifts down to 210.

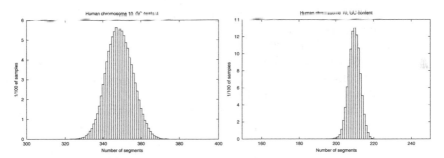

Fig. 5.4. Marginal posterior distribution of the number of segments m in the GC content of human chromosome 10. Prior distribution of m is the geometric distribution with (left) hyperparameter 0.5 and (right) 0.9999.

Figure 5.5 shows an approximation of the posterior mean of GC content for the case $\gamma = 0.5$. It was obtained by computing $\alpha(t_j) = \frac{1}{k}\sum_{i=1}^{k}\alpha^i(t_j)$ for 2,000 pre-defined locations t_j along the DNA sequence, where $\alpha^i(t_j)$ is the value of $\alpha(t_j)$ in ith sample. That is, the posterior mean $E_f(\alpha(t_j))$ is approximated by averaging over $k = 1,000,000$ sample values:

$$E_f(\alpha(t_j)) = \int_0^{100} \alpha(t_j)f(\alpha, t_j)\, d\alpha \approx \frac{1}{k}\sum_{i=1}^{k}\alpha^i(t_j). \tag{5.8}$$

Figure 5.4 shows that the number of segments is fairly large, even for the case $\gamma = 0.9999$. Thus the existence of segment structure for chromosome 10

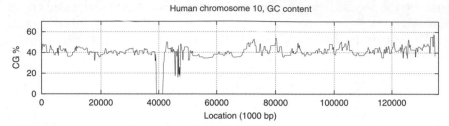

Fig. 5.5. Posterior mean of the GC content in human chromosome 10 obtained by computing $\alpha(t_j) = \frac{1}{k}\sum_{i=1}^{k}\alpha^i(t_j)$ for 2000 predefined locations t_j along the DNA sequence. The number of samples $k = 1,000,000$.

with respect to GC content is doubtful. The next example considers a case where a segment structure apparently exists.

5.3.2 Modeling ORF and SNP Densities in the Human Genome

Next we consider modeling event sequence data, the ORF and SNP densities in the human genome. A more detailed example of intensity modeling of event sequence data is given in [112].

The event sequence is modeled as a Poisson process with a time-dependent intensity function $\lambda(t)$. Intuitively, the intensity function expresses the average number of events in a time unit (see, e.g., [18, 161]).

Poisson loglikelihood of the event sequence S with occurrence times $t_1,\dots,t_n$, is given by (see, e.g., [163])

$$\log L(S \mid \lambda) = -(\int_{S_s}^{S_e}\lambda(t)dt) + \sum_{j=1}^{n}\ln(\lambda(t_j)). \tag{5.9}$$

We ran four similar trials, except for the prior specifications for the number of pieces m. In the last trial we also changed the prior of the intensity levels. The prior distributions were

$$
\begin{aligned}
\text{number of pieces } m &\sim \text{Geom}(\gamma),\\
\text{levels } \lambda_i &\sim \text{Gamma}(\nu,\eta),\\
\text{change points } c_i &\sim \text{Unif}(S_s, S_e).
\end{aligned} \tag{5.10}
$$

The hyperparameters of the geometric distribution are given in Table 5.1. In the first and fourth trial, large values of m were strongly weighted; in the third one we supported small values.

For the intensity levels, the gamma prior with hyperparameters $\nu = 0.005$ and $\eta = 0.5$ was used in all but the last trial. In trial 4, we used

Table 5.1. Parameter values for the different trials for modeling ORF density. Prior distribution of intensity levels λ_i was a gamma distribution; ν and η indicate the hyperparameters of the gamma distribution in each trial.

Trial	1	2	3	4
$m \sim Geom(\gamma); \gamma =$	0.001	0.5	0.9	0.001
ν	0.005	0.005	0.005	0.001
η	0.5	0.5	0.5	0.1

hyperparameters $\nu = 0.001$ and $\eta = 0.1$ instead (see Table 5.1). The expectation of the gamma distribution is ν/η, so the prior had the same mean 1/100 in all the trials. The variance, however, is ν/η^2; thus in the first three trials the prior variance was 1/200, and in the last one it was 1/100. We will return to the interesting question of the effect of priors later.

During the burn-in period, a change of the value of m, that is, inserting or deleting a segment, was proposed approximately 50,000,000 times, and during the actual simulation run nearly 400,000,000 times. In the case of the chromosome 1, for instance, a candidate state was accepted in 0.11 % of the cases. Since the acceptance-rejection rates of the other parameters were much higher, they were updated more rarely, approximately 40,000,000 times during the actual run in the case of the intensity value in the first segment λ_1, for instance. The value of parameter m was picked up at approximately every 100th iteration; that is, the sample size of m was 4,000,000.

Figure 5.6 shows the posterior average and standard deviation of the number of segments for human chromosomes 1–22 in four trials with different prior distributions. For each chromosome there are four errorbars in the figure, each of which presents the posterior average and standard deviation of the number of pieces in one trial. There are clear differences between chromosomes. The differences are not explained by the sizes of the chromosomes, though the size and the number of segments correlate. For instance, there seem to be relatively few segments in chromosome 4 and many segments in chromosomes 7 and 11. Chromosomes 16 and 18 have about the same number of segments, but the number of segments needed to model the distribution of ORFs on chromosome 16 is about twice the number of segments for chromosome 18. Still, there seems to be a lot of variation in chromosome 18 within a single trial as well as between the trials. The variation is also remarkably large in chromosome 1, while chromosome 15 is divided into 16 or 17 segments in all the trials. The segmentations of chromosomes 21 and 22 stay almost the same as well.

Figure 5.7 shows the posterior averages and deviations of the intensities of ORF occurrence frequency for chromosomes 15 and 18. There are clear segment boundaries in the chromosomes, indicating that various parts of the chromosomes are qualitatively different. The 16 or 17 segments of chromosome 15 that resulted in all the trials can easily be identified in the figure.

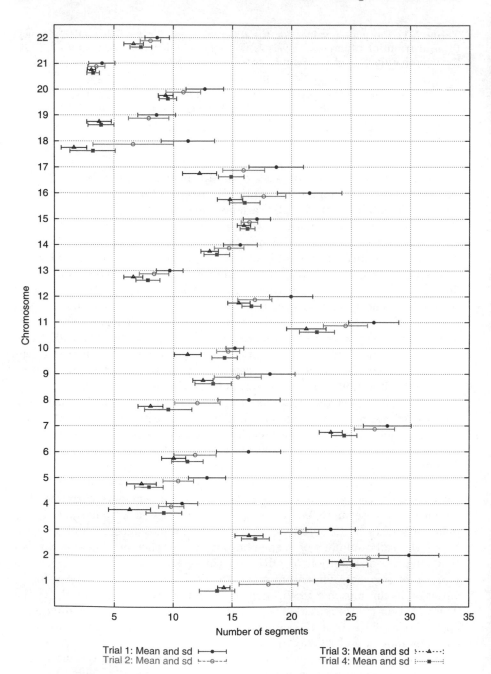

Fig. 5.6. The posterior average and standard deviation of the number of segments for ORF occurrences on human chromosomes 1–22 in four different trials. For the parameter values, see Table 5.1.

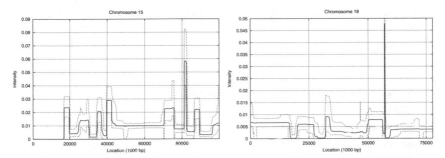

Fig. 5.7. The posterior means and 99% percentiles of the intensity of ORF occurrence in human chromosomes 15 and 18.

Chromosome 18 has many sharp change points and boundaries with smaller variation between them. The slight changes inside the relatively stable periods explain the instability of number of segments in the different trials.

The Bayesian framework and RJMCMC methods provide a conceptually sound way of evaluation between models on the whole space of segmentations. The likelihood of the model can always be improved by adding more parameters to the model. By supplying prior probabilities to all the combinations of the model parameters, the problem is shifted in Bayesian analysis to investigating the joint probability distribution of the data and the parameters. The question then takes the form of whether the advantage gained in likelihood by adding more parameters exceeds the possible loss in prior probabilities.

From the point of view of data mining, a particularly interesting problem in segmentation and clustering more generally is finding the optimal number of segments based on the given data. In a typical data mining problem, the number of data is large, and there is little previous knowledge on the process generating the data.

In the experiments on the ORF distribution, the results clearly indicate differences between different chromosomes. The priors for the number of segments are less informative in the first and fourth trials. In the second trial small values were given considerably higher probability, and they were emphasized even more strongly in the third trial. While giving higher prior probabilities to smaller segment counts naturally decreases the expected number of segments, the magnitude of the effect seems to be quite different in different chromosomes.

An important aspect is that the posterior distribution of the number of segments may be influenced more by the prior specification of the intensity levels than the prior for the dimension of the model. This is because in the higher dimension the joint prior density of the model consists of the product of one more prior densities of intensity levels than in the lower dimension.

This fact may cause problems when estimating the number of segments. Assume, for instance, that very little prior knowledge is available as to the possible intensity values. Accordingly, we would like to give wide uniform prior distributions to the intensity levels. This practice would make sense if the model dimension is fixed. However, for models with variable dimension, inserting a new segment causes the joint density to drop more the wider the prior distribution is.

The fourth trial illustrates this effect on the ORF distribution example. Gamma$(0.005, 0.5)$ priors were specified for the intensity levels λ_i in all the trials except for the fourth one, for which Gamma$(0.001, 0.1)$ distribution was used instead. The prior distribution of the last trial doubles the prior variance of the intensity levels. In all chromosomes, this change of prior has a stronger impact on the posterior number of segments than increasing the hyperparameter of the geometric prior of the number of segments from 0.001 to 0.5.

The sequence of SNP occurrences provides an example of a dataset where segmentation is of no use for obtaining a condensed representation of the data. Still, the RJMCMC methods can be used to model the continuous intensity. Figure 5.8 shows examples of intensities of the SNP occurrences from chromosomes 10 and 14. Only a few constant periods can be found as the posterior average of the number of segments is several thousand in both cases.

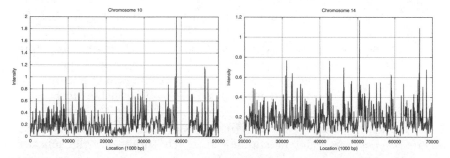

Fig. 5.8. The posterior means and 99% percentiles of the intensity of SNP occurrence in human chromosomes 10 and 14.

5.3.3 Modeling Interaction of Different Factors

In this section we model the influence of GC content on the intensity of ORF occurrence. We extend the piecewise constant intensity model of section 5.3.2 as follows. In regions where GC content exceeds a parameter value β, we increase the intensity by γ. The parameters β and γ are estimated from the GC and ORF data.

Hence, the intensity of ORF occurrence $\lambda(t)$ is given by

$$\lambda(t) = \begin{cases} \lambda_0(t) & \text{if } GC(t) < \beta \\ \lambda_0(t) + \gamma & \text{if } GC(t) \geq \beta \end{cases}$$

$\lambda_0(t)$ is a piecewise constant function as in Equation 5.10. The joint distribution of the model parameters $\theta = (m, \lambda_{0,1}, \dots, \lambda_{0,m}, c_{0,1}, \dots, c_{0,m-1}, \beta, \gamma)$, event sequence data S_1, and time series data S_2 is

$$P(\theta, S_1, S_2) = P(\beta)P(\gamma)P(m)P(\lambda_{0,j}, c_{0,j}|m)P(S_1|\lambda_{0,j}, c_{0,j}, \beta, \gamma, S_2).$$

Figure 5.9 shows a graphical representation of the model.

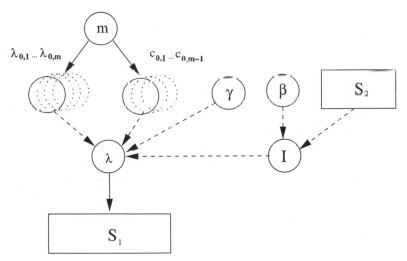

Fig. 5.9. Graphical representation of the model for the interaction between GC content and ORF occurrence. S_1 is the sequence of ORF occurrences, and S_2 is the GC content computed at every 1000th base. I is an indicator function: $I(t) = 1$ if $(GC(t) \geq \beta)$, and $I(t) = 0$ otherwise.

The GC content was computed by taking the proportion of bases C and G in the window of 250 kbp around every 1000th base in the DNA sequence. This resulted in a time series of 134,788 observations.

We ran two trials. The only difference between them was in the prior specifications of the number of segments m. We chose $m \sim \text{Geom}(0.5)$ in the first trial. In the second one we supported smaller values by setting $m \sim \text{Geom}(0.9)$. For the other parameters the prior distributions were

- $\gamma \sim \text{Unif}(0, 10)$,

- $\beta \sim \mathrm{Unif}(1, 60)$ (largest value of GC content in data was 59.5),
- intensity levels $\lambda_{0,j} \sim \mathrm{Gamma}(0.5, 0.25)$,
- change points $c_{0,j} \sim \mathrm{Unif}(S_s, S_e)$ (start and end points of the DNA sequence).

Figure 5.10 shows the positive correlation of γ and β in both trials, which strongly suggests dependence between GC content and ORF occurrence. The values of γ are larger in the second trial. The reason is that adding segments is relatively "cheap" in the first trial. Thus, the variation of intensity of ORF occurrence can be mostly explained by the piecewise constant baseline intensity $\lambda_0(t)$. Inserting a new segment is more costly in the second trial, resulting in higher values of γ. Figure 5.11 reveals the negative correlation of γ and the number of segments m, particularly clear in the second trial.

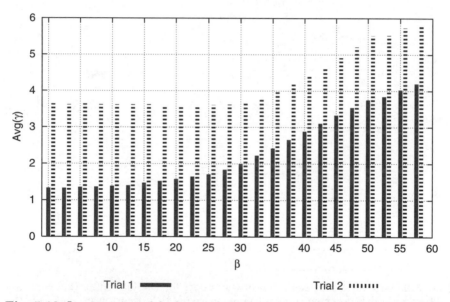

Fig. 5.10. Interaction model: the average of γ in the two trials, given $\beta \leq 2.5$ (the leftmost bar), $2.5 < \beta \leq 5.0$ (the next bar), and so on.

5.4 Concluding Remarks

We have described the use of reversible jump Markov chain Monte Carlo (RJMCMC) methods for finding piecewise constant descriptions of sequential data. The method provides posterior distributions on the number of segments in the data and thus gives a much broader view on the potential data than methods (such as dynamic programming) that aim only

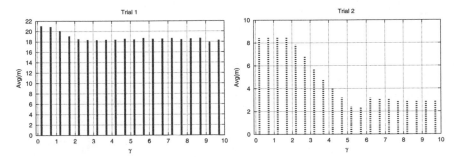

Fig. 5.11. Interaction model: the average number of segments m in the first trial (left), and in the second trial (right), given $\gamma \leq 0.5$ (the leftmost bar), $0.5 < \gamma \leq 1$ (the next bar), and so on. Note the different scales of the y axes.

at finding a single optimal solution. RJMCMC methods are also widely applicable: many different types of models can be used without any large changes in the method. On the other hand, MCMC methods can be more difficult to implement than discrete optimization techniques, and monitoring convergence of the simulations is not trivial.

We gave a few example applications showing how the methods can be used for biological data. The experiments on the GC content along human chromosome 10 showed no clear segment structure. The result is probably due to the relatively coarse resolution of the underlying data: we utilized GC content computed on 250 kb windows. The segment structure on GC content (so-called isochores) might be evident only on smaller scales. Similarly, the evidence on segment structure of the distribution of SNPs is weak. The situation is quite different for the distribution of ORFs. The results show that the number of segments on different chromosomes varies in interesting ways, and the numbers are remarkably constant even for drastic changes in the priors. We also showed how more complex models including interaction terms can be built.

The usefulness of RJMCMC methods is currently limited by the difficulty of implementation. It might be interesting to search for some less powerful but easier methods that could be used for sequence analysis.

Chapter 6

Gene Mapping by Pattern Discovery

Petteri Sevon, Hannu T. T. Toivonen, and
Päivi Onkamo

Summary

The objective of gene mapping is to localize genes responsible for
a particular disease or trait. We consider association-based gene
mapping, where the data consist of markers genotyped for a sample
of independent case and control individuals. In this chapter we
give a generic framework for nonparametric gene mapping based on
pattern discovery. We have previously introduced two instances of
the framework: haplotype pattern mining (HPM) for case–control
haplotype material and QHPM for quantitative trait and covariates. In
our experiments, HPM has proven to be very competitive compared to
other methods. Geneticists have found the output of HPM useful, and
today HPM is routinely used for analyses by several research groups. We
review these methods and present a novel instance, HPM-G, suitable for
directly analyzing phase-unknown genotype data. Obtaining haplotypes
is more costly than obtaining phase-unknown genotypes, and our
experiments show that although larger samples are needed with HPM-
G, it is still in many cases more cost-effective than analysis with
haplotype data.

6.1 Introduction

The first step in discovering genetic mechanisms underlying a disease is to find
out which genes, or more precisely, which polymorphisms, are involved. Gene
mapping, the topic of this chapter, aims at finding a statistical connection
between the trait under study and one or more chromosomal regions likely
to be harboring the disease susceptibility (DS) genes. Chromosomal regions
that cosegregate with the trait under study are searched for in DNA samples

from patients and controls. Even though the coding parts of the genes—the exons—cover only a small fraction of the human genome, the search cannot be restricted to them: polymorphisms affecting disease risk may reside in the introns or promoter regions quite far from the exons, having an effect on the expression level or splicing of the gene.

All the important simple monogenic diseases have already been mapped, or at least it is well known how it can be done. The general interest is shifting toward complex disorders, such as asthma or schizophrenia, where individual polymorphisms have rather weak effects. There may be epistatic interaction between several genes, and some mechanisms may be triggered by environmental factors. Complex disorders are also challenging clinically: it is of primary importance that the diagnoses are based on identical criteria. Systematic noise caused by inconsistent definitions for symptoms could severely hinder the search for the genetic component of the disorder. The mutation does not always cause the complex disorder (lowered penetrance), or the same disorder may be caused by other factors (phenocopies). There are other stochastic processes involved, such as recombinations and mutations, and genealogies are usually known only a few generations back. For these reasons, only probabilistic inferences can be made about the location of the DS genes.

In this chapter we present haplotype pattern mining (HPM), a method of gene mapping that utilizes data mining techniques. The chapter is organized as follows. First, we review the basic concepts in genetics and gene mapping in section 6.2. Next, we give an abstract generic algorithm for HPM in section 6.3 and present and evaluate three instances of that in section 6.4. Finally, we give a summary of related work in section 6.5 and close with a discussion in section 6.6.

6.2 Gene Mapping

Markers. *Markers* provide information about genetic variation among people. They are polymorphic sites in the genome, for which the variants an individual carries can be identified by laboratory methods. The location of a marker is usually called a *locus* (pl. *loci*). The variants at a marker are called *alleles*. We will use small-integer numbers to denote alleles throughout the chapter. The array of alleles in a single chromosome at a set of markers is called a *haplotype*.

Example 6.2.1. Let M1, M2, M3, and M4 be markers located in this order along chromosome 1. Let the alleles at these marker loci in a given instance of chromosome 1 be 1, 3, 2, and 1, respectively. The haplotype for this chromosome over all the markers is [1 3 2 1], and the haplotype over markers M2 and M4, for instance, is [3 1].

Marker data are used only for making inferences about the genealogical history of the chromosomes in the sample; the actual disease-predisposing polymorphisms are not typically expected to be among the markers. If two chromosomes have the same allele at a marker, the allele may be identical by descent (IBD), inherited from a relatively recent common ancestor. It is possible that two copies of same allele have different mutation histories, in which case the two alleles are said to be identical by state (IBS). On the other hand, different alleles at a marker in a pair of chromosomes do not completely exclude the possibility of a recent common ancestor; the marker may have mutated recently in one of the two lineages, or there might have been a genotyping error.

Linkage. The concept of *linkage* is crucial for gene mapping. In meiosis the human chromosomes are organized as homologous pairs lined up next to each other. In a random recombination process, these aligned chromosomes may form crossovers and exchange parts. Recombination can be modeled with reasonable accuracy as a Poisson process. The number of crossovers over a given genetic distance d follows Poisson distribution with mean d, and the distance between two consecutive crossovers follows exponential distribution with intensity parameter d. As a consequence, loci close to each other in the same chromosome are closely linked, and crossovers in between are rare. Genetic distances between loci are measured in Morgans (M): one Morgan is the distance at which the expected number of crossovers in a single meiosis is one. The relationship between genetic distance and physical distance measured in base pairs (bp) is such that on the average roughly 1 Mb corresponds to 1 cM, but the ratio varies a lot throughout the genome.

Linkage disequilibrium. Because of recombinations, in a hypothetical infinite randomly mating population all markers would eventually be in *linkage equilibrium*, totally uncorrelated. The opposite phenomenon—*linkage disequilibrium* (LD)—may arise from many different sources; random drift due to finite population size, recent population admixture, population substructure, and so on. From a gene-mapping perspective, utilizable LD in present population results from chromosomes sharing fragments where no crossovers have taken place since the most recent common ancestor. Genetic bottlenecks, where an initially small population has gone through a relatively long period of slow growth followed by rapid expansion, are an important source for this type of LD. As the initial population is quite small, only a handful of copies of a mutation, the founder mutations, may have entered the bottleneck in different founder haplotypes. The effect of drift is at its strongest during the period of slow growth, skewing the distribution of the founder mutation frequencies. Consequently, only a few of the founder mutations are likely to be present in the current population in significant numbers. Small isolated founder populations such as Kainuu in northeastern Finland or the

French Canadians are examples of recent bottlenecks. The whole Caucasian population is thought to have gone through a bottleneck approximately 50,000 years ago as they migrated out of Africa [89]. LD decays over time, as the chromosomes become more fragmented and conserved regions become shorter (Figure 6.1). The expected length of a region conserved over g generations is 2 M/g. LD resulting from the "out of Africa" bottleneck can still be observed over a 100 kb range.

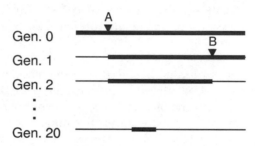

Fig. 6.1. Evolution of a chromosomal region over 20 generations. The thicker line represents fragments from the original chromosome at generation 0. In the first two meioses, crossovers at locations A and B have replaced the ends of the chromosome by material from other chromosomes. After 20 generations only a short fragment of the original chromosome has remained intact.

For an investigator, linkage disequilibrium is both a friend and an enemy. Because of the confounding effect, nearby polymorphisms are correlated, and other markers can be used as surrogates for the disease susceptibility mutation. Therefore a reasonably dense map of markers covering the genomic region under study can be sufficient for gene mapping. Furthermore, without LD all polymorphic loci would be independent of each other, leading to an unbearable multiple testing problem. On the other hand, LD makes it extremely hard to tell which polymorphism is behind the trait. Recent studies [329] show that in Caucasian populations the genome consists of blocks of 20–100 kb, where there are effectively only a handful of different haplotypes in each and no crossovers can be observed. It may be impossible to map polymorphisms inside a block, yet a single block can contain several genes.

Gene mapping paradigms. Family studies using marker data from extended pedigrees or sib pairs are based on detecting crossovers using a sparse marker map. Roughly, the idea is to predict the location of the DS gene to be where the marker alleles cosegregate with the trait value. However, due to the relatively small number of crossovers observable in pedigrees, the resolution of such studies is not particularly good. Therefore family-based linkage analysis is used as the first step of a mapping project to guide which regions to focus on in subsequent analyses.

Case–control studies of independent individuals can in principle take advantage of a much larger number of historical crossovers in the (unknown) genealogy leading to the observed sample. It is possible to get only indirect evidence of these crossovers in the form of shared patterns apparently inherited from a common ancestor, adding to the uncertainty of the analysis.

The concept of IBD generalizes to chromosomal regions: a region is IBD in a homologous pair of chromosomes if no crossovers have occurred in either of the lineages since the most recent common ancestor. As a result, haplotypes for any set of markers within the IBD region are identical save for marker mutations. Multimarker haplotypes are more informative than single alleles, and consequently haplotype sharing is more convincing evidence of IBD status.

All the chromosomes bearing a mutation inherited from a common ancestor also share a varying amount of the surrounding region IBD (Figure 6.2). All case–control methods are based on detecting haplotypes corresponding to these IBD regions and their association to the trait. In the proximity of the DS gene, LD can be increased artificially via the selection of the study subjects. If the affected subjects are overrepresented in the sample, the set of haplotypes will be enriched with the haplotype bearing the DS mutation. This is particularly useful if the causal mutation is rare.

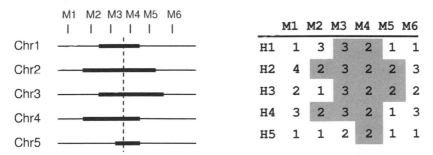

Fig. 6.2. Chromosomes (in a set) that are IBD at the location denoted by the vertical dashed line also share a varying length of the surrounding sequence (left). This sharing is reflected by the corresponding haplotypes (right).

Acquisition of data. The two most common types of markers are single-nucleotide polymorphisms (SNPs) and short tandem repeats (STRs), also known as microsatellites, where the number of repeats of a short sequence, typically 2–4 bases, varies. STRs are the more informative of the two, as the number of alleles may be more than a dozen. The number of alleles in SNPs is 2, but SNPs are much more frequent in the genome. They thus enable denser marker maps and are more suitable for fine mapping. SNPs are also more stable than STRs. Mutation rates for SNPs are estimated at 10^{-8} per meiosis, whereas for STRs they can be as high as 10^{-3}.

The human genome is organized in 22 pairs of homologous chromosomes (autosomes) and a pair of sex chromosomes. A marker residing in an autosome or in the pseudoautosomal region of the sex chromosomes has two instances in any individual. The process of reading the alleles at a marker is called *genotyping*, and the pair of alleles is the *genotype* at the marker. Current laboratory techniques produce *phase-unknown* genotypes; there is no telling which of the two alleles is of paternal or maternal origin. The term *genotype* also applies to any set of markers; a multimarker genotype is the array of the single-marker (phase-unknown) genotypes.

Since laboratories produce phase-unknown genotype data, haplotypes are not readily available for analysis. Haplotypes can be inferred from the genotypes of relatives. The most common procedure for obtaining case–control haplotype data is to genotype family trios consisting of the parents and a child. Assuming that the genotypes are known for all three, the phases of the alleles of the child can be determined in all cases but the one in which all three have a similar heterozygous genotype at the marker.

Example 6.2.2. Assume that the phase-unknown genotypes over two markers in a family trio are

	M1	M2
father	1,2	1,2
mother	2,3	1,2
child	2,3	1,2

For the first marker we can infer the alleles that the child has inherited from the mother(3) and the father(2), but for the second marker there is no way to determine the phases.

Additionally, the nontransmitted parental alleles are also determined. As a result, four independent haplotypes can be obtained from a trio: the two transmitted and the two nontransmitted pseudohaplotypes. Note that the nontransmitted pseudohaplotypes are the complements of the transmitted haplotypes with respect to the parental genotypes and do not necessarily correspond to any real chromosomes.

At the present time, the cost of genotyping in a large-scale mapping study is considerable. The need to detect DS genes in relatively small samples motivates the development of more powerful methods for in silico analysis of marker data.

6.3 Haplotype Patterns as a Basis for Gene Mapping

In this section we present a general framework, haplotype pattern mining (HPM), for gene mapping based on haplotype patterns. HPM tests each marker for association based on haplotype sharing around it. HPM looks for

patterns in the marker data that could be informative about the location
of a DS gene. Since the information is essentially contained in haplotypes
reflecting IBD sharing in a part of a chromosome, the patterns are haplotypes
over subsets of the marker map that are likely to correspond to such IBD
regions.

In the following subsections we first present the generic HPM algorithm
in terms of three components: language $\mathcal{L}$ of haplotype patterns, qualification
predicate q over $\mathcal{L}$, and marker scoring function s. Then we give a detailed
description for each of the components.

6.3.1 Outline of the Algorithm

The input for HPM consists of marker data (either a set of haplotypes, a set of
phase-unknown genotypes, or a combination set of both) and the associated
trait values. Optionally, the input may also include a set of explanatory
covariates, such as body mass index, age, sex, blood measurements, and so on.
Formally, let $M = \{1, \ldots, m\}$ be the marker map and D be an $n \times m$ matrix
of marker data; its columns correspond to markers, and its rows correspond
to observations, which may be haplotypes or genotypes. If the ith observation
is a haplotype, then $D_{ij} \in \mathcal{A}_j \cup \{0\}$; otherwise $D_{ij} \in (\mathcal{A}_j \cup \{0\})^2$. $\mathcal{A}_j$ is the
set of alleles at marker j, and 0 denotes a missing allele value. With genotype
data, the order of the alleles in a pair is insignificant. Let Y be the vector of
trait values associated with the haplotypes and genotypes. The trait may be
dichotomous or quantitative. In the case of haplotypes derived from a trio,
the trait value of the child can be used for the transmitted haplotypes, and
the trait value of the respective parent can be used for the nontransmitted
haplotypes. Let X be the matrix containing additional covariates.

The generic HPM works as follows. First, all potentially interesting
haplotype patterns are searched for. Let $\mathcal{L}$ be a language of haplotype
patterns, and q be a qualification predicate over $\mathcal{L}$: $q(\boldsymbol{p})$ is true iff $\boldsymbol{p}$ is a
potentially interesting pattern in the given dataset. Practical choices for q
set a lower bound for the number of occurrences of a pattern in the dataset.
Second, a score is calculated for each marker based on the relevant subset
of potentially interesting patterns. For a given marker, only patterns that
are likely to reflect IBD sharing at the marker are taken into account. Let
$s : 2^{\mathcal{L}} \times \mathrm{Perm}(Y) \to \mathbb{R}$ be a scoring function. $\mathrm{Perm}(Y)$ denotes the set
of all permutations of vector Y. The score for marker j given trait vector
Y is $s(Q \cap R_j, Y)$, where Q is the set of potentially interesting patterns
and $R_j \subseteq \mathcal{L}$ is the set of patterns that are relevant at marker j. Finally,
the statistical significance of the scores is measured, resulting in a P value
for each marker and an overall P value corrected for testing over multiple
markers. This necessitates the definition of a null hypothesis, and a means
for comparing the observed scores to the distribution of the scores under the
null hypothesis.

HPM does not model the process generating the trait values or marker data. Therefore we can test only the association between the trait and features of the marker data. The null hypothesis "The values of the trait vector are independent of the haplotypes and genotypes" can be tested by randomizing the relationship between the two using a permutation test. We require q to be invariant with respect to permutations of the trait vector. This way we can enumerate the set of patterns satisfying q once, and use the set for calculating the markerwise scores in the permuted data as well.

The algorithm for generic HPM is given in Figure 6.3. The markerwise P value can be used for predicting the location of the DS gene. The marker with the lowest P value is a natural choice for a point estimate. The corrected P value is good for assessing whether there is a DS gene in the investigated region in the first place or not.

Algorithm: Generic HPM
Input: Pattern language $\mathcal{L}$, qualification predicate q, scoring function s, marker data D, trait vector Y and possibly covariates X.
Output: Markerwise scores y_j and P values P_j for each marker j, a corrected overall P value.

Method

1. Find all potentially interesting patterns: $Q = \{\boldsymbol{p} \in \mathcal{L} \mid q(\boldsymbol{p})\}$.
2. Compute the score for each marker $j : y_j = s(Q \cap R_j, Y)$.
3. For $i \in \{1, \dots, r\}$, where r is the number of iterations in the permutation test, do
4.   generate a randomly permuted trait vector $Y^{(i)} \in \mathrm{Perm}(Y)$.
5.   compute the score for each marker $j : y_j^{(i)} = s(Q \cap R_j, Y^{(i)})$.
6. Compute markerwise P values for each marker by contrasting the observed scores to the samples drawn from the null distributions.
7. Compute an overall corrected P value for the best finding.

Fig. 6.3. Algorithm for generic HPM. Details are given in the text.

6.3.2 Haplotype Patterns

Haplotype patterns serve as discriminators for chromosomal regions that are potentially shared IBD by a set of chromosomes in the dataset. Language $\mathcal{L}$ of haplotype patterns consists of haplotypes over subsets of the marker map, with a few constraints. Marker maps with over hundred markers are not uncommon today; in the near future maps of several thousand of markers can be expected. The number of possible haplotypes grows exponentially with the number of markers in the map. It is not possible to consider all the possible haplotypes in the analysis, but on the other hand, not all haplotype patterns are biologically conceivable. Meaningful patterns correspond to IBD sharing between chromosomes, so markers included in a pattern should form a contiguous block. Allowing a restricted number of wildcards within a pattern may be desirable, as there may be marker mutations breaking an otherwise IBD region, or there may be markers having a lot of missing or erroneous allele values. Additionally, haplotypes extending over very long genetic distances are highly unlikely to survive over many generations and meioses, and therefore the set of patterns to be considered can be restricted with an upper limit for the genetic distance between the leftmost and rightmost markers that are assigned with an allele.

Let $p = [p_1 \cdots p_m]$ be a haplotype pattern, where $p_j \in \mathcal{A}_j \cup \{*\}$, $\mathcal{A}_j$ is the set of alleles at marker j, and $*$ is a wildcard symbol that matches any allele in the data. Pattern p overlaps marker j, or marker j is within pattern p, if j is between the leftmost and rightmost markers bound in p (inclusive). Length of p can be defined as either (1) the genetic distance between the leftmost and rightmost marker bound in p or (2) the number of markers between and including the leftmost and rightmost marker bound in p. We define language $\mathcal{L}$ of patterns as set of such vectors $p = [p_1 \cdots p_m]$, where length$(p) \leq \ell$ and either (1) the number of wildcards $(*)$ within p is at most w or (2) the number of stretches of consecutive wildcards within p is at most g and the length of such stretches is at most ℓ_G. Pattern parameters ℓ, w, g, and ℓ_G are given by the user.

Haplotype i matches pattern p iff for all markers j holds: $p_j = *$ or $p_j = D_{ij}$. The frequency of pattern p, freq(p), is the number of haplotypes matching p. With genotype data things are more complicated; a match is certain only if at most one of the markers assigned with an allele in the pattern is heterozygous in a genotype. A match is possible if at least one of the alleles at each marker in the genotype matches the corresponding allele in the pattern. One possibility for handling the uncertain cases is optimistic matching, where a genotype matches a pattern if any of the possible haplotype configurations matches it: genotype i matches pattern p iff for all markers j holds: $p_j = *$ or $p_j = g_1$ or $p_j = g_2$, where $(g_1, g_2) = D_{ij}$. In section 6.4.3 we will show that this simplistic approach works surprisingly well. More elaborate schemes are possible, e.g., genotypes can be weighted by 2^{1-n}, where n is the number of heterozygous markers in the genotype which are also assigned with an allele in the pattern.

Example 6.3.1. Let $p = [* * 1 * 2 *]$ be a haplotype pattern over markers $(1, \ldots, 6)$. The pattern p overlaps markers 3, 4 and 5 and is matched by, for example, haplotype $[3 2 1 4 2 0]$ and genotype $[(1,1) (1,2) (1,1) (2,4) (1,2) (2,3)]$. Genotype $[(1,1) (1,2) (1,2) (2,4) (1,2) (2,3)]$ may match p, depending whether allele 1 at marker 3 and allele 2 at marker 5 are from the same chromosome or not. With optimistic matching, we consider this possible match as a match.

In the instances of HPM we have used, the qualification predicate is based on a minimum frequency: $q(\boldsymbol{p}) \equiv \mathrm{freq}(\boldsymbol{p}) \geq f_{\min}$, where the minimum frequency is either given by the user or derived from other parameters and some summary statistics of the data, such as sample size and the number of disease-associated and control observations.

6.3.3 Scores

The purpose of the scoring function is to produce a test statistic for each marker, measuring total association of the marker to the trait over all haplotype patterns that are relevant at the marker. The higher the score, the stronger the association. We define the set R_j of relevant patterns at marker j as the set of patterns overlapping marker j.

A very simple—yet powerful—scoring function, used in [403, 404], counts the number of strongly disease-associated patterns overlapping the marker:

$$s(Q_j, Y') = |\{\boldsymbol{p} \in Q_j \mid A(\boldsymbol{p}, Y') \geq a_{\min}\}|, \tag{6.1}$$

where $Q_j = Q \cap R_j$ and $A(\cdot)$ is a measure for pattern–trait association or correlation. The association threshold $a_{\min}$ is a user-specified parameter. Table 6.1 illustrates the procedure.

Table 6.1. This table illustrates the computation of markerwise scores with association threshold $Z_{\min} = 3$. The patterns are ordered by the strength of association. Note that the wildcards within a pattern are included in the score for that marker.

Pattern	M1	M2	M3	M4	M5	M6	Z
$\boldsymbol{p}_1$	*	*	2	*	1	*	5.8
$\boldsymbol{p}_2$	*	1	2	1	3	*	4.4
$\boldsymbol{p}_3$	*	2	2	*	1	*	4.0
$\boldsymbol{p}_4$	1	2	2	*	1	*	3.4
$\boldsymbol{p}_5$	*	1	2	1	3	3	2.8
Score	1	3	4	4	4	0	

Another scoring function, used in [306, 359], measures the skew of the distribution of pattern–trait association in the set of overlapping patterns. The skew is defined as a distance between the P values of pattern–trait association tests for the patterns in Q_j and their expected values if there was no association:

$$s(Q_j, Y') = \frac{1}{k} \sum_{i=1}^{k} (P_i(Y') - U_i) \log \frac{P_i(Y')}{U_i}, \tag{6.2}$$

where $k = |Q_j|$, $P_1(Y'), \ldots, P_k(Y')$ is the list of P values sorted into ascending order, and $U_1, \ldots, U_k$ are the expected ranked P values assuming that there is no association and that patterns are independent, $U_i = \frac{i}{k+1}$.

Both scoring functions consider each pattern as an independent source of evidence. In reality, the patterns are far from independent, but the assumption of independence is a useful approximation. An ideal scoring function would take the structure in Q_j into account.

In all current instances of HPM, the scoring function measures the pattern–trait association independently for each pattern. A pattern whose occurrence correlates with the trait is likely to do well in discriminating the chromosomes bearing the mutation. A meaningful test for this correlation depends on the type of data. With a dichotomous trait, e.g., affected–unaffected, association can be simply tested using the Z-test (or χ^2-test) or Fisher's exact test for a 2-by-2 contingency table, where the rows correspond to the trait value and the columns to the occurrence of the pattern:

	M	N	Σ
A	n_{AM}	n_{AN}	n_A
U	n_{UM}	n_{UN}	n_U
Σ	n_M	n_N	n

Let us assume that there are n_M observations that match pattern p and n_N observations that do not match p, and that there are n_A affected and n_U unaffected observations in total. Let the frequencies in the 2-by-2 contingency table, where the rows correspond to the trait value (A or U) and the columns to matching (M) or not matching (N) p, be n_{AM}, n_{AN}, n_{UM}, and n_{UN}, respectively. The value of the test statistic

$$Z = \frac{(n_{AM}n_{UN} - n_{UM}n_{AN})\sqrt{n}}{\sqrt{n_M n_N (n_{AM} + n_{AN})(n_{UM} + n_{UN})}} \tag{6.3}$$

is approximately normally distributed. A one- or two-tailed test can be used. A one-tailed test is appropriate for patterns with a positive correlation to the trait. Assuming that there are no missing alleles in the data, it is possible to derive a lower bound for pattern frequency given the association threshold

$$f_{\min} = \frac{n_A n x}{n_C n + nx}, \tag{6.4}$$

where x is the association threshold for χ^2 statistic or the Z threshold squared (see [403] for details). No pattern with a frequency lower than $f_{\min}$ can be strongly associated. Even if there are missing alleles, this lower bound can be used—it is not imperative that all the strongly associated patterns satisfy q.

With a quantitative trait, the two-sample t-test can be used for identical means between the group of chromosomes matching the pattern and those not matching it. The number of degrees of freedom (number of chromosomes minus two) is usually large enough to justify the use of the Z-test instead of the t-test.

If explanatory covariates are included in the data, a linear model can be formulated,

$$Y_i = \alpha_1 X_{i1} + \ldots + \alpha_k X_{ik} + \alpha_{k+1} I_i + \alpha_0, \tag{6.5}$$

where Y_i is the trait value for chromosome i, X_{ij} is the value of the jth covariate for the ith observation, and I_i is an indicator variable for the occurrence of the tested pattern. Its value is 1 if the pattern matches the ith observation, otherwise 0. The significance of the pattern as an explanatory variable can be tested by comparing the best-fit model to the best-fit model where $\alpha_{k+1} = 0$.

Missing alleles in the observations are dealt with in a conservative manner: if an allele is missing at a marker bound in pattern p and there is a mismatch in any other marker, then the observation is counted as a mismatch. Otherwise we cannot know for sure whether p occurs in the observation, and to avoid any bias we ignore the observation when calculating the association for pattern p.

6.3.4 Searching for Potentially Interesting Haplotype Patterns

Let $\preceq$ be a generalization relation in $\mathcal{L}$: $p \preceq p'$ if any observation matching p' also matches p. The predicate q is monotonous in $\preceq$ if $p \preceq p' \wedge q(p') \Rightarrow q(p)$, which is true for $q(p) \equiv \text{freq}(p) \geq f_{\min}$. With monotonous q, set Q of patterns satisfying q can be efficiently enumerated using data-mining algorithms [5] or standard depth-first search (implementation for HPM given in [404]). Otherwise, a monotonous auxiliary predicate q_m such that $q(p) \Rightarrow q_m(p)$ can be introduced. The set of patterns satisfying q_m can be enumerated as described above, and each of these patterns can then be individually tested for q.

With some choices for q and s, it is possible that pattern p does not contribute to the score of any marker in any permutation of Y even if $q(p)$ holds. Marginal speed-up can be achieved if q in step 1 of the algorithm is replaced with $q' : q'(p) \equiv q(p) \wedge \exists j, Y' \in \text{Perm}(Y) : p$ contributes to $s(Q \cap R_j, Y')$.

Example 6.3.2. Let us assume a Z-test is used with a dichotomous trait, $q(p) \equiv \text{freq}(p) \geq f_{\min}$, and $s(Q', Y') = |\{p \in Q' \mid Z(p, Y') \geq Z_{\min}\}|$. The maximum value attainable for Z can be calculated based on the numbers of matching and nonmatching observations. If the maximum value is below the association threshold $Z_{\min}$, the pattern is rejected. Given n, n_M, n_N, n_A, and n_U, the largest Z value is achieved when n_{AM} and n_{UN} are maximized: if $n_M \geq n_A$, then $n_{AM} = n_A, n_{UM} = n_M - n_A, n_{AN} = 0$, and $n_{UN} = n_N$, else if $n_M \geq n_C$, then $n_{AM} = n_M, n_{UM} = 0, n_{AN} = n_N - n_C$, and $n_{UN} = n_C$;

otherwise $n_{AM} = n_M, n_{UN} = n_N$, and $n_{AN} = n_{UM} = 0$. If negative associations are considered, the minimum value of the Z statistic has to be calculated as well. This can be done analogously by swapping A and U in the formulae. A similar procedure is possible for Fisher's exact test.

6.3.5 Evaluating Statistical Significance

With real data, the allele frequencies and marker spacing vary across the marker map. Consequently, the distribution of scores varies as well, and the scores as such are not necessarily a good indicator of the location of the DS gene. Instead, the significances of the markerwise scores should be evaluated. HPM computes empirical P values for the markers using a permutation test. Figure 6.4 illustrates a successful localization with simulated data.

Let $y_j^{(1)}, \dots, y_j^{(r)}$ be the sample from the score distribution for marker j under the null hypothesis, and let y_j be the observed score at the marker. The empirical P value for the marker is then

$$\hat{P} = \frac{|\{i \in \{1, \dots, r\} \mid y_j^{(i)} \geq y_j\}|}{r}.$$

As always with permutation tests, the number of iterations should be sufficiently large for the P value estimates to be accurate. $\hat{P} \sim \frac{1}{r}\text{Bin}(r, P)$, and its standard deviation is $\sqrt{\frac{1}{r}P(1-P)}$. As a rule of thumb, at the desired significance level at least 50 iterations should have a score greater than the critical value, e.g., at $\alpha = 0.05$ at least 1,000 iterations should be performed.

The markerwise P values are not corrected for testing over multiple markers, and they should be understood as a means of ranking the markers only. However, a single corrected P value for the best finding can be obtained with another permutation test using the smallest markerwise P value as the test statistic. This P value can also be used to answer the question whether there is a DS gene in the investigated region in the first place or not. The two nested permutations can be carried out efficiently at the cost of a single test (see [360] for details).

6.4 Instances of the Generalized Algorithm

We present three instances of the generalized HPM algorithm. The original version for haplotype data and dichotomous traits [403, 404] and QHPM for quantitative traits and covariates [359, 306] have been previously published. In this section we introduce a third instance—HPM-G for phase-unknown genotype data.

We demonstrate the performance of the three instances in various settings using simulated data. We used the Populus simulation package [403, 305] for

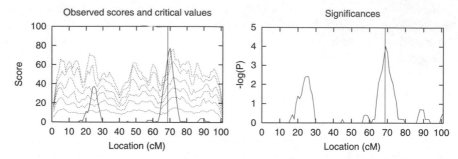

Fig. 6.4. The graph on the left shows the scores (solid line) and critical values at significance levels $\alpha = 0.001, 0.002, 0.005, 0.01, 0.02$ and 0.05 (dotted lines) over 101 evenly spaced markers. The graph on the right shows the negated logarithms (base 10) of the corresponding P values. The vertical line denotes the correct location of the DS gene.

generating realistic data sets for the analyses. In each of the simulations a small isolated founder population was generated, growing exponentially from an initial 100 people to 100,000 people over 20 generations. In each setting, a single 100 cM chromosome was simulated. The marker maps consisted either of 101 microsatellite markers or 301 SNP markers equidistantly spaced over the chromosome. A denser map was used with SNP markers because a single SNP marker is much less informative than a microsatellite marker. Each simulation was repeated 100 times to facilitate power analysis. We are interested in the localization power as a function of the tolerated prediction error. For example, in Figure 6.5a the 60% curve at 2 cM shows that for 70% of the replicates the predicted location was no more than 2 cM off the correct location. At the scale of the data sets, a mapping result is considered acceptable if it narrows down the 100 cM chromosome into a 20 cM or smaller region.

We did not apply permutation tests in the power analyses but used the scores as a basis for the localization instead: the point estimate for the gene location is the marker with the highest score. This way we were able to carry out the power analyses in much less time. Because there was no variation in the marker density over the chromosome and the alleles in the initial population were drawn from the same distribution for each marker, the score distributions are likely to be quite similar for all markers. We have previously shown that on this kind of data it does not make much difference whether the localization is based on the P values or the scores [403].

6.4.1 Original HPM for Haplotype Data and Dichotomous Trait

In the original version of HPM for haplotype data and dichotomous trait, we use the simple scoring function that counts the number of strongly

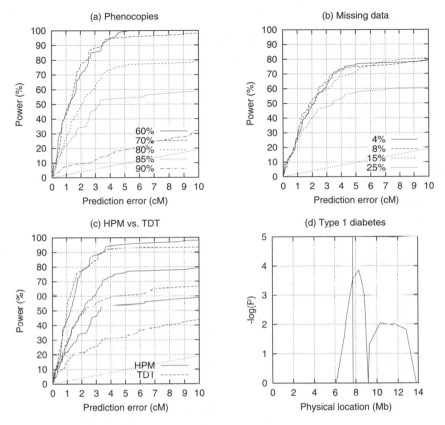

Fig. 6.5. Performance of HPM. (a) Effect of phenocopy rate on localization accuracy. (b) Effect of the number of missing alleles on localization accuracy. (c) Comparison between HPM and the multipoint TDT of Genehunter2. Phenocopy rates were at 80%, 85%, and 90%. The dotted curve at the bottom of every power graph denotes the power of random guessing. (d) Successful localization on real Type 1 diabetes data. The vertical line shows the correct location.

associated patterns, described in Equation 6.1. The χ^2-test is used for measuring pattern–trait association, and only positively associated patterns are considered. The frequency threshold is derived from the association threshold x using Equation 6.4.

The marker map consisted of microsatellite markers each with one common allele with frequency 0.4 and four alleles with frequency 0.15. The frequency of the disease-predisposing mutation was approximately 2% in each data set. The ascertainment of data was conducted as follows: 100 trios with an affected child were randomly chosen from the final population. The haplotypes were reconstructed from the trios and all uncertain alleles were set to zero denoting a missing value. The parameters for HPM were the same for all experiments: maximum length for patterns was seven markers, association threshold was nine, and one gap of up to two markers was allowed. The execution time was less than 1 second without the permutation test and about 20 seconds with 1000 permutations for a single replicate on a Pentium 4 at 1.4 GHz.

First, we simulated datasets with different phenocopy rates ranging from 60% to 90%. The results in Figure 6.5a show that the localization power reaches its maximum at a phenocopy rate between 60% and 70% and decreases steadily with increasing phenocopy rate, as expected.

Next, we assessed the effect of missing data by randomly removing 2%, 5%, and 10% of the marker genotypes in the data with an 80% phenocopy rate prior to haplotype reconstruction. This procedure resulted in approximately 8%, 15%, and 25% of missing alleles in the haplotype data. Due to haplotyping ambiguities, $\sim 4\%$ of the alleles were missing even if there had not been any missing genotypes in the trios. The results in Figure 6.5b show that up to 15%, there is practically no loss in power, which demonstrates remarkable tolerance for missing data.

To put the results into perspective, we compared HPM to TDT of Genehunter2 [232]. With TDT we considered haplotypes up to four markers in length (maximum in Genehunter2), and used the centerpoint of the best haplotype as the point estimate. The results (Figure 6.5c) show that at a phenocopy rate of 80% there is virtually no difference between the methods, but at higher rates HPM is clearly superior.

Finally, we showcase the method on a real Type I diabetes data set [25, 403]. There are 25 markers spanning a region of 14 Mb in the data. Two DS genes are known to reside in the region, very close to each other. We downsampled the original data set consisting of 385 sib-pair families to 100 trios (half the data size used in [403]). The results obtained with 100,000 permutations are shown in Figure 6.5d. The marker closest to the genes gives the second best P value 0.00014. The corrected overall P was 0.0015, indicating that the observed association is highly unlikely to be a coincidence.

6.4.2 QHPM for Quantitative Trait and Covariates

The diagnostics of a complex disease are often based on a combination of symptoms and quantitative measurements. For example, a possible diagnosis is $(X_1 \geq A \wedge (X_2 \geq B \vee S))$, where X_1 and X_2 are values of two quantitative subtraits and S is a proposition for a symptom. Different patients may have completely different genetic contributors and pathogenesis. It may be easier to find the quantitative trait loci (QTLs) affecting each of the subtraits independently than to try to map all the DS genes directly based on the affection status only.

The original HPM can cope only with a dichotomous trait. Generally, dichotomization of a quantitative variable wastes much of the information. Additionally, the power of the analysis is sensitive to the cut-off point.

There may be other information about the subjects available, for example, environmental and other nongenetic factors, e.g., smoking or nutritional habits, and measurements that are not related to the diagnosis criteria. To be able to fully utilize the available data, a method should be capable of using a quantitative trait as the response variable and using the other measurements as explanatory covariates.

QHPM is a version of HPM designed to meet the criteria mentioned earlier. It uses the linear model given in Equation 6.5 for measuring pattern–trait association and the scoring function given in Equation 6.2. We next assess the performance of QHPM on simulated data and compare it to QTDT [1], an accommodated version of TDT. The results have been previously published in [306].

The simulations were carried out in the manner described in section 6.4.1, except that there were only four alleles for each marker: one common allele with initial frequency 0.4 and three alleles with frequency 0.2. The disease-predisposing mutation was inserted into six randomly chosen chromosomes in the initial population. Liability for the disease was calculated using the formula

$$L = Ag + e_1 + e_2 + r_1 + C,$$

where g is an indicator variable for the presence of the mutation in the individual, e_1 and e_2 are environmental factors, and r_1 is a random component. The parameter values e_1, e_2, and r_1 are drawn from standard normal distribution for each individual. The strength of the genetic effect is determined by A. The probability of being affected was given by the *expit* function

$$P(\text{Affected}) = \frac{e^L}{1 + e^L}.$$

Two models were considered, an easy model with $A = 5$ and a difficult model with $A = 2$. The value of C was adjusted so that the prevalence of the disease is 5%. Additionally, five different quantitative variables were calculated from the formula

$$Q_j = jg + e_1 + e_2 + r_2,$$

where $j \in \{1, \ldots, 5\}$ determines the strength of the genetic effect and r_2 is a random component drawn from the uniform distribution in [0,1]. The sample was ascertained based on the affection status; 200 trios with an affected child were randomly selected from the final population.

The maximum length of patterns was set to seven markers, and a single one-marker gap was allowed. Minimum pattern frequency $f_{\min}$ was 10. The results in Figure 6.6 show that QHPM clearly outperforms QTDT with the difficult model. With the easy model, QHPM has a slight edge with Q_5 and Q_3, whereas with Q_2, QTDT gives better results. Q_1 turned out to be too difficult for mapping; neither method could do better than random guessing with either the easy or the difficult model.

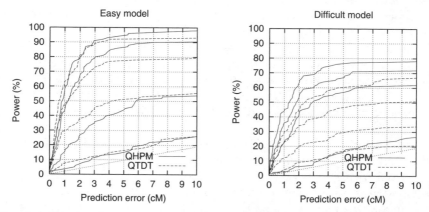

Fig. 6.6. The localization powers of QHPM (solid lines) vs. QTDT (dashed lines) are illustrated for (left) the easy model and (right) the difficult model. The curves correspond to quantitative traits Q_5, Q_3, Q_2 and Q_1 in top-down order.

6.4.3 HPM-G for Phase-Unknown Genotype Data

Haplotype data is not always easy to obtain; typically the haplotypes are inferred based on genotypes of family members. The most cost-effective way to obtain haplotypes for a case–control study is to genotype family trios, from each of which four independent haplotypes can be extracted. The efficiency of genotyping is $2/3$, as there in fact are six haplotypes in a trio and two of them are read twice. The parents need to be recruited; however, if they are deceased or not willing to participate, genotyping of these additional individuals is laborious and elevates the study expenses. Moreover, the phases cannot always be determined in a trio. Using phase-unknown genotype data directly for mapping, no extra individuals need to be genotyped, and no data are missing due to haplotyping ambiguities. Additionally, recruiting problems are alleviated and there is more freedom in selecting the cases and controls, including the ratio between the two classes.

The abstract formulation of HPM allows it to be easily adapted for genotype data. HPM for genotype data (HPM-G) is identical to the original version, with the exception that optimistic pattern matching is used. All the matches in the real haplotypes are found, but so is a large number of spurious matches, which introduce noise to the markerwise scores. Consequently, the number of frequent patterns found by HPM-G is typically an order of magnitude larger than the number found by HPM.

To compare HPM-G to HPM, we simulated both microsatellite and SNP data sets in the way described in section 6.4.1. The datasets were ascertained with equal costs of genotyping, assuming that the haplotypes for HPM are reconstructed from family trios. The haplotype data sets consisted of 200 disease-associated and 200 control haplotypes, derived from 100 trios. The dataset for HPM-G consisted of 150 affected and 150 control genotypes. In both cases, 300 individuals need to be genotyped.

The parameters used in section 6.4.1 were used as a basis for parameter settings. With SNP data, the maximum length of patterns was increased to 19 markers to give an equal maximum genetic length of 6 cM. We used a 50% elevated association threshold for HPM-G, as the expected number of mutation carriers in the genotype datasets was 50% higher than that in the haplotype datasets. The execution time of HPM-G was about 4 seconds with microsatellite data, or $6\frac{1}{2}$ minutes with SNP data, for a single replicate (Pentium 4, 1.4 GHz). With 1000 permutations, the execution times are approximately 4 minutes and 6 hours, respectively. The execution time of HPM with SNP data was 6 seconds without the permutation test and 3 minutes and 40 seconds with 1000 permutations.

We compared the two methods at four different phenocopy rates with both microsatellite and SNP data. From the results shown in Figure 6.7a, we can conclude that with microsatellite data HPM-G can tolerate slightly higher phenocopy rates than HPM with equal genotyping costs. With SNP data the methods are evenly matched (Figure 6.7b), but the execution time of HPM-G is much higher. This is due to the fact that with SNP data the number of spurious matches grows considerably.

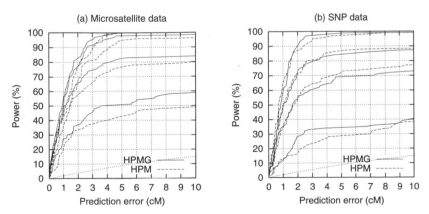

Fig. 6.7. Comparison of HPM-G and HPM with different phenocopy rates—70%, 80%, 85%, and 90%—in top-down order. (a) Localization accuracy on microsatellite data. (b) Localization accuracy on SNP data.

6.5 Related Work

Fine-scale mapping of disease genes by linkage disequilibrium has been researched intensively since the 1990s. Lazzeroni [243] gives a good overview of the work until 2000. The earliest work relied on methods that measure association between the disease status and one marker at a time or, in other words, the LD between a marker locus and the implicit disease locus [101, 159]. The disease gene is then predicted to be close to the locus with the highest association. Composite likelihood methods by Devlin et al. [102] and Terwilliger [397] consider several markers at a time but do not utilize any haplotype information.

Service et al. [358] and McPeek and Strahs [272] were among the first to suggest LD-based haplotype analysis methods. The model by Service et al. analyzes the LD of the disease to three markers at a time and estimates the disease locus with respect to the three marker loci. McPeek and Strahs are closer to the HPM approach: their method is based on an analysis of the length of haplotype sharing among disease chromosomes. Zhang and Zhao have extended the method to handle phase-unknown genotype data [451]. These methods, like most of the previous haplotype-based methods, are statistically elegant but computationally demanding. They tend to be exponential in the number of markers and sometimes in the number of haplotypes.

The implicit assumption of independent haplotypes in the methods mentioned may be very unrealistic in some populations. Parametric methods by Lam et al. [239] and Morris et al. [279] and nonparametric TreeDT by Sevon et al. [360] model the genealogical relationships among the observed haplotypes.

F-HPM, a variant of HPM, has been suggested independently by Zhang et al. [452]. It extends HPM to use pedigree data and quantitative traits by using a quantitative pedigree disequilibrium test proposed by the same authors.

Linkage analysis is an alternative for LD analysis in gene mapping. The idea, roughly, is to analyze pedigree data and find out which loci are inherited with the disease. Due to the lower effective number of recombinations, linkage analysis is less suitable than LD analysis for fine mapping. Transmission/disequilibrium tests (TDT) [382] are a well-established way of testing both association and linkage in a sample where LD exists between the disease locus and nearby marker loci.

6.6 Discussion

Gene mapping, the problem of locating disease-predisposing genes, is one of the early steps in many medical genetics studies that ultimately aim at prevention and cure of human diseases. The completion of the human DNA sequence gives a lot of useful information about the genome, in particular about polymorphisms, whether potentially disease-predisposing or just useful as markers in gene mapping studies. Availability of the human DNA sequence does not remove the gene mapping problem, however: we cannot tell from the DNA sequence alone which gene or polymorphism is associated with which trait.

From a data mining perspective, the datasets are small. They are, however, growing fast in dimensionality (number of markers), so mapping methods need to be scalable in that respect. Discovery of new knowledge is also an important aspect, even if our discussion has concentrated on predicting the gene location. Geneticists are interested in the patterns that show strong correlation with a disease, and they often investigate them manually, e.g., by constructing possible genealogies to test the plausibility of a DS gene. Strongly disease-correlated patterns or suitable disjunctions of them can sometimes also be useful as putative gene tests before the gene is actually located.

We described haplotype pattern mining, a flexible and generic algorithm for nonparametric gene mapping. It is based on searching for genetic patterns that are strongly associated with the trait under study and on mapping the disease gene to the genetic region with the most evidence for trait association. HPM incorporates several characteristic components of a typical data mining task:

- Definition of an application-specific pattern language
- Searching for frequent patterns
- Evaluating the strength of rules of form *pattern* → *trait*

In principle, HPM falls into the category of predictive data mining applications. There is a single variable, the trait, that we attempt to explain using the marker data and possibly other covariates. However, instead of having the classification or regression accuracy as the objective, we are more interested in the patterns that are used for prediction and where they are located.

Even though datasets are expected to grow as laboratory techniques evolve, the pattern search step will probably not become an issue with HPM in the near future. The computational burden mainly results from the subsequent analysis of the pattern set. With a large set of patterns, the permutation test procedure may be quite time consuming. We already saw that with phase-unknown SNP genotype data the execution times were several hours. Ideas for more efficient handling of patterns, e.g., closed patterns, could be utilized to speed up the permutation test.

An advantage of HPM is that it is model-free, as it does not require any— potentially misleading—explicit assumptions about population or mode of inheritance. Experiments show that HPM tolerates high degrees of missing data and high phenocopy rates. By introducing HPM-G for phase-unknown genotype data, we have significantly extended the scope of HPM: it can now handle dichotomous or quantitative traits, covariates, SNP and microsatellite markers, and haplotype or genotype data in any combinations. HPM has a clear advantage over many parametric methods: as a by-product HPM gives an explicit list of disease-associated patterns accompanied by a variety of statistics. This output is found very informative for the geneticists.

Gene mapping is an iterative process: starting with the whole genome, the search successively narrows down the region potentially harboring the DS genes. New markers are added and possibly new patients are recruited at each iteration. The first stage—the genome scan—is customarily conducted as a family study, using linkage analysis, resulting in candidate regions of 20 to 30 cM. HPM is best suited to the next stage, where the candidate regions are further reduced to only few centiMorgans. However, our results on simulated datasets indicate that with a dense enough marker map, HPM could actually be used for a full genomewide search, at least in populations where LD is expected to extend over several centiMorgans. This may become feasible in the near future as genotyping becomes less expensive, and the costs of extra genotyping may become insignificant compared to the costs and difficulties associated with recruitment of families for linkage analysis. Experiments reported in [359] suggest that HPM could be applied to fine mapping as well—however, proper assessment of the potential for fine mapping is yet to be done. HPM has been applied in a number of gene mapping studies. The most recent breakthrough is the identification of an asthma susceptibility gene.

Acknowledgments

The authors have developed HPM with Vesa Ollikainen, Kari Vasko, Heikki Mannila, and Juha Kere. Many thanks to Vesa Ollikainen for providing us with the simulated datasets and some of the analysis results for the experiments with HPM and QHPM.

Chapter 7
Predicting Protein Folding Pathways

Mohammed J. Zaki, Vinay Nadimpally,
Deb Bardhan, and Chris Bystroff

Summary

A structured folding pathway, which is a time-ordered sequence of
folding events, plays an important role in the protein folding process
and hence in the conformational search. Pathway prediction thus gives
more insight into the folding process and is a valuable guiding tool for
searching the conformation space. In this chapter, we propose a novel
"unfolding" approach for predicting the folding pathway. We apply
graph-based methods on a weighted secondary structure graph of a
protein to predict the sequence of unfolding events. When viewed in
reverse, this process yields the folding pathway. We demonstrate the
success of our approach on several proteins whose pathway is partially
known.

7.1 Introduction

Proteins fold spontaneously and reproducibly (on a time scale of milliseconds)
into complex three-dimensional (3D) globules when placed in an aqueous
solution, and the sequence of amino acids making up a protein appears to
completely determine its three-dimensional structure [16, 249]. At least two
distinct though interrelated tasks can be stated.

1. *Structure Prediction Problem:* Given a protein amino acid sequence
   (i.e., linear structure), determine its three-dimensional folded shape (i.e.,
   tertiary structure).
2. *Pathway Prediction Problem:* Given a protein amino acid sequence and
   its three-dimensional structure, determine the time-ordered sequence of
   folding events, called the folding pathway, that leads from the linear
   structure to the tertiary structure.

The structure prediction problem is widely acknowledged as an open problem, and a lot of research in the past has focused on it. The pathway prediction problem, on the other hand, has received almost no attention. It is clear that the ability to predict folding pathways can greatly enhance structure prediction methods. Folding pathway prediction is also interesting in itself since protein misfolding has been identified as the cause of several diseases, such as Creutzfeldt-Jacob disease, cystic fibrosis, hereditary emphysema, and some cancers. In this chapter we focus on the pathway prediction problem. Note that while there have been considerable attempts to understand folding intermediates via molecular dynamics and experimental techniques, to the best of our knowledge ours is one of the first works to *predict* folding pathways.

Traditional approaches to protein structure prediction have focused on detection of evolutionary homology [13], fold recognition [56, 370], and where those fail, ab initio simulations [372] that generally perform a conformational search for the lowest energy state [369]. However, the conformational search space is huge, and, if nature approached the problem using a complete search, a protein would take millions of years to fold, whereas proteins are observed to fold in milliseconds. Thus, a structured folding pathway, i.e., a time-ordered sequence of folding events, must play an important role in this conformational search [16]. The nature of these events, whether they are restricted to "native contacts," i.e., contacts that are retained in the final structure, or whether they might include nonspecific interactions, such as a general collapse in size at the very beginning, were left unanswered. Over time, the two main theories for how proteins fold became known as the "molten globule/hydrophobic collapse" (invoking nonspecific interactions) and the "framework/nucleation-condensation" model (restricting pathways to native contacts only).

Strong experimental evidence for pathway-based models of protein folding has emerged over the years, for example, experiments revealing the structure of the "unfolded" state in water [276], burst-phase folding intermediates [82], and the kinetic effects of point mutations ("phi values" [300]). These pathway models indicate that certain events always occur early in the folding process and certain others always occur later (Figure 7.1).

Currently, there is no strong evidence that specific nonnative contacts are required for the folding of any protein [75]. Many simplified models for folding, such as lattice simulations, tacitly assume that nonnative contacts are "off pathway" and are not essential to the folding process [227]. Therefore, we choose to encode the assumption of a "native pathway" into our algorithmic approaches. This simplifying assumption allows us to define potential folding pathways based on a known three-dimensional structure. We may further assume that native contacts are formed only once in any given pathway.

Knowledge of pathways for proteins can give important insight into the structure of proteins. To make pathway-based approaches to structure prediction a reality, plausible protein folding pathways need to be predicted.

(SSEs; namely, α-helices and β-strands), and it also captures nonlocal interactions giving clues to its tertiary structure. For example, clusters of contacts represent certain secondary structures: α-helices appear as bands along the main diagonal since they involve contacts between one amino acid and its four successors; β-sheets are thick bands parallel or antiparallel to the main diagonal. Moreover, a contact map is rotation and translation invariant, an important property for data mining. It is also possible to recover the 3D structure from contact maps [415].

7.2.2 Graphs and Minimum Cuts

An undirected graph $G(V, E)$ is a structure that consists of a set of vertices $V = \{v_1, v_2, \cdots, v_n\}$ and a set of edges $E = \{e_i = (s, t) | s, t \in V\}$; i.e., each edge e_i is an unordered pair of vertices. A *weighted graph* is a graph with an associated weight function $W : E \to \Re^+$ for the edge set. For each edge $e_i \in E$, $W(e_i)$ is called the *weight* of the edge e_i.

A *path* between two vertices $s, t \in V$ is an ordered set of vertices $\{v_1, v_2, ..., v_k\}$ such that $v_1 = s$, $v_k = t$ and for every $1 \le j < k$, $(v_j, v_{j+1}) \in E$. Two vertices $s, t \in V$ are said to be *connected* in G if there exists a path between s and t. A *connected component* K is a maximal set of vertices $K \subseteq V$ such that for every $s, t \in K$, s and t are connected in G. A graph is said to be a connected graph if $\forall s, t \in V$, s and t are connected.

Let $G = (V, E)$ be a simple undirected, connected, weighted graph. An *(edge) cut* C is a set of edges $C \subseteq E$, which when removed from the graph, partitions the graph into two connected components V_1 and V_2 (with $V_1 \bigcap V_2 = \emptyset$, $V_1 \bigcup V_2 = V$, $V_1 \ne \emptyset$, $V_2 \ne \emptyset$). An edge *crosses* the cut if its endpoints are in different partitions of the cut. The *capacity* of the edge cut C is the sum of the weights of edges crossing the cut, given as $W(C) = \sum_{e \in C} W(e)$.

A cut C is an *s-t cut* if vertices s and t are in different partitions of the cut. A *minimum s-t cut* is an s-t cut of minimum capacity. A *(global) minimum cut (mincut)* is a minimum s-t cut over all pairs of vertices s and t. Note that mincut need not be unique.

7.2.3 Weighted SSE Graph

A protein can be represented as a *weighted secondary structure element graph (WSG)*, where the vertices are the SSEs that make up the protein and the edges denote proximity relationship between the secondary structures. Furthermore, the edges are weighted by the strength of the interaction between two SSEs. Following the convention used in protein topology or TOPS diagrams [389, 427], we use triangles to represent β-strands and circles to represent α-helices.

To correctly model the secondary structure elements and their interaction, the edge construction and their weights are determined from the protein's contact map. The edge weights are determined as follows: we determine the list of SSEs and their sequence positions from the known 3D structure taken from the Protein Data Bank (PDB).[1] Every SSE is a vertex in the WSG. Let $V = \{v_1, v_2, \cdots, v_n\}$ denote a protein with n SSEs. Each SSE v_i has starting $(v_i.s)$ and ending $(v_i.e)$ sequence positions, where $1 \leq v_i.s < v_i.e \leq N$ and N is the length of the protein.

Let v_i and v_j be a pair of SSEs. Let the indicator variable $b(v_i, v_j) = 1$ if v_i and v_j are consecutive on the protein backbone chain, else $b(v_i, v_j) = 0$. The number of contacts between the two SSEs in the contact map is given as $\kappa(v_i, v_j) = \sum_{i=v_i.s}^{v_i.e} \sum_{j=v_j.s}^{v_j.e} C(i, j)$. An edge exists between two SSEs if there are a positive number of contacts between them, i.e., $\kappa > 0$, or if the two SSEs are linked on the backbone chain. The weight assigned to the edge (v_i, v_j) is given as follows: $W(v_i, v_j) = \Delta \times b(v_i, v_j) + \kappa(v_i, v_j)$, where Δ is some constant. In our study we set Δ as the average number of (nonzero) contacts between SSEs, i.e., $\Delta = \frac{S}{|S|}$, where $S = \{\kappa(v_i, v_j) > 0 \mid v_i, v_j \in V\}$. This weighting scheme gives higher weights to backbone edges and also to SSEs with greater bonding between them. The backbone edges are given higher weight since they represent strong covalent bonds, while the other contacts represent weaker noncovalent bonds. An example WSG for protein 2IGD is shown in Figure 7.3. The thick lines denote backbone edges. SSEs are arranged from the N-terminus (start) to the C-terminus (end) and numbered as given in the PDB file. 2IGD has 5 SSEs, $\beta_2\beta_1\alpha_1\beta_4\beta_3$, arranged from the N-terminus to the C-terminus.

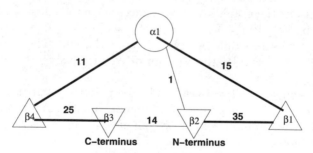

Fig. 7.3. WSG for protein 2IGD.

7.3 Predicting Folding Pathways

In this section we outline our approach to predicting the folding pathway of a protein using the idea of "unfolding." We use a graph representation of a protein, where a vertex denotes a secondary structure and an edge denotes

[1]http://www.rcsb.org/pdb/

the interactions between two SSEs. The edges are weighted by the strength of the SSE interactions obtained from the *protein contact map*. The intuition behind our approach is to break as few contacts as possible and to avoid splitting an SSE held at both ends. Among several choices, the best option is to pick one that has the least impact on the remaining part of the protein. Through a series of *minimum cuts* on the weighted graph, we predict the most likely sequence of *unfolding* events. Reversing the unfolding steps yields plausible pathways for protein folding. A detailed description of our approach follows.

7.3.1 Unfolding via Mincuts

The intuition behind the unfolding process stems from the belief that unfolding occurs by *breaking as few contacts as possible*. Given a weighted SSE graph for a protein, a mincut represents the set of edges that partition the WSG into two components that have the smallest number of contacts (i.e., bonds) between them. Hence, minimum capacity edge cuts on WSGs can help us determine the points in the protein where unfolding is likely to occur.

The problem of determining the mincuts of weighted graphs is a well-studied problem in graph theory (sec [8] for a comprehensive review). We chose the Stoer-Wagner (SW) [390] deterministic polynomial-time mincut algorithm since it is very simple and yet is one of the fastest current methods, running in time $O(|V||E|+|V|^2 \log |V|)$. It relies on the following observation: either the global mincut is an *s-t* mincut or it is not. In the former case, if we find the *s-t* mincut, we are done. In the latter case, it is sufficient to consider a mincut of $G - \{s, t\}$.

The SW algorithm works iteratively by merging vertices until only one merged vertex remains. In each phase i, SW starts with an arbitrary vertex $Y = \{a\}$ and adds the most highly connected vertex $z \notin Y$ to the current set Y, given as $z = argmax_z\{\sum_{x \in Y} W(z, x)\}$. This process is repeated until $Y = V$. At this stage the *cut of the phase*, denoted C_i, is calculated as the cut that separates the vertex added last to Y (i.e., the vertex t) from the rest of the current graph. At the end of each phase, the two vertices added last to Y, say s and t, are merged into a single node st (i.e., the edges connecting them are removed) and for any $x \in V, W(x, st) = W(x, s) + W(x, t)$. The global mincut is the minimum cut over all phases, given as $C = argmax_i\{W(Ci)\}$.

As an example, consider the WSG for 2IGD shown in Figure 7.3. Let's assume that the starting vertex is $a = \alpha_1$, i.e., $Y = \{\alpha_1\}$. The next SSE to be picked is β_1 since it has the highest weight of connection to α_1 (thus, $Y = \{\alpha_1, \beta_1\}$). Out of the remaining vertices, β_2 has the highest weight of connection to Y ($W(\beta_2, Y) = 36$), so $Y = \{\alpha_1, \beta_1, \beta_2\}$. The last two vertices to be added to Y are $s = \beta_3$ and $t = \beta_4$. At this point phase 1 is over, and the weight of the phase 1 cut is $W(C_i) = \sum_{x \in V} W(\beta_4, x) = 36$. We now merge β_3 and β_4 to get a new st node, as shown in Figure 7.4

(left). We next proceed through three more phases (again assuming that we start at vertex $a = \alpha_1$), as shown in Figure 7.4. The lowest mincut weight among all the phases is $W(C) = 25$, corresponding to the mincut $C = \{(\beta_2, \beta_3), (\alpha_1, \beta_4)\}$, which partitions the WSG into two components $V_1 = \{\alpha_1, \beta_1, \beta_2\}$, and $V_2 = \{\beta_3, \beta_4\}$.

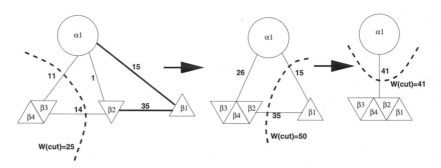

Fig. 7.4. SW algorithm for mincut of protein 2IGD.

According to our model an unfolding event is a set of edges that form a mincut in the WSG $G = (V, E)$ for a protein. Our algorithm to predict the unfolding event is called UNFOLD, and it works as follows. First, a mincut C for the initial WSG is determined; ties are broken arbitrarily. This gives the first event in the unfolding process. The edges that form this cut are deleted from the WSG, yielding two new connected subgraphs $G_1 = (V_1, E_1)$ and $G_2 = (V_2, E_2)$, where V_1 and V_2 are the two partitions resulting from the mincut C and $E_i = \{(u, v) \in E | u, v \in V_i\}$. We recursively process each subgraph to yield a sequence of mincuts corresponding to the unfolding events. This sequence when reversed produces our prediction for the folding pathway for the given protein. Figure 7.5 shows the pseudocode for the complete UNFOLD algorithm to determine the unfolding events for a given protein.

As an example of how UNFOLD works, consider again protein 2IGD. We determined that the first unfolding event (mincut) partitions its WSG into two groups of SSEs $V_1 = \{\beta_2, \beta_1, \alpha_1\}$ and $V_2 = \{\beta_4, \beta_3\}$. After recursive processing, UNFOLD produces a sequence of mincuts that can easily be visualized as a tree shown in Figure 7.6. Here each node represents a set of vertices that make up a graph obtained in the recursive application of UNFOLD, and the children of a node are the partitions resulting from the mincut, whose value appears in brackets next to the node. For example, the node $\beta_2\beta_1\alpha_1$ is partitioned into $\beta_2\beta_1$ and α_1, which has a mincut value of 25. If we proceed from the leaf nodes of the tree to the root, we obtain the predicted folding pathway of 2IGD. We find that SSEs β_2 and β_1 fold to form an antiparallel β-sheet. Simultaneously, SSEs β_3 and β_4 may also form a parallel β-sheet. SSE α_1 then forms a $\beta_2\alpha_1\beta_1$ arrangement, and then

```
//G is a graph with weight function W
UNFOLD (G = (V, E), W : E → ℜ⁺):
    C = SW-MinCut(G, W);
    G₁ = (V₁, E₁); G₂ = (V₂, E₂);
    if (|V₁| > 1) UNFOLD(G₁, W);
    if (|V₂| > 1) UNFOLD(G₂, W);

SW-MinCut(G = (V, E), W : E → ℜ⁺):
    while (|V| > 1)
        W(Cᵢ) = MinCutPhase(G, W);
    return C = argminᵢ{W(Cᵢ)};

MinCutPhase(G = (V, E), W : E → ℜ⁺):
    Y = {some a ∈ V};
    while (|Y| ≠ |V| − 2)
        Y = Y ∪ {z = argmaxᵤ{Σ_{x∈Y} W(z, x)}};
    Shrink G by merging s, t ∈ G − Y;
    return cut-of-the-phase (from t);
```

Fig. 7.5. UNFOLD algorithm.

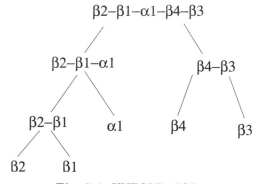

Fig. 7.6. UNFOLD 2IGD.

the whole protein comes together by forming a parallel β-sheet between β_2 and β_3. We should be careful not to impose a *strict* linear timeline on the unfolding events predicted by UNFOLD; rather, allowance should be made for several folding events to take place simultaneously. However, there may be intermediate stages that must happen before higher order folding can take place. We show that our approach is particularly suited to provide insights into such intermediate folding states.

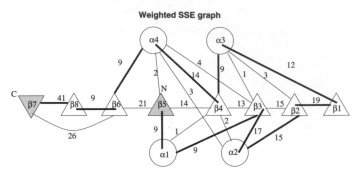

Fig. 7.7. Dihydrofolate reductase (4DFR): weight SSE graph.

7.3.2 Detailed Example: Dihydrofolate Reductase (4DFR)

Although no one has determined the precise order of appearance of secondary structures for any protein, evidence supports intermediate stages in the pathway for several well-studied proteins, including specifically for the protein dihydrofolate reductase (PDB 4DFR; 159 residues), a two-domain α/β enzyme that maintains pools of tetrahydrofolate used in nucleotide metabolism [78, 173, 202].

Experimental data indicate that the adenine-binding domain, which encompasses the two tryptophans Trp-47 and Trp-74, is folded and is an intermediate essential in the folding of 4DFR, and the event of folding the adenine-binding domain happens early in the folding of 4DFR [173]. Figures 7.7 and 7.8 show the WSG, unfolding sequence, and a series of intermediate stages in the folding pathway of protein 4DFR. Trp-47 and Trp-74 lie in SSEs α_2 and β_1, respectively. According to the mincut-based UNFOLD algorithm, the vertex set $\{\beta_2, \alpha_2, \beta_3, \beta_1\}$ lies on the folding pathway, in agreement with the experimental results!

We can see from Figure 7.7 that 4DFR has four α-helices and eight β-strands. The WSG shows the interactions weights among the different SSEs (the bold lines indicate the backbone). Applying UNFOLD to 4DFR yields the sequence of cuts shown. For clarity, the unfolding sequence tree has been stopped when there are no more than three SSEs in any given node. The remaining illustrations show some selected intermediate stages on the folding pathway by reversing the unfolding sequence.

We find that SSE groups $\beta_2\alpha_2\beta_3$ and $\beta_6, \beta_8, \beta_7$ are among the first to fold (Figure 7.9), suggesting that they might be the folding initiation sites. Next β_1 joins $\beta_2\alpha_2\beta_3$, in agreement with the experimental results [78], as shown in Figure 7.10; the Trp-47 and Trp-74 interaction is also shown, and the other group now becomes $\beta_5, \beta_6, \beta_8, \beta_7$. The final native structure including $\alpha_3\beta_4\alpha_4$ and α_1 is shown in Figure 7.11. We again underscore that the results should not be taken to imply a *strict* folding timeline, but rather as a way to understand major events that are mandatory in the folding pathway. On

Unfolding sequence

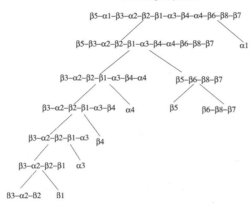

β5–α1–β3–α2–β2–β1–α3–β4–α4–β6–β8–β7

β5–β3–α2–β2–β1–α3–β4–α4–β6–β8–β7   α1

β3–α2–β2–β1–α3–β4–α4   β5–β6–β8–β7

β3–α2–β2–β1–α3–β4   α4   β5   β6–β8–β7

β3–α2–β2–β1–α3   β4

β3–α2–β2–β1   α3

β3–α2–β2   β1

Fig. 7.8. Dihydrofolate reductase (4DFR): unfolding sequence.

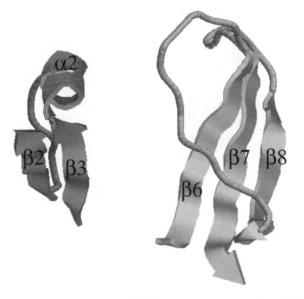

Fig. 7.9. Dihydrofolate reductase (4DFR): early stages in the folding pathway.

such experimentally verified case is the $\{\beta_2, \alpha_2, \beta_3, \beta_1\}$ group that is known to fold early, and our approach was able to predict that.

7.4 Pathways for Other Proteins

To establish the utility of our methodology we predict the folding pathway for several proteins for which there are known intermediate stages in the folding pathway.

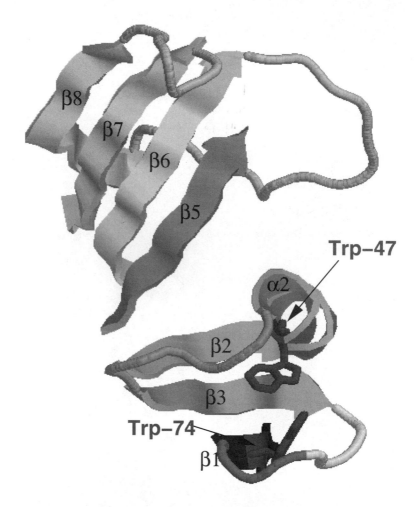

Fig. 7.10. Dihydrofolate reductase (4DFR): intermediate stages in the folding pathway.

Bovine pancreatic trypsin inhibitor (PDB 6PTI; 58 residues) is a small protein containing two α-helices and two β-strands [217]. It is known that the unfolding pathway of this protein involves the loss of the helix structure followed by the beta structure. Applying UNFOLD to 6PTI, we found that indeed $\beta_2\beta_3$ remain together until the end.

Chymotrypsin inhibitor 2 (PDB 2CI2; 83 residues) is also a small protein, with one helix and four strands arranged in sequence as follows: $\beta_1\alpha_1\beta_4\beta_3\beta_2$. Previous experimental and simulation studies have suggested an early displacement of β_1 and a key event in the disruption of the hydrophobic

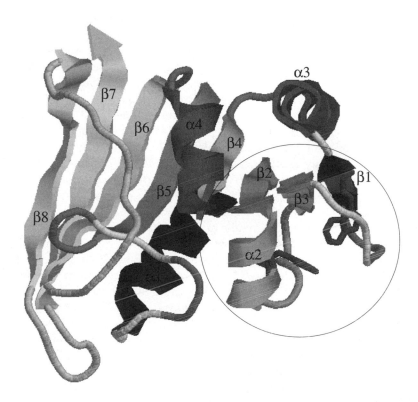

Fig. 7.11. Dihydrofolate reductase (4DFR): final stages and native structure of the folding pathway.

core formed primarily by α_1 and the strands β_3 and β_4 [242]. UNFOLD predicts that β_1 is the first to go, while $\beta_3\beta_4$ remain intact until the end.

The activation domain of human procarboxypeptidase A2 (PDB 1O6X) has 81 residues, with two α and three β strands arranged as follows: $\beta_2\alpha_1\beta_1\alpha_2\beta_3$. The folding nucleus of 1O6X is made by packing α_2 with $\beta_2\beta_1$ [417]. We found that the unfolding sequence indeed retains $\beta_2\beta_1\alpha_2$ and then finally $\beta_2\beta_1$.

The pathway of cell cycle protein p13suc1 (PDB 1SCE; 112 residues) shows the stability of $\beta_2\beta_4$ interaction even though β_4 is the strand involved in domain swapping [11]. 1SCE has four domains with seven SSEs (three α and four β). The β_{4C} of domain C interacts with the β_2 of domain A, and vice versa (the same is true for domains B and D). We found that $\beta_1\beta_2\beta_{4C}$ is the last to unfold.

β-Lactoglobulin (PDB 1CJ5; 162 residues) contains ten strands and three helices. Beta strands F, G and H are formed immediately, once the refolding starts [238], and were thus identified as the folding core of 1CJ5. In the predicted unfolding sequence obtained for 1DV9, we found that the SSEs

$\beta_8, \beta_9, \beta_{10}$ corresponding to the F, G, and H beta strands remain together until the last stages of unfolding.

Interleukin-1β (PDB 1I1B; 153 residues) is an all-β protein with twelve β-strands. Experiments indicate that strands $\beta_6\beta_7\beta_8$ are well folded in the intermediate state and $\beta_4\beta_5$ are partially formed [78]. We found $\beta_4\beta_5$ and $\beta_6\beta_7$ to be among the last unfolding units, including $\beta_8\beta_9$.

Myoglobin (PDB 1MBC; from sperm whale; 153 residues) and leghemoglobin (PDB 1BIN; from soybean; 143 residues), both belonging to the globin family of heme binding proteins, share a rather low sequence similarity but highly similar structure. Both are all-α proteins with eight helices, denoted $\alpha_1(A)\alpha_2(B)\alpha_3(C)\alpha_4(D)\alpha_5(E)\alpha_6(F)\alpha_7(G)\alpha_8(H)$. In [298], the researchers observed that the main similarity of their folding pathways is in the stabilization of the G and H helices in the burst phase of folding intermediates. However, the details of the folding pathways are different. In 1MBC intermediate additional stabilizing interactions come from helices A and B, while in 1BIN they come from part of the E helix. Running UNFOLD on 1MBC indeed finds that $\alpha_7(G)\alpha_8(H)$ remain together until the very last. For 1BIN we found a pathway passing through $\alpha_1(A)\alpha_2(B)\alpha_7(G)\alpha_8(H)$. UNFOLD was thus able to detect the similarity in the folding pathways but not the details. For that we ran UNFOLD many times with different contact thresholds, and we enumerated all exact mincuts and those mincuts within some ϵ of a mincut. From these different pathways we counted the number of times a given group of SSEs appears together. We found that $\alpha_5(E)$ showed a tendency to interact with $\alpha_8(H)$ in 1BIN but never for 1MBC. This seems to hint at the results from experiments [298].

Protein acylphosphatase (PDB 2ACY; 98 residues), with two α and five β SSEs ($\beta_2\alpha_1\beta_4\beta_3\alpha_2\beta_1\beta_5$), displays a transition state ensemble with a marked tendency for the β-sheets to be present, particularly β_3 and β_4, and while α_2 is present, it is highly disordered relative to rest of the structure [416]. UNFOLD finds that $\beta_2\beta_1$ remain intact until the end of unfolding, passing through a stage that also includes $\beta_3, \beta_4, \alpha_2$. To gain further insight, we ran UNFOLD many times (as described for 1MBC and 1BIN), and we found that there was a marked tendency for $\beta_3\beta_4$ to be together in addition to $\beta_2\beta_1$, and β_3 also interacted with α_2.

The twitchin immunoglobulin superfamily domain protein (PDB 1WIT; 93 residues) has a β-sandwich consisting of nine β-strands and one very small helix. The folding nucleus consists of residues in the structural core $\beta_3\beta_4\beta_7\beta_9\beta_{10}$ centered on β_3 and β_9 on opposite sheets [77]. We found in many runs of UNFOLD that this group does indeed have a very high tendency to remain intact.

7.5 Conclusions

In this chapter we developed automated techniques to predict protein folding pathways. We construct a weighted SSE graph for a protein where each vertex is an SSE and each edge represents the strength of contacts between two SSEs. We used a repeated mincut approach (via the UNFOLD algorithm) on the WSG graph to discover strongly interrelated groups of SSEs, and we then predicted an (approximate) order of appearance of SSEs along the folding pathway.

Currently we consider interactions only among the α-helices and β-strands. In the future we also plan to incorporate the loop regions in the WSG and see what effect this action has on the folding pathway. Furthermore, we plan to test our folding pathways on the entire collection of proteins in the PDB. We would like to study different proteins from the same family and see if our method predicts consistent pathways; both similarities and dissimilarities may be of interest. We also plan to make our software available online so that other researchers can try the UNFOLD predictions before embarking on time-consuming experiments and simulations.

One limitation of the current approach is that the UNFOLD algorithm (arbitrarily) picks only one mincut out of perhaps several mincuts that have the same capacity. It would be interesting to enumerate all possible mincuts recursively and construct all the possible folding pathways. The appearance of some mincuts on several pathways might provide stronger evidence of intermediate states.

Another limitation is that all native interactions are considered energetically equivalent, and thus large stabilizing interactions are not differentiated. Nevertheless the simplified model is based on topology and it helps investigate how much of the folding mechanism can be inferred from the native structure alone, without worrying about energetic difference. Further justification for our model comes from the fact that many independent lines of investigation indicate that protein folding rates and mechanisms are largely determined by the topology of the protein [27], which is captured by our WSG model.

Acknowledgments

This work was supported in part by NSF Career Award IIS-0092978, DOE Career Award DE-FG02-02ER25538, NSF grant EIA-0103708, and NSF grant EIA-0229454.

Chapter 8
Data Mining Methods for a Systematics of Protein Subcellular Location

Kai Huang and Robert F. Murphy

Summary

Proteomics, the comprehensive and systematic study of the properties of all expressed proteins, has become a major research area in computational biology and bioinformatics. Among these properties, knowledge of the specific subcellular structures in which a protein is located is perhaps the most critical to a complete understanding of the protein's roles and functions. Subcellular location is most commonly determined via fluorescence microscopy, an optical method relying on target-specific fluorescent probes. The images that result are routinely analyzed by visual inspection. However, visual inspection may lead to ambiguous, inconsistent, and even inaccurate conclusions about subcellular location. We describe in this chapter an automatic and accurate system that can distinguish all major protein subcellular location patterns. This system employs numerous informative features extracted from the fluorescence microscope images. By selecting the most discriminative features from the entire feature set and recruiting various state-of-the-art classifiers, the system is able to outperform human experts in distinguishing protein patterns. The discriminative features can also be used for routine statistical analyses, such as selecting the most typical image from an image set and objectively comparing two image sets. The system can also be applied to cluster images from randomly tagged genes into statistically indistinguishable groups. These approaches coupled with high-throughput imaging instruments represent a promising approach for the new discipline of location proteomics.

8.1 Introduction

8.1.1 Protein Subcellular Location

The life sciences have entered the post-genome era where the focus of biological research has shifted from genome sequences to protein functionality. With whole-genome drafts of mouse and human in hand, scientists are putting more and more effort into obtaining information about the entire proteome in a given cell type. The properties of a protein include its amino acid sequences, its expression levels under various developmental stages and in different tissues, its 3D structure and active sites, its functional and structural binding partners, and its subcellular location. Protein subcellular location is important for understanding protein function inside the cell. For example, the observation that the product of a gene is localized in mitochondria will support the hypothesis that this protein or gene is involved in energy metabolism. Proteins localized in the cytoskeleton are probably involved in intracellular trafficking and support. The context of protein functionality is well represented by protein subcellular location.

Proteins have various subcellular location patterns [250]. One major category of proteins is synthesized on free ribosomes in the cytoplasm. Soluble proteins remain in the cytoplasm after their synthesis and function as small factories catalyzing cellular metabolites. Other proteins that have a target signal in their sequences are directed to their target organelle (such as mitochondria) via posttranslational transport through the organelle membrane. Nuclear proteins are transferred through pores on the nuclear envelope to the nucleus and mostly function as regulators. The second major category of proteins is synthesized on endoplasmic reticulum(ER)-associated ribosomes and passes through the reticuloendothelial system, consisting of the ER and the Golgi apparatus. Some stay in either the ER or the Golgi apparatus, and the others are further directed by targeting sequences to other organelles such as endosomes or lysosomes. Protein subcellular location patterns often result from steady states or limit cycles and can also change under specific conditions. Proteins are continuously being synthesized, localized, and finally degraded. This process forms the distribution of a protein inside the cell. In addition, intracellular signal transduction pathways often involve translocation of either specific signal or cargo proteins among compartments and intercellular signal transduction employs endocytosis and exocytosis of certain signal proteins. The static and dynamic properties of protein subcellular location patterns provide a significant challenge for machine learning and data mining tools.

8.1.2 Experimental Methods to Determine Protein Subcellular Location

Several experimental methods have been developed to determine protein subcellular location, such as electron microscopy, subcellular fractionation, and fluorescence microscopy. Although electron microscopy provides the finest resolution, sample preparation is slow and it cannot be used for living cells. Subcellular fractionation provides only coarse separation of proteins among major cellular compartments. The most common and powerful method for analyzing the distributions of specific proteins or molecules is fluorescence microscopy. Fluorescence microscopy relies on light emitted by fluorescent dyes that are coupled to target proteins or molecules. These dyes are small molecules with special fluorescent characteristics so that they can emit fluorescence within certain wavelengths given specific illumination. Two filters are needed in fluorescence microscopy, namely, the excitation filter and the emission filter. An illumination light is first passed through the excitation filter so that only specific wavelengths that can excite the fluorescent dye are allowed to reach the specimen. The emission filter is then used to filter the emission spectrum to clean out any excitation wavelengths and only allow fluorescence from the dye to pass through.

How to make the target protein fluorescent is the key part of fluorescence microscopy. Two methods are often used to target fluorescent dyes to proteins or other macromolecules. The first is immunofluorescence, which employs antibodies as intermediates that can bind to the target protein specifically. Cells are first fixed and permeabilized so that antibodies conjugated with fluorescent dyes can enter the cell and bind to the target protein. Two antibodies are often used in immunofluorescence. A primary antibody binds to the target protein specifically and then several secondary antibodies that are conjugated with a fluorescent dye bind to the primary antibody to increase the labeling efficiency.

Different dyes can bind to different secondary antibodies and therefore to different primary antibodies and target proteins. This principle not only applies to antibodies but also applies to drugs that can bind to specific proteins. Fluorescent dyes can be conjugated with drugs that bind to a target protein; e.g., dye-coupled phalloidin can be used to label the actin cytoskeleton. Immunofluorescence requires fixing and permeabilizing cells and is therefore not suitable for live cell imaging. The other method is gene tagging, which attaches a DNA sequence coding a fluorescent protein to a gene of interest. The resulting gene will be expressed as a chimeric protein with intrinsic fluorescence. The tagging can be directed to a specific gene or done randomly. Random tagging is good for labeling unknown proteins and extensive random tagging along with fluorescence microscopy can be used to generate a database of fluorescence microscope images of all or many proteins expressed in a given cell type [200, 201, 233, 334, 396]. We have coined the term location proteomics [73] to describe the automated, proteomewide analysis of protein subcellular location.

Different microscope systems are available for fluorescence microscopy [388]. Low-cost widefield microscope systems collect fluorescence emitted from the whole depth of the specimen with fast acquisition. Deconvolution is required to remove out-of-focus fluorescence from the slice of interest. Confocal scanning microscopes automatically remove out-of-focus fluorescence using a pinhole on the detector. Image acquisition speed is limited by scan speed. A variation on this is the spinning disk confocal microscope, which employs a rotating array of pinholes to facilitate fast focusing and image acquisition. Each microscope system has its own advantages, and the choice of which to use is determined by the application.

In an unpolarized cell, which is relatively flat relative to the depth of field of a microscope objective, a 2D image of a labeled protein usually captures sufficient information about its subcellular location pattern. However, a 2D slice can be misleading in a polarized cell, where proteins show quite different distributions from one cell surface to the other. Three-dimensional images are therefore more useful for analyzing protein distribution patterns in polarized cells.

Current fluorescence microscope systems allow simultaneous imaging of multiple fluorescence channels in both 2D and 3D. Different labels can be used simultaneously during the imaging, which provides contrast information to some landmark such as the cell nucleus. Images of each fluorescent probe are normally collected separately using optical filters (e.g., resulting in a gray-scale image of the amount of fluorescence of probe 1 and a gray-scale image of the amount of fluorescence of probe 2). For display, these separate images are frequently combined to create a false-color image in which, for example, the gray-scale image of one probe is copied into the green channel of an output image and the gray-scale image of a second probe is copied into the red channel.

8.1.3 Overview of Data Mining Methods for Predicting Protein Subcellular Location

Computational approaches to protein location have taken two forms. The first is prediction of location primarily from sequence including prediction using an N-terminal signal peptide [418], functional domain compositions [76, 280], amino acid composition [185, 293], and evidence combined from both sequences and expression levels [106]. The most significant problem with this approach is the currently limited knowledge of the spectrum of possible location patterns. Supervised prediction schemes are limited to assigning new proteins to existing location classes based on their sequence. The situation is analogous to that in structural proteomics a decade or more ago before the major protein fold classes were identified.

The second, complementary approach is automated determination of protein location directly from experimental data. As discussed in section 8.1.2, fluorescence microscopy is the most powerful method for determining protein location, and we [44, 45, 46, 288, 414] and others [90] have described systems for classifying subcellular patterns in fluorescence microscope images.

This chapter focuses on data mining in protein fluorescence microscope images. The image acquisition process is described first. We then introduce subcellular location features (SLFs) computed from images that can capture the characteristics of different protein subcellular location patterns. SLFs are robust for different cell shapes and orientations and are adaptable across various cell types, sample preparations, fluorescence microscopy methods, and image resolutions. Third, work on classical supervised learning of location patterns using SLF is described. The use of various data mining tools such as feature reduction and classifier ensembles to improve classification performance is presented. Systematic statistical analysis comparing different protein subcellular location patterns in image sets can be simplified by carrying out distance computation and statistical tests on the SLF. Finally, we describe the use of unsupervised learning methods to group all proteins expressed in a given cell type into clusters with statistically indistinguishable patterns. The identification of informative features using supervised learning on known classes represents a useful (and we would say required) step in validating the use of these features for exploratory data mining. The result of applying these methods proteomewide is a systematics for protein patterns that is the goal of location proteomics.

8.2 Methods

8.2.1 Image Acquisition

Cell biologists evaluating subcellular location patterns may view anywhere from a few to dozens of cells under a microscope, but the number of images saved is usually limited to a few examples for presentation and publication. In contrast, development and evaluation of methods for location proteomics have required the collection of a sufficient number of digital images to permit statistically meaningful results to be obtained. Our group has used four collections of images for this purpose, which are described here and summarized in Table 8.1. Links for downloading the image collections can be found at http://murphylab.web.cmu.edu/data.

2D Protein Fluorescence Microscope Image Collections

2D CHO. For the initial demonstration of the feasibility of automating subcellular pattern classification, we collected four sets of fluorescence microscope images of Chinese hamster ovary (CHO) cells. In one set, nuclear DNA was labeled with Hoechst 33258; in the other three sets, a specific protein was labeled by immunofluorescence[45]. Antibodies against the Golgi protein giantin, the yeast nucleolar protein NOP4, the lysosomal protein LAMP2, and the microtubule protein tubulin were used. The number of images collected for each protein ranged from 33 to 97. For each field (which

Table 8.1. Summary of the image collections discussed in this chapter.

Data set	No. of classes	Microscopy method	Objective	Pixel size in original field (μm)	No. of colors per image	Ref.
2D CHO	5	Deconvolution	100X	0.23	1	[45]
2D HeLa	10	Deconvolution	100X	0.23	2	[46]
3D HeLa	11	Confocal scanning	100X	0.0488	3	[414]
3D 3T3	46	Spinning disk confocal	60X	0.11	1	[73]

were chosen to include primarily one cell), three optical slices separated by 0.23 micron in focus position were taken. Nearest-neighbor deconvolution was used to remove out-of-focus fluorescence from the central slice [4]. The resulting images were cropped to remove any partial cells along the edge so that only a single-cell region remained. The most common pixel intensity in an input image was subtracted from all pixels in the image to remove the background fluorescence (the most common pixel value was used as background based on the assumptions that cells typically occupy less than half of the total area of the image and that variation in pixel intensity is greater in the cell than in the background). The images were then thresholded so that all pixels below four times the background value were set to zero. Figure 8.1 shows example processed images taken from the 2D CHO collection.

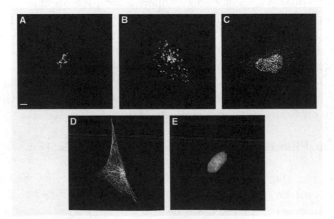

Fig. 8.1. Example images from the 5-class CHO cell image collection depicting five major subcellular location patterns: (A) giantin, (B) LAMP2, (C) NOP4, (D) tubulin, and (E) DNA. From reference [45].

2D HeLa. For a more complete testing of the capabilities and limits of automated subcellular location analysis, a similar immunofluorescence approach was used to acquire a larger image collection of the human cell line HeLa. This line was used because more antibodies are available for human than for hamster cells and because the cells are larger and better spread than CHO cells. Nine different proteins located in major subcellular organelles were labeled, and DNA was labeled in each sample using a distinguishable fluorescent probe. The proteins included a protein located in the endoplasmic reticulum membrane, the Golgi proteins giantin and Gpp130, a protein on the mitochondria outer membrane, the nucleolar protein nucleolin, the lysosomal protein LAMP2, transferrin receptor (primarily localized in endosomes), and the cytoskeletal proteins beta-tubulin and f-actin. The two Golgi proteins were included to test the ability of the automated methods to distinguish similar patterns. The number of images per protein ranged from 73 to 98. The same fluorescence microscope and nearest neighbor deconvolution method used for the CHO set was applied to the HeLa images. The same preprocessing steps of cropping, background subtraction, and thresholding were applied, but an automated threshold selection method [331] was used rather than the fixed multiple method used previously. A separate DNA class was created by making synthetic two color images in which both colors contained the same DNA image (the DNA images collected in parallel with giantin were used). Figure 8.2 shows example processed images taken from the 2D HeLa image collection.

3D Protein Fluorescence Microscope Image Collections

3D HeLa. To acquire the 3D image collection, we used a three-laser confocal laser scanning microscope that is able to remove out-of-focus fluorescence while taking an image. The same nine proteins used in the 2D HeLa set were imaged. For each protein, parallel images of DNA and total protein were obtained using additional fluorescent probes so that three-color images were obtained. Every 3D image in the set consisted of 14 to 24 2D slices and the dimensions of each voxel in the resulting 3D stack was $0.049 \times 0.049 \times 0.2$ microns. Between 50 and 58 3D images were collected for each protein. Automatic cell segmentation was performed by employing a seeded watershed algorithm on the total protein channel using the centers of the nuclei (calculated using the DNA channel) as seeds. After segmentation, the images were further processed by background subtraction and automated thresholding. Figure 8.3 shows an example image taken from the 3D HeLa image collection. A synthetic DNA class was created by copying the DNA image, and a synthetic "cytoplasmic" class was created by copying the total protein image.

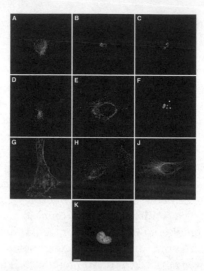

Fig. 8.2. Example images from 2D HeLa cell image collection depicting ten major subcellular location patterns. The target proteins include (A) an ER protein, (B) the Golgi proteins giantin, (C) Gpp130, (D) a lysosomal protein LAMP2, (E) a mitochondrial protein, (F) a nucleolar protein nucleolin, (G) filamentous actin, (H) an endosomal protein transferrin receptor, (J) tubulin, and (K) DNA. Scale bar=$10\mu m$. From reference [46].

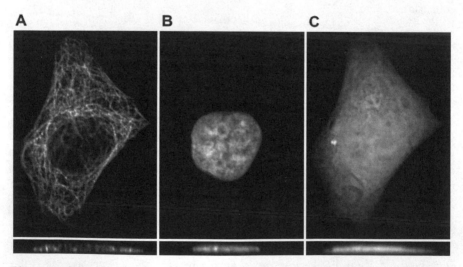

Fig. 8.3. An example image from the 3D HeLa cell image collection. Each image comprises three channels labeling (A) a specific target protein (tubulin), (B) total DNA, and (C) total protein. Summed projections onto the X–Y and X–Z planes are shown. From reference [414].

3D 3T3. As mentioned previously, random tagging can provide an image library of all proteins expressed in a cell type. For example, CD tagging [200] introduces a CD cassette into the genome through a genetically engineered retroviral vector. The coding sequence of a green fluorescence protein (GFP) is enclosed in the CD cassette and a GFP-tagged fusion protein will be expressed if (and only if) the CD cassette is inserted into an intron of a gene. Cell lines expressing properly tagged genes can be isolated by selection for GFP expression. The sequence of the tagged gene can be determined later and identified by sequence homology search. We have used a library of CD-tagged lines derived from 3T3 cells [201] to build a collection of single-color 3D images for 46 tagged clones [73]. Between 16 and 33 3D images were collected for each clone, where each voxel represents $0.11 \times 0.11 \times 0.5$ microns in space. Since no DNA or total protein images were available to permit automated cropping, manual cropping was conducted followed by background subtraction and thresholding. Figure 8.4 shows example processed images taken from the 3D 3T3 image collection.

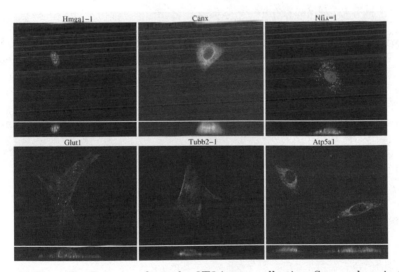

Fig. 8.4. Example 3D images from the 3T3 image collection. Summed projections onto the X–Y and X–Z planes are shown for proteins representing six of the major subcellular patterns found by cluster analysis [73].

8.2.2 Subcellular Location Features (SLFs)

Traditional image classification in computer vision frequently involves knowledge representation of an image by features such as color, frequency, and texture. These generalized features have been successfully used in classification of natural scenes, human faces, and so on. Complex image preprocessing, however, is employed in these problems so that variances in illuminations, translations, and orientations are removed and all input images are normalized. Therefore, no specific requirement is imposed on these generalized features. Cells are more variable than objects in natural scenes or faces. They can have widely varying morphologies, and the images taken for a specific protein can be affected by sample preparation and fluorescence microscopy methods. No image-processing methods for removing these sources of variation have been described. As a result, the features that are suitable for describing protein fluorescence microscope images should be invariant to translation and rotation of the cell in the field and be robust to different cell shapes, cell types, and fluorescence microscopy methods. The design of the subcellular location features (SLFs) was based on these constraints, although some generalized features such as wavelets are also considered. These features are designed for single-cell images, although some of them can also be adapted to multicell images.

Features for 2D Images

Zernike moment features. Zernike moment features [220], defined on the unit circle, describe the similarity of an input image to a set of Zernike polynomials. They were first used for analyzing subcellular patterns in our initial work with the 2D CHO images [44, 45]. We use a transformation that maps a rectangular image $f(x, y)$ to a unit circle with a user-supplied cell radius r centered on the center of fluorescence (c_x, c_y) of the cell and removes pixels outside that circle:

$$f'(x', y') = f(x, y)w(x', y'), \quad x' = \frac{x - C_x}{r}, \quad y' = \frac{y - C_y}{r}, \tag{8.1}$$

where

$$C_x = \frac{\sum_{x,y} x f(x, y)}{\sum_{x,y} f(x, y)}, \quad C_y = \frac{\sum_{x,y} y f(x, y)}{\sum_{x,y} f(x, y)} \tag{8.2}$$

and $w(x', y')$ is a unit circle mask function:

$$w(x', y') = \begin{cases} 1, & p^2 + q^2 \leq 1 \\ 0, & \text{otherwise} \end{cases} \tag{8.3}$$

where $p = x'$ and $q = y'$.

The Zernike moment, Z_{nl}, is calculated as a dot product between the normalized image and a Zernike polynomial with degree n and angular dependence l,

$$Z_{nl} = \frac{n+1}{\pi} \sum_{x'} \sum_{y'} V_{nl}^*(x', y') f'(x', y'), \tag{8.4}$$

where V_{nl}^* is the complex conjugate of V_{nl},

$$V_{nl}(x', y') = \sum_{m=0}^{\frac{n-1}{2}} (-1)^m \frac{(n-m)!}{m!(\frac{n-2m+l}{2})!(\frac{n-2m-l}{2})!} (p^2+q^2)^{\frac{n}{2}-m} e^{jl\theta}, \tag{8.5}$$

and $p = x'$, $q = y'$, $0 \le l \le n$, $n - l$ is even, $\theta = tan^{-1}(\frac{y'}{x'})$, and $j = \sqrt{-1}$.

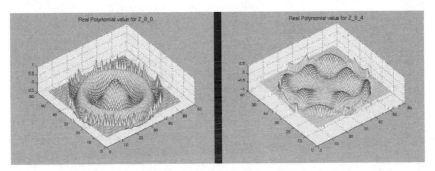

Fig. 8.5. Example Zernike polynomials (Z_{80} and Z_{84}).

Figure 8.5 shows examples of two of the Zernike polynomials. The image transformation to a unit circle makes the moments invariant to translations and scales, and features invariant to orientation of the cell can then be obtained by calculating magnitudes. We use $|Z_{nl}|$ for $0 \le n \le 12$, resulting in 49 Zernike moment features.

Haralick texture features. Texture features measure repetitive local patterns in an image. Just as some characteristics of biomolecular sequences can be represented by treating them as a Markov chain in which the probability of a particular sequence element depends only on the prior sequence element, so images can be simplistically represented using a gray-level cooccurrence matrix. This is an $N_g \times N_g$ matrix (where N_g is the number of gray levels in the image) where each element $p(i, j)$ represents the probability of observing a pixel with gray level i occurring adjacent to a pixel with gray level j. Haralick [169] defined 14 features that can be computed from the cooccurrence matrix to describe image texture. Table 8.2 shows the 13 of these features that we have used in our work.

Adjacency can be defined in horizontal, vertical, and two diagonal directions in a 2D image. To achieve rotational invariance, texture features can be calculated from separate cooccurrence matrices and then averaged

Table 8.2. Definitions of 13 Haralick texture features that can be computed from a gray-level cooccurrence matrix [169], $p(i,j)$.

Feature name	Definition
1. Angular second moment	$\sum_i \sum_j p(i,j)^2$
2. Contrast	$\sum_{n=0}^{N_g-1} n^2 \{\sum_{i=1}^{N_g} \sum_{j=1}^{N_g} p(i,j)\}, |i-j|=n$
3. Correlation	$\frac{\sum_i \sum_j (ij)p(i,j) - \mu_x \mu_y}{\sigma_x \sigma_y}$, where μ_x, μ_y, σ_x, and σ_y are the means and standard deviations of the marginal probability density functions p_x and p_y
4. Sum of squares: variance	$\sum_i \sum_j (i-\mu)^2 p(i,j)$
5. Inverse difference moment	$\sum_i \sum_j \frac{1}{1+(i-j)^2} p(i,j)$
6. Sum average	$\sum_{i=2}^{2N_g} i p_{x+y}(i)$, where x and y are the coordinates of an element in the cooccurrence matrix and $p_{x+y}(i)$ is the probability summing to $x+y$
7. Sum variance	$\sum_{i=2}^{2N_g} (i-f_8)^2 p_{x+y}(i)$
8. Sum entropy	$-\sum_{i=2}^{2N_g} p_{x+y}(i) log\{p_{x+y}(i)\}$
9. Entropy	$-\sum_i \sum_j p(i,j) log(p(i,j))$
10. Difference variance	$\sum_{i=0}^{N_g-1} i^2 p_{x-y}(i)$
11. Difference entropy	$-\sum_{i=0}^{N_g-1} p_{x-y}(i) log\{p_{x-y}(i)\}$
12. Info. measure of correlation 1	$\frac{H_{XY} - H_{XY1}}{max\{H_X, H_Y\}}$, where $H_{XY} = -\sum_i \sum_j p(i,j) log(p(i,j))$, H_X and H_Y are the entropies of p_x and p_y, $H_{XY1} = -\sum_i \sum_j p(i,j) log\{p_x(i)p_y(j)\}$ $H_{XY2} = -\sum_i \sum_j p_x(i)p_y(j) log\{p_x(i)p_y(j)\}$
13. Info. measure of correlation 2	$(1 - exp[-2(H_{XY2} - H_{XY})])^{\frac{1}{2}}$

across the four directions. These features were first used to describe subcellular location patterns in our work on the 2D CHO images, both by themselves and in combination with Zernike moment features [45].

Since the cooccurrence matrix captures second-order image statistics, the Haralick texture features are intrinsically invariant to translations (within digitization error). However, the features are sensitive to the number of gray levels and the pixel size in the image. To find the largest pixel size and the optimal number of gray levels acceptable for protein location analysis, we conducted a series of experiments involving resampling and requantizing gray-level images from the 2D HeLa image collection [289]. The result showed that an image with 1.15 microns/pixel and 256 gray levels generates the most discriminative Haralick features. Since most fluorescence microscopes give higher resolution than 1.15 microns/pixel and fluorescence intensity readings greater than 256, we have proposed using these settings to calculate texture features robust to variation in image acquisition conditions [289]. To do this, input images can be resampled to 1.15 microns/pixel and binned in 256 gray levels before building the cooccurrence matrix.

SLFs. To permit unambiguous references to specific feature combinations, we have created a nomenclature for feature sets and individual features [46]. The convention is for feature sets to be referred to by SLF (subcellular location feature) followed by a number (e.g., SLF1) and for individual features to be referred to by the set number followed by the index of that feature within that set (e.g., SLF1.7). Features used in new feature sets can be defined recursively until their original definition is reached (e.g., SLF5.1 is the same as SLF1.3). SLF1 was the first feature set designed specifically for describing protein subcellular patterns in fluorescence microscope images [46]. The features in SLF1 were based on the image properties that a human expert pays attention to when classifying protein patterns. For instance, the pattern for an endosomal protein such as transferrin receptor (see Figure 8.2) shows more fluorescence objects than other patterns, making the number of fluorescence objects in the image a good feature to distinguish endosomes from other location patterns. Similarly, other morphological and geometric features such as object size and the average distance between objects and the center of fluorescence of the image are used in SLF1 as well as features derived from edge finding and the convex hull of the image.

When a parallel DNA image is available, additional features can be calculated, describing the distance between objects and the center of fluorescence of DNA and the overlap between the protein fluorescence and the DNA fluorescence. The six DNA features, along with the 16 features in SLF1, form feature set SLF2. Feature set SLF3 was defined as a combination of SLF1, Zernike moment features, and Haralick texture features and feature set SLF4 as a combination of SLF2, Zernike, and Haralick [46]. As improvements and additions are made, new sets have been defined. SLF7 starts from SLF3, incorporates the intensity scale- and pixel size-normalized Haralick features described, and includes six new features measuring object skeletons and nonobject fluorescence [289]. Table 8.3 gives brief descriptions of each of the features. This set is appropriate for single-color protein images, and SLF7 can be combined with the six DNA features in SLF2 (SLF2.17–22) to describe protein images that have a parallel DNA image.

Wavelet features. Wavelets decompose an input image locally by many basis functions with different scales. They have been successfully used in image denoising, compression, and classification [67]. Recently we have explored the use for protein pattern analysis of two sets of wavelet features that are commonly used in computer vision, Daubechies 4 wavelet features and Gabor wavelet features [186]. These wavelet features are not invariant to cell translation and rotation, and therefore a procedure for rotating each image to a common frame of reference is needed. For this purpose we rotate the image so that its principal axis aligns with the y coordinate axis and perform an additional 180° rotation if necessary so that the x skewness (the third central moment of x) is positive.

Table 8.3. All current features for analysis of 2D images (these are the SLF7 feature set augmented by the six DNA features from SLF2). The SLF number is a composite index for each feature including both the feature set name and an index; e.g., SLF2.21 stands for the 21st feature in feature set SLF2.

SLF number	Feature description
SLF1.1	Number of fluorescence objects in the image
SLF1.2	Euler number of the image (no. of holes minus no. of objects)
SLF1.3	Average number of above-threshold pixels per object
SLF1.4	Variance of the number of above-threshold pixels per object
SLF1.5	Ratio of the size of the largest to the smallest object
SLF1.6	Average object distance to the cellular center of fluorescence (COF)
SLF1.7	Variance of object distances from the COF
SLF1.8	Ratio of the largest to the smallest object to COF distance
SLF7.9	Fraction of the nonzero pixels that are along an edge
SLF7.10	Measure of edge gradient intensity homogeneity
SLF7.11	Measure of edge direction homogeneity 1
SLF7.12	Measure of edge direction homogeneity 2
SLF7.13	Measure of edge direction difference
SLF1.14	Fraction of the convex hull area occupied by protein fluorescence
SLF1.15	Roundness of the convex hull
SLF1.16	Eccentricity of the convex hull
SLF2.17	Average object distance from the COF of the DNA image
SLF2.18	Variance of object distances from the DNA COF
SLF2.19	Ratio of the largest to the smallest object to DNA COF distance
SLF2.20	Distance between the protein COF and the DNA COF
SLF2.21	Ratio of the area occupied by protein to that occupied by DNA
SLF2.22	Fraction of the protein fluorescence that colocalizes with DNA
SLF3.17-SLF3.65	Zernike moment features
SLF3.66-SLF3.78	Haralick texture features
SLF7.79	Fraction of cellular fluorescence not included in objects
SLF7.80	Average length of the morphological skeleton of objects
SLF7.81	Average ratio of object skeleton length to the area of the convex hull of the skeleton
SLF7.82	Average fraction of object pixels contained within its skeleton
SLF7.83	Average fraction of object fluorescence contained within its skeleton
SLF7.84	Average ratio of the number of branch points in skeleton to length of skeleton

Daubechies 4 wavelet features

Wavelet features are computed from discrete wavelet transformation of an image, which captures information from both the spatial and frequency domains of an image. The discrete wavelet transformation (DWT) decomposes an image to a detailed resolution and a coarse approximation by employing a scaling function and a wavelet function (corresponding to a low-pass and a high-pass filter, respectively). Since an image is a 2D signal, filter convolutions are conducted on the columns and the rows of an image sequentially. In other words, the columns of an input image are first convolved with the high-pass and low-pass filters in the DWT. The rows of the resulting images are convolved again with the high-pass and low-pass filters. Therefore, four convolved images can be obtained after each DWT decomposition. These four images correspond to four frequency groups: low-frequency component, high-frequency component in the x direction, high-frequency component in the y direction, and high-frequency component in the diagonal direction. The useful information is contained in the three high-frequency components. The low-frequency component can be further decomposed by using the same procedure, and four new components are obtained again. At each level of decomposition, we store the three high-frequency components and decompose the low-frequency component. We computed features from the tenth level of decomposition. In other words, an image was transformed by the discrete Daubechies 4 wavelet transformation ten times. At each level, the average energy of each of the three high-frequency components is stored as a feature. Therefore, three features are obtained for each level (x, y, and diagonal), giving a total of 30 features. The scaling function and the wavelet function of the Daubechies wavelets are specified as follows:

$$\varphi(x) = \sum_{k} \alpha_k^0 \cdot \varphi(nx - k) \tag{8.6}$$

$$\psi^r = \sum_{k} \alpha_k^r \cdot \varphi(nx - k), \quad r = 1, \ldots, n-1, \tag{8.7}$$

where n is the level order, α stands for Daubechies wavelets coefficients, and k is the translation variable. These functions are shown in Figure 8.6.

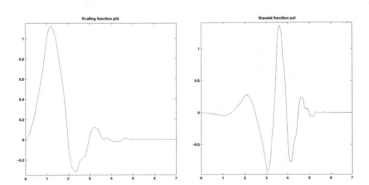

Fig. 8.6. Daubechies 4 wavelet functions. The left panel shows the scaling function that generates the mother wavelet function on the right.

Gabor wavelet features

The filters generated from the Gabor function, whose orientations and scales can be customized, capture image derivative information such as edges and lines [266]. A 2D Gabor function is a 2D Gaussian modulated by an complex exponential:

$$
g(x, y) = (\frac{1}{2\pi\sigma_x\sigma_y})\exp\left\{-\frac{1}{2}\left(\frac{x^2}{\sigma_x^2} + \frac{y^2}{\sigma_y^2}\right) + i2\pi Wx\right\}, \tag{8.8}
$$

where W is the frequency bandwidth of Gabor filters. The basis set formed by Gabor functions is complete but nonorthogonal. To generate Gabor filters as 2D wavelets, a filter bank can be formed by rotating and dilating a mother wavelet $g(x', y')$:

$$
g_{mn}(x, y) = a^{-m}g(x', y'),
$$
$$
a > 1, \quad m = 0, \dots, S-1, \quad n = 0, \dots, K-1 \tag{8.9}
$$

with

$$
\begin{aligned}
x' &= a^{-m}(x\cos\theta + y\sin\theta) \\
y' &= a^{-m}(-x\sin\theta + y\cos\theta) \\
\theta &= n\pi/K \\
\alpha &= (U_h/U_l)^{1/(S-1)} \\
W &= U_h,
\end{aligned}
$$

where S and K are the total number of scales and orientations respectively, q is the orientation angle, α is the scale factor, and U_h and U_l are the upper and lower interested-center frequencies and are normally set to 0.4 and 0.05 respectively to reduce redundancy in the frequency space [266]. The variances along the x axis and y axis can be computed as

$$
\sigma_x = \frac{1}{2\pi}\left\{\left(\frac{\alpha-1}{\alpha+1}\right)\left(\frac{U_h}{\sqrt{2\ln 2}}\right)\right\}^{-1} \quad \text{and}
$$
$$
\sigma_y = \frac{1}{2\pi}\left\{\tan\left(\frac{\pi}{2K}\right)\sqrt{\frac{U_h^2}{2\ln 2} - (2\pi\sigma_x)^{-2}}\right\}^{-1} \tag{8.10}
$$

We can convolve an input image with a Gabor filter with scale m and orientation n and take the mean and standard deviation of the response as texture features. We have used five different scales and six different orientations yielding a total of 60 Gabor texture features.

Features for 3D Images

3D variants of SLF2. The morphological and geometric features in SLF2 involve 2D object finding and distance calculation. We have created 3D counterparts of these features using 3D object finding and distance calculation. Features dependent on area are straightforwardly converted to use volume, but we chose not to replace 2D distance directly with 3D distance. We do so because while for 2D images we consider orientation in the plane of the microscope slide to be unimportant (thus using only the magnitude of a distance vector as a feature), for 3D images it is inappropriate to consider distance in the slide plane to be equivalent to distance along the microscope axis. Therefore, for each feature in SLF2 involving distance, we created two 3D features: the unsigned magnitude of the distance component in the slide plane and the signed magnitude of the distance component along the microscope axis (z). The result was feature set SLF9, consisting of 28 features capturing morphological and geometrical information in 3D protein fluorescence microscope images [414]. Half of the features in SLF9 depend on a parallel DNA image.

3D Haralick texture features. Four cooccurrence matrices along horizontal, vertical, and diagonal directions are built when computing 2D Haralick texture features. For 3D images, voxel adjacency can occur in 13 different directions and therefore 13 cooccurrence matrices need to be constructed to calculate average values of the same 13 Haralick texture features we have used previously. To retrieve more information from the textures, the range between the maximum and the minimum in the 13 directions was employed as a new feature. The combination of average and range for each of the 13 Haralick features gives a total of 26 3D texture features [73].

3D edge features. In the interest of computational simplicity, we derived 3D edge features by applying edge finding on each 2D slice of a 3D image and combining them to form 3D edge features (SLF11.15-11.16). Feature set SLF11 (Table 8.4) was created by combining the 14 DNA-independent features from SLF9 with the 3D texture and edge features.

Feature Normalization

When used for classification, we normalize each feature to have zero mean and unit variance using the values from the training set, and then the same mean and variance are used to normalize the features in the test set.

Table 8.4. All current features for analysis of 3D images (these are the SLF11 feature set augmented by the 14 DNA features from SLF9).

SLF number	Feature description
SLF9.1	Number of fluorescent objects in the image
SLF9.2	Euler number of the image
SLF9.3	Average object volume
SLF9.4	Standard deviation of object volumes
SLF9.5	Ratio of the max object volume to min object volume
SLF9.6	Average object distance to the protein center of fluorescence (COF)
SLF9.7	Standard deviation of object distances from the protein COF
SLF9.8	Ratio of the largest to the smallest object to protein COF distance
SLF9.9	Average object distance to the COF of the DNA image
SLF9.10	Standard deviation of object distances from the COF of the DNA image
SLF9.11	Ratio of the largest to the smallest object to DNA COF distance
SLF9.12	Distance between the protein COF and the DNA COF
SLF9.13	Ratio of the volume occupied by protein to that occupied by DNA
SLF9.14	Fraction of the protein fluorescence that colocalizes with DNA
SLF9.15	Average horizontal distance of objects to the protein COF
SLF9.16	Standard deviation of object horizontal distances from the protein COF
SLF9.17	Ratio of the largest to the smallest object to protein COF horizontal distance
SLF9.18	Average vertical distance of objects to the protein COF
SLF9.19	Standard deviation of object vertical distances from the protein COF
SLF9.20	Ratio of the largest to the smallest object to protein COF vertical distance
SLF9.21	Average object horizontal distance from the DNA COF
SLF9.22	Standard deviation of object horizontal distances from the DNA COF
SLF9.23	Ratio of the largest to the smallest object to DNA COF horizontal distance
SLF9.24	Average object vertical distance from the DNA COF
SLF9.25	Standard deviation of object vertical distances from the DNA COF
SLF9.26	Ratio of the largest to the smallest object to DNA COF vertical distance
SLF9.27	Horizontal distance between the protein COF and the DNA COF
SLF9.28	Signed vertical distance between the protein COF and the DNA COF
SLF11.15	Fraction of above-threshold pixels that are along an edge
SLF11.16	Fraction of fluorescence in above-threshold pixels that are along an edge
SLF11.17/30	Average/range of angular second moment
SLF11.18/31	Average/range of contrast
SLF11.19/32	Average/range of correlation
SLF11.20/33	Average/range of sum of squares of variance
SLF11.21/34	Average/range of inverse difference moment
SLF11.22/35	Average/range of sum average
SLF11.23/36	Average/range of sum variance
SLF11.24/37	Average/range of sum entropy
SLF11.25/38	Average/range of entropy
SLF11.26/39	Average/range of difference variance
SLF11.27/40	Average/range of difference entropy
SLF11.28/41	Average/range of info measure of correlation 1
SLF11.29/42	Average/range of info measure of correlation 2

8.2.3 Supervised Learning for Protein Subcellular Location

A supervised learning problem usually involves finding the relationship between the predictors X and the dependent variable Y, namely $Y = f(X)$. A typical supervised learning system takes a training data set and models the predictors as its inputs and the dependent variables as its outputs. The learning process is characterized by modifying the relationship f' learned by the system with regard to the difference between system prediction $f'(x_i)$ and expected output y_i so that the system will generate close enough predictions to the desired outputs. The performance of a classifier is often evaluated as the average accuracy on a test set. In our work, we use the average accuracy over all test set instances (images), which, since the number of instances per class is roughly similar, is close to the average performance over all classes.

Given the definitions of various feature sets in the previous section, we can transform a protein fluorescence microscope image to a number of features and train a classifier to learn the relationship between these features and the protein subcellular location patterns. We first introduce classification on 5-class CHO images by using a neural network classifier.

Classification of 5-Class 2D CHO Images

As the first trial of automatic recognition of protein subcellular location patterns in fluorescence microscope images, a back-propagation neural network with one hidden layer and 20 hidden nodes was trained using Zernike moment features computed from the 2D CHO set [44, 45]. The images were divided into three sets (training/stop training/test) as follows: giantin 47/4/26, DNA 39/4/36, LAMP2 37/8/52, NOP4 25/1/7, tubulin 25/3/23. The neural network was trained on the training set and the training was stopped when the sum of squared error on the stop set reached a minimum. The test set was then used to evaluate the network. Table 8.5 shows the confusion matrix averaged over eight trials.

Table 8.5. Confusion matrix for test data using a neural network classifier with Zernike moment features on the 2D CHO images. The average classification accuracy is 87% on eight random trials and the corresponding training accuracy is 94%. Data from reference [45].

True class	Output of the classifier				
	Giantin	DNA	LAMP2	NOP4	Tubulin
Giantin	**97%**	0%	3%	0%	0%
DNA	3%	**93%**	0%	3%	0%
LAMP2	12%	2%	**70%**	10%	7%
NOP4	0%	0%	0%	**88%**	13%
Tubulin	0%	0%	12%	4%	**85%**

Each element in a confusion matrix measures how much a classifier gets "confused" between two classes. For instance, Table 8.5 shows that the neural network classifier incorrectly considers 12% of the LAMP2 images to represent a Giantin pattern. Each percentage at the diagonal of the matrix is the recall of the classifier for the corresponding class. The precision of the classifier for a specific class can be computed by dividing the number of correctly classified images on that class by the column-sum of images of the class in the matrix. Due to rounding, the sum of each row in a confusion matrix might not equal 100%. The average recall achieved by Zernike moment features and the back-propagation neural network is much higher than that of a random classifier, 20%. A similar neural network classifier trained using Haralick texture features in place of the Zernike moment features gave a similar overall accuracy [45].

The recognition of the 5 subcellular location patterns in 2D CHO image set showed that Zernike moment features and Haralick texture features are able to capture appropriate information from fluorescence microscope images and a trained classifier was able to give relatively accurate prediction on previously unseen images.

Classification of 10-Class 2D HeLa Images

To test the applicability of automated classification to protein fluorescence microscope images for other patterns and cell types, we conducted supervised learning on the 10-class 2D HeLa image collection. This collection not only contains location patterns covering all major cellular organelles, it also includes patterns that are easily confused by human experts (such as giantin and gpp130). The SLF3 and SLF4 feature sets previously described were developed for these studies, but only modest classifier accuracies were obtained with these whole sets. This result was presumably due to having insufficient training images to determine decision boundaries in the large feature space. Significant improvement in classifier performance can often be obtained by selecting a smaller number of features from a large set. Here we will first review methods for decreasing the size of the feature space, then review various classifiers that can be applied to the features, and finally describe comparison of these approaches for the 2D HeLa collection.

Feature reduction. There are two basic approaches to feature reduction: feature recombination and feature selection. The former recombines the original features either linearly or nonlinearly according to some criterion to reach a smaller set of features. The latter explicitly selects a small set of features from the original set by using some heuristic search. Following are descriptions of four methods from each category that are widely used for feature reduction.

Feature recombination

1. Principal component analysis (PCA), probably the first feature recombination method adapted for data mining, captures the linear relationships among the original features. It projects the input data into a lower-dimensional space so that most of the data variance is preserved. To do that, the covariance matrix A of the input data is first constructed:

$$A = \frac{1}{n} \sum_{j=1}^{n} x_j x_j^T, \tag{8.11}$$

where $x_j (j = 1, \dots, n)$ represents the m-dimensional feature vector of the jth image and n is the total number of images. The basis of the low-dimensional space is formed by choosing the eigenvectors of the covariance matrix A that correspond to the largest k eigenvalues. By projecting the original data onto this new space, we get a $k(k < m)$-dimensional feature space in which the data are spread as much as possible.

2. Unlike the linear relationships obtained by PCA, nonlinear principal component analysis (NLPCA) is often used to obtain nonlinear combinations of the input features that capture as much of the information in the original set as possible. A five-layer neural network is often used to extract nonlinearly combined features [108]. In this network, the data set serves as both the inputs and the desired outputs. The second layer nonlinearly maps the input features to some space, and the middle layer of k nodes recombines these features linearly. The reverse operation is carried out at the fourth layer to attempt to make the outputs of the network equal its inputs. The training of the neural network stops when the sum of squared error stops decreasing. The first three layers are separated as a new neural network. By feeding the original data, the new network will generate k nonlinear recombined features as its outputs.

3. Another way to extract nonlinearly combined features is to use kernel principal component analysis (KPCA). KPCA is similar to PCA except that it first applies a nonlinear kernel function to the original data to map them to a new high-dimensional space in which normal PCA is conducted [354]. The assumption is that nonlinear relationships among original features can be captured through the nonlinear kernel transformation (represented as Φ below). A dot product matrix K can be constructed by taking dot products between any two data points in the new feature space,

$$K(i, j) = \Phi(x_i) \bullet \Phi(x_j) \quad i, j \in 1, 2, \dots, n, \tag{8.12}$$

where x_i is the m-dimensional feature vector describing the ith image and $\Phi(x_i)$ is new feature vector in the high-dimensional space. This matrix K is similar to the covariance matrix A used in normal PCA. Eigenvalue decomposition is further conducted on K resulting in a group of eigenvectors that form the new basis of the high-dimensional space. Projecting the original data to the new space will give us the nonlinear recombined features. The maximum number of new features is determined by the total number of data points n, as can be seen in the definition of K. Therefore, KPCA is not only a feature reduction method but can also work as a feature expansion method.

4. In ideal pattern recognition, the input variables, features, should be statistically independent from each other so that the information representation efficiency is maximized. Independent component analysis (ICA) is used to extract statistically independent features from the original data [108]. Given n m-dimensional data points, we can define a source matrix s and a transformation matrix B as

$$D = sB, \tag{8.13}$$

where D is an $n \times m$ original data matrix, s is an $n \times d$ source matrix containing d independent source signals, and B is a $d \times m$ transformation matrix. We can assume that s is formed by a linear transformation of D followed by a nonlinear mapping [108]:

$$s = f(WD + w_0), \tag{8.14}$$

where W and w_0 are weights involved in the linear transformation and f is often chosen as a sigmoid function. Solving W and w_0 requires choosing a cost function that measures the independence of the d source signals. Nongaussianity is often used as the cost function.

Feature selection

A brute-force examination of all possible subsets of some larger feature set is an NP-hard problem. Therefore, either sequential or randomized heuristic search algorithms are used in feature selection. A classifier or some global statistic computed from the data is often employed to evaluate each selected feature subset. The feature selection process can go forward or backward or in both directions.

1. A classical measurement of feature goodness is information gain ratio, a criterion from the decision tree theory. Given a data set D with m features, the information gain ratio of feature X_i is defined as [275]

$$Gain(D, X_i) = \frac{Entropy(D) - \sum_{v \in V_i} \frac{D_v}{D} Entropy(D_v)}{-\sum_{v \in V_i} \frac{D_v}{D} log \frac{D_v}{D}},$$
$$i = 1, 2, \ldots, m \tag{8.15}$$

where V_i is the set of all possible values that X_i can have and D_v represents
the data subset in which X_i has the value of v. The gain ratio of a feature
measures how much more information will be gained by splitting a decision
tree node on this feature. It is more advantageous than normal information
gain because it penalizes features that are different at every data point. A
simple ranking of features by their gain ratios can help identify the "best"
features.

2. Every data set has more or less self-similarity, which can be measured
by its intrinsic dimensionality. The intrinsic dimensionality of a self-similar
data set should be much less than the actual dimension in its feature
space. Therefore, those features that do not contribute to the intrinsic
dimensionality are candidates to be dropped. One way to determine the
intrinsic dimensionality of a data set is to compute its fractal dimensionality,
also known as correlation fractal dimensionality [407]. A feature selection
scheme can be formed by considering the goodness of each feature by
measuring how much it will contribute to the fractal dimensionality. An
algorithm, FDR (fractal dimensionality reduction), implements this idea by
employing a backward elimination process where the feature whose deletion
changes the fractal dimensionality the least gets dropped each time until no
more features can decrease the total fractal dimensionality by a minimum
amount [407]. This algorithm can be used for both labeled and unlabeled
data, and it also gives an approximate final number of features we should
keep, which is the fractal dimensionality of the original data.

3. In a well-configured classification problem, it can be found that different
classes are far apart from each other in the feature space where each class is
also tightly packed. The job of a classifier is made much easier by features
that have this property. Stepwise discriminant analysis [203] uses a statistic,
Wilks's Λ, to measure this property of a feature set. It is defined as

$$\Lambda(m) = \frac{|W(X)|}{|T(X)|}, \quad X = [X_1, X_2, \ldots, X_m], \tag{8.16}$$

where X represents the m features currently used and the within-group
covariance matrix W and the among-group covariance matrix T are defined
as

$$W(i,j) = \sum_{g=1}^{q} \sum_{t=1}^{n_g} (X_{igt} - \bar{X}_{ig})(X_{jgt} - \bar{X}_{jg}), \quad i,j \in 1,2,\ldots,m \tag{8.17}$$

$$T(i,j) = \sum_{g=1}^{q} \sum_{t=1}^{n_g} (X_{igt} - \bar{X}_i)(X_{jgt} - \bar{X}_j), \quad i,j \in 1,2,\ldots,m, \tag{8.18}$$

where i and j represent the ith and jth features, X_{igt} is the ith feature value
of the data point t in the class g, $\bar{X}_{ig}$ is the mean value of the ith feature

in the class g, $\bar{X}_i$ is the mean value of the ith feature in all classes, q is the total number of classes, and n_g is the number of data points in the class g. Since Wilks's Λ is a group statistic, an F statistic is often used to convert it to the confidence of including or removing a feature for the current feature set. A feature selection process can be formed according to the F statistic at each step by starting from the full feature set.

All these methods provide a criterion for adding or subtracting a feature and follow a sequential, deterministic path through the feature space. This search can be either forward (starting with no features and adding one at each step), backward (starting with all features and removing one at each step), or forward-backward, in which we choose whether to add or subtract at each step. Both the forward and the backward methods are greedy and therefore limited in the number of possibilities considered (making them efficient). The forward-backward method is one order less greedy so that initial, nonoptimal inclusions of features can be reversed.

4. As an alternative to these deterministic methods, we can incorporate random choice into a search strategy. A genetic algorithm is often used for this purpose [440]. It treats each possible feature subset as a bit string, with 1 representing inclusion of the feature. The initial pool of bit strings is randomly generated, and all strings go through mutation and crossover at each generation. At the end of each generation, a classifier is applied as the fitness function to rank all feature subsets at that generation according to their prediction errors. The feature subsets giving lowest error are selected as well as some lower-performing subsets that are selected under predefined probability. The selection process will stop if either the maximum number of generations is reached or no more improvement can be observed between generations. Figure 8.7 shows an outline of the genetic algorithm approach.

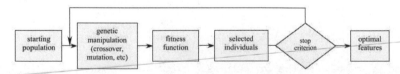

Fig. 8.7. Flow chart of feature selection using genetic algorithms.

Classifiers

Support vector machines (SVMs)

Support vector machines are generalized linear classifiers. A linear classifier looks for a hyperplane, a linear decision boundary, between two classes if one exists. It will perform badly if the optimal decision boundary is far from

linear. Sometimes there are many possible linear classifiers to separate two classes making the choice between them difficult. Therefore, there are two constraints in classical linear classifiers, namely the linear decision boundary constraint and the optimal choice among several candidates. Support vector machines were designed to solve these two problems in linear classifiers. The same kernel trick used in KPCA is applied in support vector machines. The original feature space is transformed to a very high, sometimes infinite, dimensional space after a kernel mapping. The nonlinear decision boundary in the original feature space can be close to linear in the new feature space by applying a nonlinear kernel function. To choose the optimal linear boundary in the new high-dimensional space, a support vector machine selects the maximum-margin hyperplane that maximizes the minimum distance between the training data and the hyperplane. Intuitively, this hyperplane will prevent overfitting by reducing its representation to a small number of data points lying on the boundary. The maximum-margin criterion was proved to minimize the upper bound on the VC dimension of a classifier, an objective goodness measurement of a classifier [410].

Support vector machines can model very complex decision boundaries in the original feature space through the kernel trick. A kernel function K is defined as the inner product of two data points in the new feature space Φ (Equation 8.12) and should satisfy Mercer's conditions [158]:

$$K(r, x') = \sum_{m}^{\infty} \alpha_m \Phi_m(x) \Phi_m(x'), \quad \alpha_m \geq 0,$$

$$\int \int K(x, x') g(x) g(x') dx dx' > 0, \quad g \in L_2 \tag{8.19}$$

As reviewed before [158], the final discriminant function can be represented as

$$f(x) = sgn(\sum_{i=1}^{l} \alpha_i y_i K(x_i, x) + b) \tag{8.20}$$

with $b = -\frac{1}{2} \sum_{i=1}^{l} \alpha_i y_i K(x_i, x_r + x_s)$, where x_r and x_s are support vectors located at the boundary of the maximum margin satisfying

$$\alpha_r, \alpha_s > 0, \quad y_r = -1, \quad y_s = 1.$$

This system can be solved as a constrained quadratic programming problem,

$$\alpha^* = argmin \frac{1}{2} \sum_{i=1}^{l} \sum_{j=1}^{l} \alpha_i \alpha_j y_i y_j K(x_i, x_j) - \sum_{k=1}^{l} \alpha_k, \tag{8.21}$$

with constraints

$$C \geq \alpha_i \geq 0, \qquad i = 1, \ldots, l$$
$$\sum_{j=1}^{l} \alpha_j y_j = 0$$

Different kernel functions are available, such as linear, polynomial, rbf, exponential-rbf, and neural network kernels. The kernel parameters can be selected by cross-validation:

$$K(x_i, x_j) = \langle x_i, x_y \rangle \qquad \text{linear kernel}$$
$$K(x_i, x_j) = (\langle x_i, x_j \rangle + 1)^d \qquad \text{polynomial kernel}$$
$$K(x_i, x_j) = exp\left(-\frac{\|x_i - x_j\|^2}{2\sigma^2}\right) \qquad \text{radial basis kernel}$$
$$K(x_i, x_j) = exp\left(-\frac{\|x_i - x_j\|}{2\sigma^2}\right) \qquad \text{exponential radial basis kernel}$$

To expand the binary SVM to K-class SVM, three methods are often used [231, 318, 411]. The max-win strategy creates K binary SVMs, each distinguishes class i versus non-i. The class that has the highest score will be selected as the predicted target. The pairwise strategy creates a total of $K(K-1)/2$ binary classifiers between every pair of classifiers and each classifier gets one vote. The predicted target will be the class that gets the most votes. The DAG (directed acyclic graph) strategy puts the $K(K-1)/2$ binary classifiers in a rooted binary DAG. At each node, a data point is classified as non-i if the class i loses. The predicted target is the one that is left after tracing down the tree from the root.

AdaBoost

As shown in support vector machine learning, not all training data are equally useful for forming the decision boundary. Some of the training data are easily distinguished and some require a finely tuned boundary. AdaBoost is a classifier that manipulates the weights on the training data during training. It employs a base learner generator that generates a simple classifier such as a neural network or decision tree that is trained with a differently weighted set of training data at each iteration. More weight will be put on the wrongly classified data points and less weight on the correctly classified data points. Therefore, each base classifier is trained toward those hard examples from the previous iteration. The final classifier merges all base learners under some weighting scheme. Following is the AdaBoost training process [349].

Given a binary classification problem with m two-dimensional data points: $(x_1, y_1), \ldots, (x_m, y_m)$, where $x_i \in X, y_i \in Y = \{-1, +1\}$.
Uniform weight for each data point $D_1(i) = \frac{1}{m}$.
For $t = 1, \ldots, T$:

Train the rule generator using distribution D_t.
Generate base rule $h_t : X \to \Re$.
Choose $\alpha_t \in \Re$.
Update:

$$D_{t+1}(i) = \frac{D_t(i)exp(-\alpha_t y_i h_t(x_i))}{Z_t}, \qquad (8.22)$$

where Z_t is the sum of all numerators such that D_{t+1} represents a probability.
Each base classifier tries to minimize the training error ϵ_t, where

$$\epsilon_t = Pr_{i \in D_t}[h_t(x_i) \neq y_i],$$

and the weight α_t associated with each data point can be updated as

$$\alpha_t = \frac{1}{2} \ln(\frac{1 - \epsilon_t}{\epsilon_t}).$$

The final discriminant function is

$$H(x) = sign \left(\sum_{t=1}^{T} \alpha_t h_t(x) \right). \qquad (8.23)$$

Similar to SVM, AdaBoost was designed as a binary classifier and several multiclass variants have been made [132, 350].

Bagging

Bagging, also called bootstrap aggregation, is a classifier that bootstraps an equally weighted random sample from the training data at each iteration [104]. Unlike AdaBoost, which pays special attention to previously hard examples, bagging works by averaging performances of a base classifier on different random samples of the same training data. It has been shown that some classifiers such as neural network and decision trees are easily skewed by small variations in the training data. By averaging out the random variances from repetitive bootstrapping, the base classifier will be more robust and therefore give more stable prediction results. The outputs of the resulting base classifiers from all iterations are finally averaged to give the prediction $H(x)$:

$$H(x) = sign(\sum_{t=1}^{T} h_t(X_t)/T), \qquad (8.24)$$

where X_t is a bootstrap sample from the training data, $h_t(X_t)$ is a binary classifier learned from the sample X_t, and T is the total number of iterations.

Mixtures-of-Experts

A mixtures-of-experts classifier employs a divide-and-conquer strategy to assign individual base classifiers to different partitions of the training data [197, 424]. It models the data generation process as

$$P(Y \mid X) = \sum_Z P(Z \mid X)P(Y \mid X, Z), \tag{8.25}$$

where Y stands for the targets, X represents the input variables, and Z is a hidden variable representing local experts related to each data partition. The generation of the dependent variables can be regarded as two steps: first, individual local experts are assigned to different partitions of the training data with probability $P(Z|X)$; second, the target variable is calculated given the local data and experts as $P(Y|X, Z)$. The first step is modeled using a gating network and the second step can involve various classifiers as local experts. The final output of a mixtures-of-experts classifier can be regarded as combining the outputs from each local expert weighted by the probability of assigning a data partition to that expert.

Majority-voting classifier ensemble

Although theoretically sound, every classifier has some constraints in its performance; more important, each suffers from overfitting given limited training data. A classifier ensemble can alleviate these problems by compensating for the weakness of a classifier with the strengths of other classifiers, assuming that the errors made by individual classifiers are not fully correlated [104]. Majority voting is a simple and common choice when fusing different classifiers. It performs as well as more complex trainable methods such as Bayesian voting and the evaluation set method [226].

Results for feature reduction. To find the best feature reduction method for our problem, the eight feature reduction methods described earlier were compared, starting with the 2D feature set SLF7. We used a support vector machine classifier with Gaussian kernel ($\sigma^2 = 50, c = 20$) along with tenfold cross validation to evaluate different numbers of features chosen by each method [187]. A summary of the results is shown in Table 8.6.

The mother feature set, SLF7, contains 84 features that can achieve an average prediction accuracy of 85.2% on the support vector machine classifier with tenfold cross validation. From Table 8.6, we can see that the four feature selection methods perform generally better than the four feature recombination methods. To statistically compare the performance of feature reduction to that of the original feature set, we conducted a paired t-test

Table 8.6. Summary of results from eight feature reduction methods evaluated by a multiclass support vector machine classifier with radial basis kernel on the 2D HeLa collection. The starting point for feature reduction was set SLF7. The P values for the hypothesis that a given method shows higher accuracy than the original 84 features are shown where relevant. Data from reference [187].

Method	Minimum number of features for over 80% accuracy	Highest accuracy (number of features)	P value of paired t-test against the result from the original 84 features
None	n/a	85.2% (all 84)	
PCA	17	83.4% (41)	
NLPCA	none found	75.3% (64)	
KPCA	17	86.0% (117)	0.38
ICA	22	82.9% (41)	
Information Gain	11	86.6% (72)	0.08
SDA	8	87.4% (39)	0.02
FDR	18	86.2% (26)	0.15
Genetic Algorithm	none found	87.5% (43)	0.04

on the tenfold cross validation results [275] between each feature reduction method and the mother feature set. Only stepwise discriminant analysis and a genetic algorithm achieve statistically significant ($P \leq 0.05$) improvements over the SLF7 feature set under a 95% confidence level, although the genetic algorithm approach is much more computationally demanding. SDA also generates the smallest feature subset that can achieve an average accuracy over 80%. This subset, consisting of only eight features, is defined as SLF12 and has the potential to serve as a multimedia basis set for indexing in an R-tree or a KD-tree enabling image content retrieval from protein image databases. Considering both speed and effectiveness, stepwise discriminant analysis should be regarded as the best feature reduction method among the eight, which achieves significant improvement in prediction accuracy using less than half of the original features. Perhaps by coincidence, SDA was the approach used in our initial work on the 2D HeLa image collection [46]. All the work described below uses SDA as the feature selection method.

Our initial work on classification of the 2D HeLa image collection used a neural network classifier with one hidden layer and 20 hidden nodes [46]. We have used this classifier as a reference point for comparing the value of various features sets as the sets have been developed. Table 8.7 summarizes this comparison. As discussed earlier, SLF2 consists of morphological, edge, hull, and DNA features. SLF4 includes the Zernike moment features and Haralick texture features as well, and the inclusion of these features increases the average accuracy by 5% over SLF2 alone. Selecting a subset from SLF4 by SDA (to form SLF5) further increases the average accuracy by 2%. The addition of the nonobject fluorescence and object skeleton features in SLF7 [289] provides an additional 5% boost in performance once SDA is used.

SLF2, SLF4, and SLF5 all require a parallel DNA image to calculate features that provide protein localization information relative to the cell

Table 8.7. Average performance of a neural network classifier with one hidden layer and 20 hidden nodes on the 2D HeLa dataset with various feature sets. N/A, not available.

Feature sets	Requires DNA image?	Number of features	tenfold cross validation accuracy using a neural network classifier (%)	
			On test set	On training set
SLF2	yes	22	76	89
SLF4	yes	84	81	95
SLF5	yes	37 by SDA from SLF4	83	95
SLF13	yes	31 by SDA from SLF7+DNA	88	N/A
SLF3	no	78	79	94
SLF8	no	32 by SDA from SLF7	86	N/A

nucleus. Because of the value of the cell nucleus as a stable and central reference point, location patterns can be distinguished more easily using these additional features. We can see how much these features contribute to the overall classification performance by comparing SLF3 and SLF4 (which differ only in the presence of the DNA features). These sets differ by 2% in average accuracy. Comparing SLF8 and SLF13 (which also differ only in the DNA features) confirms that the benefit of the DNA features is a 2% increase in average performance.

Results for different classifiers. The classification results presented so far were achieved by using a single neural network classifier with one hidden layer and 20 hidden nodes or with an SVM. To determine whether results could be improved using other classification approaches, we tested the eight different classifiers described [186]. The base learner in AdaBoost, bagging, and mixtures-of-experts was the same, a neural network classifier with one hidden layer [81]. The parameters associated with each classifier were determined by cross validation. After optimizing each classifier, we created a majority-voting classifier involving the best choices of the eight classifiers (the majority-voting classifier performs better than each single classifier in all our experiments).

We focused our efforts on two feature sets, SLF13 and SLF8, because they were the best feature sets with and without DNA features. Table 8.8 shows the optimal majority-voting classifier selected for each feature set with statistical comparison to the previously used neural network classifier. For SLF13, the best classifiers selected from the eight are an rbf-kernel support vector machine, an AdaBoost classifier, and a mixtures-of-experts classifier. The average accuracies were compared to the corresponding value from Table 8.7 by the paired t-test. Significant improvement ($P \leq 0.5$) was observed by upgrading the neural network classifier to a majority-voting classifier under a 95% confidence level. The mean and standard deviation of the pairwise classifier error correlation coefficients were also listed in the table. The small correlation in the classification errors made by the eight classifiers explains the advantage of creating a majority-voting classifier. Similarly, an ensemble comprising an exponential rbf-kernel support vector machine, an AdaBoost classifier, and a bagging classifier performed significantly better than the previous neural network on SLF8.

Table 8.8. Performance of the optimal majority-voting classifiers for feature sets SLF13 and SLF8 on the 2D HeLa dataset. Data from reference [186].

Feature set	Classifier	Pairwise classifier error correlation coefficients	Tenfold cross validation accuracy (%)	P value of paired t-test
SLF13	Rbf-kernel SVM AdaBoost Mixtures-of-experts	$0.1 + 0.06$	90.7	3.0×10^{-3}
SLF8	Exp rbf-kernel SVM AdaBoost Bagging	0.09 ± 0.06	89.4	3.0×10^{-4}

Improved classification using wavelet features. The Gabor and Daubechies wavelet features described earlier are sufficiently different from the previous SLF features that they may extract previously unused information from the fluorescence microscope images. We therefore examined whether they could improve classification accuracy on the 2D HeLa image set. Stepwise discriminant analysis was performed on a combined feature set including SLF7, Gabor wavelet features, and Daubechies 4 wavelet features with and without DNA features. Two new feature sets were defined: SLF15, the best 44 features selected by SDA from the full feature set except DNA features, and SLF16, the best 47 features selected by SDA from the full feature set including DNA features. The incremental evaluations generating the two new feature sets were conducted using the optimal majority-voting classifiers listed in Table 8.8. Finally, we considered again all possible choices of the eight classifiers in majority-voting ensembles for these two new feature sets. The optimal majority-voting classifiers are shown in Table 8.9. The performances of the new majority-voting classifiers were compared to those of the previous majority-voting classifiers in Table 8.8. Statistically significant improvement was observed for SLF15 compared to SLF8, but the improvement from SLF13 to SLF16 was not significant. The benefit of DNA features previously estimated at 2% decreased after using majority-voting classifiers and adding new features. The confusion matrix of the majority-voting classifier for SLF16 is shown in Table 8.10. Both giantin and Gpp130 can be distinguished over 80% of the time, and so can the endosome and lysosome patterns.

Table 8.9. Performance of the optimal majority-voting classifiers for feature sets SLF15 and SLF16 on the 2D HeLa dataset. Data from reference [186].

Feature set	Classifier	Pairwise classifier error correlation coefficients	Tenfold cross validation accuracy (%)	P value of paired t-test
SLF15	Rbf-kernel SVM Exponential Rbf-Kernel SVM Polynomial-kernel SVM	0.1 ± 0.06	91.5	0.02
SLF16	Neural network Linear-kernel SVM Exprbf-kernel SVM Polynomial-kernel SVM AdaBoost	0.1 ± 0.07	92.3	0.08

Table 8.10. Confusion matrix of the optimal majority-voting classifier for SLF16 on the 2D HeLa dataset. Data from reference [186].

True class	Output of the classifier (%)									
	DNA	ER	Gia	Gpp	Lam	Mit	Nuc	Act	TfR	Tub
DNA	**99**	1	0	0	0	0	0	0	0	0
ER	0	**97**	0	0	0	2	0	0	0	1
Gia	0	0	**91**	7	0	0	0	0	2	0
Gpp	0	0	14	**82**	0	0	2	0	1	0
Lam	0	0	1	0	**88**	1	0	0	10	0
Mit	0	3	0	0	0	**92**	0	0	3	3
Nuc	0	0	0	0	0	0	**99**	0	1	0
Act	0	0	0	0	0	0	0	**100**	0	0
TfR	0	1	0	0	12	2	0	1	**81**	2
Tub	1	2	0	0	0	1	0	0	1	**95**

Through this section, we have shown how we optimized our feature sets and our classifiers such that the classification performance on the 2D HeLa image set was improved. We also trained a human classifier on the same data set, obtaining the results shown in Table 8.11 with an average classification accuracy of 83% [290]. This is much lower than the current 92% achieved by using our machine learning approaches. Although the human expert appears to have a little better understanding of the mitochondria and the endosome patterns, his performance when distinguishing giantin and Gpp130 was equivalent to random choice. Thus our methods capture some information that a human expert may not be able to appreciate.

Classification of 11-Class 3D HeLa Images

As mentioned above, 3D protein fluorescence microscope images can provide more information and are more reliable to represent protein subcellular distribution in polarized cells. We therefore extended our features to 3D

Table 8.11. Confusion matrix of a human classifier on the 2D HeLa dataset. Data from reference [290].

True class	Output of the classifier (%)									
	DNA	ER	Gia	Gpp	Lam	Mit	Nuc	Act	TfR	Tub
DNA	**100**	0	0	0	0	0	0	0	0	0
ER	0	**90**	0	0	3	6	0	0	0	0
Gia	0	0	**56**	36	3	3	0	0	0	0
Gpp	0	0	53	**43**	0	0	0	0	3	0
Lam	0	0	6	0	**73**	0	0	0	20	0
Mit	0	3	0	0	0	**96**	0	0	0	0
Nuc	0	0	0	0	0	0	**100**	0	0	0
Act	0	0	0	0	0	0	0	**100**	0	0
TfR	0	13	0	0	3	0	0	0	**83**	0
Tub	0	3	0	0	0	0	0	3	0	**93**

images and trained a neural network classifier to recognize the location patterns [413].

The first feature set we used to classify the 11-class 3D HeLa image set was SLF9, which contains 28 features describing morphological and geometrical information in 3D images. A neural network classifier with one hidden layer and 20 hidden nodes was employed. The average recall across 11 classes after 50 cross-validation trials was 91%, which is as good as the 2D classification result. We then applied stepwise discriminant analysis on SLF9 and the best nine features returned by SDA were defined as SLF10. The same neural network classifier was trained on SLF10 and the average performance is shown in Table 8.12 after 50 cross-validation trials.

Table 8.12. Confusion matrix of a neural network classifier with one hidden layer and 20 hidden nodes on the 3D HeLa dataset using feature set SLF10. Data from (Velliste and Murphy, in preparation).

True class	Output of the classifier (%)										
	Cyt	DNA	ER	Gia	Gpp	Lam	Mit	Nuc	Act	TfR	Tub
Cyt	**100**	0	0	0	0	0	0	0	0	0	0
DNA	0	**99**	0	0	0	0	0	0	0	0	0
ER	0	0	**95**	0	0	0	0	0	0	2	2
Gia	0	0	0	**91**	2	7	0	0	0	0	0
Gpp	0	0	0	7	**92**	1	0	0	0	0	0
Lam	0	0	0	0	3	**94**	0	0	0	2	0
Mit	0	0	0	2	0	1	**95**	0	2	1	0
Nuc	0	0	0	0	0	0	0	**100**	0	0	0
Act	0	0	3	1	0	0	4	0	**90**	2	0
TfR	0	0	2	0	0	4	2	0	2	**89**	1
Tub	0	0	4	0	0	0	0	0	0	3	**93**

These results are the first in which the patterns giantin and Gpp130 can be distinguished at better than 90% accuracy. The discrimination between endosomes and lysosomes was also much higher than the best results from 2D classification. Recognizing the actin pattern was still more challenging for

3D images than for 2D images. The average prediction accuracy across 11 classes was 94%.

Classification of Sets of HeLa Images

Biologists often take a set of images under each experimental condition to increase the reliability of any conclusions. A set of images from the same preparation is often taken for every protein. For computational analysis, we have shown that creating sets of images drawn from staining the same protein can dramatically improve classification accuracy [46]. For this purpose the same neural network classifier was used to classify sets of images randomly chosen from each class in the test set. Each set was classified as the dominant class assigned to individual images in the set. An unknown label was assigned to a set if no dominant class could be found. Table 8.13 shows the average performance for classifying sets of 10 images from the 2D HeLa set with SLF5 features. Most classes can be discriminated more than 97% of the time except for the endosome pattern, which is often confused with the lysosome pattern. The two closely related patterns giantin and Gpp130 can be distinguished more than 98% of the time. Indeed, endosome and lysosome have more location similarity than giantin and Gpp130 from the results shown so far. Most errors were due to failing to find a dominant prediction by plurality rule. The average performance for the sets of 10 images using SLF5 was 98%, much higher than the average 83% achieved with single protein images using the same feature set.

Table 8.13. Confusion matrix of a neural network classifier with one hidden layer and 20 hidden nodes for classifying sets of 10 images from the 2D HeLa dataset using the SLF5 feature set. Data from reference [46].

True	Output of the classifier (%)										
class	DNA	ER	Gia	Gpp	Lam	Mit	Nuc	Act	TfR	Tub	Unk
DNA	100	0	0	0	0	0	0	0	0	0	0
ER	0	100	0	0	0	0	0	0	0	0	0
Gia	0	0	98	0	0	0	0	0	0	0	1
Gpp	0	0	0	99	0	0	0	0	0	0	1
Lam	0	0	0	0	97	0	0	0	1	0	2
Mit	0	0	0	0	0	100	0	0	0	0	0
Nuc	0	0	0	0	0	0	100	0	0	0	0
Act	0	0	0	0	0	0	0	100	0	0	0
TfR	0	0	0	0	6	0	0	0	88	0	6
Tub	0	0	0	0	0	0	0	0	0	100	0

Similar enhancement of accuracy was also observed for the 3D HeLa images (Table 8.14). Using a set size of 9, we achieved nearly perfect classification accuracy of 99.7% with the feature set SLF9.

Table 8.14. Confusion matrix of a neural network classifier with one hidden layer and 20 hidden nodes for classifying sets of 9 images from the 3D HeLa dataset using the feature set SLF9. Data from (Velliste and Murphy, in preparation).

True class	Output of the classifier (%)										
	DNA	ER	Gia	Gpp	Lam	Mit	Nuc	Act	TfR	Tub	Unk
DNA	100	0	0	0	0	0	0	0	0	0	0
ER	0	99	0	0	0	0	0	0	0	1	0
Gia	0	0	100	0	0	0	0	0	0	0	0
Gpp	0	0	0	99	0	0	0	0	0	0	0
Lam	0	0	0	0	100	0	0	0	0	0	0
Mit	0	0	0	0	0	100	0	0	0	0	0
Nuc	0	0	0	0	0	0	100	0	0	0	0
Act	0	0	0	0	0	0	0	100	0	0	0
TfR	0	0	0	0	0	0	0	0	100	0	0
Tub	0	1	0	0	0	0	0	0	0	99	0

8.2.4 Statistical Analysis for Image Sets

The high accuracy achieved in supervised learning of protein subcellular location patterns illustrates that the subcellular location features are good descriptors of protein fluorescence microscope images. This finding lends strong support to applying the subcellular location features in other applications such as hypothesis tests on image sets. Statistical analysis on image sets is often desirable for biologists in interpreting and comparing experimental results quantitatively. Two statistical analyses will be described in this section, objective selection of the most representative microscope image from a set [270] and objective comparison of protein subcellular distributions from two image sets [335].

Objective Selection of Representative Microscope Images

Current fluorescence microscopy techniques allow biologists to routinely take many images in an experiment. However, only a few images can be included in a report, which forces biologists to select representative images to illustrate their experimental results. Prior to the work described here, no objective selection method was available to authors, and readers of an article would typically have little information about the criteria that were used by the authors to select published images.

To address this situation, we have described a method in which each protein fluorescence microscope image is represented by SLF features and distance metrics are defined on the feature space to quantify image similarity [270]. The most representative image is the one that is the closest to the centroid of the image set in the feature space (the mean feature vector of an image set), and all other images are ranked by distance from this centroid. We tested variations on this approach using mixed sets of protein patterns and observed that the best results were obtained using outlier rejection methods so that the centroid can be reliably estimated. Figure 8.8 shows example images for the Golgi protein giantin chosen by some of the typicality methods. The giantin images with scattered structure were ranked as least typical while those with compact structure were ranked as most typical. This ranking is consistent with biological knowledge about the Golgi complex, which decomposes during mitosis or under abnormal cell conditions. (The cell in panel G appears to be compact but on close inspection has a single dim vesicle, which may indicate the onset of Golgi breakdown and which makes the pattern atypical.)

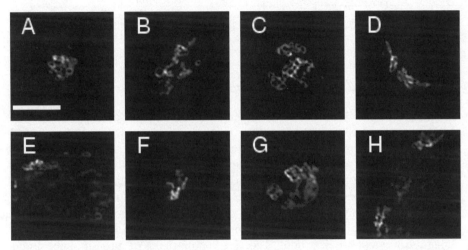

Fig. 8.8. Application of typicality ranking to a diverse image set. Giantin images ranking high in typicality (A–D) and ranking low in typicality (E–H) were chosen by the methods described in the text. From reference [270].

Objective selection of representative data points has general interest in data mining. In our problem, we are aiming at the best microscope image to represent a set acquired from experiments. In information retrieval, a summary that represents an article can be generated by selecting several sentences from the article objectively. Both distance metric and features are important for a successful selection. The results showed that Mahalanobis distance is a better distance metric than Euclidean distance. The ability to correctly select the most typical images from contaminated image sets assures the reliability of image typicality ranking in uncontaminated sets.

Objective Comparison of Protein Subcellular Distributions

Proteins can change their subcellular location patterns under different environmental conditions. Biologists are often interested in such changes caused by pharmacological treatments or hormones. Traditionally, visual examination was employed to compare the fluorescence microscope image sets from two or more different conditions. This method was not very sensitive and was not suitable for objective and quantitative analysis of protein subcellular location changes. With the development of protein subcellular location features, objective and quantitative analysis of protein subcellular distributions has become possible. Instead of comparing two image sets visually, a subcellular location feature matrix can be calculated for each image set and statistical techniques can be applied to compare the two feature matrices. We used two statistical hypothesis tests for this task, namely univariate t-test and Hotelling T^2-test [229]. The Hotelling T^2-test is a multivariate counterpart of the univariate t-test; it yields a statistic following an F distribution with two degrees of freedom: the total number of features and the total number of images in the two sets minus the total number of features. The critical F value given a confidence level can be compared to the F value from Hotelling T^2-test of two image sets.

To characterize this approach, we used the 2D HeLa image collection. Each image was described by the feature set SLF6 (a combination of Zernike moment features and SLF1). We first compared all pairs of classes in the 2D HeLa set and the results are shown in Table 8.15. All class pairs were regarded as distinguishable since their F values were larger than the critical value. The distribution of the F values corresponded well to the classification results. Giantin and Gpp130 as well as endosome and lysosome patterns were the least distinguishable in both classification and image sets comparison. The well-classified DNA pattern was also the easiest pattern to be distinguished from all other image sets with an average F value of 180 across nine comparisons. To examine whether the Hotelling T^2-test as we applied it was not only able to distinguish different patterns but also able to correctly recognize indistinguishable patterns, we chose the two largest classes, tfr and phal, and randomly sampled two equal subsets from each class 1000 times. The Hotelling T^2-test was conducted to compare the two sets drawn from the same class and the results are summarized in Table 8.16. The average F value for each class is less than the critical F value and less than 5% of the total of 1000 comparisons failed (as expected for a 95% confidence interval). Therefore, the method we employed to compare two image sets is able to identify two same protein subcellular location distributions.

One question that might be asked is whether the difference identified by the statistical test in closely related patterns is due to artifactual protocol differences rather than significant subcellular distribution change. To address this question, we conducted the same test on two image sets prepared under different experimental conditions. One image set was acquired by tagging giantin with an antibody collected from rabbit antiserum and the other by mouse antigiantin monoclonal antibody. The F value with 95% confidence level from these two sets was 1.04 compared to the critical value 2.22.

Table 8.15. Hotelling T^2-test comparing all class pairs in the 2D HeLa dataset using SLF6. The critical F values with 95% confidence level range from 1.42 to 1.45 depending on the number of images in each pair. Note that all pairs of classes are considered to be different at that confidence level. Data from reference [335].

Class	No. of images	DNA	ER	Gia	Gpp	Lam	Mit	Nuc	Act	TfR
DNA	87									
ER	86	83.2								
Gia	87	206.1	34.7							
Gpp	85	227.4	44.5	2.4						
Lam	84	112.2	13.8	10.7	11.4					
Mit	73	152.4	8.9	39.2	44.5	15.9				
Nuc	73	79.8	39.8	17.2	15.1	14.5	46.6			
Act	98	527.2	63.5	325.3	354.0	109.8	16.0	266.4		
TfR	91	102.8	7.4	14.8	15.6	2.8	9.2	20.5	29.1	
Tub	91	138.3	10.8	63.0	72.2	18.4	7.0	49.4	22.4	5.5

Table 8.16. Hotelling T^2-test comparing 1000 image sets randomly selected from each of the two classes using SLF6. Data from reference [335].

	tfr	phal
Average F	1.05	1.05
Critical F(0.95)	1.63	1.61
Number of failing sets out of 1000	47	45

Therefore, potential minor differences introduced by experimental protocols were appropriately ignored by the method.

Various features in SLF6 might contribute differently to distinguish two distributions. We therefore conducted a univariate t-test on each feature and computed the confidence level of each feature change. The results on giantin and Gpp130 image sets are shown in Table 8.17. Features that describe the shape of the pattern and object characteristics account for the major distinction between giantin and Gpp130.

The objective comparison of protein subcellular distributions by subcellular location features and statistical tests enables automatic and reproducible analysis. The sensitivity and reliability of this method have been proved by experiments comparing both different and identical protein subcellular distributions. The method can be used to study different effects of hormones or pharmacological agents on the subcellular location of certain target proteins. It also has potential in high-throughput drug screening where the relationship between various candidate chemicals and target genes can be studied quantitatively in terms of subcellular distribution.

8.2.5 Unsupervised Clustering for Location Proteomics

Data clustering is an important tool for studying unlabeled data. It often involves segmenting the data into subgroups by introducing some

Table 8.17. Most distinguishable features evaluated by a univariate t-test on each feature in SLF6 from comparing two image sets: giantin and Gpp130. Data from reference [335].

Feature	Confidence level at which feature differs
Eccentricity of the ellipse equivalent to the protein image convex hull	99.99999
Convex hull roundness	99.9999
Measure edge direction homogeneity 1	99.9873
Average object size	99.9873
Average object distance to the center of fluorescence	99.9873
Ratio of largest to smallest object to image center of fluorescence distance	99.9873

distance/similarity measurement so that the examples in the same subgroup have more similarity than those in other subgroups. The most trivial segmentation is to isolate each data point as its own cluster, which provides the best within-group similarity. To avoid trivial segmentation, constraints are often introduced in data clustering algorithms such as the minimum size of a cluster and the maximum number of clusters. Given a distance metric, data clustering can also be regarded as a graph separation problem where each node represents a data point and each edge represents the distance between two nodes. Various graph partitioning criteria have been proposed such as min-cut [435], average-cut [346] and normalized-cut [366].

The organization of clusters can be either flat or hierarchical. Nonhierarchical clustering algorithms such as K-means and Gaussian mixture models partition data into separate subgroups without any hierarchical structure. The number of total clusters in these algorithms is either fixed by the user or determined by some statistical criterion. On the contrary, hierarchical clustering algorithms require only a metric definition. Agglomerative algorithms start from all data points, merge similar ones from each immediate lower level, and finally reach a single cluster root. Divisive algorithms, on the other hand, go in the opposite direction. The advantage of a hierarchical structure is that different number of clusters can be obtained at each level so that we can choose the optimal number of clusters intuitively. The subcellular location features have been proved to be able to measure the similarity of protein subcellular location patterns. They define a metric space for clustering protein fluorescence microscope images according to their location similarity. In this section, we will describe how these features are used to build a subcellular location tree (SLT) that is a major goal of location proteomics.

Clustering the 10-Class 2D HeLa Images

Biologists have been studying tree structures of protein families and the evolution of organisms for a long time. Trees provide a clear view of how every element is related to each other. Similar to the sequence similarity metric for a phylogenetic tree, we can employ the location similarity metric described by SLF features to create a subcellular location tree for different proteins. As a first attempt, we applied an average linkage agglomerative hierarchical clustering algorithm to create a dendrogram (subcellular location tree) for the 10 protein subcellular location patterns in the 2D HeLa image set [289]. The feature set we used was SLF8, containing 32 features. For each class of images, we calculated its mean feature vector and the feature covariance matrix. The distance between each class pair was the Mahalanobis distance between the two mean feature vectors. A dendrogram was then created based on the Mahalanobis distances by an agglomerative clustering method (Figure 8.9). As expected, both giantin and Gpp130 were grouped first followed by the lysosome and endosome patterns. The grouping of tubulin and the lysosome and endosome patterns also agrees with biological knowledge in that both lysosomes and endosomes are thought to be involved in membrane trafficking along microtubules.

Clustering the 3D 3T3 Image Set

Instead of clustering only 10 protein subcellular location patterns, we can imagine applying the algorithm used earlier to cluster all proteins expressed in a given cell type. As mentioned before, the 3D 3T3 image set was created by the CD tagging project [200, 201, 396], whose goal is to tag all expressed proteins in this cell type. Since the project is ongoing, we applied our clustering method on an early version of the CD-tagging protein database containing 46 different proteins [73].

The number of 3D images in each of the 46 clones ranges from 16 to 33, which makes the effect of a single outlier noticeable. To obtain robust estimation of the mean feature vector for each class, we first conducted outlier removal from the 3D 3T3 image set. Either a Q-test (when a clone has fewer than 10 cells) or a univariate t-test (more than 10 cells per clone) was carried out on each feature. A cell was regarded as an outlier if any one of its features failed the test. After outlier removal, we ended up with 660 full cell images for 46 clones, each of which has 9 to 22 cells.

We first clustered the 46 clones by using the 14 SLF9 features that do not require a DNA label. All 14 features were z-scored across all clones so that they had mean zero and variance one. Euclidean distances computed from pairs of class mean feature vectors were employed as the distance metric in an agglomerative clustering method to create the dendrogram shown in Figure 8.10. There are two nuclear protein clusters in the tree: Hmga1-2,

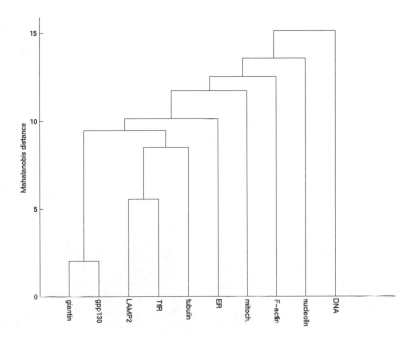

Fig. 8.9. Subcellular location tree created by an average linkage agglomerative hierarchical clustering algorithm for the 10 protein subcellular location patterns from the 2D HeLa dataset. From reference [289].

Hmga1-1, Unknown-9, Hmgn2-1, and Unknown-8; Ewsh, Unknown-11, and SimilarToSiahbp1. Two representative images were selected from these two clusters (Figure 8.11). Apparently, one cluster is exclusively localized in the nucleus while the other has some cytoplasmic distribution outside the nucleus, which made these two nuclear protein clusters distinguishable.

To select the optimal number of clusters from Figure 8.10, we applied a neural network classifier with one hidden layer and 20 hidden nodes to classify the 46 clones by using the 14 SLF9 features. The average recall after 20 cross validations was 40%, which indicated that many clones were hardly distinguishable. To choose a cutting threshold for the tree, we examined the confusion matrix of the classifier and found that those clones separated below 2.8 z-scored Euclidean distance can hardly be distinguished by the classifier. By choosing a cutting threshold of 2.8, the tree shown in Figure 8.10 can be reduced to 12 clusters, which was consistent with the result obtained by using the K-means algorithm and Akaike information criterion on the same data. By grouping images from 46 clones to the new 12 clusters, the same neural network gave an average performance of 71% across 12 classes.

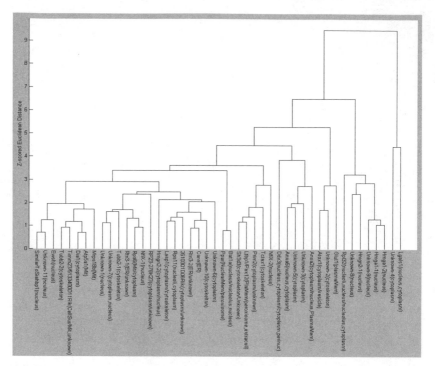

Fig. 8.10. Subcellular location tree created for 46 clones from the 3D 3T3 collection by using 14 of the SLF9 features. The protein name (if known) is shown for each clone, followed by the presumed location pattern from the relevant literature. Independently derived clones in which the same protein was tagged are shown with a hyphen followed by a number (e.g., Hmga1-2 is clone 2 tagged in Hmga1). From reference [73].

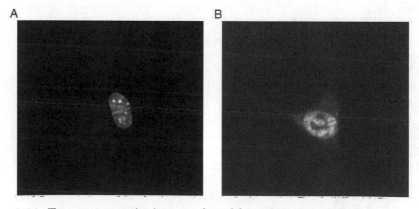

Fig. 8.11. Two representative images selected from the two nuclear protein clusters shown in Figure 8.10. (A) Hmga1-1. (B) Unknown-11. From reference [73].

The second feature set we used for clustering the 46 clones was the 42-dimensional SLF11, which contains 14 SLF9 features that do not require a DNA label, 2 edge features, and 26 3D Haralick texture features. Just as for supervised learning, data clustering can also benefit from feature selection. Therefore, we employed stepwise discriminant analysis coupled with the same neural network classifier used earlier to select the features from SLF11 that can distinguish the 46 classes as well as possible. Figure 8.12 shows the average classification results of sequential inclusion of features ranked by SDA. The first 14 features ranked by SDA can give 70% average accuracy, while a comparable 68% can be achieved by using the first 10 features.

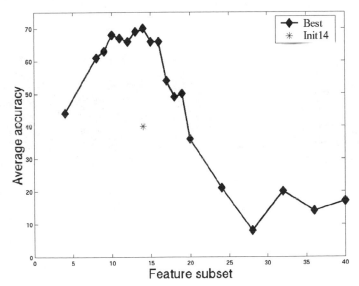

Fig. 8.12. Determination of minimum number of features for adequate discrimination of the 3D 3T3 clones. The average performance of a neural network classifier after 20 cross validation trials is shown as a function of the number of features used from those selected by stepwise discriminant analysis (SDA). From reference [73].

By using the top 10 features selected from SLF11 by SDA, we ran the same clustering algorithm on the 46 3T3 clones. Figure 8.13 shows a new tree generated from clustering the same data by the new features. The previous two nucleus protein clusters still remained mostly the same. The new clone added in the second cluster, Unknown-7, has a hybrid location pattern in both nucleus and cytoplasm, which agrees with our previous observation of the distinction between the two clusters.

The tree created by clustering 3T3 clones from the CD tagging project provides a systematic representation of observed subcellular location

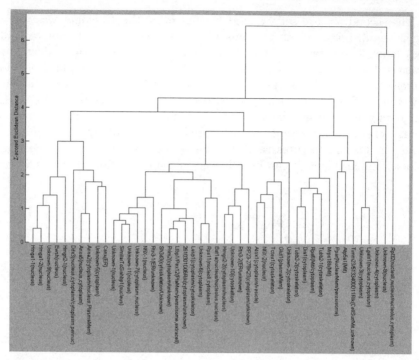

Fig. 8.13. Subcellular location tree created for 46 clones from the 3D 3T3 set by using the top 10 features selected from SLF11 by SDA. The results shown are for the same clones as in Figure 8.10. From reference [73].

patterns. By examining the tree, the characteristics of an unknown protein may be deduced from nearby proteins with known functions and similar location pattern. The sensitivity of the subcellular location features assures the distinction and separation of patterns in the tree with subtle location differences.

8.3 Conclusion

In this chapter, we have described the intensive application of machine learning methods to a novel problem in biology. The successful application of supervised learning, statistical analysis, and unsupervised clustering all depended on informative features that were able to capture the essence of protein subcellular location patterns in fluorescence microscope images. Our automatic image interpretation system coupled with high-throughput random-tagging and imaging techniques provide a promising and feasible capability for decoding the subcellular location patterns of all proteins in a given cell type, an approach we have termed "location proteomics." The systematic approach we have described is also adaptable to other data mining areas in bioinformatics, in which a successful system should be able to address all the aspects of a learning problem, such as feature design and extraction, feature selection, classifier choice, statistical analysis, and unsupervised clustering.

Acknowledgments

The original research described in this chapter was supported in part by research grant RPG-95-099-03-MGO from the American Cancer Society, by NSF grants BIR-9217091, MCB-8920118, and BIR-9256343, by NIH grants R01 GM068845 and R33 CA83219, and by a research grant from the Commonwealth of Pennsylvania Tobacco Settlement Fund. K.H. was supported by a Graduate Fellowship from the Merck Computational Biology and Chemistry Program at Carnegie Mellon University established by the Merck Company Foundation.

Chapter 9
Mining Chemical Compounds

Mukund Deshpande, Michihiro Kuramochi, and
George Karypis

Summary

In this chapter we study the problem of classifying chemical compound
datasets. We present a substructure-based classification algorithm that
decouples the substructure discovery process from the classification
model construction and uses frequent subgraph discovery algorithms
to find all topological and geometric substructures present in the
dataset. The advantage of this approach is that during classification
model construction, all relevant substructures are available allowing
the classifier to intelligently select the most discriminating ones. The
computational scalability is ensured by the use of highly efficient
frequent subgraph discovery algorithms coupled with aggressive feature
selection. Experimental evaluation on eight different classification
problems shows that our approach is computationally scalable and on
the average outperforms existing schemes by 10% to 35%.

9.1 Introduction

Discovering new drugs is an expensive and challenging process. Any new
drug should not only produce the desired response to the disease but should
do so with minimal side effects and be superior to the existing drugs on
the market. One of the key steps in the drug design process is to identify the
chemical compounds (widely referred to as *"hit"* compounds) that display the
desired and reproducible behavior against the disease [247] in a biological
experiment. The standard technique for discovering such compounds is to
evaluate them with a biological experiment, known as an assay. The 1990s
saw the widespread adoption of high-throughput screening (HTS), which

uses highly automated techniques to conduct the biological assays and can be used to screen a large number of compounds. Though in principle HTS techniques can be used to test each compound against every biological assay, it is never practically feasible for the following reasons. First, the number of chemical compounds that have been synthesized or can be synthesized using combinatorial chemistry techniques is extremely large. Evaluating this large set of compounds using HTS can be prohibitively expensive. Second, not all biological assays can be converted to high-throughput format. Third, in most cases it is hard to find all the desirable properties in a single compound, and chemists are interested in not just identifying the hits but studying what part of the chemical compound leads to desirable behavior so that new compounds can be rationally synthesized.

The goal of this chapter is to develop computational techniques based on classification that can be used to identify the hit compounds. These computational techniques can be used to replace or supplement the biological assay techniques. One of the key challenges in developing classification techniques for chemical compounds stems from the fact that the properties of the compounds are strongly related to their chemical structure. However, traditional machine learning techniques are suited to handling datasets represented by multidimensional vectors or sequences and cannot handle the structural nature of the chemical structures.

In recent years two classes of techniques have been developed for solving the chemical compound classification problem. The first class builds a classification model using a set of physicochemical properties derived from the compounds structure, called quantitative structure-activity relationships (QSAR) [14, 167, 168], whereas the second class operates directly on the structure of the chemical compound and in the attempt to automatically identify a small number of chemical substructures that can be used to discriminate between the different classes [41, 99, 193, 236, 436]. A number of comparative studies [222, 384] have shown that techniques based on the automatic discovery of chemical substructures are superior to those based on QSAR properties and require limited user intervention and domain knowledge. However, despite their success, a key limitation of these techniques is that they rely on heuristic search methods to discover these substructures. Even though such approaches reduce the inherently high computational complexity associated with these schemes, they may lead to suboptimal classifiers in cases in which the heuristic search failed to uncover substructures that are critical for the classification task.

In this chapter we present a substructure-based classifier that overcomes the limitations associated with existing algorithms. One of the key ideas of this approach is to decouple the substructure discovery process from the classification model construction step and use frequent subgraph discovery algorithms to find all chemical substructures that occur a sufficiently large number of times. Once the complete set of these substructures has been identified, the algorithm then proceeds to build a classification model based on them. The advantage of such an approach is that during classification model construction, all relevant substructures are available, allowing the classifier to intelligently select the most discriminating ones. To ensure that such an approach is computationally scalable, we use recently developed [234, 236], highly efficient frequent subgraph discovery algorithms coupled with aggressive feature selection to reduce the amount of time required to build as well as to apply the classification model. In addition, we present a substructure discovery algorithm that finds a set of substructures whose geometry is conserved, further improving the classification performance of the algorithm.

We experimentally evaluated the performance of these algorithms on eight different problems derived from three publicly available datasets and compared their performance against that of traditional QSAR-based classifiers and existing substructure classifiers based on SUBDUE [84] and SubdueCL [149]. Our results show that these algorithms, on the average, outperform QSAR-based schemes by 35% and SUBDUE-based schemes by 10%.

The rest of the chapter is organized as follows. Section 9.2 provides some background information related to chemical compounds, their activity, and their representation. Section 9.3 provides a survey of the related research in this area. Section 9.4 provides the details of the chemical compound classification approach. Section 9.5 experimentally evaluates its performance and compares it against other approaches. Finally, section 9.6 outlines directions of future research and provides some concluding remarks.

9.2 Background

A chemical compound consists of different atoms held together via bonds adopting a well-defined geometric configuration. Figure 9.1a represents the chemical compound flucytosine from the DTP AIDS repository [107]. It consists of a central aromatic ring and other elements like N, O, and F. The representation shown in the figure is a typical graphical representation that most chemists work with.

There are many different ways to represent chemical compounds. The simplest representation is the molecular formula that lists the various atoms making up the compound; the molecular formula for flucytosine is $C4H4FN3O$. However, this representation is woefully inadequate for capturing the structure of the chemical compound. It was recognized early on that it was possible for two chemical compounds to have an identical molecular formula but completely different chemical properties [139]. A more sophisticated representation can be achieved using the SMILES [425] representation; it not only represents the atoms but also represents the bonds between different atoms. The SMILES representation for flucytosine

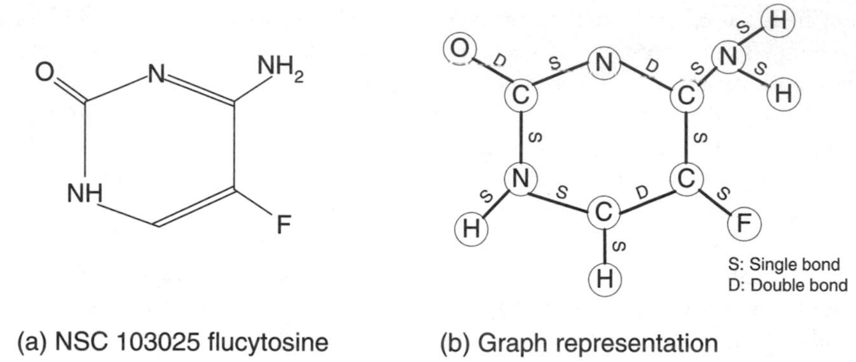

(a) NSC 103025 flucytosine   (b) Graph representation

Fig. 9.1. Chemical and graphical representation of flucytosine.

is `Nc1nc(O)ncc1F`. Though SMILES representation is compact, it is not guaranteed to be unique; furthermore, the representation is quite restrictive to work with [230].

The activity of a compound largely depends on its chemical structure and the arrangement of different atoms in 3D space. As a result, effective classification algorithms must be able to directly take into account the structural nature of these datasets. In this chapter we represent each compound as undirected graphs. The vertices of these graphs correspond to the various atoms, and the edges correspond to the bonds between the atoms. Each of the vertices and edges has a label associated with it. The labels on the vertices correspond to the type of atoms and the labels on the edges correspond to the type of bonds. As an example, Figure 9.1b shows the representation of flucytosine as graph model. We will refer to this representation as the *topological graph* representation of a chemical compound. Note that such representations are quite commonly used by many chemical modeling software applications and are referred as the *connection table* for the chemical compound [247].

In addition, since chemical compounds have a physical three-dimensional structure, each vertex of the graph has a 3D coordinate indicating the position of the corresponding atom in 3D space. However, there are two key issues that need to be considered when working with the compound's 3D structure. First, the number of experimentally determined molecular geometries is limited (about 270,000 X-ray structures in the Cambridge Crystallographic Database compared to 15 million known compounds). As a result, the 3D geometry of a compound needs to be computationally determined, which may introduce a certain amount of error. To address this problem, we use the Corina [138] software package to compute the 3D coordinates for all the chemical compounds in our datasets. Corina is a rule- and data-based system that has been experimentally shown to predict the 3D structure of compounds with high accuracy. Second, each compound can have multiple low-energy conformations (i.e., multiple 3D structures) that need to be taken into account to achieve the highest possible classification performance. However, due to time constraints, in this study we do not take into account these multiple conformations but instead use the single low-energy conformation that is returned by Corina's default settings. However, as discussed in section 9.4.1, the presented approach for extracting geometric substructures can be easily extended to cases in which multiple conformations are considered as well. Nevertheless, despite this simplification, as our experiments in section 9.5 will show, incorporating 3D structure information leads to measurable improvements in the overall classification performance. We will refer to this representation as the *geometric graph* representation of a chemical compound.

The meaning of the various classes in the input dataset is application dependent. In some applications, the classes will capture the extent to which a particular compound is toxic, whereas in other applications they may capture the extent to which a compound can inhibit (or enhance) a particular factor and/or active site. In most applications, each of the compounds is assigned to only one of two classes, which are commonly referred to as the *positive* and *negative* classes. The compounds of the positive class exhibit the property in question, whereas the compounds of the negative class do not. Throughout this chapter we will be restricting ourselves to only two classes, though all the techniques described here can be easily extended to multiclass as well as multilabel classification problems.

Another important aspect of modeling chemical compounds is the naming of single and double bonds inside aromatic rings. Typically in an aromatic ring of a chemical compound, though the number of single and double bonds is fixed, the exact position of double and single bonds is not fixed, because of the phenomenon of resonance [139]. It is worth noting that the exact position of double and single bond in an aromatic ring does not affect the chemical properties of a chemical compound. To capture this uncertainty in the position of single and double bonds, we represent all the bonds making up the aromatic ring with a new bond type called the *aromatic bond*. Another aspect of the chemical compounds is that the number of hydrogen bonds connected to a particular carbon atom can usually be inferred from the bonds connecting the carbon atom [139]. Therefore, in our representation we do not represent the hydrogen atoms that are connected to the carbon atoms. Such hydrogen atoms are referred as nonpolar hydrogen atoms. Note that these transformations are widely used by many chemistry modeling tools and are usually referred to as *structure normalization* [247].

9.3 Related Research

In the early 1960s, the pioneering work of Hansch et al. [167, 168] demonstrated that the biological activity of a chemical compound is a function of its physicochemical properties. These physicochemical properties are usually derived from the compound's structure and are called quantitative structure-activity relationships (QSAR). Examples of physicochemical properties include the molecular weight, total energy, dipole moment, solvent accessible area, and so on. Over the years a number of different QSAR properties has been developed and they are used extensively to model and analyze chemical compounds within the pharmaceutical industry.[1] The amount of time required to compute QSAR properties varies from property to property. Some of them can be computed very fast (e.g., molecular weight), while others require time-consuming numerical simulations (e.g., dipole moment, total energy) that can be performed only for small datasets.

In QSAR-based classification methods, each chemical compound is transformed into a vector of numerical values corresponding to the various QSAR properties. After this transformation, any traditional classifier capable of handling numerical features can be used for the classification task. Early research on QSAR-based classification methods focused primarily on regression-based techniques [131, 167]; however, more sophisticated classifiers have also been used. For example, Andrea and Kalayeh [15] show that neural networks can achieve better accuracies over regression-based techniques, whereas An and Wang [14] report that decision tree classifiers applied on QSAR features outperform those based on neural networks and logistic regression.

The key challenge in using QSAR-based approaches stems from the fact that the classification performance relies, to a large extent, on the a priori identification of the relevant QSAR properties that capture the structure-activity relationships for the particular classification problem. Identifying this relevant set of QSAR properties requires considerable domain expertise and extensive experimentation. To overcome this problem, different techniques have been developed that operate directly on the structure of the chemical compound and try to automatically identify a small number of chemical substructures that can be used to discriminate between the different classes.

One of the earlier approaches that follows this paradigm is based on inductive logic programming (ILP) [283]. In this approach the chemical compound is expressed using first-order logic. Each atom is represented as a predicate consisting of atomID and the element, and a bond is represented as a predicate consisting of two atomIDs. Using this representation, an ILP system discovers rules (i.e., conjunction of predicates) that are good for discriminating the different classes. Since these rules consist of predicates describing atoms and bonds, they essentially correspond to substructures that are present in the chemical compounds. The pioneering work in this field was done by King et al. in the early 1990s [221, 222]. They applied an ILP system, Golem [284], to study the behavior of 44 trimethoprin

---

[1]For example, GAUSSIAN, a widely used software tool for analyzing and predicting chemical structures, contains over 50 QSAR properties.

analogues and their observed inhibition of *Escherichia coli* dihydrofolate reductase. They reported an improvement in classification accuracy over the traditional QSAR-based models. Srinivasan et al. [384] present a detailed comparison of the features generated by ILP with the traditional QSAR features used for classifying chemical compounds. They show that for some applications features discovered by ILP approaches lead to a significant lift in the performance. Besides improved classification performance, an additional advantage of these structure-based approaches is that the discovered rules (i.e., substructures) can be easily understood by experts and could be used to check the correctness of the model and to provide insights in the chemical behavior of the compounds.

Though ILP-based approaches are quite powerful, the high computational complexity of the underlying rule-induction system limits the size of the dataset to which they can be applied. Furthermore, they tend to produce rules consisting of relatively small substructures (usually three to four atoms [95, 223]), limiting the size of the structural constraints that they impose and hence affecting the classification performance. Another drawback of these approaches is that in order to reduce their computational complexity, they employ various heuristics to prune the explored search space [282], potentially missing substructures that are important for the classification task. One exception is the WARMR system [95, 223] that is specifically developed for chemical compounds and discovers all possible substructures above a certain frequency threshold. However, WARMR's computational complexity is very high and can only be used to discover substructures that occur with relatively high frequency.

One of the fundamental reasons limiting the scalability of ILP-based approaches is the first-order logic-based representation that they use. This representation is much more powerful than is needed to model chemical compounds and discover substructures. For this reason a number of researchers have explored the much simpler graph-based representation of the chemical compound's topology and transformed the problem of finding chemical substructures to that of finding subgraphs in this graph-based representation [41, 193, 436]. Probably the most well-known approach is the SUBDUE system [84, 180]. SUBDUE finds patterns that can effectively compress the original input data based on the minimum description length (MDL) principle by replacing those patterns with a single vertex. To narrow the search space and improve its computational efficiency, SUBDUE uses a heuristic beam search approach, which quite often results in failing to find subgraphs that are frequent. The SUBDUE system was also later extended to classify graphs and was referred to as SubdueCL [149]. In SubdueCL, instead of using minimum description length as a heuristic, a measure similar to confidence of a subgraph is used as a heuristic.

Finally, another heuristics-based scheme targeted for chemical compounds is MOLFEA [230]. In this scheme each chemical compound is represented as a SMILES string and is thought of as sequence of SMILES objects. This representation simplifies the problem to discovering frequently occurring subsequences.

9.4 Classification Based on Frequent Subgraphs

The previous research on classifying chemical compounds (discussed in section 9.3) has shown that techniques based on the automatic discovery of chemical substructures are superior to those based on QSAR properties and require limited user intervention and domain knowledge. However, despite their success, a key limitation of both the ILP-based and the subgraph-based techniques is that they rely on heuristic search methods to discover the substructures to be used for classification. As discussed in section 9.3, even though such approaches reduce the inherently high computational complexity associated with the schemes, they may lead to suboptimal classifiers in cases in which the heuristic search fails to uncover substructures that are critical for the classification task.

To overcome this problem, we developed a classification algorithm for chemical compounds that uses the graph-based representation and limits the number of substructures that are pruned a priori. The key idea of our approach is to decouple the substructure discovery process from the classification model construction step and use frequent subgraph discovery algorithms to find all chemical substructures that occur a sufficiently large number of times. Once the complete set of substructures has been identified, our algorithm then proceeds to build a classification model based on them. To a large extent, this approach is similar in spirit to the recently developed frequent-itemset-based classification algorithms [100, 251, 255] that have been shown to outperform traditional classifiers that rely on heuristic search methods to discover the classification rules.

The overall outline of our classification methodology is shown in Figure 9.2. It consists of three distinct steps: feature generation, feature selection, and classification model construction. During the feature generation step, the chemical compounds are mined to discover the frequently occurring substructures that correspond to either topological or geometric subgraphs. These substructures are then used as the features by which the compounds are represented in the subsequent steps. During the second step, a small set of features is selected so that the selected features can correctly discriminate between the different classes present in the dataset. Finally, in the last step, each chemical compound is represented using this set of features, and a classification model is constructed. The rest of this section describes these three steps in detail.

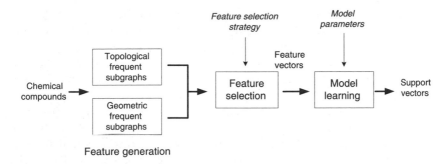

Feature generation

Fig. 9.2. Frequent subgraph-based classification framework.

9.4.1 Feature Generation

Our classification algorithm finds substructures in a chemical compound database using two different methods. The first method uses the topological graph representation of each compound whereas the second method is based on the corresponding geometric graph representation (discussed in section 9.2). In both these methods, our algorithm uses the topological or geometric connected subgraphs that occur in at least $\sigma\%$ of the compounds to define the substructures.

There are two important restrictions on the type of the substructures that are discovered by our approach. The first has to do with the fact that we are interested only in substructures that are connected, and it is motivated by the fact that connectivity is a natural property of such patterns. The second has to do with the fact that we are interested only in frequent substructures (as determined by the value of σ), as this ensures that we do not discover spurious substructures that will in general not be statistically significant. Furthermore, this minimum support constraint also helps in making the problem of frequent subgraph discovery computationally tractable.

Frequent topological subgraphs. Developing frequent subgraph discovery algorithms is particularly challenging and computationally intensive as graph and/or subgraph isomorphisms play a key role throughout the computations. Nevertheless, in recent years, four different algorithms have been developed capable of finding all frequently occurring subgraphs with reasonable computational efficiency. These are the AGM algorithm developed by Inokuchi et al. [193], the FSG algorithm developed by members of our group [234], the chemical substructure discovery algorithm developed by Borgelt and Berthold [41], and the gSpan algorithm developed by Yan and Han [436]. The enabling factors to the computational efficiency of these schemes have been (1) the development of efficient candidate subgraph generation schemes that reduce the number of times the same candidate subgraph is generated, (2) the use of efficient canonical labeling schemes to represent the various subgraphs, and (3) the use of various techniques developed by the data mining community to reduce the number of times subgraph isomorphism computations need to be performed.

In our classification algorithm we find the frequently occurring subgraphs by using the FSG algorithm. FSG takes as input a database D of graphs and a minimum support σ and finds all connected subgraphs that occur in at least $\sigma\%$ of the graphs. FSG, initially presented in [234], with subsequent improvements presented in [236], uses a breadth-first approach to discover the lattice of frequent subgraphs. It starts by enumerating small frequent graphs consisting of one and two edges and then proceeds to find larger subgraphs by joining previously discovered smaller frequent subgraphs. The size of these subgraphs is increased by adding one edge at a time. The lattice of frequent patterns is used to prune the set of candidate patterns, and it only explicitly computes the frequency of the patterns that survive this downward closure pruning. Despite the inherent complexity of the problem, FSG employs a number of sophisticated techniques to achieve high computational performance. It uses a canonical labeling algorithm that fully makes use of edge and vertex labels for fast processing and various vertex invariants to reduce the complexity of determining the canonical label of a graph. These canonical labels are then used to establish the identity and total order of the frequent and candidate subgraphs, a critical step of redundant candidate elimination and downward closure testing. It uses a sophisticated scheme for candidate generation [236] that minimizes the number of times each candidate subgraph is generated and also dramatically reduces the generation of subgraphs that fail the downward closure test. Finally, for determining the actual frequency of each subgraph, FSG reduces the number of subgraph isomorphism operations by using TID lists [109, 365, 445, 446] to keep track of the set of graphs that supported the frequent patterns discovered at the previous level of the lattice. For every candidate, FSG takes the intersection of TID lists of its parents and performs the subgraph isomorphism only on the graphs contained in the resulting TID list. As the experiments presented in section 9.5 show, FSG is able to scale to large datasets and low support values.

Frequent geometric subgraphs. Topological substructures capture the connectivity of atoms in the chemical compound, but they ignore the 3D shape (3D arrangement of atoms) of the substructures. For certain classification problems the 3D shape of the substructure might be essential for determining the chemical activity of a compound. For instance, the geometric configuration of atoms in a substructure is crucial for its ability to bind to a particular target [247]. For this reason we developed an algorithm that finds all frequent substructures whose topology as well as geometry is conserved.

There are two important aspects specific to the geometric subgraphs that need to be considered. First, since the coordinates of the vertices depend on a particular reference coordinate axis, we would like the discovered geometric subgraphs to be independent of the coordinate axes; i.e., we are interested in geometric subgraphs whose occurrences are translation and rotation invariant. This dramatically increases the overall complexity of the geometric subgraph discovery process, because we may need to consider all possible geometric configurations of a single pattern. Second, while determining if a geometric subgraph is contained in a bigger geometric graph, we would like to allow some tolerance when we establish a match between coordinates, ensuring that slight deviations in coordinates between two identical topological subgraphs do not lead to the creation of two geometric subgraphs. The amount of tolerance (r) should be a user-specified parameter. The task of discovering such r-tolerant frequent geometric subgraphs dramatically changes the nature of the problem. In traditional pattern discovery problems such as finding frequent itemsets, sequential patterns, and/or frequent topological graphs, there is a clear definition of what a pattern is, given its set of supporting graphs. On the other hand, in the case of r-tolerant geometric subgraphs, there are many different geometric representations of the same pattern (all of which will be r-tolerant isomorphic to each other). The problem becomes not only that of finding a pattern and its support but also finding the right representative for this pattern. The selection of the right representative can have a serious impact on correctly computing the support of the pattern. For example, given a set of subgraphs that are r-tolerant isomorphic to each other, the one that corresponds to an *outlier* will tend to have a lower support than the one corresponding to the *center*. These two aspects of geometric subgraphs makes the task of discovering the full-fledged geometric subgraphs extremely hard [235].

To overcome this problem we developed a simpler, albeit less discriminatory, representation for geometric subgraphs. We use a property of a geometric graph called the *average interatomic distance* that is defined as the average Euclidean distance between all pairs of atoms in the molecule. Note that the average interatomic distance is computed between all pairs of atoms irrespective of whether a bonds connects the atoms or not. The average interatomic distance can be thought of as a geometric signature of a topological subgraph. The geometric subgraph consists of two components, a topological subgraph and an interval of average interatomic distance associated with it. A geometric graph contains this geometric subgraph if it contains the topological subgraph and the average interatomic distance of the embedding (of the topological subgraph) is within the interval associated with the geometric subgraph. Note that this geometric representation is also translation and rotation invariant, and the width of the interval determines the tolerance displayed by the geometric subgraph. We are interested in discovering geometric subgraphs that occur in more than $\sigma\%$ of the graphs and whose interval of average interatomic distance is bound by r.

Since a geometric subgraph contains a topological subgraph, for the geometric subgraph to be frequent, the corresponding topological subgraph has to be frequent as well. This allows us to take advantage of the existing approach to discovering topological subgraphs. We modify the frequency-counting stage of the FSG algorithm as follows. If a subgraph g is contained in a graph t, then all possible embeddings of g in t are found and the average interatomic distance for each of these embeddings is computed. As a result, at the end of the frequent subgraph discovery, each topological subgraph has a list of average interatomic distances associated with it. Each one of the average interatomic distances corresponds to one of the embeddings, i.e., a geometric configuration of the topological subgraph. This algorithm can be easily extended to cases in which there are multiple 3D conformations associated with each chemical compound (as discussed in section 9.2) by simply treating each distinct conformation as a different chemical compound.

The task of discovering geometric subgraphs now reduces to identifying geometric configurations that are frequent enough, i.e., identify intervals of average interatomic distances such that each interval contains the minimum number geometric configurations (it occurs in $\sigma\%$ of the graphs) and the width of the interval is smaller than the tolerance threshold (r). This task can be thought of as 1D clustering on the vector of average interatomic distances so that each cluster contains items above the minimum support and the spread of each cluster is bounded by the tolerance r. Note that not all items will belong to a valid cluster as some of them will be infrequent. In our experiments we set the value of r to be equal to half the minimum distance between any two pairs of atoms in the compounds.

To find such clusters, we perform agglomerative clustering on the vector of average interatomic distance values. The distance between any two average interatomic distance values is defined as the difference in their numeric values. To ensure that we get the largest possible clusters, we use the maximum-link criterion function for deciding which two clusters should be merged [214]. The process of agglomeration is continued until the interval containing all the items in the cluster is below the tolerance threshold (r). When we reach a stage where further agglomeration would increase the spread of the cluster beyond the tolerance threshold, we check the number of items contained in the cluster. If the number of items is above the support threshold, then the interval associated with this cluster is considered as a geometric feature. Since we are clustering one-dimensional datasets, the clustering complexity is low. Some examples of the distribution of the average interatomic distance values and the associated clusters are shown in Figure 9.3. Note that the average interatomic distance values of the third example are uniformly spread and lead to no geometric subgraph.

Note that this algorithm for computing geometric subgraphs is approximate in nature for two reasons. First, the average interatomic distance may map two different geometric subgraphs to the same average interatomic

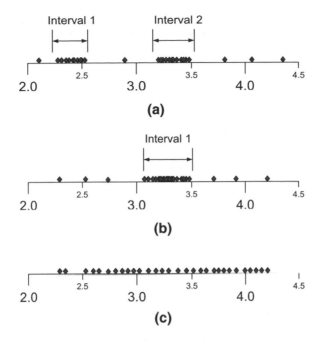

Fig. 9.3. Some examples of the one-dimensional clustering of average interatomic distance values.

distance value. Second, the clustering algorithm may not find the complete set of geometric subgraphs that satisfy the r tolerance. Nevertheless, as our experiments in section 9.5 show, the geometric subgraphs discovered by this approach improve the classification accuracy of the algorithm.

Additional considerations. Even though FSG provides the general functionality required to find all frequently occurring substructures in chemical datasets, a number of issues need to be addressed before FSG can be applied as a black-box tool for feature discovery in the context of classification. One issue is selecting the right value for σ, the support constraint used for discovering frequent substructures. The value of σ controls the number of subgraphs discovered by FSG. Choosing a good value of σ is especially important for a dataset containing classes of significantly different sizes. In such cases, to ensure that FSG is able to find features that are meaningful for all the classes, it must use a support that depends on the size of the smaller class.

For this reason we first partition the complete dataset, using the class label of the examples, into class-specific datasets. We then run FSG on each of these *class datasets*. This partitioning of the dataset ensures that sufficient subgraphs are discovered for class labels that occur rarely in the dataset. Next, we combine subgraphs discovered from each class dataset. After this step, each subgraph has a vector that contains the frequency with which it occurs in each class.

9.4.2 Feature Selection

The frequent subgraph discovery algorithm described in section 9.4.1 discovers all the substructures (topological or geometric) that occur above a certain support constraint (σ) in the dataset. Though the discovery algorithm is computationally efficient, it can generate a large number of features. A large number of features is detrimental for two reasons. First, it could increase the time required to build the model. But more important, a large number of features can increase the time required to classify a chemical compound, as we need to first identify which of the discovered features it contains before we can apply the classification model. Determining whether a compound contains a particular feature or not can be computationally expensive as it may require a subgraph isomorphism operation. This problem is especially critical in the drug discovery process where the classification model is learned on a small set of chemical compounds and is then applied to large chemical compound libraries containing millions of compounds.

One way of solving this problem is to follow a heuristic subgraph discovery approach (similar in spirit to previously developed methods [84, 149]) in which during the subgraph discovery phase itself, the discriminatory ability of a particular subgraph is determined, and the discovery process is terminated as soon as a subgraph is generated that is less discriminatory than any of its subgraphs. By following this approach, the total number of features will be substantially reduced, achieving the desired objective. However, the limitation to such an approach is that it may fail to discover and use highly discriminatory subgraphs. This is because the discriminatory ability of a subgraph does not (in general) consistently increase as a function of its size, and subgraphs that appear to be poor discriminators may become very discriminatory by increasing their size. For this reason, to develop an effective feature selection method, we use a scheme that first finds all frequent subgraphs and then selects among them a small set of discriminatory features. The advantage of this approach is that during feature selection all frequent subgraphs are considered regardless of when they were generated and whether or not they contain less or more discriminatory subgraphs.

The feature selection scheme is based on the *sequential covering paradigm* used to learn rule sets [275]. To apply this algorithm, we assume that each discovered substructure corresponds to a rule, with the class label of the substructure as the *target attribute*. Such rules are referred to as *class rules* in [255]. The sequential covering algorithm takes as input a set of examples and the features discovered from these examples, and it iteratively applies the feature selection step. In this step the algorithm selects the feature that has the highest estimated accuracy. After selecting this feature, all the examples containing this feature are eliminated and the feature is marked as selected. In the next iteration of the algorithm, the same step is applied but on a smaller set of examples. The algorithm continues in an iterative fashion until either all the features are selected or all the examples are eliminated.

In this chapter we use a computationally efficient implementation of the sequential covering algorithm known as CBA [255]. This algorithm proceeds by first sorting the features based on confidence and then applying the sequential covering algorithm on the sorted set of features. One of the advantages of this approach is that it requires a minimal number of passes on the dataset and hence is very scalable. To obtain better control over the number of selected features, we use an extension of the sequential covering scheme known as *classification based on multiple rules* (CMAR) [251]. In this scheme, instead of removing the example after it is covered by the selected feature, the example is removed only if it is covered by δ selected features. The number of selected rules increases as the value of δ increases; an increase in the number of features usually translates into an improvement in the accuracy as more features are used to classify a particular example. The value of δ is specified by the user and provides a means to the user for controlling the number of features used for classification.

9.4.3 Classification Model Construction

Our algorithm treats each subgraph discovered in the previous step as a feature and represents the chemical compound as a frequency vector. The ith entry of this vector is equal to the number of times (frequency) that feature occurs in the compound's graph. This mapping into the feature space of frequent subgraphs is performed for both the training and the test dataset. Note that the frequent subgraphs were identified by mining *only* the graphs of the chemical compounds in the training set. However, the mapping of the test set requires that we check each frequent subgraph against the graph of the test compound using subgraph isomorphism. Fortunately, the overall process can be substantially accelerated by taking into account the frequent subgraph lattice that is also generated by FSG. In this case, we traverse the lattice from top to bottom and visit only the child nodes of a subgraph if that subgraph is isomorphic to the chemical compound.

Once the feature vectors for each chemical compound have been built, any one of the existing classification algorithms can potentially be used for classification. However, the characteristics of the transformed dataset and the nature of the classification problem itself tends to limit the applicability of certain classes of classification algorithms. In particular, the transformed dataset will most likely be high dimensional, and second, it will be sparse, in the sense that each compound will have only a few of these features and each feature will be present in only a few of the compounds. Moreover, in most cases the positive class will be much smaller than the negative class, making it unsuitable for classifiers that primarily focus on optimizing the overall classification accuracy.

In our study we built the classification models using support vector machines (SVMs) [411], as they are well suited for operating in such sparse and high-dimensional datasets. An additional advantage of SVM is that it allows us to directly control the cost associated with the misclassification of examples from the different classes [278]. This allows us to associate a higher cost for the misclassification of positive instances, thus biasing the classifier to learn a model that tries to increase the true positive rate at the expense of increasing the false positive rate.

9.5 Experimental Evaluation

We experimentally evaluated the performance of our classification algorithm and compared it against that achieved by earlier approaches on a variety of chemical compound datasets. The datasets, experimental methodology, and results are described in subsequent sections.

9.5.1 Datasets

We used three different publicly available datasets to derive a total of eight different classification problems. The first dataset was initially used as a part of the Predictive Toxicology Evaluation Challenge [383] which was organized as a part of PKDD/ECML 2001 Conference.[2] It contains data published by the U.S. National Institute for Environmental Health Sciences, consisting of bioassays of different chemical compounds on rodents to study the carcinogenicity (cancer inducing) properties of the compounds [383]. The goal was to estimate the carcinogenicity of different compounds on humans. Each compound is evaluated on four kinds of laboratory animals (male mice, female mice, male rats, female rats) and is assigned four class labels each indicating the toxicity of the compound for that animal. There are four classification problems, one corresponding to each of the rodents, and they will be referred as *P1*, *P2*, *P3*, and *P4*.

The second dataset was obtained from the National Cancer Institute's DTP AIDS Antiviral Screen program [107, 230].[3] Each compound in the dataset is evaluated for evidence of anti-HIV activity. The screen utilizes a soluble formazan assay to measure protection of human CEM cells from HIV-1 infection [426]. Compounds able to provide at least 50% protection to the CEM cells were retested. Compounds that provided at least 50% protection on retest were listed as *moderately active* (CM, confirmed moderately active). Compounds that reproducibly provided 100% protection were listed as

---

[2]http://www.informatik.uni-freiburg.de/~ml/ptc/.
[3]http://dtp.nci.nih.gov/docs/aids/aids_data.html.

confirmed active (CA). Compounds neither active nor moderately active were listed as *confirmed inactive* (CI). We formulated three classification problems on this dataset. In the first problem we consider only *confirmed active* (CA) and *moderately active* (CM) compounds and then build a classifier to separate these two compounds; this problem is referred as *H1*. For the second problem we combine *moderately active* (CM) and *confirmed active* (CA) compounds to form one set of *active* compounds, then build a classifier to separate these *active* and *confirmed inactive* compounds; this problem is referred as *H2*. In the last problem we use only *confirmed active* (CA) and *confirmed inactive* compounds and build a classifier to categorize these two compounds; this problem is referred as *H3*.

The third dataset was obtained from the Center for Computational Drug Discovery's anthrax project at the University of Oxford [330]. The goal of this project was to discover small molecules that would bind with the heptameric protective antigen component of the anthrax toxin and prevent it from spreading its toxic effects. A library of small-sized chemical compounds was screened to identify a set of chemical compounds that could bind with the anthrax toxin. The screening was done by computing the binding free energy for each compound using numerical simulations. The screen identified a set of 12,376 compounds that could potentially bind to the anthrax toxin and a set of 22,400 compounds that were unlikely to bind to the chemical compound. The average number of vertices in this dataset is 25 and the average number of edges is also 25. We used this dataset to derive a two-class classification problem whose goal is to correctly predict whether or not a compound will bind the anthrax toxin or not. This classification problem is referred to as *A1*.

Some important characteristics of these datasets are summarized in Table 9.1. The right-hand side of the table displays the class distribution for different classification problems; for each problem the table displays the percentage of positive class found in the dataset for that classification problem. Note that both the DTP-AIDS and the anthrax datasets are quite large, containing 42,687 and 34,836 compounds, respectively. Moreover, in the case of DTP-AIDS, each compound is also quite large, having on an average 46 atoms and 48 bonds.

9.5.2 Experimental Methodology and Metrics

The classifications results were obtained by performing five-way cross validation on the dataset, ensuring that the class distribution in each fold is identical to the original dataset. For the SVM classifier we used the SVMLight library [206]. All the experiments were conducted on a 1500MHz Athlon MP processor with 2 GB of memory.

Since the positive class is significantly smaller in size than the negative class, using *accuracy* to judge a classifier would be incorrect. To get a better understanding of the classifier performance for different cost settings, we

Table 9.1. Characteristics of the various datasets. N is the number of compounds in the database. $\bar{N}_A$ and $\bar{N}_B$ are the average number of atoms and bonds in each compound. $\bar{L}_A$ and $\bar{L}_B$ are the average number of atom and bond types in each dataset; $\max N_A/\min N_A$ and $\max N_B/\min N_B$ are the maximum/minimum number of atoms and bonds over all the compounds in each dataset.

	Toxic.	Aids	Anthrax	Class dist. (% +ve class)	
N	417	42,687	34,836	**Toxicology**	
$\bar{N}_A$	25	46	25	P1: Male mice	38.3%
$\bar{N}_B$	26	48	25	P2: Female mice	40.9%
$\bar{L}_A$	40	82	25	P3: Male rats	44.2%
$\bar{L}_B$	4	4	4	P4: Female rats	34.4%
$\max N_A$	106	438	41	**AIDS**	
$\min N_A$	2	2	12	H1: CA/CM	28.1%
$\max N_B$	1	276	44	H2: (CA+CM)/CI	3.5%
$\min N_B$	85	1	12	H3: CA/CI	1.0%
				Anthrax	
				A1: active/inactive	35%

obtain the ROC curve [319] for each classifier. The ROC curve plots the false positive rate (x axis) versus the true positive rate (y axis) of a classifier; it displays the performance of the classifier without regard to class distribution or error cost. Two classifiers are compared by comparing the area under their respective ROC curves, a larger area under the curve indicating better performance. The area under the ROC curve will be referred by the parameter A.

9.5.3 Results

Varying minimum support. The key parameter of the proposed frequent substructure-based classification algorithm is the choice of the minimum support (σ) used to discover the frequent substructures (either topological or geometric). To evaluate the sensitivity of the algorithm on this parameter, we performed a set of experiments in which we varied σ from 10% to 20% in 5% increments. The results of these experiments are shown in Table 9.2 for both topological and geometric substructures.

From Table 9.2 we observe that as we increase σ, the classification performance for most datasets tends to degrade. However, in most cases this degradation is gradual and correlates well with the decrease on the number of substructures that were discovered by the frequent subgraph discovery algorithms. The only exception is the H2 problem for which the classification performance (as measured by ROC) degrades substantially as we increase the minimum support from 10% to 20%. Specifically, in the case of topological subgraphs, the performance drops from 70.1 down to 59.0, and in the case of geometric subgraphs it drops from 76.0 to 58.1.

These results suggest that lower values of support are in general better as they lead to better classification performance. However, as the support decreases, the number of discovered substructures and the amount of time required increase. Thus, depending on the dataset, some experimentation

Table 9.2. Varying minimum support threshold (σ). A denotes the area under the ROC curve and N_f denotes the number of discovered frequent subgraphs.

D	$\sigma=10.0\%$				$\sigma = 15.0\%$				$\sigma = 20.0\%$			
	Topo.		Geom.		Topo.		Geom.		Topo.		Geom.	
	A	N_f	A	N_f	A	N_f	A	N_f	A	N_f	A	N_f
P1	66.0	1211	65.5	1317	66.0	513	64.1	478	64.4	254	60.2	268
P2	65.0	967	64.0	1165	65.1	380	63.3	395	64.2	217	63.1	235
P3	60.5	597	60.7	808	59.4	248	61.3	302	59.9	168	60.9	204
P4	54.3	275	55.4	394	56.2	173	57.4	240	57.3	84	58.3	104
H1	81.0	27034	82.1	29554	77.4	13531	79.2	8247	78.4	7479	79.5	7700
H2	70.1	1797	76.0	3739	63.6	307	62.2	953	59.0	139	58.1	493
H3	83.9	27019	89.5	30525	83.6	13557	88.8	11240	84.6	7482	87.7	7494
A1	78.2	476	79.0	492	78.2	484	77.6	332	77.1	312	76.1	193

Dset	Optimized σ					
	Topo.		Geom.		Per class	$Time_p$
	A	N_f	A	N_f	σ	(sec)
P1	65.5	24510	65.0	23612	3.0, 3.0	211
P2	67.3	7875	69.9	12673	3.0, 3.0	72
P3	62.6	7504	64.8	10857	3.0, 3.0	66
P4	63.4	25790	63.7	31402	3.0, 3.0	231
H1	81.0	27034	82.1	29554	10.0, 10.0	137
H2	76.5	18542	79.1	29024	10.0, 5.0	1016
H3	83.9	27019	89.5	30525	10.0, 10.0	392
A1	81.7	3054	82.6	3186	5.0, 3.0	145

may be required to select the proper value of the support that balances these conflicting requirements (i.e., low support but reasonable number of substructures).

In our study we performed such experimentation. For each dataset we kept decreasing the value of support down to the point after which the number of features that were generated was too large to be efficiently processed by the SVM library. The resulting support values, number of features, and associated classification performance are shown in Table 9.2 under the header "Optimized σ." Note that for each problem two different support values are displayed corresponding to the supports that were used to mine the positive and negative class, respectively. Also, the last column shows the amount of time required by FSG to find the frequent subgraphs and provides a good indication of the computational complexity at the feature discovery phase of our classification algorithm.

Comparing the ROC values obtained in these experiments with those obtained for $\sigma = 10\%$, we can see that as before, the lower support values tend to improve the results, with measurable improvements for problems in which the number of discovered substructures increased substantially. In the rest of our experimental evaluation we will be using the frequent subgraphs that were generated using these values of support.

Varying misclassification costs. Since the number of positive examples is in general much smaller than the number of negative examples, we performed a set of experiments in which the misclassification cost associated with each positive example was increased to match the number of negative examples. That is, if n^+ and n^- are the number of positive and negative examples, respectively, the misclassification cost β was set equal to $(n^-/n^+ - 1)$ (so that $n^- = \beta n^+$). We refer to this value of β as the EqCost value. The classification performance achieved by our algorithm using either topological or geometric subgraphs for $\beta = 1.0$ and $\beta = $ EqCost is shown in Table 9.3. Note that the $\beta = 1.0$ results are the same with those presented in Table 9.2.

Table 9.3. Area under the ROC curve obtained by varying the misclassification cost. $\beta = 1.0$ indicates the experiments in which each positive and negative example had a weight of one, and $\beta = $ EqCost indicates the experiments in which the misclassification cost of the positive examples was increased to match the number of negative examples.

Dataset	Topo		Geom	
	$\beta = 1.0$	$\beta = $ EqCost	$\beta = 1.0$	$\beta = $ EqCost
P1	65.5	65.3	65.0	66.7
P2	67.3	66.8	69.9	69.2
P3	62.6	62.6	64.8	64.6
P4	63.4	65.2	63.7	66.1
H1	81.0	79.2	82.1	81.1
H2	76.5	79.4	79.1	81.9
H3	83.9	90.8	89.5	94.0
A1	81.7	82.1	82.6	83.0

From the results in this table we can see that, in general, increasing the misclassification cost so that it balances the size of positive and negative class tends to improve the classification accuracy. When $\beta = $ EqCost, the classification performance improves for four and five problems for the topological and geometric subgraphs, respectively. Moreover, in the cases in which the performance decreased, that decrease was quite small, whereas the improvements achieved for some problem instances (e.g., P4, H1, and H2) were significant. In the rest of our experiments we will focus only on the results obtained by setting $\beta = $ EqCost.

Feature selection. We evaluated the performance of the feature selection scheme based on sequential covering (described in section 9.4.2) by performing a set of experiments in which we varied the parameter δ that controls the number of times an example must be covered by a feature before it was removed from the set of yet to be covered examples. Table 9.4 displays the results of these experiments. The results in the column labeled "Original" show the performance of the classifier without any feature selection. These results are identical to those shown in Table 9.3 for $\beta = $ EqCost and are included here to make comparisons easier.

Two key observations can be made by studying the results in this table. First, as expected, the feature selection scheme is able to substantially reduce the number of features. In some cases the number of features that was selected

Table 9.4. Results obtained using feature selection based on sequential rule covering. δ specifies the number of times each example needs to be covered before it is removed, A denotes the area under the ROC curve, and N_f denotes the number of features that were used for classification.

Topological features										
Dataset	Original		$\delta = 1$		$\delta = 5$		$\delta = 10$		$\delta = 15$	
	A	N_f	A	N_f	A	N_f	A	N_f	A	N_f
P1	65.3	24510	65.4	143	66.4	85	66.5	598	66.7	811
P2	66.8	7875	69.5	160	69.6	436	68.0	718	67.5	927
P3	62.6	7504	68.0	171	65.2	455	64.2	730	64.5	948
P4	65.2	25790	66.3	156	66.0	379	64.5	580	64.1	775
H1	79.2	27034	78.4	108	79.2	345	79.1	571	79.5	796
H2	79.4	18542	77.1	370	78.0	1197	78.5	1904	78.5	2460
H3	90.8	27019	88.4	111	89.6	377	90.0	638	90.5	869
A1	82.1	3054	80.6	620	81.4	1395	81.5	1798	81.8	2065
Geometric features										
Dataset	Original		$\delta = 1$		$\delta = 5$		$\delta = 10$		$\delta = 15$	
	A	N_f	A	N_f	A	N_f	A	N_f	A	N_f
P1	66.7	23612	68.3	161	68.1	381	67.4	613	68.7	267
P2	69.2	12673	72.2	169	73.9	398	73.1	646	73.0	265
P3	64.6	10857	71.1	175	70.0	456	71.0	241	66.7	951
P4	66.1	31402	68.8	164	69.7	220	67.4	609	66.2	819
H1	81.1	29554	80.8	128	81.6	396	81.9	650	82.1	885
H2	81.9	20024	80.0	525	80.4	1523	80.6	2467	81.2	3249
H3	94.0	30525	91.3	177	92.2	496	93.1	831	93.2	1119
A1	83.0	3186	81.0	631	82.0	1411	82.4	1827	82.7	2106

decreased by almost two orders of magnitude. Also, as δ increases, the number of retained features increases; however, this increase is gradual. Second, the overall classification performance achieved by the feature selection scheme when $\delta \geq 5$ is quite comparable to that achieved with no feature selection. The actual performance depends on the problem instance and whether or not we use topological or geometric subgraphs. In particular, for the first four problems (P1, P2, P3, and P4) derived from the PTC dataset, the performance actually improves with feature selection. Such improvements are possible even in the context of SVM-based classifiers as models learned on lower dimensional spaces will tend to have better generalization ability [100]. Also note that for some datasets the number of features decreases as δ increases. Even though this is counterintuitive, it can happen in the cases in which due to a higher value of δ, a feature that would have been skipped is now included in the set. If this newly included feature has relatively high support, it will contribute to the coverage of many other features. As a result, the desired level of coverage can be achieved without the inclusion of other lower-support features. Our analysis of the selected feature sets showed that for the instances in which the number of features decreases as δ increases, the selected features have indeed higher average support.

Topological versus geometric subgraphs. The various results shown in Tables 9.2–9.4 also provide an indication on the relative performance of topological versus geometric subgraphs. In almost all cases, the classifier that is based on geometric subgraphs outperforms that based on topological subgraphs. For some problems, the performance advantage is marginal, whereas for other problems, geometric subgraphs lead to measurable improvements in the area under the ROC curve. For example, if we consider the results shown in Table 9.3 for $\beta = $ EqCost, we can see the geometric subgraphs lead to improvements that are at least 3% or higher for P2, P3, and H3, and the average improvement over all eight problems is 2.6%. As discussed in section 9.4.1, these performance gains are due to the fact that conserved geometric structure is a better indicator than just its topology of a chemical compound's activity.

9.5.4 Comparison with Other Approaches

We compared the performance of our classification algorithm with the performance achieved by the QSAR-based approach and the approach that uses the SUBDUE system to discover a set of substructures.

Comparison with QSAR. As discussed in section 9.3, there is a wide variety of QSAR properties, each of which captures certain aspects of a compound's chemical activity. For our study, we have chosen a set of 18 QSAR properties that are good descriptors of the chemical activity of a compound, and most of them have been previously used for classification purposes [14]. A brief description of these properties is given in Table 9.5. We used two programs to compute these attributes: the geometric attributes, like solvent-accessible area, total accessible area/volume, total Van der Waal's accessible area/volume, were computed using the program SASA [246]; the remaining attributes were computed using Hyperchem software.

Table 9.5. QSAR properties.

Property	Dim.	Property	Dim.
Solvent accessible area	Å^2	Moment of inertia	*none*
Total accessible area	Å^2	Total energy	*kcal/mol*
Total accessible volume	Å^3	Bend energy	*kcal/mol*
Total Van der Waal's area	Å^2	Hbond energy	*kcal/mol*
Total Van der Waal's volume	Å^3	Stretch energy	*kcal/mol*
Dipole moment	*Debye*	Nonbond energy	*kcal/mol*
Dipole moment comp. (X, Y, Z)	*Debye*	Estatic energy	*kcal/mol*
Heat of formation	*Debye*	Torsion energy	*kcal/mol*
Multiplicity	*Kcal*	Quantum total charge	*eV*

We used two different algorithms to build classification models based on these QSAR properties. The first is the C4.5 decision tree algorithm [324] that has been shown to produce good models for chemical compound classification based on QSAR properties [14], and the second is the SVM algorithm that was used to build the classification models in our frequent substructure-based approach. Since the range of values of the different QSAR properties can be significantly different, we first scaled them to be in the range of $[0, 1]$

prior to building the SVM model. We found that this scaling resulted in some improvements in the overall classification results. Note that C4.5 is not affected by such scaling.

Table 9.6 shows the results obtained by the QSAR-based methods for the different datasets. The values shown for SVM correspond to the area under the ROC curve and can be directly compared with the corresponding values obtained by our approaches (Tables 9.2–9.4). Unfortunately, since C4.5 does not produce a ranking of the training set based on its likelihood of being in the positive class, it is quite hard to obtain the ROC curve. For this reason, the values shown for C4.5 correspond to the precision and recall of the positive class for the different datasets. Also, to make the comparisons between C4.5 and our approach easier, we also computed the precision of our classifier at the same value of recall as that achieved by C4.5. These results are shown under the columns labeled "Freq. sub. prec." for both topological and geometric features and were obtained from the results shown in Table 9.3 for β = EqCost. Note that the QSAR results for both SVM and C4.5 were obtained using the same cost-sensitive learning approach.

Table 9.6. Performance of the QSAR-based classifier.

Dataset	SVM	C4.5		Freq. sub. prec.	
	A	Precision	Recall	Topo	Geom
P1	60.2	0.4366	0.1419	0.6972	0.6348
P2	59.3	0.3603	0.0938	0.8913	0.8923
P3	55.0	0.6627	0.1275	0.7420	0.7427
P4	45.4	0.2045	0.0547	0.6750	0.8800
H1	64.5	0.5759	0.1375	0.7347	0.7316
H2	47.3	0.6282	0.4071	0.7960	0.7711
H3	61.7	0.5677	0.2722	0.7827	0.7630
A1	49.4	0.5564	0.3816	0.7676	0.7798

Comparing both the SVM-based ROC results and the precision/recall values of C4.5, we can see that our approach substantially outperforms the QSAR-based classifier. In particular, our topological subgraph-based algorithm does 35% better compared to SVM-based QSAR and 72% better in terms of the C4.5 precision at the same recall values. Similar results hold for the geometric subgraph-based algorithm. These results are consistent with those observed by other researchers [222, 384] that showed that substructure-based approaches outperform those based on QSAR properties.

Comparison with SUBDUE and SubdueCL. Finally, to evaluate the advantage of using the complete set of frequent substructures over existing schemes that are based on heuristic substructure discovery, we performed a series of experiments in which we used the SUBDUE system to find the substructures and then used them for classification. Specifically, we performed two sets of experiments. In the first set, we obtained a set of substructures using the standard MDL-based heuristic substructure discovery approach of

Table 9.7. Performance of the SUBDUE and SubdueCL-based approaches.

Dataset	SUBDUE			SubdueCL		
	A	N_f	$Time_p$	A	N_f	$Time_p$
P1	61.9	1288	303sec	63.5	2103	301sec
P2	64.2	1374	310sec	63.3	2745	339sec
P3	57.4	1291	310sec	59.6	1772	301sec
P4	58.5	1248	310sec	60.8	2678	324sec
H1	74.2	1450	1,608sec	73.8	960	1002sec
H2	58.5	901	232,006sec	65.2	2999	476,426sec
H3	71.3	905	178,343sec	77.5	2151	440,416sec
A1	75.3	983	56,056sec	75.9	1094	31,177sec

SUBDUE [180]. In the second set, we used the substructures discovered by the more recent SubdueCL algorithm [149] that guides the heuristic beam search using a scheme that measures how well a subgraph describes the positive examples in the dataset without describing the negative examples.

Even though there are a number of parameters controlling SUBDUE's heuristic search algorithm, the most critical among them are the width of the beam search, the maximum size of the discovered subgraph, and the total number of subgraphs to be discovered. In our experiments, we spent a considerable amount of time experimenting with these parameters to ensure that SUBDUE was able to find a reasonable number of substructures. Specifically, we changed the width of the beam search from 4 to 50 and set the other two parameters to high numeric values. Note that in the case of SubdueCL, to ensure that the subgraphs were discovered that described all the positive examples, the subgraph discovery process was repeated by increasing the value of the beam width at each iteration and removing the positive examples that were covered by subgraphs.

Table 9.7 shows the performance achieved by SUBDUE and SubdueCL on the eight different classification problems along with the number of subgraphs it generated and the amount of time it required to find these subgraphs. These results were obtained by using the subgraphs discovered by either SUBDUE or SubdueCL as features in an SVM-based classification model. Essentially, our SUBDUE and SubdueCL classifiers have the same structure as our frequent subgraph-based classifiers, the only difference being that the features now correspond to the subgraphs discovered by SUBDUE and SubdueCL. Moreover, to make the comparisons as fair as possible, we used $\beta = $ EqCost as the misclassification cost. We also performed another set of experiments in which we used the rule-based classifier produced by SubdueCL. The results of this scheme were inferior to those produced by the SVM-based approach and we do not report them here.

Comparing SUBDUE with SubdueCL, we can see that the latter achieves better classification performance, consistent with the observations made by other researchers [149]. Comparing the SUBDUE and SubdueCL-based results with those obtained by our approach (Tables 9.2–9.4), we can see that in almost all cases both our topological and geometric frequent subgraph-based algorithms lead to substantially better performance. This is true both in the cases in which we performed no feature selection and in the cases in which we used the sequential covering-based feature selection scheme. In particular, comparing the SubdueCL results against the results shown in Table 9.4 without any feature selection, we can see that on the average, our topological and geometric subgraph-based algorithms do 9.3% and 12.2% better, respectively. Moreover, even after feature selection with $\delta = 15$ that results in a scheme that has a comparable number of features to those used by SubdueCL, our algorithms are still better by 9.7% and 13.7%, respectively. Finally, if we compare the amount of time required by either SUBDUE or SubdueCL to that required by the FSG algorithm to find all frequent subgraphs (Table 9.2), we can see that despite the fact that we are finding the complete set of frequent subgraphs, our approach requires substantially less time.

9.6 Conclusions and Directions for Future Research

In this chapter we presented a highly effective algorithm for classifying chemical compounds based on frequent substructure discovery that can scale to large datasets. Our experimental evaluation showed that our algorithm leads to substantially better results than those obtained with existing QSAR- and substructure-based methods. Moreover, besides this improved classification performance, the substructure-based nature of this scheme provides chemists with valuable information as to which substructures are most critical for the classification problem at hand. For example, Figure 9.4 shows the three most discriminating substructures for the PTC, DTP AIDS, and anthrax datasets that were obtained by analyzing the decision hyperplane produced by the SVM classifier. A chemist can then use this information to understand the models and potentially use it to design better compounds.

The classification algorithms presented in this chapter can be improved along three different directions. First, as already discussed in section 9.2, our current geometric graph representation utilizes a single conformation of the chemical compound, and we believe that the overall classification performance can be improved by using all possible low-energy conformations. Such conformations can be obtained from existing 3D coordinate prediction software, and as discussed in section 9.4.1, they can be easily incorporated in our existing framework. Second, our current feature selection algorithms focus only on whether or not a particular substructure is contained in a compound; they do not take into account how these fragments are distributed over different parts of the molecule. Better feature selection algorithms can be developed by taking this information into account so that to ensure that the entire (or most of) molecule is covered by the selected features. Third, even though the proposed approaches significantly outperformed that based on QSAR, our analysis showed that there is a significant difference as to which compounds are correctly classified by the substructure- and QSAR-based

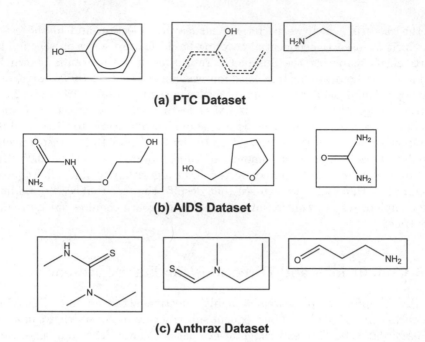

(a) PTC Dataset

(b) AIDS Dataset

(c) Anthrax Dataset

Fig. 9.4. Three most discriminating substructures for the (a) PTC, (b) AIDS, and (c) anthrax datasets.

approaches. For example, Figure 9.5 shows the overlap among the different correct predictions produced by the geometric, topological, and QSAR-based methods at different cutoff values for the anthrax dataset. From these results, we can see that there is a great agreement between the substructure-based approaches, but there is a large difference among the compounds that are correctly predicted by the QSAR approach, especially at the top 1% and 5%. These results suggest that better results can be potentially obtained by combining the substructure- and QSAR-based approaches.

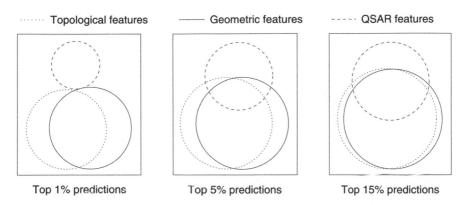

Fig. 9.5. Venn diagrams displaying the relation between the positive examples that were correctly classified by the three approaches at different cutoff values for the anthrax dataset. The different cutoffs were obtained by looking at only the top 1%, 5%, and 15% of the ranked predictions. Each circle in the Venn diagrams corresponds to one of the three classification schemes and the size of the circle indicates the number of positive examples correctly identified. The overlap between two circles indicates the number of common correct predictions.

Part IV

Biological Data Management

Chapter 10
Phyloinformatics:
Toward a Phylogenetic Database

Roderic D. M. Page

Summary

Much of the interest in the "tree of life" is motivated by the notion that we can make much more meaningful use of biological information if we query the information in a phylogenetic framework. Assembling the tree of life raises numerous computational and data management issues. Biologists are generating large numbers of evolutionary trees (phylogenies). In contrast to sequence data, very few phylogenies (and the data from which they were derived) are stored in publicly accessible databases. Part of the reason is the need to develop new methods for storing, querying, and visualizing trees. This chapter explores some of these issues; it discusses some prototypes with a view to determining how far phylogenetics is toward its goal of a phylogenetic database.

10.1 Introduction

Cracraft [87] defined *phyloinformatics* as "an information system that is queried using the hierarchical relationships of life." Much of the interest in the "tree of life" [391] is motivated by the notion that we can make much more meaningful use of biological information if we query the information in a phylogenetic framework. Rather than being limited to queries on single species or arbitrarily defined sets of species, phyloinformatics aims to query data using sets of evolutionarily related taxa (Figure 10.1).

Implementing such a system raises a number of issues, several of which have been discussed at various workshops.[1] My aim in this chapter is

---

[1] Examples include the tree of life workshops held at Yale and the Universities of California at Davis and Texas at Austin (reports available from http://taxonomy.zoology.gla.ac.uk/rod/docs/tol/) and the tree of life workshop at DIMACS (http://dimacs.rutgers.edu/Workshops/Tree/).

to explore some of the database and data visualization issues posed by phylogenetic databases. In particular I discuss taxonomic names, supertrees, and navigating phylogenies. I review some recent work in this area and discuss some prototypes with a view to determining how far phylogenetics is toward its goal of a phylogenetic database.

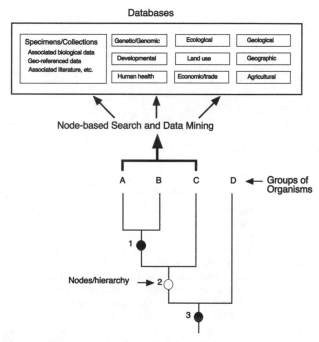

Fig. 10.1. Diagram illustrating a "phyloinformatic search strategy." Instead of undertaking searches on a single taxa at a time, queries would use sets of related taxa, such as the taxa A–C in the subtree rooted at node 2. From reference [87].

10.1.1 Kinds of Trees

It is useful to distinguish between at least two different kinds of trees—classifications and phylogenies. Figure 10.2 shows a classification and a phylogeny for the plant order Nymphaeales (waterlilies).

Classification. A Linnaean classification can be represented as a rooted tree with all nodes labeled. Each node has a "rank," such as order, family, genus, or species (see Figure 10.2). Although the relative position of a rank in the taxonomic hierarchy is fixed, ranks are essentially arbitrary in that they are rarely comparable across different taxonomic groups. For example,

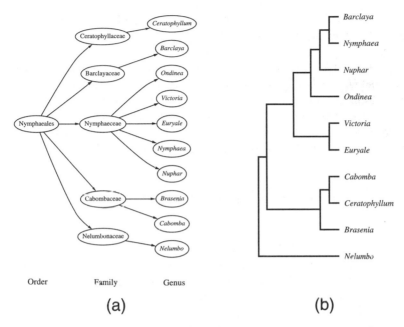

Order   Family   Genus

(a)   **(b)**

Fig. 10.2. (a) Classification and (b) phylogenctic tree for the plant order Nymphaeales (waterlilies). Adapted from reference [458].

a fish genus may be a few thousand years old, whereas an insect genus may be more than 40 million years old. There have been some attempts to make ranks comparable by assigning taxa of similar age to the same rank [22], but to date these attempts have met with little enthusiasm.

A different response to this issue is to abandon ranks altogether [97]. Without wishing to get embroiled in that debate [299], it is worth pointing out that a useful consequence of having a small, fixed number of taxonomic ranks is that the height of any classification tree (the number of nodes from any leaf to the root) is limited. In the International Code of Botanical Nomenclature there arc 25 distinct ranks [456]; the NCBI taxonomy database [37, 428][2] has 28 ranks (including the rank "no rank"). Having a tree of limited height may be an advantage in visualizing very large trees (see section 10.6).

Phylogenies. Phylogenetic trees may be inferred using a wide variety of methods [310], and can have several different representations. Unlike classifications, internal nodes of phylogenetic trees need not be labeled, nor are there any ranks (see Figure 10.2). Often the internal nodes and/or edges of a phylogeny are decorated with measures of support (such as bootstrap values or Bayesian posterior probabilities). The edges of a phylogeny typically

---

[2]http://www.ncbi.nlm.nih.gov/Taxonomy/taxonomyhome.html

have a "length," which measures the amount of evolutionary change that is estimated to have occurred along that edge.

Tree of Life. The tree of life is the phylogeny of every organism, both alive and extinct. As such it is the holy grail of phylogenetics. It may prove equally elusive, if only because the metaphor of a tree is a gross simplification of the complex picture of intertwined trees that emerges once lateral gene transfer is taken into account [432]. In this sense, the tree of life is an abstraction that serves as a useful metaphor for navigation (as, indeed, do classifications).

10.2 What Is a Phylogenetic Database For?

There are a least two distinct goals of a phylogenetic database: archival storage and analysis. The requirements for meeting these two goals are in many respects quite different. Archiving can be as simple as storing plain text data files, but analysis requires considerable care in data curation if the database is to support useful computational tasks.

10.2.1 Archival Storage

The first goal of a phylogenetic database is to act as a repository of published phylogenetic analyses, including data and trees. Currently, TreeBASE³ [314] is the only database that tackles this problem in anything resembling a satisfactory way. The NCBI's GenBank stores only molecular sequences. The same organization's PopSet database stores sets of sequences (and sometimes alignments), but they are difficult to access in formats useful to phylogenetists, and they can be incomplete. They also lack phylogenetic trees. The EMBL's WebAlign database [257] is similarly inadequate. Unlike TreeBASE, Popset and WebAlign are limited to sequence data, which is a subset of the range of data types employed by systematists.

   Another trend in recent years is the archiving of data by journal publishers as "supplementary material" for a publication. Although it is a commendable idea, it is in reality a poor option. Journals may store data in nonstandard formats (e.g., formatted tables of data), and they frequently use file formats such as HTML and PDF, which need to be converted before being used. Last, there is no guarantee, especially given the volatile nature of the publishing industry, that these archives will be stable in the long term.

What to archive? A phylogenetic database would ideally store individual data sets and the trees resulting from phylogenetic analysis of the data. In practice, this ideal raises problems. Some methods of analysis, such as parsimony, can yield many thousands of trees. Should a database store all

---

³http://www.treebase.org

these trees? One approach would be to store a summary of the trees, and indeed, authors of papers typically summarize their trees using consensus trees (as a consequence, TreeBASE often contains consensus trees). However, whereas for some systematists a successful phylogenetic analysis yields a single, well-supported, phylogenetic tree, others argue that our best estimate of evolutionary history is a probability distribution of trees (for an overview see [184]). Bayesian methods [190] can generate sets of $10^4 - 10^6$ trees, each of which has a nontrivial probability of being the "true tree." Although these trees can be summarized using a consensus tree, in many applications of Bayesian analysis we are interested in the complete set of trees. For example, we may want to evaluate an evolutionary hypothesis of interest over all trees yielded by Bayesian analysis. The implication is that it would be desirable to store all the trees, especially if the analysis that yielded the trees was itself time consuming.

Given the implications for storage space, it would be useful to develop compression techniques for trees. These techniques are likely to save considerable space as the trees are typically quite similar to each other. Nor should we confine our attentions to trees—networks may be better descriptors of the data, in which case they would need to be stored.

Metadata. A phylogenetic database needs to store information about the analyses that generated the trees stored in that database. At present no formal definition of such phylogenetic "metadata" has been proposed. TreeBASE stores some information on the type of analysis performed (whether it was parsimony or likelihood), but ideally a database would store details of the model of evolution used and any relevant parameter values. Because most phylogeny programs have command line interfaces with options set by the user or support a command language such as NEXUS [261], it should be relatively straightforward to extract metadata for an analysis from the data file used to construct the trees. If metadata is stored, then there is scope for automated comparison of the properties of different phylogenetic methods, a topic that generates much debate within the phylogenetics community.

Data formats. The existence of multiple data formats is an issue that has plagued bioinformatics, especially sequence analysis. Phylogenetics has suffered from this problem to a lesser extent, due in large part to the creation of the NEXUS format [261], which is extensible and for which software libraries are available.[4] This format has been adopted by a number of software authors, and it has been put forward as a candidate for interoperability between bioinformatics tools [192]. As a consequence, the phylogenetics community has been less excited by XML than some other disciplines in

---

[4]For example, the Nexus Class Library, http://hydrodictyon.eeb.uconn.edu/ncl/

bioinformatics [2]. XML standards have been proposed (e.g., [145]) but have yet to be widely adopted.

10.2.2 Analysis

Among the most basic questions one might ask of a phylogenetic database are those that concern the phylogeny of a group of organisms: What is the current best estimate of the phylogeny? Which data are available? For which taxa do we need more information? We can also ask questions concerning methodology: Which methods give the most robust trees? Which methods disagree most often about relationships? What kinds of data yield the best estimates of phylogenies? More general questions, such as the distribution of tree shapes and other properties of trees (e.g., edge lengths), could be asked of large numbers of trees, which could be used to inform probabilistic methods of tree reconstruction and assist inference of evolutionary processes.

Addressing these kinds of questions requires that data are adequately annotated and curated and are accessible to analytical and visualization tools. Some of the problems to be addressed are discussed here.

10.3 Taxonomy

Fundamental to any phylogenetic database is a consistent organismal taxonomy. The effort to achieve it is one of the longest running projects in biology [121] and also one of the most contentious [147]. A naive approach to the problem of building a list of species names is simply to compile all scientific names that have been published, and indeed there have been some highly publicized attempts to do so [142]. However, this approach is inadequate because an organism can have several different names (synonyms), and the same name may be applied to different organisms (e.g., the genus *Morus* is used for both a plant and a bird). Furthermore, different authors may have different conceptions of what taxa are covered by the same name (see the example of albatrosses in section 10.3.2). There may also be variations in how the same name is spelled.

As just one example of the problems taxonomic names can cause databases, the species *Pelecanoides garnotii* is present in the ITIS database (taxonomic serial number 174666) but not in the NCBI taxonomy database. However, the NCBI list contains *Pelecanoides garnoti* (taxonomy ID number 79637), which differs from the ITIS name in missing the last "i." These names refer to the same bird, the Peruvian diving petrel, but these two databases use different spellings of the taxonomic name. The phylogenetic database TreeBASE also has this bird, but it is stored as "Pelecanoides garnoti AF076073" (TreeBase taxon T9334), a combination of scientific name and GenBank accession number. Searches on "Pelecanoides garnoti" in TreeBASE fail to return this taxon. Until such instances are dealt with, efforts to link different databases together using taxonomic names will be thwarted.

Lack of taxonomic consistency also makes it difficult to develop meaningful computational challenges or contests. For example, Michael Sanderson proposed the following supertree challenge as part of the "Deep Green Challenges":[5]

> The TreeBASE database currently contains over 1000 phylogenies with over 11,000 taxa among them. Many of these trees share taxa with each other and are therefore candidates for the construction of composite phylogenies, or "supertrees," by various algorithms. A challenging problem is the construction of the largest and "best" supertree possible from this database. "Largest" and "best" may represent conflicting goals, however, because resolution of a supertree can be easily diminished by addition of "inappropriate" trees or taxa.

Computationally this challenge is very interesting; however, from a biologist's perspective the results will have little meaning in the absence of a consistent taxonomy in TreeBASE.

10.3.1 Taxonomic Assertions

At the core of any effort to establish a taxonomic name server is a data model of taxonomic names that can accommodate the ambiguity caused by the same name meaning different things in different contexts. One solution is to represent a taxonomic concept as a (name, reference) pair (Figure 10.3). A name is any validly published name, e.g. *Rhea pennata* or *Pteroicnemia pennata*. A reference is a dated usage of the name, such as in a publication or a database. A "potential" taxon [38] or "assertion" [322] is the pairing of a name and reference. This model enables a database to store information on different usages of the same name and provides a mechanism for incorporating synonyms by linking assertions together. For example, an assertion can contain a pointer to a valid assertion for the corresponding name [322]. The principle strength of the assertion model is that it provides a way to associate a name with the context in which the name is used. Consequently, taxonomic name servers would ideally provide assertions rather than simply taxonomic names.

Fig. 10.3. Model for a taxonomic concept ("assertion") as the intersection of a name and a reference. From reference [322].

---

[5]http://www.life.umd.edu/labs/delwiche/deepgreen/DGchallenges.html

10.3.2 Higher Taxa and Classifications

Higher taxa are sets of lower taxa. It follows that if one searches a database for a higher taxon, or family, one expects to find all instances of genera in the database that belong to that family. However, the expectation will be met only if the database contains information on taxonomic classification. TreeBASE, for example, has no taxonomic structure, which can lead to frustrating searches. To illustrate, a search on the taxonomic name "Aves" (birds) yields four studies (TreeBASE accession numbers S281, S880, S296, and S433), none of which focuses on birds (although all four studies do contain at least one bird). However, this search has not recovered all the bird studies in TreeBASE. For example, studies S375 (on swiftlets) and S351(on albatrosses) are just some of the avian datasets that are stored in TreeBASE but that are not accessible by searching on higher taxa.

While the lack of taxonomic hierarchy in TreeBASE is a limitation, it does simplify the developer's task as it avoids the thorny problem of which taxonomic classification to use. In many groups of organisms there exist different, mutually incompatible classifications. As a consequence, the same name may have very different meanings in different classifications. For example, Figures 10.4 and 10.5 show two classifications of albatrosses. The Robertson and Nunn [332] classification (Figure 10.4) recognizes four genera, *Diomedea*, *Phoebastria*, *Phoebetria*, and *Thalassarche*, whereas the NCBI's taxonomy database (Figure 10.5) recognizes just *Diomedea* and *Phoebetria*. Consequently, searching GenBank for *Diomedea* would return sequences for taxa that a user following the Robertson and Nunn classification would not regard as belonging to *Diomedea*.

Furthermore, biological classifications follow rules that need to be encoded into databases in order to maintain consistency. For example, a species belongs to a single genus, and the species name includes the name of the genus to which it belongs. The NCBI taxonomy does not always follow this rule. Returning to albatrosses, the NCBI classification shown in Figure 10.5 includes species such as *Thalassarche bulleri* as members of the genus *Diomedea*. However, if *Thalassarche bulleri* is the species name then *Thalassarche* is the genus, not *Diomedea*. From a nomenclatural point of view, the albatross taxonomy in GenBank is invalid.

Ideally a database would support multiple classifications so that the user can choose a preferred classification as the basis of a query. The database would also be able to translate between different classifications. Current database systems are not ideally suited to this task (for a detailed discussion see [326]). It would also be desirable to be able to compare different classifications. Similar issues arise in the comparison of topical hierarchies and ontologies [406]; hence methods developed to tackle those problems might be usefully applied to biological classification.

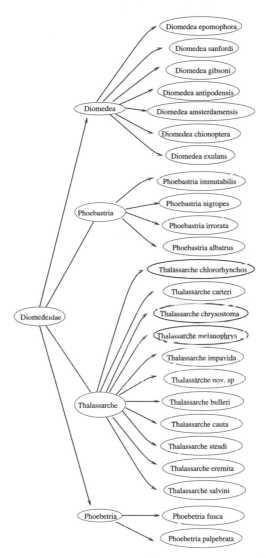

Fig. 10.4. Classification of albatrosses (family Diomedeidae) represented as directed acyclic graphs, based on Robertson and Nunn [332]. Compare with the classification in Figure 10.5.

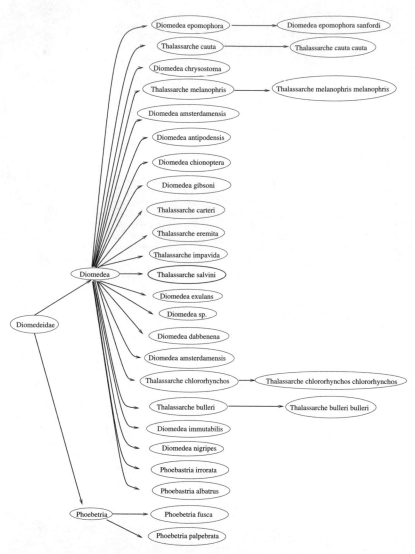

Fig. 10.5. Classification of albatrosses (family Diomedeidae) based on the NCBI taxonomy tree. Compare with the classification in Figure 10.4.

10.3.3 Classification of Data

The issues of consistent nomenclature apply to data as well as taxa. For database queries to be meaningful it is important that consistent names are used for the same sources of data. It is not uncommon for the same gene to have several different names in the sequence databases. For example, the mitochondrial cytochrome b gene may be variously referred to as "cyt b" or "cytochrome b." The genomics community is moving to standardize gene nomenclature (e.g., [420]). For other kinds of data similar issues arise. Morphological data tends to be described in an idiosyncratic fashion, although efforts are being made to standardize nomenclature (see the Structure of Descriptive Data subgroup of the International Working Group on Taxonomic Databases).[6] This project raises issues similar to those being tackled by the Gene Ontology Consortium.[7]

10.4 Tree Space

A phylogenetic database is, in part, a collection of trees. Questions naturally arise about the properties of this set of trees, how we can navigate it, and how we can summarize information shared by sets of trees.

10.4.1 Cluster Graphs

The degree of overlap between trees can be visualized using a cluster graph [345], where the nodes represent individual trees. Two nodes, x and y, are connected by an edge if, for some fixed k, the corresponding trees have at least k leaves in common. At a minimum we need two leaves in common to construct a supertree. If we construct a cluster graph for $k = 2$ and the graph is not connected, then we cannot construct a supertree for all the trees of interest.

We can explore the degree of overlap in a set of input trees by constructing cluster graphs for different values of k and finding the components of the graphs. For real data the results can be disappointing. Figure 10.6 shows an example for birds based on 143 generic-level phylogenies for birds assembled from the literature [241]. If we require minimal overlap (i.e., $k = 2$), almost all (129) of the phylogenies form a single component, with a few isolated studies remaining. As we increase the amount of minimum overlap required, this component gets progressively smaller, until $k = 5$, when the set of 143 bird trees fragments into two components with 27 and 29 trees, respectively, and numerous smaller components (Figure 10.7). Given that the degree of taxonomic overlap between input trees is a key predictor of the accuracy

---

[6]http://www.tdwg.org/sddhome.html

[7]http://www.geneontology.org/

of the derived supertree [43, 71], then the greater the degree of overlap the better the resulting supertree is likely to be. For the bird example, overlap comes at the price of being able to construct supertrees for a only limited number of taxa using subsets of the original sets of trees. For $k = 5$, over a third of the input trees do not overlap with any other tree and hence have to be discarded.

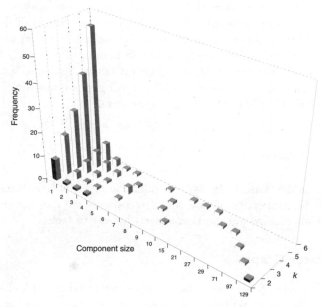

Fig. 10.6. Size distributions of components of cluster graphs for 143 genus-level bird phylogenies constructed for different levels of overlap. Data from reference [241].

10.5 Synthesizing Bigger Trees

A supertree method takes a set of trees with overlapping leaves and constructs a larger tree that contains all the leaves in the input trees (Figure 10.8). Supertree methods are receiving increasing attention [42], motivated in part by considerations of computational complexity. Although the phylogenetic community has made a lot of progress in developing sophisticated search algorithms, some of which scale to tens of thousands of sequences, constructing trees on the scale of the tree of life does not look feasible at present. One approach to this problem is to adopt a divide-and-conquer strategy: build smaller trees and assemble them into a larger tree. This is the supertree approach. For this argument to be compelling,

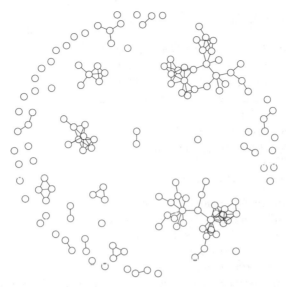

Fig. 10.7. Cluster graph for 143 bird trees for $k = 5$ (data as for Figure 10.6). Each node represents a tree, and a pair of trees is connected by an edge if the trees share at least five taxa in common. Note that the graph is not connected and contains numerous isolated trees.

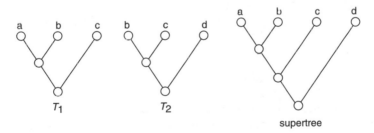

Fig. 10.8. Two input trees T_1 and T_2 and a supertree.

supertree algorithms must be more efficient than tree-building algorithms. The only polynomial time supertree algorithms to date are ONETREE [7] and MINCUTSUPERTREE [357]. The most popular algorithm for supertrees, matrix representation parsimony (MRP) [31, 325], is NP-complete, as are others such as minimum flipping [71] and compatibility methods [148]. The attractiveness of a polynomial time algorithm is that it can be used to construct supertrees quickly as part of queries on phylogenetic databases.

10.5.1 MINCUTSUPERTREE

Semple and Steel's [357] MINCUTSUPERTREE algorithm takes a set of k rooted trees $\mathcal{T}$ and a set of species $S = \cup_{i=1}^{k} \mathcal{L}(T_i) = \{x_1, \ldots, x_n\}$, where $\mathcal{L}(T_i)$ is the set of leaves in tree T_i. The algorithm recursively constructs the graph $S_{\mathcal{T}}$. The nodes in $S_{\mathcal{T}}$ are terminal taxa, and nodes a and b are connected if a and b are in a proper cluster in at least one of the input trees (i.e., if there is a tree in which the most recent common ancestor of a and b is not the root of that tree). The algorithm proceeds as follows:

> **procedure** MinCutSupertree($\mathcal{T}$)

1. **if** $n = 1$ **then return** a single node labeled by x_1.
2. **if** $n = 2$ **then return** a tree with two leaves labeled by x_1 and x_2.
3. Otherwise, construct $S_{\mathcal{T}}$ as described.
4. **if** $S_{\mathcal{T}}$ is disconnected **then**
   Let S_i be the components of $S_{\mathcal{T}}$.
   else Create graph $S_{\mathcal{T}}/E_{\mathcal{T}}^{\mathrm{max}}$ and delete all edges in $S_{\mathcal{T}}/E_{\mathcal{T}}^{\mathrm{max}}$ that are in a minimum cut set of $S_{\mathcal{T}}$. Let S_i be the resulting components of $S_{\mathcal{T}}/E_{\mathcal{T}}^{\mathrm{max}}$.
5. **for** each component S_i **do**
   $T_i = MinCutSupertree(\mathcal{T}|S_i)$, where $\mathcal{T}|S_i$ is the set of input trees with any species not in S_i pruned.
6. Construct a new tree $\mathcal{T}$ by connecting the roots of the trees T_i to a new root r.
7. **return** T

end

The key difference between the ONETREE algorithm and MINCUTSUPER TREE lies in step 4. In ONETREE if the graph $S_{\mathcal{T}}$ is connected (i.e., comprises a single component) then the algorithm exits, returning the result that the input trees are not consistent. Semple and Steel modify ONETREE by ensuring that $S_{\mathcal{T}}$ yields more than one component by using minimum cuts. In a connected graph G, a set of edges whose removal disconnects the graph is a *cut set*. If each edge in G has a weight assigned to it, then a cut set with the smallest sum of weights is a *minimum cut* of the graph. Note that Semple and Steel find minimum cuts not of $S_{\mathcal{T}}$ but rather of an associated graph $S_{\mathcal{T}}/E_{\mathcal{T}}^{\mathrm{max}}$, which they construct as follows:

1. Weight each edge (a, b) in $S_{\mathcal{T}}$ by the number of trees in $\mathcal{T}$ in which a and b are in the same proper cluster.
2. Let $E_{\mathcal{T}}^{\mathrm{max}}$ be the set of edges that have weight k, where k is the number of trees in $\mathcal{T}$.
3. Merge any nodes in $S_{\mathcal{T}}$ that are connected by edges in $E_{\mathcal{T}}^{\mathrm{max}}$.

For example, given the two input trees in Figure 10.9, the edge (a, b) in $S_{\mathcal{T}}$ has a weight of 2, and hence the nodes a and b are merged. This procedure ensures that any nesting found in all the input trees $\mathcal{T}$ will be in the supertree returned by MINCUTSUPERTREE.[8]

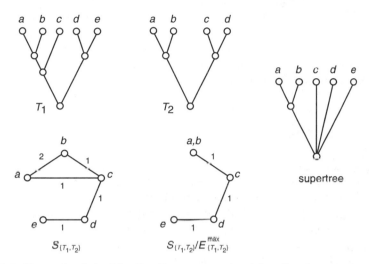

Fig. 10.9. Example of the MINCUTSUPERTREE algorithm showing two input trees T_1 and T_2, and the graphs $S_{\mathcal{T}}$ and $S_{\mathcal{T}}/E_T^{\max}$. The graph $S_{\mathcal{T}}/E_{\mathcal{T}}^{\max}$ has three minimum cut sets, which yield the components $\{a, b\}, \{c\}, \{d\}$, and $\{e\}$, which in turn yield a supertree. From reference [309].

Modified mincut supertrees. Although MINCUTSUPERTREE is fast, it can produce somewhat paradoxical results [309]. It also does not perform as well as MRP and minimum flipping methods [71]. Modifications to the original algorithm (described in [309]) improve its performance somewhat.

10.5.2 Supertrees and Distances

The degree of overlap between trees is a crude measure of tree similarity—two trees may share the five leaves but completely disagree on the relationships among those leaves. Hence it would be desirable to use a more refined measure of tree similarity. Among those that have been used in the context of navigating large sets of trees are the partition metric [333] used in Tree Set Viz, and the TreeRank measure [422]. There are several other measures that

---

[8]Note that while in Semple and Steel's original algorithm each input tree in $\mathcal{T}$ can have a weight $w(T)$ assigned to it, for simplicity here I consider only the case where all trees have the same unit weight.

could be investigated, including quartet and triplet measures [93], agreement subtrees [120], and matchings [103].

One appealing definition of a supertree is that it minimizes some distance function between the supertree and the set of input trees [71]. Hence, we could define a tree space based on a given metric and a corresponding supertree method. Although Figure 10.7 is not an ordination, it resembles the diagrams produced by the Tree Set Viz program [228].[9] This program enables the user to navigate a set of trees (all with the same leaf set) and select subsets of trees for further analysis (such as constructing a consensus tree). This approach could be extended to accommodate trees with overlapping leaf sets, where users would select trees for supertree construction.

10.6 Visualizing Large Trees

A major challenge facing tree of life projects is visualizing very large trees. Programs such as TreeView [308] are limited by the size of computer screen or printed paper and typically can adequately display trees with a few hundred leaves. Displaying trees with orders of magnitude more leaves is a problem that has received a lot of attention in the computer science literature. Various methods have been proposed, including hyperbolic tree browsing [240] and SpaceTree [317]. Figure 10.10 shows a classification for birds displayed using a hyperbolic tree. Figure 10.11 shows the same classification visualized using SpaceTree. The two visualizations have rather different properties. The hyperbolic tree enables the user to get a sense of the whole tree very quickly, especially as it can be navigated by "dragging" nodes on the screen. However, the spatial distortion introduced by hyperbolic geometry can be a little disorienting. In contrast, SpaceTree is perhaps more intuitive. Rather than distort space, it collapses large subtrees, which reveal themselves when the user clicks on them. A SpaceTree is easy to navigate, albeit at the cost of numerous mouse clicks.

10.7 Phylogenetic Queries

Given one or more trees there are a number of queries that biologists might wish to formulate [294]. Some simple queries are shown in Figure 10.12. For example, given a node in a tree, we might wish to find all its ancestors (i.e., find that node's "lineage"). Given two nodes, we could seek their least common ancestor (LCA; often in the biological literature this ancestor is referred to as the "most recent common ancestor," MRCA). Often the subtree rooted at $LCA(A, B)$—the "minimum spanning clade" [294]—of A and B will

---

[9]http://comet.lehman.cuny.edu/treeviz/

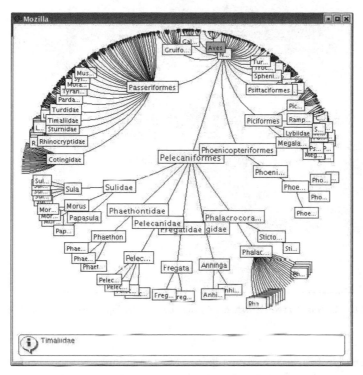

Fig. 10.10. Hyperbolic tree drawn using the TreeBolic applet (http://treebolic.sourceforge.net/en/home.htm). The tree is the classification for birds (class Aves) taken from the NCBI taxonomy and generated by the Glasgow Name Server (http://darwin.zoology.gla.ac.uk/~rpage/ToL/).

be of interest. A path length query returns the number of nodes on the path between two nodes.

The least common ancestor (LCA) query is central to the notion of a "phylogenetic classification" [97]. Under this model, a classification is not a hierarchy of nested nodes of a given rank. Instead, taxonomic groups are defined by statements such as "the Nymphaeceae are all descendants of the most recent common ancestor of *Nymphaea* and *Euryale*." In this sense, a phylogenetic classification can be viewed as simply a set of named LCA queries.

10.7.1 SQL Queries on Trees

SQL (Structured Query Language) is the standard database query language, but it is not particularly adept at handling trees. However, there are ways to query trees in SQL, either using extensions to the language or preprocessing the trees. For example, Nakhleh et al. [294] evaluate the performance of

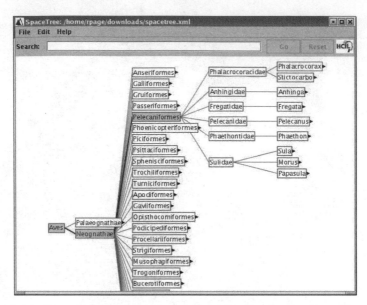

Fig. 10.11. Same tree shown in Figure 10.10 displayed using SpaceTree [317].

recursive Datalog queries implemented in Oracle SQL. This approach requires only parent-child relationships to be stored in a database; however, it makes use of features not available in many SQL implementations. Other approaches to querying trees involve preprocessing the tree to store additional information about the nodes. The "nested sets" model [69] assigns a pair of numbers to each node in the tree that record the order in which the node is visited during a depth-first traversal of the tree (Figure 10.13a). These numbers have several nice properties. For leaf nodes the difference between the right and left visitation numbers is 1. The subtree rooted at a node n can be recovered by finding all nodes whose left visitation number lies within the range of the left and right visitation numbers of node n. For example, in Figure 10.13a the subtree rooted at the node with visitation numbers $(3, 12)$ comprises all nodes with left visitation numbers $3 < l < 12$.

Another approach is to use "genealogical identifiers" [376] (also called "classification notation" [30]). For each node we compute a string representation of the path from that node to the root of the tree (the "path+filename" notation used in file systems and Web addresses is an example of the use of genealogical identifiers). A simple way to construct an identifier is to assign to each node n a unique number in the range $1 \ldots k$, where k is the number of children of the parent of node n. For example, the left descendant of the root in Figure 10.13b is numbered "1" and the right descendant is labeled "2." We then make labels by appending the node's number to the label of its parent (the root has label " "). In Figure 10.13b

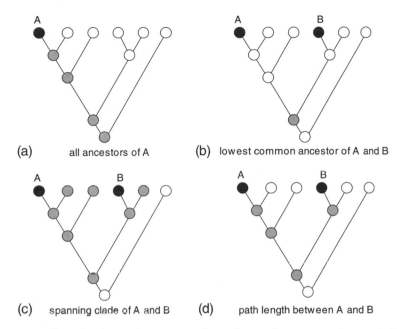

Fig. 10.12. Some basic queries on trees. In each tree the query nodes are indicated as solid dots, and nodes matching the query are shown in light gray. (a) Find all ancestors of node A. (b) Find the least common ancestor (LCA) of A and B. (c) Find the minimum spanning clade of A and B. (d) Find the path length between A and B.

we label the two immediate descendants of the root "/1" and "/2," the two descendants of "/1" are labeled "/1/1" and "/1/2," and so on (the forward slash "/" is a separator). Finding a subtree in SQL becomes a simple string search; for example, the nodes in the subtree rooted at the node labeled "/1/1" are found by this SQL statement:

```
SELECT FROM nodes
WHERE (gi LIKE "/1/1%") AND (gi < "/1/10") ;
```

where gi is the genealogical identifier. Other tree operations are also straightforward. For example, the LCA of any two nodes A and B is the node with the genealogical identifier corresponding to the longest common substring in the genealogical identifier's of A and B (and which includes the start of the genealogical identifier). For example, the LCA of nodes labeled "/1/1/1/1" and "/1/1/2" in Figure 10.13 is the node labeled "/1."

The relative merits of nested set and genealogical identifiers have been discussed by Sofer [376] and Ballew et al. [30]. The latter opted for nested sets for their implementation of a thesaurus, based on performance considerations.

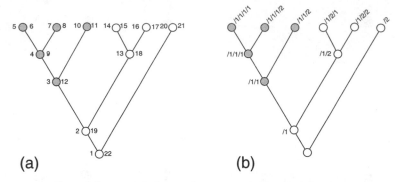

Fig. 10.13. Two different labeling schemes to facilitate SQL queries on rooted trees. In each tree the same subtree is shaded light gray. (a) Labeling nested sets assigns to each node a left and right visitation number. The labeling is created by a depth-first traversal of the tree that records for each node when that node was first encountered (left number) and when the traversal last visited that node (right number). (b) Genealogical identifier labels are constructed by appending a node's label to that of its immediate parent. In this example, each node is labeled by its position in the list of children of each parent.

10.7.2 Phylogenetic Query Language

Given that SQL is not ideally suited to querying trees, perhaps we need a phylogenetic query language. Jamil et al. [199] describe some work on developing a query language that supports SELECT, JOIN, and SUBSET queries on trees.

The SELECT query selects a subset of trees that match one or more criteria. Simple queries would retrieve trees containing one or more taxa (for example, find all trees for birds). More elaborate queries would find trees based on structure (e.g., find all trees that have humans more closely related to chimps than to gorillas) [361, 364] or within some specified distance of a tree [422].

A phylogenetic JOIN query joins two trees together using a pair of nodes, one from each tree. For example, we could join two trees together where the root node of the first tree is a leaf in the second tree, thus creating a larger, combined tree. This is, of course, an instance of the supertree problem discussed in section 10.5. For the JOIN operation to be possible, there must exist a supertree of which the two trees are subtrees. This can be determined in polynomial time using the ONETREE algorithm [7]. A logical extension of the JOIN query would be to extend it to cover cases where the two input trees are incompatible. For instance, a JOIN query could return the largest shared subtree. There is considerable scope for developing a family of JOIN queries and the corresponding family of supertrees. There are also possible parallels with tree-adjoining grammars [207].

SUBSET queries retrieve part of a given tree. The spanning clade query in Figure 10.12c is a simple example of a SUBSET query.

10.8 Implementation

Many of the ideas outlined in this chapter have been implemented in various prototypes by different research groups. In several cases, the results are not robust products but are better characterized as "proof of concept" tools.

10.8.1 Taxonomic Databases

Major taxonomic databases that make their data publically available include the Integrated Taxonomic Information System (ITIS)[10] and the NCBI's Taxonomy database.[11] Data from these two databases, together with classifications from other sources, are incorporated in the Glasgow Name Server,[12] which is a test bed for methods for comparing and visualizing classifications. The classifications shown in Figures 10.10 and 10.11 were generated using that server.

10.8.2 Supertrees

The mincut supertree algorithm (section 10.5.1) has been implemented in the C++ programming language and is available from http://darwin.zoology. gla.ac.uk/~rpage/supertree. The code makes extensive use of the Graph Template Library (GTL),[13] which provides a Standard Template Library (STL) based library of graph classes and algorithms. The program reads trees in either NEXUS or Newick format, and outputs a supertree. There is also a Web interface to the program,[14] and the program has been integrated into TreeBASE.

Source code and executables for the minimum flipping supertree method [71] are available from the Iowa State University Supertree Server.[15] There are several programs that can encode sets of trees as binary characters suitable for analysis by matrix representation parsimony, such as RadCon and Supertree.

10.8.3 Tree Queries

TreeBASE contains a tree searcher [361] that uses ATreeGrep [364] to find trees that share a specified subtree. A similar prototype that queries a user-provided database of trees has been implemented by Kenneth Jackson.[16] The Glasgow Name Server uses genealogical identifier labels (see Figure 10.13) to find subtrees in classifications, which are then displayed in a range of formats (see e.g., Figures 10.10 and 10.11).

---

[10] http://www.itis.usda.gov/
[11] ftp://ftp.ncbi.nlm.nih.gov/pub/taxonomy
[12] http://darwin.zoology.gla.ac.uk/~rpage/ToL/
[13] http://www.infosun.fmi.uni-passau.de/GTL/
[14] http://darwin.zoology.gla.ac.uk/cgi-bin/supertree.pl
[15] http://genome.cs.iastate.edu/supertree/index.html
[16] http://students.dcs.gla.ac.uk/students/jacksonk/project.html

10.8.4 Tree Visualization

The methods discussed in section 10.6 are just two of a number of visualization tools that could be employed to display large trees. There is a growing literature on evaluating tree and graph visualization tools [174, 316]. Other approaches include 3D hyperbolic trees [285],[17] the TreeWiz program [338],[18] and displaying trees in semiimmersive 3D environments [341]. More recently, tree visualization methods have begun to incorporate tools for comparing trees [286]. Both hyperbolic viewers and SpaceTree have been used in taxonomic and phylogenetic contexts, and two of the three datasets for the INFOVIS 2003 contest Visualization and Pairwise Comparison of Trees[19] are phylogenies or classifications.

10.9 Prospects and Research Problems

This rather superficial survey has covered just some of the issues involved in implementing a phylogenetic database. However, it is clear that many of the elements needed by a phyloinformatic system are either available or would not be too difficult to implement. The challenge is to integrate the tools into a useful package. A major topic not covered here is the acquisition, annotation, curation, and storage of data. In some respects, this task represents a greater obstacle than the development of tools to query and visualize the data. Following are some of the topics that need further work.

10.9.1 Storing Large Numbers of Trees Efficiently

In section 10.2.1 it was mentioned that Bayesian methods [190] can generate very large numbers of (i.e., more than a million) trees in a single analysis. These trees are sampled from a Markov chain. It would be useful to store these trees in a database, but the practice would rapidly consume a lot of storage. Typically the trees will be very similar to each other, and the same tree topologies will occur many times. Is it possible to compress the trees so that the storage space requirements are reduced but individual trees can still be recovered quickly? Can a method be developed that does not lose information on where in the chain a given tree occurred?

10.9.2 Database Models

Most taxonomic databases, such as ITIS and the NCBI taxonomy, use relational databases. An open question is whether this technology is the most

---

[17]http://graphics.stanford.edu/~munzner/h3/

[18]http://www.eml.org/english/staff/homes/ulla/rost.html

[19]http://www.cs.umd.edu/hcil/iv03contest/index.shtml

appropriate for the task. Taxonomic databases need to be able to store trees and other graphs and to handle the semantics of classifications (for example, the rules concerning the names of species and genera mentioned in section 10.3.2). For an introduction to the issues see Raguenaud and Kennedy [326].

10.9.3 Tree Matching

Comparing competing classifications (e.g., Figures 10.4 and 10.5) involves tree comparison and matching. While unordered tree matching is NP-complete, there are constrained variants that are tractable [409]. There is considerable scope in employing these methods to quantitatively compare classifications.

10.9.4 Searching Tree Space

Searching a database of trees may benefit from using metric-space indexing [274]. It would be interesting to investigate the implications of the structure of the tree space in phylogenetic databases [315] for metric-space indexing.

Acknowledgments

I thank the editors for inviting me to contribute this chapter. In developing the ideas presented here I've greatly benefited from attending NSF-funded workshops at the University of California at Davis (2000) and DIMACS at Rutgers University (2003). I'm indebted to Mike Sanderson and Mel Janowitz, respectively, for inviting me to those events. My thinking on taxonomic name databases has been influenced by Richard Pyle's unpublished draft schema [322]. I thank James Cotton, Vince Smith, and anonymous reviewers for their helpful comments.

Chapter 11
Declarative and Efficient Querying on Protein Secondary Structures

Jignesh M. Patel, Donald P. Huddler, and
Laurie Hammel

Summary

In spite of the many decades of progress in database research, surprisingly scientists in the life sciences community still struggle with inefficient and awkward tools for querying biological datasets. This work highlights a specific problem involving searching large volumes of protein datasets based on their secondary structure. In this chapter we define an intuitive query language that can be used to express queries on secondary structure and develop several algorithms for evaluating these queries. We have implemented these algorithms in Periscope, which is a native database management system that we are building for declarative querying on biological datasets. Experiments based on our implementation show that the choice of algorithms can have a significant impact on query performance. As part of the Periscope implementation, we have also developed a framework for optimizing these queries and for accurately estimating the costs of the various query evaluation plans. Our performance studies show that the proposed techniques are very efficient and can provide scientists with interactive secondary structure querying options even on large protein datasets.

11.1 Introduction

The recent conclusion of the Human Genome Project has served to fuel an already explosive area of research in bioinformatics that is involved in deriving meaningful knowledge from proteins and DNA sequences. Even with the full human genome sequence now in hand, scientists still face the challenges of determining exact gene locations and functions, observing interactions between proteins in complex molecular machines, and learning the structure and function of proteins through protein conservation, just to name a few. The progress of this scientific research in the increasingly vital fields of functional genomics and proteomics is closely connected to the research in the database community; analyzing large volumes of genetic and biological datasets involves being able to maintain and query large genetic and protein databases. If efficient methods are not available for retrieving these biological datasets, then unfortunately the progress of scientific analysis is encumbered by the limitations of the database system.

This chapter looks at a specific problem of this nature that involves methods for searching protein databases based on secondary structure properties. This work is a part of the Periscope project at the University of Michigan, in which we are investigating methods for declarative querying on biological datasets. In this chapter, we define a problem that the scientific community faces regarding searching on protein secondary structure, and we develop a query language and query-processing techniques to efficiently answer these queries. We have built a secondary structure querying component, called Periscope/PS^2, based on the work described in this chapter, and we also describe a few experimental and actual user experiences with this component of Periscope.

11.1.1 Biological Background

Proteins have four different levels of structural organization, primary, secondary, tertiary, and quaternary; the latter two are not considered in this chapter. The primary structure is the linear sequence of amino acids that makes up the protein; this is the structure most commonly associated with protein identification [321]. The secondary structure describes how the linear sequence of amino acids folds into a series of three-dimensional structures. There are three basic types of folds: alpha-helices (h), beta-sheets (e), and turns or loops (l). Because these three-dimensional structures determine a protein's function, knowledge of their patterns and alignments can provide important insights into evolutionary relationships that may not be recognizable through primary structure comparisons [307]. Therefore, examining the types, lengths, and start positions of its secondary structure folds can aid scientists in determining a protein's function [10].

11.1.2 Scientific Motivation

The discovery of new proteins or new behaviors of existing proteins necessitates complex analysis in order to determine their function and classification. The main technique that scientists use in determining this information has two phases. The first phase involves searching known protein databases for proteins that "match" the unknown protein. The second phase involves analyzing the functions and classifications of the similar proteins in an attempt to infer commonalities with the new protein [10]. These phases may be intertwined as the analysis of matches may provide interesting results that could be further explored using more refined searches.

This simplification of the searching process glosses over the actual definition of protein similarity. The reason is that no real definition of protein similarity exists; each scientist has a different idea of similarity depending on the protein structure and search outcome goal. For example, one scientist may feel that primary structure matching is beneficial, while another may be interested in finding secondary structure similarities in order to predict biomolecular interactions [196]. In addition to these complications, there is a plethora of differing opinions even within same-structure searches. One scientist may want results that exactly match a small, specific portion of the new protein, while another may feel that a more relaxed match over the entire sequence is more informative.

What is urgently needed is a set of tools that are both *flexible* regarding posing queries and *efficient* regarding evaluating queries on protein structures. Whereas there are a number of public domain tools, such as BLAST, for querying genetic data and the primary structure of proteins [12, 13, 218, 429, 454], to the best of our knowledge there are no tools available for querying on the secondary structure of proteins. This chapter addresses this void and focuses on developing a *declarative* and *efficient* search tool based on secondary structure that will enable scientists to encode their own definition of secondary structure similarity.

11.1.3 Chapter Organization

In this chapter, we first define a simple and intuitive query language for posing secondary structure queries based on segmentation. We identify various algorithms for efficiently evaluating these queries and show that depending on the query selectivities and segment selectivities, the choice of the algorithm can have a dramatic impact on the performance of the query.

Next we develop a query optimization framework to allow an optimizer to choose the optimal query plan based on the incoming query and data characteristics. As the accuracy of any query optimizer depends on the accuracy of its statistics, for this application we need to accurately estimate both the segment and the overall result selectivities. We develop histograms for estimating these selectivities and demonstrate that these histograms are very accurate and take only a small amount of space to represent.

Finally, we implement our techniques in Periscope, a native DBMS that we have developed for querying on biological datasets, and in this chapter, we also present results from actual uses of this search technique.

11.2 Protein Format

The first task to perform is to establish the format for representing proteins in our system. This format largely depends on the prediction tool that is used to generate the secondary structure of proteins in our database. For the majority of known proteins, their secondary structure is just a predicted measure. To obtain the secondary structure for a given protein, therefore, it is usually necessary to enter its primary structure into a prediction tool that will return the protein's predicted secondary structure.

The tool used to predict the secondary structure information for the proteins in our database is Predator [134]. Predator is a secondary structure prediction tool based on the recognition of potentially hydrogen-bonded residues in a single amino acid sequence. Even though, we use this particular tool, our query-processing techniques can work with other protein prediction tools as well.

Predator returns the protein name, its length in amino acids, its primary structure, and its predicated secondary structure along a number in the range 0–9 for each position. This number indicates the probability that the prediction is accurate for the given position. We add a unique id to each protein for internal purposes. Figure 11.1 contains a portion of a sample protein in our database.

Name:	$t2\_1296$
Id:	1
Length:	554
Primary structure:	MSAQISDSIEEKRGFFT..
Secondary structure:	LLLLEELLLLLLLHHHH..
Probability:	99755577763445443..

Fig. 11.1. Sample protein.

11.3 Query Language and Sample Queries

Next we determine the types of queries that are useful to scientists in examining secondary structure properties and design a query language to express these queries. Based on interviews with scientists who regularly perform secondary structure protein analysis, we are able to formulate three initial classes of queries and a query language.

11.3.1 Query Language

As these queries are defined, an intuitive query language begins to emerge. Because only three types of secondary structure can occur in a protein sequence, helices (h), beta-sheets (e), and turns or loops (l), and as these types normally occur in groups as opposed to changing at each position, it is natural to characterize a portion of a secondary structure sequence by its type and length. For example, because the sequence hhhheeeelll is more likely to occur than helhelehle, it is intuitive to identify the first sequence as three different segments: 4 h's, 4 e's and 3 l's.

The formal process for posing a query is to express the query as a sequence of *segment predicates*, each of which must be matched in order to satisfy the query. A quick note on terminology: throughout this chapter we refer to segment predicates either as query predicates or simply predicates. Each segment predicate in the query is described by the type and the length of the segment. It is often necessary to express both the upper and lower bounds on the length of the segment instead of the exact length. Finally, in addition to the three type possibilities, h, e, and l, we also use a fourth type option, ?, which stands for a gap segment and allows scientists to represent regions of unimportance in a query. The formal query language is defined in Figure 11.2. We will now look at three important classes of queries that can be expressed using the language defined.

```
Query → Segments
Segments → Segment*
Segment → <type lb ub>
Type → e | h | l | ?
lb → any integer >= 0
ub → any integer >= 0 | ∞
Segment Constraint: lb <= ub
```

Fig. 11.2. Query language definition.

11.3.2 Exact Match Queries

In the simplest situations, scientists would like to find all proteins that contain an exact query sequence. An example of such a query is

find all proteins that contain 'hhheeeelll', or 3 h's followed by 4 e's followed by 3 l's

The user would express this query as a sequence of three predicates: {< $h33 >< e44 >< l33 >$}. Our algorithms take the exactness of these predicates literally; they do not return matches that are a part of a larger sequence. For example, the sequence hhhheeeelll would not be returned as a match for the example query because it contains four h's at the beginning of the sequence, not three as specified in the first query predicate.

11.3.3 Range Queries

While exact matching is important, in some cases it may be sufficient to find matches of approximate length. For example, one might want to pose the following query:

> *find all proteins that contain a loop of length 4 to 8 followed by a helix of length 7 to 10*

Here the exact position where the amino acids stop looping and start to form a helix is not as important as the fact that there is a loop followed by a helix. This range query would be expressed as {<l 4 8><h 7 10>}. Note that this example provides the motivation for expressing both the upper and lower bounds of the segment length.

11.3.4 Gap Queries

Another feature scientists would like to be able to express in their queries is the existence of gaps between regions of importance. For example, one scientist may be interested in matching two portions of a query protein exactly but may not care if the connecting positions hold any similarity. One of the big drawbacks of current primary structure search tools is that there is no effective way to specify gaps in the query sequence. Using our query language, these gaps can easily be expressed. The query sequence {<h 4 6><? 0 ∞ ><l 5 5>} would solve the gap query:

> *find all proteins that contain a helix of length 4 to 6 followed at some point by a loop of length 5*

These three classes of queries provide an initial functionality for our system to solve; we will look at more complex queries in our future work.

11.4 Query Evaluation Techniques

This section describes four methods for evaluating the types of queries just defined. The first approach uses a protein scan and the last three utilize a segmentation technique similar to that described in section 11.3 that represents proteins as sequences of segments. Section 11.5 will provide details about a statistics-based query optimizer that chooses between these methods.

11.4.1 Complex Scan of Protein Table (CSP)

The first approach performs a scan of the protein table itself. Before proceeding with the details of the scan, we will first describe the schema that is used to store proteins in the protein table. The schema for the protein table is

```
table   protTbl (
        name                    char(30),
        id                      int primary key,
        length                  int,
        primary_structure       char(length),
        secondary_structure     char(length),
        probability             int(length));
```

The descriptions for these fields are the same as in Figure 11.1. The latter three fields are character or integer arrays, where *length* is the length of the protein in amino acids.

The general plan for the scan is that each protein in the database is retrieved, its secondary structure is scanned, and its information is returned if the secondary structure matches the query sequence. The matching is performed using a nondeterministic finite state machine (FSM) technique similar to that used in regular expression matching [371]. Each secondary structure is input to the FSM one character at a time until either the machine enters a final (matching) state or it is determined that the input sequence does not match the query sequence.

As protein sequences can be long, sometimes consisting of thousands of amino acids, it is common for a query sequence to match more than once in a given protein. Scientists are interested in each match, not just each matching protein. In other words, if a sequence matches a given protein in two distinct positions, each of these places must be reported separately. To achieve this result, our algorithm checks for all possible occurrences in each protein by running the FSM matching test once for each position in the protein's secondary structure.

The FSM itself is constructed once for each query. In our algorithm the FSM consists of a lookup table with next-state assignments for the three possible types of inputs as well as information regarding the final, or matching, and exiting, or nonmatching, states. This complex scan of the protein table is able to solve any of the three types of queries described in section 11.3 containing any number of predicates.

11.4.2 General Segmentation Technique

The last three approaches are based on a segmentation scheme that represents proteins as a sequence of segments. This segmentation technique is similar to the one described in [312] in which the interest is in retrieving sequences of integers. The idea is to break the secondary structure of a protein into segments of like types. These segments are stored in a separate segment table. Along with the type and length of each segment, the protein id of the segment's originating protein and the start position of the segment in that protein are also stored. The corresponding segment table schema, then, is

> table segTbl (
> segment_id   int primary key,
> id   int,
> type   char,
> length   int,
> start_position   int,
> foreign key (id)   references protTbl (id));

A multiattribute B+-tree index is built on the segment table's type and length attributes. A clustered B+-tree index is also built on the protein id of the protein table to facilitate protein retrieval. Tables 11.1 and 11.2 show an example of several small protein entries with their corresponding segment tuples.

Table 11.1. Sample protein table.

name	id	len	primary	secondary	prob.
A	1	5	mtgpi	lleee	99401
B	2	6	liffki	hhheee	983121

Table 11.2. Sample segment table.

seg id	id	type	length	start position
1	1	l	2	1
2	1	e	3	3
3	2	h	3	1
4	2	e	3	4

The remaining three query evaluation techniques all incorporate some variation on the following plan description to produce proteins that satisfy a given query. In general, each nongap predicate of a query can be evaluated using either a scan of the segment table or a probe of the segment index. Once individual matching segments of the query have been retrieved, they can be merged based on their protein id; the start position information can then be used to satisfy the ordering constraints between segments to produce the final matching results.

In all three techniques, once the matching protein ids have been found, they must still be joined with the protein table in order to obtain the actual proteins. This is accomplished through an index-nested loops join (INLJ) of the protein ids with the B+-tree index built on the protein id attribute of the protein table. These protein ids (obtained from the segment predicate matches) are first sorted in order to improve the performance of the INLJ. This join provides quick retrieval of the actual proteins stored in the protein table, especially as the B+-tree index is clustered on the protein id attribute.

This segmentation query plan can be conveyed in standard database terminology through SQL queries using the segment and protein tables. We now present an example of each of the three types of queries in our query language along with their corresponding SQL translations. The exact match query {<e 8 8><h 6 6>} is expressed in SQL as

> select * from protTbl p, segTbl s1, segTbl s2
> where s1.type = 'e' and s1.length = 8
> and s2.type = 'h' and s2.length = 6
> and s1.id = s2.id and s1.id = p.id
> and s2.start_pos - (s1.start_pos + s1.length) = 0

Note that the start position information is utilized to account for the predicate ordering. The range query {<e 8 10><l 6 7>} is essentially the same as the exact match query only with range bounds on the length constraints instead of single equality bounds, as shown here:

> select * from protTbl p, segTbl s1, segTbl s2
> where s1.type = 'e' and s1.length BETWEEN 8 and 10
> and s2.type = 'l' and s2.length BETWEEN 6 and 7
> and s1.id = s2.id and s1.id = p.id
> and s2.start_pos - (s1.start_pos + s1.length) = 0

Queries involving gaps become a little more complicated because the start position information must also be utilized to account for the gap constraints as well as the predicate ordering. The query {<e 8 10><? 3 5><h 2 2>} is expressed as

> select * from protTbl p, segTbl s1, segTbl s2
> where s1.type = 'e' and s1.length BETWEEN 8 and 10
> and s2.type = 'h' and s2.length = 2
> and s1.id = s2.id and s1.id = p.id
> and s2.start_pos - (s1.start_pos + s1.length) <= 5
> and s2.start_pos - (s1.start_pos + s1.length) >= 3

We will now describe the remaining three query evaluation techniques, which all incorporate the methodologies of the foregoing plan with some minor variations.

Simple scan of segment table (SSS). In this technique the entire segment table is scanned for segments that match the most highly selective predicate of the query. All the segments returned by the scan then participate in the aforementioned INLJ to retrieve their actual proteins. It is important to note that the retrieved proteins do not yet match the query, as there may be other query predicates that have not yet been tested. If there are additional predicates in the query, each protein is scanned using the FSM technique described in section 11.4.1 to produce the final matching result.

Index scan of segment index (ISS). The index scan query plan is essentially identical to the SSS method with one exception. While the SSS method uses a scan of the segment table to produce segments matching the most highly selective predicate, the ISS method instead utilizes the B+-tree index built on the type and length attributes of the segment table to retrieve segments that match the most highly selective predicate. Once these matching segments have been found, an INLJ with the protein table id index and a possible complex scan (for queries with more than one predicate) are performed in the same fashion as in the SSS plan.

Multiple index scans of segment index (MISS(n)). The final method described in this chapter, the multiple index scan technique, is a generalization of the ISS plan. The basic change is that instead of performing only one index probe, the B+-tree index is now probed n times with the n most highly selective query predicates, where n can range from two to the total number of nongap predicates in the query. We will refer to this value of n as the MISS number. The segment results of each individual index probe are sorted, first by protein id and then by start position, and written to separate files.

The newly written files then participate in an n-way sort-merge join to find query segments with the same protein id. At this point the start position information is used to determine whether the segments occur in the correct order within the protein and if the proper gap constraints between them are met. If the segments match the query constraints, then the corresponding protein id is returned. As with the previous two plans, the protein id then participates in an INLJ with the protein id index followed by a possible complex scan to test for any remaining query predicates.

11.5 Query Optimizer and Estimation

When a query is posed to Periscope, the system must decide which of the four plans should be used to evaluate the given query. In this section we present the framework of the query optimizer that is used to make this decision. As in the classic System R paper, our query optimizer utilizes cost functions that model the CPU and I/O resources of each plan [21, 356]. We also have a slightly simpler method of query optimization that uses heuristic cutoffs to determine the most efficient query plan. Both the cost functions and heuristic cutoffs take as input the estimations of the selectivity of each of the query predicates and the selectivity of the result. Traditional database management systems utilize histograms to provide such estimations [194, 195, 198, 287, 356]. The unique, restricted nature of the segment query language and the composition of protein secondary structure allows the Periscope query optimizer to incorporate these standard techniques and expand the estimation capabilities of histograms beyond their typical capacity. We utilize two histograms in our current implementation: a basic one to determine the selectivities of the query predicates and a more complex one to estimate the resulting protein selectivity. Section 11.5.1 introduces the basic histogram and section 11.5.2 describes the complex histogram. Sections 11.5.3 and 11.5.4 explain how the query optimizer uses these histograms in the heuristic cutoff and cost function methods, respectively.

11.5.1 Basic Histogram

The basic histogram contains information about the number of segments in the segment table for a given type and length pair. As there are only three possible types, e, h, and l, and as the segments are usually relatively small in length, it is neither space nor time consuming to maintain exact counts for the majority of protein segments. The basic histogram is stored in the form of a $k \times 3$ matrix, where k is the number of length buckets in the histogram and the second dimension has one value for each of the three possible types, e, h, and l. For example, position [7][2] holds the number of <h 7 7> segments.[1] The last bucket is used to represent all segments with length greater than or equal to k. For range predicates, an estimate is computed by summing the counts in the appropriate range of buckets. This estimate is *exact* for all segment predicates that are less than k in length.

In our current implementation, the number of buckets is set to 100, since segments rarely have a length of longer than one hundred positions. This size is also small enough to ensure a compact storage representation for the histogram. Segments over a length of 100 are considered to have a default low selectivity.

This histogram may be populated during or immediately following the loading of the segment table. Updates can be performed on each new protein addition without significant time penalty. With the protein dataset that we use for our experimentation, which contains 248,375 proteins and their associated 10,288,769 segments, this histogram requires only 13 seconds to

---

[1] Note that the numbering of the rows and columns in the matrix starts from 1 instead of 0. As there is no practical reason for being able to express segments of length 0, segments of length 1 are the smallest segments we consider. We want to keep the segment length identical to the associated histogram row number, so the row numbering starts with 1; the column numbering also starts with 1 (and ends at 3) for uniformity.

build and is created immediately after the loading of the segment table. The time spent by the query optimizer in estimating query predicate selectivities using this histogram is minimal, less than a millisecond on average. In terms of space requirements, the histogram contains information about more than 99% of all segments and occupies only 1.2 KB of disk space.

11.5.2 Complex Histogram

The second histogram, which has a more complex structure, is used to estimate the selectivity of the entire query result, not just of a given query predicate. This calculation procedure surpasses traditional histogram estimation techniques in that it finds the probability of *multiple* attributes occurring in a specific order in the same string, possibly separated by gap positions. This estimation technique is in contrast to traditional histograms that are used to estimate the occurrence of a single attribute [194, 195, 356] or multiple *unordered* substrings [198].

Description. The complex histogram is stored as a four-dimensional matrix; the first dimension corresponds to the protein id attribute, the second dimension to the start position attribute, and the third and fourth dimensions represent the same length and type attributes as in the simple histogram. Due to the large number of proteins found in protein databases and their long sequence lengths, the first two dimensions are divided into equal-width buckets to reduce space requirements. For example, in our experimental dataset with 248,375 proteins and 10,288,769 segments, we use one hundred buckets each for the first, second and third dimensions and three buckets for the fourth dimension (corresponding to the three types e, h, and l). Position [3][4][7][2], for example, holds the number of <h 7 7> segments whose starting position is in the range of the fourth starting position bucket and whose protein id lies within the third protein id bucket.

Result cardinality estimation. We will initially present our cardinality estimation algorithms using an example. Consider the query $\{<P_1><P_2>\}$, which has two predicates, P_1 and P_2. Table 11.3 shows all possible arrangements for the two predicates in a histogram with three buckets (SPB_1, SPB_2, and SPB_3) for the start position ranges 0–49, 50–99, and 100–149, respectively. For simplicity we assume here that these three start position buckets correspond to the same protein id bucket. Note that the type and length attributes of the buckets shown in the table are implicitly defined according to the definitions of the predicates P_1 and P_2.

The arrangements of these two predicates fall into two configurations. In the first configuration, the predicates match segments in distinct start position buckets. For the two-predicate example, cases 1–3 show all possible arrangements with this configuration. In the second configuration, corresponding to cases 4–6 in Table 11.3, both predicates match segments in the same bucket.

Table 11.3. Arrangement possibilities for two query predicates in three start position buckets.

	SPB$_1$ (0–49)	SPB$_2$ (50–99)	SPB$_3$ (100–149)
1	P$_1$	P$_2$	
2	P$_1$		P$_2$
3		P$_1$	P$_2$
4	P$_1$ and P$_2$		
5		P$_1$ and P$_2$	
6			P$_1$ and P$_2$

We now need formulas to estimate the number of matches in each of these cases. Once we have these formulas, the resulting cardinality will be the sum of the estimates from each of these cases. Table 11.4 contains a description of the variables that will be used in these formulas. Figure 11.3 gives the pseudocode for the general algorithm that is used to calculate the estimated result cardinality of a query. The result selectivity follows by dividing this cardinality by the total number of proteins in the database. We next present the estimations for cases in both these configurations. In the following discussion we will refer to these configurations as *distinct bucket* and *same bucket configurations*.

Table 11.4. Description of the cardinality estimation variables.

Variables	Description
$NumProtIdBuckets$	Number of protein id buckets in first dimension of histogram
$NumPosBuckets$	Number of start position buckets in second dimension of histogram
$NumProtPerBucket$	Number of proteins represented by a protein id bucket
$NumPosPerBucket$	Number of start positions represented by a start position bucket
PIB_i	ith protein id bucket
SPB_i	ith start position bucket
P_1	First predicate used in the estimation
P_2	Second predicate used in the estimation
Gap	Gap between P$_1$ and P$_2$
$X.start$	Lower bound on predicate X's range where X = P$_1$, P$_2$, or Gap
$X.end$	Upper bound on predicate X's range where X = P$_1$, P$_2$, or Gap

The calculations for both types of configurations are performed with the assumption that the segments are uniformly distributed throughout

---

This function gives the general framework for estimating the cardinality of a query using two predicates, P_1 and P_2, and the Gap between them.
double Estimate_Cardinality(P_1, P_2, Gap)
{
  double card = 0;

  // do for each protein id bucket in the histogram
  for (int i = 1; i <= NumProtIdBuckets; i++) {

    // *for each possible starting position bucket, do same bucket configuration*
    for (int j = 1; j <= NumPosBuckets; j++) {
      card += Same_Bucket(PIB_i, SPB_j, P_1, P_2, Gap);
    }

    // *for each possible starting position, do distinct bucket configuration*
    for (j = 1; j < NumPosBuckets; j++) {
      card += Distinct_Bucket(PIB_i, SPB_j, P_1, P_2, Gap, j);
    }
  }
  return card;
}

Fig. 11.3. Cardinality algorithm pseudocode.

the protein id and start position buckets. The distinct bucket configuration estimate is calculated by multiplying the number of matching first-predicate segments found in the first start position bucket by the number of second-predicate matches found in the second bucket divided by the number of protein ids in each protein id bucket. The division operation is necessary because of the uniform distribution assumption. This formula can be generalized to estimate the number of results from n predicates in n distinct start position buckets and can also incorporate gap information to automatically disregard start position buckets that do not satisfy the gap requirements. Figure 11.4 gives the pseudocode for the distinct bucket configuration algorithm.

The calculations for the same bucket configuration are more complex. When P_1 and P_2 are in the same start position bucket, P_1's start position could be anywhere within the range of that bucket. We assume a uniform distribution of the start positions of the two predicates. For each possible first-predicate start position, we calculate the chances of the second predicate being in the proceeding start positions and in the same protein. For example, in case 4, the number of proteins that match P_1 at position 9 is $n_{p1} = (1/50) \times$ (number of P_1 in SPB_1). Similarly, the number of proteins that match P_2 in positions 10 to 49 is $n_{p2} = (4/5) \times$ (number of P_2 in SPB_1). Now, assuming that there are 100 proteins in each protein id bucket, the estimated number of proteins that match the query in start position 9 for

---

This function determines the number of proteins that for a given protein id bucket (PIB$_k$) and a given start position bucket (SPB$_i$) contain P$_1$ in SPB$_i$ and P$_2$ in any subsequent start position bucket (for the same protein id bucket PIB$_k$).

$Distinct\_Bucket$(PIB$_k$, SPB$_i$, P$_1$, P$_2$, Gap, i)

{

int P$_1$_count = number of P$_1$ in PIB$_k$ and SPB$_i$ (from histogram);

int P$_2$_count;

// need to be aware of the last possible start position
// that occurs in the given position bucket (ith bucket)
int SPB$_i$_end = (i × NumPosPerBucket);

// also need to be aware of the first possible start position that occurs in SPB$_i$
int SPB$_i$_start = ((i - 1) × NumPosPerBucket) + 1;

// also need to calculate the first and last possible start positions in each
// of the subsequent start position buckets, SPB$_j$
int SPB$_j$_start, SPB$_j$_end;
double sum = 0;

// calculate for each of the following position buckets
for (int j= i+1; j < NumPosBuckets + 1; j++) {
    SPB$_j$_end = (j × NumPosPerBucket);
    SPB$_j$_start = ((j - 1) × NumPosPerBucket) + 1;

    // take gaps and predicate lengths into account
    if (SPB$_j$_start <= SPB$_i$_end + P$_1$.end + Gap.end) {
        if (SPB$_j$_end >= SPB$_i$_start + P$_1$.start + Gap.start) {
            sum += P$_2$_count (number of P$_2$ in PIB$_k$ and SPB$_i$ from histogram);
        }
        else { j = NumPosBuckets + 1; }
    }
}
double result = (P$_1$_count × sum)/NumProtPerBucket
return result;

}

Fig. 11.4. Distinct bucket configuration algorithm pseudocode.

the given protein id bucket is $(n_{p1} \times n_{p2})/100$. To get the total estimate for the start position bucket SPB$_1$, we integrate all the possible start positions. In our actual estimates we also factor the lengths of the predicates into the analysis. Figure 11.5 gives the pseudocode for the same bucket configuration algorithm.

Histogram analysis. Next we examine the accuracy of the complex histogram as well as its space and time efficiency. Figure 11.6 tests the accuracy of these complex histogram estimates by comparing the actual number of proteins that match a given query with the estimated number.

This function determines the number of proteins that for a given protein id bucket (PIB_k) and a given start position bucket (SPB_i) contain both P_1 and P_2 in the correct order with the specified gap between them.

Same_Bucket(PIB_k, SPB_i, P_1, P_2, Gap)
{
// *if P_1 and the Gap are longer than the bucket, then no matches will occur*
if (P_1.start + Gap.start) >= NumPosPerBucket { return 0; }

P_1_count = number of P_1 in PIB_k and SPB_i (from histogram);
P_2_count = number of P_2 in PIB_k and SPB_i (from histogram);

// *P_2 cannot start before the minimum range of P_1 and Gap have occurred*
int length = P_1.start + Gap.start;
double sum = 0;

for (int j = 0; j < NumPosPerBucket - length; j++) {
sum += ((NumPosPerBucket - j - length)/NumPosPerBucket)
× (P_2_count/NumProtPerBucket)
}

double result = (sum × P_1_count)/NumPosPerBucket;
return result;
}

Fig. 11.5. Same bucket configuration algorithm pseudocode.

The query tested is a three-predicate query in which the gap, or middle predicate, is varied to produce different query result selectivities. The results from the dataset of 248,375 proteins show that the histogram estimates are accurate to within approximately 80% of the actual result size. This degree of accuracy is sufficient for the optimizer's needs, as only a general idea of the selectivity is required by the cost functions and heuristics.

Next we analyze the time required to compute these estimates. For a histogram to be practical, this estimation time must be small. We performed this cardinality estimation on several seven-predicate queries with varying segment selectivities. Each of the queries has four nongap predicates that are alternated with three gap predicates. For each query we ran the cardinality estimation using two, three, and four of the nongap predicates and recorded the estimation time for each. For the two-predicate trials the two most highly selective predicates are used in the estimation; the same rule is applied in the three-predicate cases where the three most selective predicates are utilized. All four of the nongap predicates are used for the four-predicate trials. The data set used for this test consists of 56,000 proteins and 1,100,000 segments; the protein and segment tables were 56 and 66 MB in size, respectively. Figure 11.7 contains the execution time results of these cardinality estimations.

The results in Figure 11.7 show that the estimation time is small when the two or three most highly selective predicates are used to calculate

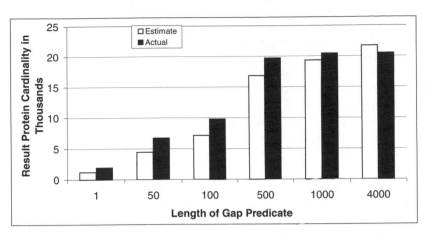

Fig. 11.6. Complex histogram accuracy, three-predicate query - {<l 15 15><? 0 X><h 24 24>}, varied gap predicate.

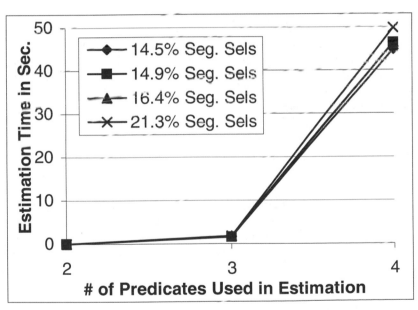

Fig. 11.7. Cardinality estimation time for seven-predicate queries with varied segment selectivities.

the estimations. With four-predicate estimations, however, the calculation time will probably surpass the query evaluation time, as validated in the experimental section because the number of calculations required is factorial in the number of query predicates and start position buckets. We also find in analyzing the accuracy of the estimations that adding the third and fourth

predicates to the estimation does not significantly improve the accuracy found
by only using two query predicates.

Thus, based on this empirical evidence, in our implementation we look
only at the two or three most highly selective predicates for estimation
purposes. In choosing to use the two most highly selective predicates over two
random query predicates, we ensure that the estimated query result space
is reduced as much as possible. Calculating the individual query predicate
selectivities to determine the two most highly selective predicates is very
efficient when the simple histogram techniques described in Section 11.5.1
are used.

In the current implementation we create the complex histogram
immediately following the loading of the segment table. The complex
histogram takes 22 seconds to load and requires 5.8 MB of disk space, which
is only 1% of the size of the segment table.

11.5.3 Heuristic Cutoff Method

Periscope's query optimizer has two different methods for determining the
most efficient query plan, a heuristic cutoff method and a cost formula
method. Both utilize the basic and complex histogram techniques described
for determining segment and result selectivities. The heuristic cutoff method,
which is simpler and less detailed, is the default technique in our current
implementation, although the cost formula technique can be turned on with
a simple flag option.

The heuristic cutoff process arose from our early experimentation with
the four query evaluation methods, in which we found that each query plan
performs differently for different queries depending on the selectivities of the
query predicates and the cardinalities of the results. Further analysis of these
performance trends allowed us to form some guidelines for choosing one query
plan over the other based on the selectivity values. These guidelines then were
translated into an algorithm that uses heuristic cutoff values to determine the
most efficient plan. The cutoff values vary from system to system and should
be established on each system through initial testing; they may also be tuned
during further experimentation stages. Figure 11.8 contains the pseudocode
for the heuristic cutoff algorithm.

The actual query optimization process using this method happens as
follows. The basic histogram is used to determine the segment selectivities
of all the nongap predicates in the query and the complex histogram is used
to calculate the result protein selectivity. These results are input into the
heuristic cutoff algorithm, which is then evaluated, and the optimal plan is
returned. The system then uses this method to evaluate the query.

Variables
Sel$_1$ - *selectivity of first query predicate*
Sel$_{MHSP}$ - *selectivity of most highly selective predicate*
Sel$_{Result}$ - *selectivity of the result (estimated using complex histogram)*
Sorted_Sel$_i$ - *selectivity of the ith most highly selective predicate*
n - *number of nongap query predicates*

Example Cutoff Values
CSPCutoff - .1% TableCutoff - 10% ResultCutoff - 50% SumCutoff - 10%

Cutoff Heuristic Algorithm
if (Sel$_1$ < CSPCutoff) { plan = CSP; }
else if (Sel$_{MHSP}$ > TableCutoff) { plan = SSS; }
else if (Sel$_{Result}$ > ResultCutoff) { plan = ISS; }
else {
plan = MISS;

// *sort nongap query predicates by selectivity with Scl$_{MHSP}$ first,*
//*store in Sorted_Sel list*
sel_sum = 0;
for (int i = 1; i <= n; i++) {
sel_sum += Sorted_Sel$_i$;
if (sel sum > SumCutoff) { miss_number = i - 1; i = n + 1; }
else if (i == n) { miss_number = n; }
}
}
return plan (and optionally, miss_number)

Fig. 11.8. Heuristic cutoff algorithm.

11.5.4 Cost Formula Method

The second method Periscope's query optimizer has for determining the most efficient query plan is the cost formula method. In this method, cost formulas are used to model the I/O time and CPU resources needed for each evaluation method for a given query. The underlying functionalities of each of the methods are similar and use a number of basic operations including index scans, table retrievals, and finite state machine matchings. We developed cost models, which are along the lines of the cost models in [356], for each of these basic operations. These models are then incorporated into the individual cost models for the various algorithms. The basic and complex histograms described in sections 11.5.1 and 11.5.2 are used to estimate the query segment selectivities and the result protein selectivity. Standard statistics such as table cardinalities and tuple sizes are maintained and used in the cost model. In addition, a number of system-dependent "fixed" constants, such as page sizes, maximum index fanout, and weighted I/O and CPU costs, are used. The following section describes the cost formulas for the basic operations that are used by the query evaluation algorithms, and section 11.5.4 details how these cost formulas are incorporated to estimate the overall cost of each algorithm.

Cost functions for basic operations. A description of the variables and constants that are used in the cost functions is given in Table 11.5.

Table 11.5. Description of the cost function variables and constants.

Variables	Description
$\|\|S\|\|$	Total number of segments
$\|\|P\|\|$	Total number of proteins
$\|S\|$	Number of segment table pages
$\|P\|$	Number of protein table pages
$\|IS\|$	Number of segment index pages
$\|IP\|$	Number of protein index pages
$\|Q\ Pages\|$	Total number of pages in all the temporary files for a given query
$Sel(P_i)$	Selectivity of the ith query predicate
$Sel(Q)$	Result selectivity of the query
N	Total number of temporary files for a given query (MISS number)
$WCPU$	Weighted time for a CPU operation
WIO	Weighted time for an I/O operation
$MaxProtFanout$	Maximum fanout of the protein id index
$MaxSegFanout$	Maximum fanout of the segment <type, len> index
$AvgLen$	Average length of a protein in amino acids
$SegSize$	Size of a segment tuple in the DBMS
$PageSize$	Size of a page in the DBMS
$MaxNumberStates$	Number of possible states the FSM can be in at one time

One of the basic operations of the query evaluation methods is the complex scan of a protein. The time required for this operation depends on the average length of the proteins, the maximum number of states the FSM can be in at a given time, and the result selectivity of the query. This cost, $Cost_{CS}$, is estimated as

$$Cost_{CS} = WCPU \times AvgLen \times MaxNumberStates \times Sel(Q)$$

A basic operation used by the SSS plan is the scan of the segment table to find matching segments. This includes both the scanning time as well as the time to compare the segments to the given query predicate. The function $Cost_{SegScan}$ calculates the time required for this basic operation. It assumes that each comparison can be done in one CPU cycle. The cost of this operation is

$$Cost_{SegScan} = WIO \times |S| + WCPU \times \|S\|$$

Another basic operation is the probing of the segment index to find matching segments; this operation also includes the retrieval of these segments. $Cost_{SegProbe}$ calculates the time required to probe the segment index and $Cost_{SegRet}$ calculates the time required to retrieve the matching segments. These functions require as input the selectivity of the given query predicate, $Sel(P_i)$. For $Cost_{SegProbe}$, the I/Os required include retrieving a fraction of the segment index pages as determined by the selectivity of the given query predicate. The CPU time required is the time to traverse to the leaf pages of the segment index to find the matching segments. Our calculation assumes that the height of the index is two. For $Cost_{SegRet}$, the I/O's required are to retrieve the data pages containing the matching segments. In the worst case, this is the maximum number of segment data pages; otherwise, it is determined by the number of matching segments, denoted by $Sel(P_i) \times ||S||$. The costs for the segment probing and retrieving operation are

$$
\begin{aligned}
Cost_{SegProbe} =&(WIO \times |IS| \times Sel(P_i)) + (WCPU \times 2 \times Sel(P_i) \times \\
&||S|| \times log(MaxSegFanout)) \\
Cost_{SegRet} =&WIO \times min(|S|, Sel(P_i) \times ||S||)
\end{aligned}
$$

A related basic operation is the probing of the protein id index to find the matching protein ids; this operation also includes the retrieval of these proteins. The functions $Cost_{ProtProbe}$ and $Cost_{ProtRet}$ perform almost the same calculations as their corresponding segment functions described in the preceding paragraph. One difference occurs in the I/O portion of the $Cost_{ProtProbe}$ function, which calculates the I/Os required to retrieve the appropriate protein index pages. In the example segment case, the matching segments are found in one portion of the index, not randomly scattered throughout. The protein ids to be retrieved using the protein id index, however, although they are sorted, will not occur in one specific portion of the index but will instead be scattered throughout. Therefore, if the number of protein ids to be retrieved is greater than the number of protein id index pages, it is possible that all the index pages may need to be retrieved. This is accounted for in the $Cost_{ProtProbe}$ equation. The costs for the protein id probing and retrieving operations are

$$
\begin{aligned}
Cost_{ProtProbe} =&(WIO \times min(|IP|, Sel(P_i) \times ||S||)) + \\
&(WCPU \times 2 \times Sel(P_i) \times ||S|| \times log(MaxProtFanout)) \\
CostProtRet =&WIO \times min(|P|, Sel(P_i) \times ||S||)
\end{aligned}
$$

Another basic operation that is used by the MISS plans is the writing of temporary files. For each of the query predicates used in the MISS methods, the resulting matching segments must be sorted and written to temporary files. The function $Cost_{Write}$ calculates the time required to write one of these temporary files. (The time required for the sorting will be described later.) $Cost_{Write}$ is based on the number of segments to be written, which also depends on the selectivity of the given query predicate, $Sel(P_i)$. The number of segments to be written is multiplied by the storage size of a segment in the database storage manager and is divided by the size of a database page to determine the number of pages necessary for the temporary file. The cost for writing a temporary file is

$$Cost_{Write} = WIO \times Sel(P_i) \times ||S|| \times SegSize/PageSize$$

The merge of these temporary files is another basic operation that is used only by the MISS plans. The function $Cost_{Merge}$ calculates the I/O and CPU time necessary to merge the temporary files by protein id and start position. It requires as input the number of temporary files (or the MISS number), the total number of pages in these temporary files, and the selectivities of each of the corresponding query predicates. The only I/O cost incurred is the time to read each page in each temporary file, denoted as $|Q\ Pages|$. The CPU time is measured here for the worst case. In the average case each of the segments in each temporary file will have to be compared to each of the other segments in the other temporary files. Therefore, the CPU time can be found by computing the product of the number of segments in each temporary file. The number of segments in the ith temporary file is $Sel(P_i) \times ||S||$. The overall cost of the file merge, then, is

$$Cost_{Merge} = WIO \times |QPages| + WCPU \times \prod_{i=1}^{n}(Sel(P_i) \times ||S||)$$

The final basic operation involves sorting, either on the protein ids or on the segment type and lengths. Both sorts are implemented as quick sorts, which in general have an execution time of $O(m\ log\ m)$. In our cost formula m represents the number of segments being sorted, which depends on the selectivity of the query predicate used. The number of segments to be sorted is denoted by $Sel(P_i) \times ||S||$. The function $Cost_{Sort}$ calculates the time required to sort a set of segments; its equation is

$$Cost_{Sort} = WCPU \times Sel(P_i) \times ||S|| \times log(Sel(P_i) \times ||S||)$$

Cost functions for query plans. Now that we have examined the costs for each of the basic functionalities of the four query evaluation methods, we will look at how these basic operations are put together to formulate the overall query plan cost functions. The following cost formulas rely on the knowledge of the segment and result selectivities that are estimated using the two histograms described in sections 11.5.1 and 11.5.2. While they are not shown as inputs to the cost formulas that follow, it is assumed that they are available for use in the cost estimation. The cost for the CSP plan, $Cost_{CSP}$, is the easiest to calculate as it involves simply scanning the protein table and performing a complex scan for each protein:

$$Cost_{CSP} = WIO \times |P| \times ||P|| \times Cost_{CS}$$

The SSS method involves scanning the segment table to retrieve segments that match the most highly selective query predicate. These segments are then sorted by protein id and participate in an index probe of the protein id index to retrieve the actual proteins. A complex scan of the proteins may then be performed based on the number of predicates in the query. The cost formula for the SSS method, $Cost_{SSS}$, follows and assumes that the value for $Sel(P_i)$ that is used in the various basic operation formulas is the selectivity of the most highly selective predicate:

$$
Cost_{SSS} = \begin{cases}
\begin{aligned}
& Cost_{SegScan} + Cost_{Sort} + \\
& Cost_{ProtProbe} + Cost_{ProtRet} + \\
& (Sel(P_i) \times ||S|| \times Cost_{CS})
\end{aligned} & \begin{aligned} & \text{if number of query} \\ & \text{predicates} > 1 \end{aligned} \\
\\
\begin{aligned}
& Cost_{SegScan} + Cost_{Sort} + \\
& Cost_{ProtProbe} + Cost_{ProtRet}
\end{aligned} & \begin{aligned} & \text{if number of query} \\ & \text{predicates} == 1 \end{aligned}
\end{cases}
$$

The ISS method involves probing the segment index to retrieve segments that match the most highly selective query predicate. These segments are also sorted by protein id and participate in an index probe of the protein id index to retrieve the actual proteins. A complex scan of the proteins may then be performed based on the number of predicates in the query. The cost formula for the ISS method, $Cost_{ISS}$, follows and assumes that the value for $Sel(P_i)$ that is used in the various basic operation formulas is the selectivity of the most highly selective predicate:

$$
Cost_{ISS} = \begin{cases}
\begin{aligned}
& Cost_{SegProbe} + Cost_{SegRet} + \\
& Cost_{Sort} + Cost_{ProtProbe} + \\
& Cost_{ProtRet} + (Sel(P_i) \times \\
& ||S|| \times Cost_{CS})
\end{aligned} & \begin{aligned} & \text{if number of query} \\ & \text{predicates} > 1 \end{aligned} \\
\\
\begin{aligned}
& Cost_{SegProbe} + Cost_{SegRet} + \\
& Cost_{Sort} + Cost_{ProtProbe} + \\
& Cost_{ProtRet}
\end{aligned} & \begin{aligned} & \text{if number of query} \\ & \text{predicates} == 1 \end{aligned}
\end{cases}
$$

The MISS method is more complicated because multiple probes of the segment index are performed; their results are written to temporary files and then merged before participating in the protein index probe. A complex scan of the proteins may then be performed if the MISS number, n, is less than the total number of predicates in the query. When calculating the cost of the MISS plan, $Cost_{MISS}$, care must be taken in specifying the selectivities that are used by the various basic operations. Both the formulas $Cost_{ProtProbe}$ and $Cost_{ProtRet}$ described in section 11.5.4 use a selectivity value, $Sel(P_i)$, to determine how many protein ids will need to be probed for and retrieved. In the SSS and ISS cost formulas, this selectivity value is simply the selectivity of the most highly selective predicate. In the MISS cost formula, however, this selectivity value represents how many protein ids are estimated to be returned from the merge of the n query predicates. $Cost_{MISS}$ assumes the worst when calculating this selectivity value by using the sum of the n segment selectivities. This is essentially saying that the number of protein ids that will be returned from the merge is the same as the total number of segments returned from the n segment index probes. Although this is an upper bound on the actual number of protein ids, it is still accurate enough to give a reasonable estimation. Therefore, it is assumed that the $Cost_{ProtProbe}$ and $Cost_{ProtRet}$ formulas will use the sum of the n query predicate selectivities as the required selectivity value. This same value also is used to determine the number of complex scans that may have to be performed at the conclusion of the MISS plan; this is shown in the $Cost_{MISS}$ formula that follows. The $Cost_{MISS}$ formula also assumes that the n predicates used in the n segment index probes, writes, and sorts are the n-most highly selective query predicates. The cost to evaluate a query using the MISS plan with a MISS number of n is

$$
Cost_{MISS} =
\begin{cases}
\begin{aligned}
&\sum_{i=1}^{n}(Cost_{SegProbe} + Cost_{SegRet} + \\
&Cost_{Sort} + Cost_{Write}) + \\
&Cost_{Merge} + Cost_{ProtProbe} + \\
&Cost_{ProtRet} + (Cost_{CS} \times \\
&\sum_{i=1}^{n}(Sel(P_i) \times \|S\|))
\end{aligned} & \begin{aligned}&\text{if number of query}\\&\text{predicates} > \text{N}\end{aligned} \\
\\
\begin{aligned}
&Cost_{SegProbe} + Cost_{SegRet} + \\
&Cost_{Sort} + Cost_{Write}) + \\
&Cost_{Merge} + Cost_{ProtProbe} + \\
&Cost_{ProtRet}
\end{aligned} & \begin{aligned}&\text{if number of query}\\&\text{predicates} == \text{N}\end{aligned}
\end{cases}
$$

The actual query optimization process for the cost formula method happens as follows. First the simple histogram is used to determine the segment selectivities of all the nongap predicates in the query and the complex histogram is used to calculate the result protein selectivity. These results are input into the different cost formulas along with the table and index information. Then the optimizer evaluates these cost formulas for the CSP, SSS, and ISS plans, as well as for each MISS(n) plan. Finally, the plan with the lowest cost formula is returned as the optimal plan and the system uses this method to evaluate the query.

11.6 Experimental Evaluation and Application of Periscope/PS²

In this section we first present an experimental performance evaluation of the tool Periscope/PS², which implements the query language and query-processing techniques described in the previous sections. Then we describe an actual case study demonstrating the use of this tool in practice.

11.6.1 Experimental Evaluation

In this section, we compare the algorithms presented in section 11.4. The goal of this section is to present a few key results for comparing the performance of the individual algorithms; more extensive performance comparison results can be found in [164]. For all the experiments presented in this section, the Periscope heuristic optimizer picks the cheapest plan.

Setup. We implemented our query evaluation techniques in Periscope, which is built on top of the SHORE storage manager from the University of Wisconsin [65]. SHORE provides various storage manager facilities including file and index management, buffer pool management, concurrency control, and transaction management. The commercial system runs on Windows; Periscope can run on either Linux or Windows. For these tests we used a Linux 2.4.13 machine with 896 MB of memory, a 1.70 GHz Intel Xeon processor, and a Fujitsu MAN3367MP hard drive with an SCSI interface and a 40 GB capacity. In both configurations SHORE is compiled for a 16 KB page size, and the buffer pool size is set to 64 MB. The numbers presented in this study are cold numbers, i.e., the queries do not have any pages cached in the buffer pool from a previous run of the system. Each of the experimental queries is run five times and the average of the middle three execution times is presented in the graphs.

In the following experimental sections, the abbreviations CSP, SSS, ISS, and MISS are all implicitly understood to be implementations of the four algorithms presented in section 11.4. When appropriate, the MISS plan will be shown for all possible numbers of query predicates from two to the total number of nongap predicates in the query, denoted by MISS(n), and the number of predicates used in the individual MISS plans will be referred to as the MISS number.

Dataset. To produce a dataset for our experiments, we first downloaded the entire PIR-International Protein Sequence Database. This database is a comprehensive, nonredundant protein database in the public domain and is extensively cross-referenced [434]. Since the PIR dataset contains only primary protein structures, we then used the Predator tool [134] to obtain predicted secondary structures. The final dataset consists of 248,375 proteins. Each protein has approximately 41 segments, which results in 10,288,769 segments. The Periscope protein and segment tables are 259 and 355 MB in size, respectively, while in the commercial system the protein table is 390 MB and the segment table is 425 MB.

Performance comparison. In this experiment we use a complex query with nine predicates in which both the result protein selectivity and the various segment selectivities stay constant. The variable in this experiment is the ordering of the nine query predicates. There are five nongap predicates, four of which have a segment selectivity of less than .03% (S) and one of which has a segment selectivity of 7% (L). The result protein selectivity is fixed at less than .1% by varying the four gap predicates, which are inserted between every two nongap predicates. Figure 11.9 shows the results of this experiment in which the position of the large query predicate varies from last in the query to first.

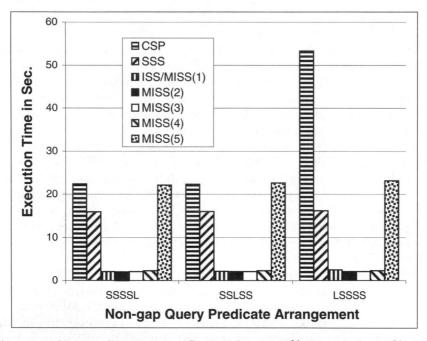

Fig. 11.9. Nine-predicate queries, S seg. sel. = ∼.03%, L seg. sel. = 7%, fixed result sel. < .1%.

The results show that the CSP method is the only method whose execution time varies widely depending on the position of the large predicate, which indicates that the execution time of the CSP method is very sensitive to the selectivity of the first predicate. Due to the nature of the FSM matching algorithm, queries in which the first predicate matches a large number of segments (like the L predicate) require the FSM to check more states. Because the leading predicate matches often, the number of times that the FSM tries to match the subsequent predicates increases, which in turn leads to longer CSP query execution times.

This test also highlights the importance of the MISS number on the performance of the MISS method. For MISS(2–4) the index is scanned for various subsets of the four most highly selective predicates, which in this test are all very selective. In MISS(5), however, the index is also scanned for the large (less selective) predicate. This adds considerable length to the execution time (recall that the MISS algorithm picks predicates based on their selectivities, not their physical order in the query).

The most efficient MISS number, in general, depends on the segment selectivities and the final protein selectivity. The MISS plan performs a number of index probes, which reduces the number of proteins to be retrieved and scanned. There is a balance between the costs incurred from performing these probes and the costs saved by the reduced number of proteins that must be retrieved. This balance is also influenced by the result protein selectivity in that the time required to perform an FSM scan of each protein is also affected by the result selectivity (we explore this effect in the next set of experiments). The cost of adding another query predicate to the MISS(k) plan is the sum of the time to scan the segment index for the $(k + 1)$th predicate, the time to sort the results by protein id and start position, and the time to add these results to the segment merge join. Evaluating the $(k + 1)$th predicate, however, will further cut down on the number of protein ids that emerge from the merge join, which in turn reduces the number of protein tuples that have to be retrieved. The reduction factor is roughly inversely proportional to the selectivity value of the added predicate. The time saved is the sum of the time to probe the id index for the eliminated proteins, the time to retrieve them, and the time to perform their complex scans. When this time saved is greater than the time incurred by adding the $(k + 1)$th predicate, the MISS number should increase to $k + 1$; otherwise it is more efficient to remain at k.

Another important point to notice in Figure 11.9 is that in many cases the optimal MISS method is *an order of magnitude faster* than the CSP method! This experiment demonstrates that having flexible query plans that adapt to query characteristics can significantly improve query response times. In addition, this experiment demonstrates that it is possible to evaluate these complex queries even on the large PIR dataset in few seconds, which allows the use of this tool in an interactive querying mode.

11.6.2 Example of Application of Periscope/PS^2

In this section, we outline an actual application of the Periscope/PS^2 tool. For this study, the PIR dataset described in section 11.6.1 was used.

Background. The common bioinformatic tasks for life scientists are to (1) infer functional similarity, (2) infer structural similarity, (3) identify domains or compact structural regions, and (4) estimate evolutionary relationships between the target under investigation and the database of characterized proteins [336]. A variety of computational tools are used for these activities; however, the majority relate to finding other database entries that share the primary sequence (i.e., the sequence of amino acids that make up the protein) similarity and assembling a multiple sequence alignment. From the alignment, complex judgments are made about the degree of "relatedness" and the functional implications of the array of potentially similar proteins [33]. If the target protein is not found to be similar in sequence to any other proteins with an experimentally determined atomic structure, the entire collection of aligned protein sequences are processed by secondary structure prediction algorithms and any common patterns noted. In some cases, the predicted secondary structure may lead to adjustments in the primary sequence alignment. This combined analysis often provides the basis for experimental decisions, for example, which example of an apparently conserved protein to clone and express, or to identify conserved regions that may bear directly on function and as such develop a "hit list" of potential point mutants. As currently practiced by working life scientists, bioinformatics analysis of proteins is not algorithmic but a complex heuristic process informed not only by the results of various database searches and computational analyses, but significantly by the individual scientist's experience and expert knowledge of the biology related to the query protein. That is, the analysis actually generates hypotheses: x is related to y, a and b share the same modular arrangement of domains, m and n are both DNA binding proteins. These hypotheses nucleate experimental work on the biological system in question.

In this context, Periscope has a variety of clear applications for life sciences researchers. A Periscope/PS^2 search string encodes local protein topology; as a consequence, the user is actually performing a direct arbitrary topological search against a database of protein topologies. To our knowledge, this search domain is unique to Periscope. Secondary structural pattern searches are of particular use for investigators studying protein structure and function. A distantly related protein or remote homolog (i.e., same superfamily but a different family; see [340] for definitions) will have low sequence similarity and perhaps escape the statistical significance threshold of the commonly used BLAST search heuristic [13]. Combining a Periscope/PS^2 search with a sequence-based search will augment the ability to select potential true homologs and perhaps analogs from unrelated proteins.

Actual example demonstrating the use of Periscope/PS^2. A standard BLASTP search performed on an experimentally uncharacterized protein, "conserved hypothetical protein from Streptococcus pyogenes" (GI 19745566), returns 14 hits. Buried in the search results in the low-confidence area, commonly referred to as the twilight zone [337], is the C3 exoenzyme of *C. botulinum* (E = 0.025), a bacterial exotoxin of considerable interest. Is our query protein truly related to the C3 exoenzymes, or is it a member of the larger superfamily of ADP-ribosylating enzymes? The sequence BLASTP query results are suggestive. The secondary structure of GI 19745566 was predicted using SAM-T99sec [213]. Based on the secondary structure prediction, several Periscope search strings were developed and used to query the combined nonredundant database described in section 11.6.1.

Table 11.6 shows the final query and a summary of each matching result. Among the Periscope results is the *C. botulinum* C3 exoenzyme (PDB code 1GZE). The uncharacterized query protein's predicted secondary structure closely matches the experimentally determined secondary structure of the C3 exoenzyme. Furthermore both proteins are of similar overall length, and the matching secondary structure spans 56% of the experimentally determined structure. Based on the combined results of low but detectable sequence similarity and common local topologies, we can hypothesize that the uncharacterized *S. pyogenes* open reading frame is a member of the ADP-ribosylating toxin family.

In summary, Periscope/PS^2 allows direct arbitrary topological searches through a simple declarative query language. This tool can (1) enhance the detection of remote protein homology, (2) provide topological information for the classification of a protein as a remote homolog vs. analog of the query, and (3) provide a unique tool for exploring loop insertions and deletions in known protein families.

11.7 Conclusions and Future Work

Knowing the secondary structure of proteins plays an important role in determining their function. Consequently, tools for querying the secondary structure of proteins are invaluable in the study of proteomics. This chapter addresses the problem of efficient and declarative querying of the secondary structure of protein datasets.

Our contributions include defining an expressive and intuitive query language for secondary structure querying and identifying various algorithms for query evaluation. To help a query optimizer pick among the various algorithms, we have also developed novel histogram techniques to determine segment and result selectivities. We have implemented and evaluated the proposed techniques in a native DBMS we have developed called Periscope. As the experimental results show, the system we have developed can query large protein databases efficiently, allowing scientists to interactively pose queries even on large datasets.

There are a number of directions for our future work, including developing algorithms to produce results in some ranked order. We would like to design a framework so that the metric used for ranking the answers can be easily customized by the user, as the model for ranking proteins is usually not fixed but instead varies among scientists and may also change frequently during the course of an experiment. The ranking metric may take into account

Table 11.6. Results for the query <h 4 6> <? 6 12> <h 6 10> <? 17 30> <h 10 15> <l 4 20> <h 7 20> <l 8 20> <h 10 20> <l 3 6> <e 4 8>.

Accession number	Description	Match
AD1845	5-methyltetrahydrofolate-homocysteine S-methyltransferase [imported] - *Nostoc* sp. (strain PCC 7120)	352 to 464
E86671	Lysine-tRNA ligase (EC 6.1.1.6) [imported] - *Lactococcus lactis subsp. lactis* (strain IL1403)	390 to 488
A38912	NAD-asparagine ADP-ribosyltransferase (EC 2.4.2.-) C3 precursor - *Clostridium botulinum* phage (strain CST)	53 to 171
E70838	Hypothetical protein Rv0200 - *Mycobacterium tuberculosis* (strain H37RV)	117 to 224
D90551	Lipoprotein [imported] - *Mycoplasma pulmonis* (strain UAB CTIP)	123 to 240
C89045	Protein B0238.6 [imported] - *Caenorhabditis elegans*	32 to 154
C82251	GGDEF family protein VC1029 [imported] - *Vibrio cholerae* (strain N16961 serogroup O1)	107 to 228
D69105	Coenzyme PQQ synthesis protein - *Methanobacterium thermoautotrophicum* (strain delta H)	139 to 252
T41643	Probable involvement in cytoskeletal organization - fission yeast (*Schizosaccharomyces pombe*)	1253 to 1361
1GZE	Chain A, structure of the *Clostridium botulinum* C3 exoenzyme (L177c mutant)	13 to 132
747707	Exoenzyme C3 [*Clostridium botulinum* D phage]	20 to 138
P15879	ARC3_CBDP mono-ADP-ribosyltransferase C3 precursor (exoenzyme C3)	53 to 171

additional information that is present in the protein, such as the positional probability of the secondary structure, which is currently one of the fields produced as output by protein structure predication tools. Techniques that have been developed for ranking results in other contexts may be applicable here [117, 118, 295].

Search engines for querying biological datasets often employ a query-by-example interface. In BLAST, one of the most popular search tools for searching genes and the primary structure of proteins, the system is presented with a query sequence and the search engine finds the best matches to the sequence. The input sequence is converted into a set of segments, and segment-matching techniques are employed to evaluate the query. While our work presented in this chapter focuses on segment-matching techniques for querying on the secondary structure of proteins, we would also like to explore the use of a query-by-example interface for our current system. Query-by-example interfaces require additional input that allows the user to influence the mapping of the query into segments to be matched. This additional input can be fairly complex; as an example the user may be allowed to specify a scoring matrix to assign weights to different portions of the input query. The "right" interface for specifying this mapping model can vary among users, and designing an interface that is both intuitive and easily specified is a challenge that we hope to undertake as part of our future work.

Experiments in the life sciences often involve querying a number of biological datasets in a variety of different ways. For example, a scientist may first query on the primary structure of a protein and then on the secondary structure or vice versa. Ideally a *combination* of both primary sequence and secondary structure searches will lead to more accurate protein function discovery [307]. This chapter addresses only the issue of efficient query-processing techniques for secondary structure. Hence the tool we have built would be an addition to the suite of biological querying tools that exist today. Developing techniques for integrated and declarative querying on all protein structures is an interesting database problem, and it is part of the long-term goal of the Periscope project.

Acknowledgments

This research has been supported in part by donations from IBM and Microsoft.

Chapter 12
Scalable Index Structures for Biological Data

Ambuj K. Singh

Summary

Bioinformatics holds great promise for the advancement of agriculture, public health, drug design, and the understanding of complex medical and biological systems. For this promise to come to fruition, new query algorithms, data models, and data management techniques need to be developed that can provide access to the varied kinds and large amounts of biological data. This chapter presents scalable index structures for DNA/protein sequences, protein structures, and pathways. After a brief discussion of sequences and structures, the focus shifts to pathways. Modeling of pathways along with their qualitative and quantitative characteristics is considered. Techniques that allow comparison and querying of static and dynamic aspects of pathways are presented.

12.1 Introduction

As a result of the recent spurt in high-throughput techniques, new biological data are being acquired at phenomenal rates. With such a rapid growth, biological datasets (e.g., sequence, structure, expression array, pathway) have become too large to be readily accessible for homology searches, mining, adequate modeling, and integrative understanding. Scalable and integrative tools that access and analyze these valuable data need to be developed.

The growth in genomic information has spurred increased interest in large-scale comparison of genetic sequences. Comparative genomics analyzes and compares the genetic material of different species to identify genes and predict their functions. Genome analysis involves comparison of sequences as large as the whole genome of a species. Phylogenetics and evolutionary studies are other important applications that use complete genetic information of different species. Shotgun assembly of a genome also requires rapid identification of overlaps across millions of reads. It is obvious that new approaches for large-scale comparison of sequences are needed.

Akin to the growth of sequence databases, protein structure databases, expression array databases, and pathway databases have also been recording significant growth. These databases are intrinsically different from sequence databases. For example, in the case of protein structures, common queries ask for the best alignment (in terms of root mean square distance) of a given query protein to a set of target database proteins. The desired alignment can be either global (i.e., using the entire query, say, for the construction of evolutionary trees or classifications), or local (i.e., using parts of the query to find the active sites). Computing the best alignment is an expensive step if it has to be repeated for all protein structures in PDB [39] or for the larger number of predicted structures [344]. Structure comparison defines the conserved core of a protein family by isolating the common ancestry of proteins. This allows one to go beyond the "twilight zone" where similarities cannot be detected reliably using sequence alone. Predicting the function of proteins *in silico* is of great benefit since it is faster and cheaper than experimentation. Characterization and understanding of protein structures is important for identification of functional motifs and understanding of principles underlying the structure and dynamics of proteins.

Just as sequence and structure databases require the design of new techniques to access, manipulate, and mine datasets, pathway databases require the design of new techniques for accessing, comparing, and manipulating large graphs. There is significant semantics attached to the nodes (substrates, products) and edges (enzymes, reaction control) of such graphs. There is also a need to identify common motifs such as modules in the constructed pathways and to make predictions based on them.

It is evident that the exploding growth in biological data is on a collision course with current database query techniques, presenting new challenges to biological database design. The new generation of databases have to (a) encompass terabytes of data, often local and proprietary, (b) answer queries involving large and complex inputs such as a complete genome, and (c) handle highly complex queries that access more than one dataset (e.g. "find all genes that are structurally similar to a given gene and express similarly over a specific DNA microarray dataset"; "find all proteins that are structurally similar to a given protein, used in a given pathway, and are expressed similarly as another given protein in a given experiment"; "find all protein pairs that are less than 30% similar at a sequence level, share a given active site, and cooccur in some metabolic pathway").

The complexity, heterogeneity, and quantity of biological data also raise difficult issues in the area of data models. Flexible and complex access to biological databases require a model in which information can be stored and queried. There is a need to develop new data models that are sensitive to the novel characteristics of biological data and queries. Current databases use ad hoc models that can answer a predefined set of queries and meet the requirements of only parts of the scientific community. The static information about the modeled entities (genes, protein structures, enhancers, and so on) needs to be coupled with dynamic information such as metabolic pathways, regulatory networks, feedback mechanisms, and protein trafficking. There is an increasing demand for the integration of diverse information sources in order to answer complex queries. For example, to understand the differences in protein localization between normal and diseased cells, one will need to understand and query the entire dynamic process, including abnormalities at the DNA level and events during transcription, translation, and signaling. Unified models will facilitate the integration of currently disparate data.

This chapter focuses on algorithms and index structure for comparative analysis of sequences, structures, and pathways. The discussion of index structures for sequences and structures is presented in the next two sections. In each case, existing techniques are surveyed and brief outline of a specific index structure is presented. Pathways are considered in detail in section 12.4. Structural comparison of pathways and analysis of their dynamic properties is presented. A brief summary appears in section 12.5.

12.2 Index Structure for Sequences

The dynamic programming solution to the problem of finding the best alignment between two sequences of lengths m and n runs in $O(mn)$ time and space [296, 374]. For large data and query sequences, this technique becomes infeasible in terms of both time and space. Many heuristics-based search tools have been developed to perform faster sequence alignment. These can be classified into two categories: (1) hash table based and (2) suffix tree based. Some of the important hash table based tools are FASTA [313], BLAST [12], PSI-BLAST [13], MegaBLAST [455], BL2SEQ [393], WU-BLAST [146], SENSEI [387], FLASH [61], PipMaker (BLASTZ) [355], BLAT [218], GLASS [32], and PatternHunter [260]. These techniques are similar in spirit: they construct a hash table on either the query sequence or the database sequence (or both) for all possible substrings of a prespecified size (say, l). The value of l varies for these search tools and for different applications (e.g., BLAST uses $l = 11$ for nucleotides and $l = 3$ for proteins.). They start by finding exactly matching substrings of length l using this hash table. In the second phase, these seeds are extended in both directions and combined, if possible, to find better alignments.

There are also a number of homology search tools based on suffix trees (see [160] for suffix tree algorithms). These include MUMmer [98], QUASAR [60], AVID [50], and REPuter [237]. QUASAR builds a suffix array on one of the sequences and counts the number of exactly matching seeds using this suffix array. If the number of seeds for a region is more than a prespecified threshold, this region is searched using BLAST. REPuter builds a suffix tree on a sequence to find repetitions on the fly. MUMmer builds the suffix tree on both sequences to find maximal unique matches. These tools are suitable for highly similar sequences. Extensive memory requirements make these tools infeasible for large-scale genome comparison.

12.2.1 Indexing Frequency Vectors

It is difficult to design scalable search techniques in the string space. We now present a scalable indexing technique [208, 210] that transforms the sequence information into a vector space with the help of *frequency vectors*, constructs an index structure on frequency vectors, and uses their proximity to identify homologous substrings.

Given a sequence over an alphabet, the number of occurrences of each symbol defines its frequency vector.   For example, if CTACCATTAG is a DNA sequence, then its frequency vector is $[3, 3, 1, 3]$ ([number of As, Cs, Gs, and Ts]). An edit operation alters a string by inserting, deleting, or modifying a symbol. An edit distance between strings can be defined as the minimum number of edit operations needed to transform one string into another. An analogous measure on frequency vectors, called *frequency distance*, can be defined. An edit operation on a string transforms its frequency vector to a neighboring point in the frequency space. The frequency distance $FD(u, v)$ between two frequency vectors u and v is the minimum number of edit operations required to transform some sequence with frequency vector u into some sequence with frequency vector v. Clearly, the frequency distance between two sequences is a lower bound of the edit distance between them. This property can be used for pruning a search for similar sequences as follows. For each sequence, its frequency vector is computed. Then, instead of computing the edit distance between two sequences, one can just compute their frequency distances, which requires less computation and main memory. If the frequency distance is above a certain threshold, then the edit distance must also be above the threshold; only if the frequency distance is below the threshold, do the actual sequences need to be compared.

To find similar regions between two genomes, one can compute for each genome the frequency vectors for all substrings that are of a certain length w, the *window size*. When frequency vectors from the two genomes are close together, it indicates that the corresponding regions of the sequence may align well. The choice of w affects the precision and speed of the technique: a larger w leads to faster computation at the risk of missing short alignments.

Multiple frequency vectors are aggregated into an index structure called the *F-index*. An F-index is a set of boxes (the number of dimensions is defined by the size of the alphabet). For a number of consecutive frequency vectors from the same sequence, their *minimum bounding rectangle (MBR)* is computed and added to the index. The maximum number of points in each box is termed its *box capacity*. For each box in the F-index, its lowest and

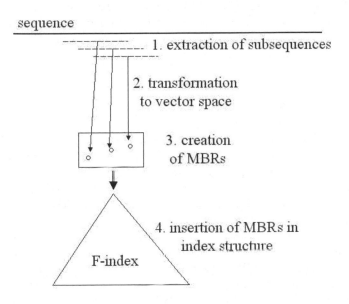

sequence

1. extraction of subsequences

2. transformation
   to vector space

3. creation
   of MBRs

4. insertion of MBRs in
   index structure

F-index

Fig. 12.1. Different steps of index creation: (1) extraction of subsequences of fixed length from database sequence, (2) transformation of information into vector space, (3) creation of an MBR, (4) insertion of MBR into F-index.

highest coordinates are stored. As the box capacity increases, the number of boxes in the F-index decreases. Thus, the memory usage of the F-index goes down. However, boxes containing more points are generally larger, leading to more false hits. The process of index creation is shown in Figure 12.1.

To align two genomes, an F-index is created on one of them and a number of points (frequency vectors) is extracted from the other. The next step is to find all box-point pairs that match. If a point and a box match, the corresponding parts of the two genomes have to be aligned. This is recorded in the *match table*, a data structure that provides a memory-efficient representation of which substrings must be aligned and is suitable for deciding on an optimal I/O schedule. The regions of good matches as identified by the match table can be used by an extensive sequence alignment tool such as BLAST [12, 13] for processing. This technique is termed MAP, for *match table based pruning*.

Experimental results show that MAP runs up to two orders of magnitude faster than BLAST without decreasing the output quality. Furthermore, MAP can work well even with small memory sizes. This drastic reduction in CPU and I/O cost makes homology searches viable on desktop PCs. The filtering and scheduling techniques of MAP can easily be used to speed up and reduce the memory requirements of any of the current local alignment tools. MAP also provides the user with a coarse-grained visualization of the similarity pattern between the sequences prior to the actual search.

12.3 Indexing Protein Structures

Structure is believed to be more closely related than sequences to the function of proteins. For example, the helical cytokines form an extended family that is undetectable by sequence comparison [143, 339, 385]. Structure comparison defines the conserved core of a protein family by isolating the common ancestry of proteins. This allows one to go beyond the "twilight zone" where similarities cannot be detected reliably using sequence alone. Predicting the function of proteins is a key challenge facing computational biology in the next few years as much of the benefits of molecular biology will depend on understanding the functions of proteins. The potential benefits of computationally predicting functions are huge since it is faster and cheaper than experimentation, thus allowing laboratories to focus on verifying computational predictions. Characterization and understanding of protein structures are important for identification of functional motifs and understanding of principles underlying the structure and dynamics of proteins.

The three-dimensional structure of protein adds insight into its molecular mechanism. For example, the structure of TATA box binding protein when it is bound to DNA not only provides information about molecular interactions but also clues about DNA binding specificity. Comparison of all structures against each other can produce new structural and functional relationships between proteins. Structure based distance measures are also critical in constructing accurate phylogenies [79, 141]. Structural alignment is also used during prediction of protein folding using threading.

The key problem in structural alignment of protein structures is to find the optimal correspondence between the atoms in two molecular structures. It is not known which molecules of one structure correspond to the other. This makes an exhaustive search intractable and heuristics are frequently employed. The root mean square distance (RMSD) between the aligned atoms of two aligned structures is typically taken as a measure of the quality of the alignment. Given a correspondence, the problem of optimally aligning two structures through rotation and translation so that the RMSD is minimized can be solved efficiently [20].

There are essentially three classes of algorithms for structural alignment of proteins [113]. The first set performs structural alignment directly at the level of constituent carbon atoms. The second group of algorithms first uses SSEs (secondary structure elements) to carry out an approximate alignment and then uses the carbon atoms. The final group of algorithms uses geometric hashing [433].

Direct alignment of carbon atoms. The simplest algorithm for structural alignment uses dynamic programming to find the optimal correspondence. Each iteration of the algorithm begins with a correspondence. The alignment that minimizes the RMSD metric for this correspondence is found. This alignment defines a score between pairs of atoms. Dynamic programming is then used to find a possibly better correspondence. The process is repeated until convergence. The *DALI* algorithm [182] uses distance matrices to align proteins. A distance matrix contains all pairwise distances between atoms of a molecule. Distance matrices of two molecules are compared to find regions of similar patterns of distances, which indicate similarities in their 3D structure. There are a number of other algorithms that align protein structures directly using carbon atoms [367, 394, 395].

Hierarchical algorithms. Hierarchical algorithms are based on rapidly identifying correspondences between small *similar* SSE fragments (consisting of 2 or 3 SSEs) across two proteins. The similarity of two fragments is defined using length and angle constraints. Fragments that do not align within a specified tolerance can be pruned away, saving considerable computation time. At the same time, fragment pairs that align well form the seed for extensive atom-level alignments. The *VAST* algorithm [263] begins with a bipartite graph: vertices on one side consist of pairs of SSEs from query protein and vertices on the other side consist of pairs of SSEs from target protein. An edge is placed between two pairs of SSEs if they can be aligned well. A maximal clique is found in this bipartite graph; this defines the initial SSE alignment. This initial alignment is extended to carbon atoms by Gibbs sampling. A nice feature of the VAST program is its ability to report on the unexpectedness of the match through P values. A P value is computed by considering the size of the match, the size of the proteins, and the quality of the alignment. A number of other algorithms in the literature are also based on hierarchical alignment [62, 368].

Geometric hashing based algorithms. Geometric hashing based algorithms choose a set of reference frames from each database protein and place the other elements of the protein in a 3D grid (hash table) based on each reference frame. Given a query protein, a set of reference frames is again chosen and the placement of elements of the query protein is computed for each query reference frame. Every time a query element and a database protein element share a grid cell, a vote is assigned to the database protein, its corresponding reference frame, and the query reference frame. A score is tallied for each database protein reference frame, and all reference frames with scores above a threshold number of votes are isolated. Each such reference frame defines an alignment between the query protein and a database protein. Further refinements can be carried out on this initial

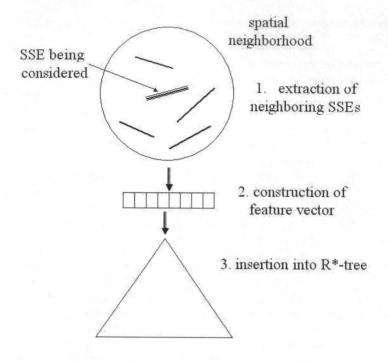

Fig. 12.2. Different steps of SSE index creation: (1) extraction of neighboring SSEs for a given SSE, (2) construction of a feature vector that summarizes the neighborhood of the SSE, (3) insertion of the feature in an R*-tree.

alignment. Implementations of this general idea differ in the way reference frames are defined. The 3D lookup algorithm [183] defines reference frames using SSEs. Another algorithm [303] defines reference frames based on carbon atoms.

12.3.1 PSI: Index Structure on SSEs

We present a hierarchical search and alignment [62] technique that is aimed at efficiently pruning proteins dissimilar to a given query. In this technique, each SSE is approximated by a vector, and triplets of spatially neighboring vectors are extracted. For each triplet, information on pairwise angle and distance (minimum and maximum) is extracted; this generates a feature vector of 9 dimensions. Later, an R*-tree [35] is built on this feature space using minimum bounding rectangles (MBRs). The process of index creation is shown in Figure 12.2.

The search technique finds high-quality seeds by pruning dissimilar proteins, achieved in four steps. First, similar triplets (of SSEs) of dataset proteins and query protein are found using the index structure. Second, a *triplet pair graph (TPG)* is constructed on the similar triplet pairs. The vertices of the TPG correspond to triplet pairs and the weight of a vertex indicates the *unexpectedness* of the match. An edge is placed between triplet pairs whose alignment is consistent. A *connected component* of the TPG corresponds to a set of triplet pairs that can be combined to find mappings of larger number of query SSEs to dataset SSEs. Next, *depth-first search* is used to find the *largest weight connected component (LWCC)* of the TPG. The LWCC of the TPG is the subset of the triplet pairs that results in the highest scoring mapping of query SSEs to dataset SSEs. Finally, a bipartite graph is constructed on the LWCC. This bipartite graph consists of SSEs from the query protein and the database protein that are present in the LWCC. The weight of an edge indicates the quality of the alignment of the corresponding pair of vertices. A largest weight graph matching algorithm [135] is run on the bipartite graph to find a mapping of the vertices in the two sets that maximize the sum of edge weights. The resulting mapping defines a seed (potential alignment) for each target protein.

Each seed defines an alignment of the query protein to a target protein in the feature space. A statistical model is developed to calculate the P value of a seed. This value corresponds to the probability of having a seed at least as good as the given one in a randomly distributed space. Therefore, small P values correspond to *unexpected* matches. Target proteins that have high P values are eliminated.

Experimental results show that this technique classified more than 88% of the superfamilies of SCOP [83] correctly. More than 98% of the results concurred with those of VAST [263]. The technique also ran 3 to 3.5 times faster than VAST's pruning step.

Protein structure search is an important emerging application. The explosive increase of the size of the structure databases and the complexity of the search algorithms make faster techniques imperative. Index-based techniques are an important step in this regard and will be widely applicable for homology searching, multiple structure alignment, and motif discovery.

12.4 Comparative and Integrative Analysis of Pathways

Biological pathways define how genes, proteins, RNAs, and other molecules cooperate and compete to produce the necessary functional activities in cells. They provide the glue for other diverse information sources such as DNA/protein sequences, protein structures, microarrays, and image data. Our current understanding of biological pathways is incomplete; there is much that is not known about causality, kinds of reactions, spatiotemporal localization of reactions and molecules, control and feedback mechanisms, and quantitative information on reaction rates and metabolite concentrations. Significant advances in understanding can come about by integrating information from multiple data sources, by comparing and contrasting the accumulated information, and by asking what-if questions of in silico models. Following are some of the current challenges in the analysis of pathways.

- Algorithms and tools for the comparison of qualitative pathway information. Logical and causal information about pathways is usually captured using graphs in which nodes and edges are annotated with genes, enzymes, and reactions. The comparison of these graphs is valuable for understanding the similarity of given pathways with respect to their inherent structure and evolutionary relationships.
- Algorithms and tools for the comparison of dynamic behavior of cell models. The simulation of quantitative pathway models results in spatiotemporal traces of attribute values (enzyme or metabolite concentration at different locations within a cell). The comparison of such traces can be informative for comparing the dynamic behavior of pathways. Integrating pathway simulations with other time-based data sources such as expression arrays and cellular images also requires the comparison of different time traces.
- New database tools for the integrated analysis of pathways. Inference of new pathways requires that multiple biological data sources such as DNA sequences, protein sequences, protein-protein interactions, protein structures, and expression arrays be integrated. To understand these diverse data sources, one needs to use a common data model and query distributed and heterogeneous information sources simultaneously.

A database of pathway models for different pathways can be used for comparative and integrative analysis. The behaviors of these pathways can be compared with each other, validated with observed data, and integrated with other information sources. With regard to the analysis of pathways, one needs to investigate the steady-state behavior as well as the dynamic response of a system. Both the time-invariant behavior and the time-variant behavior of pathways need to be considered.

Recent research on pathways has been quite broad, ranging across inference, simulation and modeling, predictions, and analysis. This section focuses on the comparative and integrative analysis of pathways. After a brief discussion of pathway models, the focus shifts to the comparison of pathways modeled as graph structures and the comparison of multidimensional time series that arise when time-variant properties of pathways are studied. The former concerns static properties of pathways while the latter concerns their dynamic properties.

12.4.1 Pathway Models

Organisms have elaborate mechanisms (pathways) for flow of energy, synthesis of complex biomolecules, degrading and transporting materials, sending and receiving signals, regulation of transcription and translation, homeostasis, apoptosis, and so on. Pathways form the basis for nearly every process of living things, from moving around and digesting food to thinking and reproducing. Not surprisingly, a large proportion of these chemical processes are shared across a wide range of organisms. Nearly all biochemical processes are catalyzed reactions, requiring the presence of enzymes, proteins obtained through transcription and translation from DNA. A complete understanding of the cellular pathways is the holy grail of systems biology since pathways determine the varied cellular functions and their breakdown leads to various diseases. The development of microarrays and high-throughput cellular imaging, which permit the measurement of spatiotemporal expression of proteins, have provided a major impetus to the study of pathways.

A large number of pathway databases are currently available, for example, KEGG [211], EcoCyc [212], and WIT [430]. KEGG (Kyoto Encyclopedia of Genes and Genomes) is a repository of metabolic pathways for organisms whose genome has been completely sequenced. It provides information on molecular and cellular biology in terms of interacting molecules or genes. EcoCyc was originally a database for metabolic pathways in *Escherichia coli*. It has been extended to other microbial organisms to produce the MetaCyc database. WIT (What Is There) is another database that provides information on gene and operon organization, as well as information about metabolic networks for completely or partially sequenced genomes.

There have been a number of approaches in recent years toward modeling the statics and dynamics of biological networks [96]. The modeling of the static and causal relationship is usually carried out through graph-based models of the kind represented in KEGG and EcoCyc. Quantitative information can be introduced into such graphs through conditional probabilities (*Bayesian networks* [133]). The on/off status of a gene in a regulatory network can be modeled through booleans in a *Boolean network* [379]. Here, the current state of the regulatory network is a set of booleans, and a set of connections (rules) defines the next state of the system. The 0-1 state of each gene has been generalized to a discrete number of states in a *logical network* [399]. A notion of *logical steady states* is defined to characterize the system when its logical state equals its *image*.

Differential equations of various kinds have been widely used to model biological pathways. Rate equations expressing the rate of change of a molecule as a function of the concentrations of other molecules can be written down [85, 412]. The dynamics of regulatory systems in terms of the feedback loops, negative (stable periodicity) or positive (multistationarity), can be studied [153, 398]. Other approaches include piecewise-linear differential equations [111], the use of power-law functions [347], and qualitative differential equations [9].

Differential equations presuppose that concentrations of molecules vary continuously and deterministically. These assumptions may not hold for small number of molecules and fluctuations in the timing of cellular events. This has led to discrete and stochastic models [19, 144]. Stochastic simulation results in a closer approximation to cellular events.

Hybrid petri nets [271], which extend petri nets by adding *continuous places and continuous transitions*, have also been used to model pathways. A *continuous place* holds a positive real number and a *continuous transition* fires continuously at a speed determined by the values in the *places*.

12.4.2 Structural Comparison of Pathways

To study the evolutionary relationships between organisms, various methods can be employed to estimate when the species may have diverged from a common ancestor. Having this information allows construction of a phylogenetic tree in which species are arranged on branches that link them according to their relationships and/or evolutionary descent. The most popular and frequently used methods of tree building can be classified into two major categories [297]: phenetic methods based on distances and cladistic methods based on characters. The former measures the pairwise distance/dissimilarity between two organisms and constructs the tree totally from the resultant distance matrix. In the latter, all possible evolutions are considered and trees are calculated using parsimony or likelihood methods.

Construction of phylogenetic trees for a group of taxa requires information about their evolutionary history. Historically, morphological data was used for inferring phylogenies. However, the abundance of DNA/RNA sequence data currently available for a variety of organisms has led to phylogenetic inference based on these data. Most of the phylogeny algorithms rely on multisequence alignments [125] of cautiously selected characteristic sequences: sequences of a single protein or single gene from each organism. Numerous studies have used the ribosomal RNA 16S sequences because these sequences exist in all organisms and are highly conserved [94, 264].

However, in spite of the success of rRNA taxonomy, the evolutionary relationships between major groups of organisms are still unclear because phylogenetic analysis of single gene sequences lacks the information to resolve deep branches in the tree. Further, misalignment and differing evolutionary rates can result in phylogenetic trees with the wrong topology. The recently completed sequences of several organism genomes provide an enormous amount of data with which to address some of these problems. Phylogenetic analysis can be made on sequence comparison of the whole genome [128] and can lead to more precise studies.

Understanding of evolutionary relationships may be further expanded by comparing higher level functional components among species, such as metabolic pathways. In such pathways, enzymes, substrates, and reactions are grouped conceptually into networks as part of a dynamic information processing system. A metabolic pathway is a series of individual chemical reactions in a living system that combine to perform one or more important functions (for example, glycolysis and the Krebs cycle). Comparative analysis of metabolic pathways in different genomes yields important information on their evolution. Studies in this direction focusing on individual pathways [129, 130] or on the entire metabolic repertoire [253] have been attempted. Such analysis allows us to measure evolution of complete processes (with different functional roles) rather than individual elements of a conventional phylogenetic analysis. We now present a *graph based* technique for constructing a phylogenetic tree using the structural information inherent in the metabolic pathways of different organisms [175].

Since evolutionary distance is based on the divergence of the elements constituting the pathways as well as the divergence of the network structure, both these aspects can be combined in formulating a measure of distance between pathways. The former aspect of the distance, i.e., the similarity between two enzymes, can be defined using the sequence similarity of the corresponding genes, or the structural similarity of the corresponding proteins or the similarity between EC (enzyme classification) numbers of the corresponding reactions [301].

Our graph based technique of building phylogenetic trees from metabolic pathways is divided into three steps [175]. In the first step, *enzyme graphs* are constructed for a specific metabolic pathway from a set of organisms under study. In the second step, a pairwise comparison of these enzyme-enzyme relational graphs is performed. This yields a distance matrix between organisms. Using this matrix, a phylogenetic tree is computed in the final step with the help of existing software packages. These steps are detailed next.

Step 1: Obtaining enzyme graphs from pathways. The collection of reactions and enzymes that an organism uses to achieve a certain metabolic function determines the architecture and topology of the pathway. Metabolic pathways can be abstracted as reaction graphs (networks) with specific graph-topological information, such as connectivity. A metabolic pathway can be represented as a directed reaction graph with substrates as vertices and directed edges denoting reactions (labeled by enzymes) between them. Given a pathway or a group of pathways, binary relations are extracted between enzymes [151, 304] as follows. Two enzymes are related if they activate reactions that share at least one chemical compound, either as substrate or as product. In the enzyme graph $G = (V, E)$ for a given pathway P, the vertex set V consists of the enzymes present in the pathway P and the set of edges E represent the enzyme-enzyme relationships of the pathway. There exists a directed edge from enzyme e_1 to enzyme e_2 in G if e_1 activates some reaction $A \to B$ (with substrate A and product B) and e_2 activates some reaction $B \to C$ (with substrate B and product C).

Step 2: Pairwise comparison of enzyme graphs. Each enzyme graph is specific to a particular organism. A distance matrix between organisms can be computed by performing a pairwise comparison of these graphs. This is achieved using a new algorithm that combines similarity between objects represented by the nodes of the graphs and information on the structure of the enzyme graph. To define a similarity measure between the enzymes of the graph, different notions of relationships between nodes of the graphs (enzymes) can be exploited: sequence similarity of the corresponding genes, structure similarity of the corresponding proteins, or similarity between EC numbers. In the experimental results presented later, the functional hierarchy of the EC number is used to express this similarity. Each of the enzymes that constitute a pathway is classified according to its EC number, which consists of four sets of numbers that categorize the type of the catalyzed chemical reaction. A similarity value of 1 is used if all four digits of the two reactions are identical, 0.75 if the three first digits are identical, 0.5 if the two first digits are identical, 0.25 if the first digit is identical, and 0 if the first digit is different. By applying a pairwise comparison to a set of N enzyme graphs, an $N \times N$ similarity matrix is obtained. The similarity scores ranging from -1 to 1 can be interpreted as distances by using the following formula: $distance = 1 - score$.

Step 3: Building phylogenetic trees from distance matrices. From the computed distance matrix, a phylogenetic tree is computed with hierarchical clustering algorithms. These cluster methods construct a tree by linking the least distant pair of taxa, followed by successively more distant taxa. There is a wide variety of distance based clustering algorithms constructed with differing sets of assumptions [342, 375]. The "neighbor joining" algorithm from the Phylip (phylogenetic inference) package [124] is used to construct the phylogenetic trees.

Experimental results. Phylogenetic trees were constructed for four different sets of organisms from the KEGG database. A set of 72 organisms was selected by removing all the organisms that have less than three enzymes present in the glycolysis and citric acid cycle pathways. A second set of 48 organisms was selected by collapsing all organisms with exactly the same network in the glycolysis and/or citric acid cycle pathways. The third set of 16 organisms is the set of organisms considered by Liao et al. [253]. The fourth set is composed of eight organisms, two of them from the eukaryota domain, two others from the archaea domain, and the remaining four from the bacteria domain. For this set of eight organisms, phylogenetic trees were derived by considering a set of pathways instead of a single pathway.

The effectiveness of this graph based technique was evaluated by comparing the produced phylogenies with the NCBI taxonomy (or the 16S rRNA based tree) and obtaining a single *similarity measure* (The *cousins* tool [450] was used for computing the similarity measures.). Comparative evaluation of the method was carried out by examining a few other existing techniques, comparing their trees again with the NCBI taxonomy to obtain their similarity measures, and comparing the similarity measures with those produced by the graph based technique. One specific alternative technique was the NCE (number of common enzymes) method motivated by [129, 130], in which phylogenetic analysis is based on the number of common enzymes between two organisms. Results are presented here only for 16 organisms based on the glycolysis pathway and 8 organisms based on carbohydrate metabolism. Complete names of organisms and other details can be found in [175].

Figure 12.3 depicts the phylogenetic tree computed for the set of 16 organisms. The two mycoplasma MGE and MGN have a low distance of 0.05 and are clustered together. They are the two closest organisms. The two archaea AFU and MJA are also grouped together. The similarity measures using the NCBI taxonomy as the standard are shown in Table 12.1 for the graph based technique and three others: NCE, 16S rRNA, and Liao et al.'s method. The graph based technique outperforms the other techniques. Table 12.2 shows the similarity measures when the 16S rRNA tree is chosen as the standard. The graph based technique again obtains the best alignment.

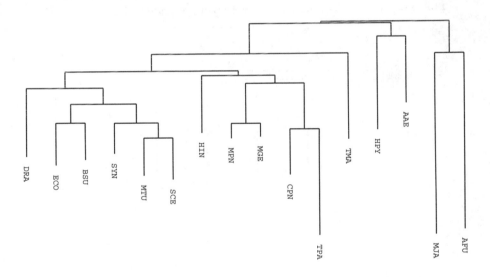

Fig. 12.3. Phylogenetic tree for 16 organisms built from comparison of glycolysis pathway.

Figure 12.4 depicts the phylogenetic trees computed for the set of 8 organisms based on carbohydrate metabolism. The two archaea AFU and MJA are the two closest organisms with a distance of 0.55. They form a separate cluster in the phylogenetic trees. The two eukaryota RNO and MMU

Table 12.1. Similarity measures based on the NCBI taxonomy for the glycolysis pathway.

Technique	Similarity
Graph based technique	0.26
NCE technique	0.19
16S rRNA	0.22
Liao et al.'s technique	0.16

Table 12.2. Similarity measures based on the 16S rRNA tree for the glycolysis pathway.

Technique	Similarity
Graph based technique	0.27
NCE technique	0.18
Liao et al.'s technique	0.12

are also grouped together with a distance of 0.78. RNO is the closest organism to MMU. In the tree, the bacteria CPE, HIN and LIN are clustered together. The proteobacteria NME has a lower distance to the archaea AFU and MJA. The three of them belong to the prokaryote classification.

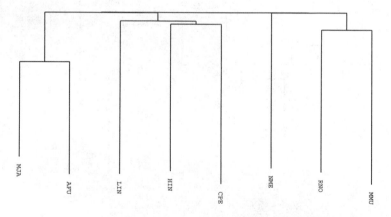

Fig. 12.4. Phylogenetic trees for the dataset of 8 organisms built from comparison of carbohydrate metabolism.

The presented graph based technique has considered only the reaction types of the enzymes in labeling the nodes and in defining node similarity. Further refinements of this general approach may lead to more accurate representation of pathways and distance computation. For example, the nodes can be labeled with enzymes and the sequence/structure distance between the corresponding proteins considered in defining distance measures. Another approach toward refining the graph representation is to include substrate information along with the reaction types to distinguish between enzymes that have the same EC number. Distance between substrates could be defined using their chemical formulae.

Computation of phylogenies is just one direct use of the pathways. Being closer to functions, pathway databases provide the clue for the ultimate understanding of biological processes. Supporting access to pathways as a part of a general query language requires a data model that is sophisticated enough to combine data from heterogeneous sources. Ultimately, one wants to answer queries such as "find all proteins that are structurally similar to protein X, which allosterically controls a reaction in the glycolysis pathway of organism Y" or "find all transcription regulatory elements for enzymes that occur in the heat shock pathway."

As the biological pathways and protein-protein interactions are understood better, the information about pathways will include qualitative as well as quantitative data. The qualitative data will include information on the enzymes, the substrates, and the type and direction of reactions. The quantitative data will include information on the rate of reactions, the flux, and the kind of control and feedback. One of the goals of systems biology is to characterize and classify the pathway information at a higher level. This is likely to result in the isolation of pathway modules or subgraphs. Providing mechanisms to store and query the pathway datasets qualitatively, quantitatively, and at multiple levels (viz. based on type of interacting modules) is one of the database challenges of the future. Aspects of quantitative comparison of pathways using their time-invariant and time-variant properties are considered next.

12.4.3 Analysis of Time-Invariant Properties of Pathways

Schilling et al. [351] propose the idea of *extreme pathways* for analyzing the inherent characteristics of pathways. They analyze the capabilities of a pathway in terms of its invariant fluxes: all possible concentrations of metabolites at steady state. A stoichiometric matrix S ($m \times n$, where m is the number of metabolites and n is the total number of inputs/outputs and reactions) is defined for each pathway. At steady state, the rate of change of metabolites is 0. This means that a steady-state flux v satisfies the equation $S.v = 0$. Furthermore, the constraints regarding internal fluxes (rates of reactions being positive) and external fluxes have to be met. All the steady-state solutions lie in the positive orthant of the null space of S, generating a convex polyhedral cone in a high-dimensional space. The extreme pathways are the rays of this cone, ensuring that each interior point can be written as their nonnegative combination. The solution for extreme pathways for a realistic pathway can be expensive, necessitating a division into subsystems that are analyzed separately and later combined under some integration constraints [352].

The formalization of extreme pathways raises a number of interesting questions: How does evolution change the extreme pathways? Is there a separate control mechanism for each extreme pathway so that the entire cone can be spanned? Answering these biological questions requires that research be carried out on the comparison of pathways based on their steady-state flux cones. Some relevant database queries may be as follows.

- Does a given flux lie within the cone of a specified pathway?
- What is the similarity of two pathways (defined by considering the volume of the intersected steady-state cones)?
- What are the most similar pathways for a given pathway (again using the steady-state flux cones)?

Clustering the steady-state cones or predicting a phylogenetic tree based on them may be other useful operations. Common to all the queries considered here is the computational complexity, in terms of both computation and memory. New index structures that can work in the high-dimensional spaces resulting from these cones need to be developed.

12.4.4 Analysis of Time-Variant Properties of Pathways

As discussed earlier, several formalisms exist for modeling pathways. No dominant technique has emerged that can represent the kinetics, the dynamics, and the logical structure of pathways. There are tradeoffs between the accuracy of the approaches and their scalability. This heterogeneity implies that mechanisms should be provided to integrate the simulations from different models. This integration needs to happen not only at a protocol level but also at a semantic level. One obvious mechanism to support semantic integration is through spatiotemporal traces. Since the different pathway models finally predict and produce spatiotemporal traces (concentrations of biomolecules at different spatial locations), comparisons across different models would be greatly enhanced if these traces could be stored in a database, queried, and compared with suitable metrics.

The pathway models produce spatiotemporal traces at different spatial and temporal resolutions. Some models assume a homogeneous environment throughout a cell, while the others can compartmentalize a cell into 3D boxes. Such compartmentalization is important for modeling the localization of processes in organelles and the transport of biomolecules. New techniques for querying and comparing spatiotemporal traces at varying spatial and temporal scales need to be developed.

There has been significant research on analysis of large collections of time-series data [219]. Both single-attribute and multiattribute traces have been considered. A multiattribute trace arises when different attributes of a cell are being quantitatively measured, possibly in different locations. Comparisons and analysis of the traces can be made in a number of ways: nearest-neighbor (NN) queries that ask for all trace points that are closest to a given query point under a defined distance metric, range queries that ask for all trace points that lie within a specified range, correlation queries that ask for all trace segments that are similar, and so on. We next present an index structure that allows flexible querying of single-attribute time series.

Accommodating queries of arbitrary lengths is important for time series databases. Such querying can be accomplished through summarizing a time series at multiple resolutions [209]. Let s be the longest time sequence in the database, where $2^b \leq |s| < 2^{b+1}$ for some integer b. Similarly, let the minimum possible length for a query be 2^a for some integer a where $a \leq b$. Let $s_1, s_2, ..., s_n$ be the time sequences in the database. As shown in Figure 12.5, the index structure stores a grid $T_{i,j}$, where i ranges from a to b and j ranges from 1 to n. Component $T_{i,j}$ is the set of MBRs for the jth sequence corresponding to window size 2^i. To obtain $T_{i,j}$, each sequence of length 2^j in sequence s_i is transformed using DFT or wavelets, and a few of the coefficients from the transformation are chosen. The transformed sequences are stored in MBRs. The ith row of the index structure is represented by R_i, where $R_i = \{T_{i,1}, ..., T_{i,n}\}$ corresponds to the set of all structures at resolution 2^i. Similarly, the jth column of the index structure is represented by C_j, where $C_j = \{T_{a,j}, ..., T_{b,j}\}$ corresponds to the set of all structures for the jth time sequence in the database. This index structure is called the *MR (multiresolution) index structure*.

The search technique partitions a given query sequence of arbitrary length into a number of subqueries at various resolutions available in the index structure. Later, it performs a *partial range query* for each of these subqueries on the corresponding row of the index structure. Given any query q of length $k \cdot 2^a$ and a range ϵ, there is a unique partitioning $q = q_1 q_2 ... q_t$, with $|q_i| = 2^{c_i}$ and $a \leq c_1 < ... < c_i \leq c_{i+1} \leq ... c_t \leq b$. This partitioning corresponds to the 1's in the binary representation of k. A search is first performed using q_1 on row R_{c_1} of the index structure. As a result of this search, a set of MBRs that lie within a distance of ϵ from q_1 is obtained. Using the distances to these MBRs, the value of ϵ for each MBR is refined, and a second query is made using q_2 on row R_{c_2} and the new value of ϵ. This process continues for the remaining rows $R_{c_3} ... R_{c_t}$.

A number of experiments were carried out on different kinds of queries and different datasets. The result for range queries on a stock market dataset are presented here, specifically precision and I/O overhead for four different techniques: sequential scan, prefix search (a competing method in which information is maintained at a fixed resolution [119]), longest prefix search (a variation of the MR index in which only a single row of the index structure is searched), and MR index. The precision and I/O (number of disk reads) is plotted as a function of the number of dimensions (coefficients) of the

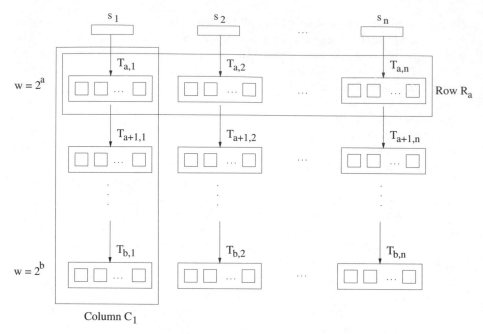

Fig. 12.5. Layout of the MR index structure.

transformed data set. Precision is defined as the number of MBRs that contain result sequences divided by the number of MBRs in the candidate set. Note that for sequential scan, the candidate set is the entire database. The performance of sequential scan is not affected by the number of dimensions.

According to the experimental results, the MR index and LPS (longest prefix search) perform better than prefix search and sequential scan for all dimensionalities. The precision of the MR index structure (Figure 12.6) is more than five times better than prefix search and more than 15 times better than sequential scan. Compared to LPS, the MR index is about 15% better for the stock market dataset. This improvement is an indication of the performance gain due to iterative reduction in query range as one traverses down the rows of the MR index structure. Figure 12.7 compares the I/O overhead of the four mentioned techniques. The number of page reads for the MR index structure is less than one-sixth of that for prefix search and less than one-seventh of that for sequential scan.

Flexible index structures such as the one discussed will be useful for comparing simulations resulting from different pathway models. Research on index structures for multiattribute time sequences and the use of other metrics besides Euclidean distance will also be relevant for the integration and comparison of pathway models.

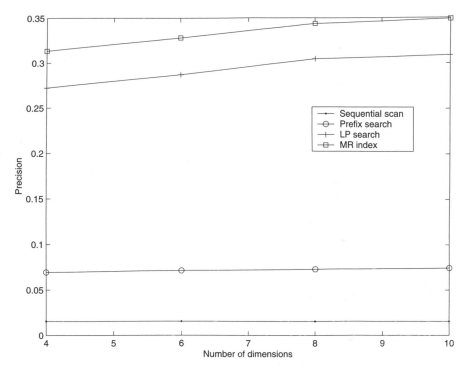

Fig. 12.6. Precision for the stock market dataset for different dimensionalities.

12.5 Conclusion

The challenges of indexing biological data are immense: accommodating different similarity metrics, use of statistics, novel data types, and support for integrative techniques. This chapter has presented a number of open problems and some specific instances of solutions.[1] However, many of the problems are open-ended and await the design of new methods. The recent emergence of bioimage data (e.g., confocal microscopy, AFM) also adds to the diversity of biological data. Finally, a word of caution regarding the development of new index structures. Although the complexity, heterogeneity, and size of biological datasets motivate faster access mechanisms, the question of quality of results remains paramount.

Acknowledgments

I would like to thank Tamer Kahveci and Orhan Camoglu for reading drafts of the chapter.

---

[1]Tools based on these methods can be accessed at http://bioserver.cs.ucsb.edu.

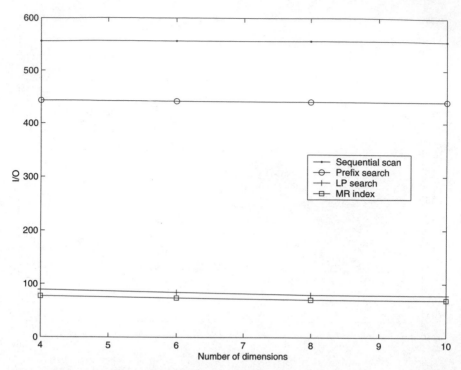

Fig. 12.7. Number of disk reads for the stock market dataset for different dimensionalities.

Glossary

AdaBoost. Classifier that uses an iterative procedure to manipulate the weights on the training data during training, putting more weight on the wrongly classified data points and less on the correctly classified ones at each iteration (chapter 8).

allele. Variant form of a marker or a gene (chapter 6).

amino acid. Any of a class of 20 molecules that are combined to form proteins in living things. The sequence of amino acids in a protein and hence protein function are determined by the genetic code (chapter 11).

bagging. Classifier that repeatedly selects a random sample from the training data and averages the outcomes of all trained classifiers (chapter 8).

base pair, kb, Mb. Two complementary bases forming a single step in a double-stranded DNA or RNA molecule. Length of DNA (or RNA) sequences is measured in base pairs (bp). 1 kb = 1000 bp, 1 Mb = 1000 kb (chapter 6).

CD tagging. Molecular biology technique that introduces a DNA sequence (the CD cassette) into genomic DNA (usually via a genetically engineered retroviral vector) so that if the CD cassette is inserted into an intron of a gene, the gene will generate a chimeric protein containing a unique protein sequence inserted into the original protein sequence (most frequently used to tag proteins with a fluorescent probe such as green fluorescent protein, GFP) (chapter 8).

classification. Tree where taxa are represented by nodes labeled by taxon name and taxon rank (chapter 10).

classifier ensemble. Macroclassifier that combines the outcomes from more than one base classifier (chapter 8).

clustering. Algorithm that groups points together based on some distance or similarity metric (chapter 3).

consensus tree. Tree summarizing the information in common to two or more trees (chapter 10).

crossover. Reciprocal breakage and reunion of two homologous chromosomes. Before reunion the partial chromosomes exchange partners (chapter 6).

DNA. Deoxyribonucleic acid; the molecules inside cells that carry genetic information and pass it from one generation to the next (chapter 11).

domain. Specific region or amino acid sequence in a protein associated with a particular function or corresponding segment of DNA (chapter 11).

feature normalization. Removing the magnitude divergence among features by expressing them on a common scale (chapter 8).

feature recombination. Producing a set of features by combining information from more than one input feature to generate each output feature (chapter 8).

feature reduction. Producing a smaller set of features from a feature set so that only informative and/or discriminative features are kept (chapter 8).

fluorescence microscopy. Method for imaging samples, such as cells, that measures the light emitted from fluorescent probes at one or more wavelengths upon exposure to light of another wavelength (chapter 8).

fractal dimensionality reduction (FDR). Feature selection method that employs fractal dimensionality as an approximation of the intrinsic dimensionality of a dataset and removes features that do not contribute to the intrinsic dimensionality of the dataset (chapter 8).

gene. Stretch of DNA coding for a protein (chapter 6).

gene mapping. Process that aims at locating a gene affecting a given trait (chapter 6).

genetic algorithm. Iterative, randomized feature selection algorithm that employs genetic operators to manipulate feature combinations so that the classification error is minimized at each iteration (chapter 8).

genotype. Genetic code of an individual. Specifically, a marker genotype is the pair of alleles at the marker, and a (phase-unknown) multimarker genotype is a vector of (unordered) allele pairs over the set of markers (chapter 6).

geometric graph. Graph representation that encodes both the connectivity between the vertices as well as the position of the vertices in the 3D space (chapter 9).

graph isomorphism. Two graphs g_1 and g_2 are isomorphic to each other if there is one-to-one mapping between all the vertices and edges of the graphs g_1 and g_2, which preserves the vertex as well as edge labels (chapter 9).

haplotype. Vector of alleles in a single chromosome over a set of markers or genes (chapter 6).

Haralick texture features. Numerical features that describe the relationship between the intensities of pixels and their adjacent pixels, calculated as various statistics of the gray-level co-occurrence matrix of the image (chapter 8).

identical by descent (IBD). Two alleles or haplotypes are identical by descent if they have been inherited from a common ancestor unchanged (chapter 6).

identical by state (IBS). Two alleles or haplotypes are identical by state if they cannot be distinguished by laboratory methods (chapter 6).

independent component analysis (ICA). Feature recombination method that retrieves statistically independent features from the original features (chapter 8).

information gain ratio. Variable that measures how much more information will be gained by splitting a decision tree node on a certain feature (chapter 8).

kernel principal component analysis. Feature recombination method that uses a kernel function to map the original features to a very high-dimensional space in which principal component analysis is conducted (chapter 8).

leaf. Node in a tree that has no descendants. Also called a *tip* or a *terminal node* (chapter 10).

linkage. Nearby markers tend to be transmitted together. Linkage between two loci can be expressed quantitatively by recombination fraction (the probability of the loci being separated in a single meiosis) (chapter 6).

linkage disequilibrium (LD). Nonrandom association of nearby markers (chapter 6).

Linnaean classification. Classification where each taxon has a rank. Taxa of lower rank are included in taxa of higher rank (chapter 10).

location proteomics. Subfield of proteomics directed toward objectively and systematically determining the subcellular location patterns of all proteins in a cell type or organism (chapter 8).

locus (pl. loci). Location of a specific marker or gene in a chromosome (chapter 6).

marker. Polymorphic stretch of DNA for which the variants can be reliably detected (chapter 6).

mixtures-of-experts. Classifier that employs the divide-and-conquer strategy to assign individual base classifiers to different partitions of a dataset (chapter 8).

Morgan, M, cM. Genetic distance between two loci measured in Morgans (M) is defined as the expected number of crossovers between the loci in a single meiosis. 1 M = 100 cM. On average, 1 cM is roughly 1 Mb, but the ratio varies a great deal throughout the genome (chapter 6).

multiple sequence alignment. Process of taking three or more sequences and forcing them to have the same length, maximizing their similarity (chapter 3).

nonlinear principal component analysis (NLPCA). Feature recombination method that employs a nonlinear transformation of the original features (chapter 8).

penetrance. Probability of the occurrence of a phenotype given a genotype (chapter 6).

phase. Parental origin of an allele, maternal or paternal (chapter 6).

phenocopy. Phenotype of nongenetic origin that appears similar to that of genetic origin (chapter 6).

phenotype. Observable characteristic or trait of an individual, e.g., presence of a disease (chapter 6).

phylogenetic classification. Classification where taxa have no rank but are instead defined with respect to a phylogenetic tree (chapter 10).

phylogeny. Tree depicting the evolutionary relationships between a set of objects, such as organisms or molecular sequences (chapter 10).

prevalence. Relative frequency of a disease in a population (chapter 6).

primary structure. Covalent backbone of a macromolecule. The order of subunits in a biological polymer, such as amino acids in a polypeptide or nucleotides in a molecule of DNA or RNA (chapter 11).

principal component analysis (PCA). Feature recombination method that employs a linear transformation of the original features (chapter 8).

protein. Molecule made up of amino acids that are needed for the body to function properly. Proteins are the basis of body structures such as skin and hair and of substances such as enzymes, cytokines, and antibodies (chapter 11).

protein contact map. Binary, symmetric matrix indicating for each pair of amino acids whether they are in contact or not (chapter 7).

protein pathway prediction. Given a protein amino acid sequence and its three-dimensional structure, determination of the time-ordered sequence of folding events, called the folding pathway, that leads from the linear structure to the tertiary structure (chapter 7).

protein structure prediction. Given a protein amino acid sequence (i.e., linear structure), determination of its three-dimensional folded shape (i.e., tertiary structure) (chapter 7).

protein subcellular location. Distribution of a protein inside a cell, especially with respect to organelles or other distinct subcellular structures (chapter 8).

protein subcellular location pattern. Statistical regularity of the subcellular location of a protein (chapter 8).

quantitative structure activity relations (QSAR). QSAR relates to the numerical properties of the molecular structure to its chemical activity; such numerical properties are usually computed via a mathematical model (chapter 9).

quaternary structure. Three-dimensional structure of a complex protein; especially refers to the way the polypeptide subunits fit together (chapter 11).

randomized tournament. Method of finding desired points in a metric space based on random choice of small subsets and elimination based on some metric (chapter 3).

rank. In a Linnaean classification each taxon has a rank, which specifies its order in the classification. Typically the highest rank is "kingdom" and the lowest rank is "subspecies" or "variety" (chapter 10).

recombination. Interchange of genetic material between two homologous chromosomes during meiosis. In humans recombination occurs by crossing over (chapter 6).

secondary structure. Folded, coiled or twisted shape a polypeptide or polynucleotide chain takes on when hydrogen bonds form between adjacent parts of the molecule (chapter 11).

secondary structure element (SSE). Either an α-helix or β-strand, two of the most common secondary structures found in proteins (chapter 7).

sequence alignment. Process of lining up two or more sequences to achieve maximal levels of identity (and conservation, in the case of amino acid sequences) for the purpose of assessing the degree of similarity and the possibility of homology (chapter 11).

stepwise discriminant analysis (SDA). Feature selection method that selects features that can separate different classes from one another while keeping each class as tightly packed as possible (chapter 8).

structure of chemical compound. Three-dimensional arrangement of atoms and bonds in a chemical compound (chapter 9).

subcellular location features (SLFs). Numbers derived from applying various functions to fluorescence microscope images in order to describe the properties of protein subcellular location patterns (chapter 8).

subcellular location tree (SLT). Rooted tree generated by hierarchical clustering of a set of images representing many different protein subcellular location patterns (chapter 8).

supertree. Tree that contains all the leaves found in a set of trees with overlapping leaves. For example, given the trees (a,(b,c)) and (b,(c,d)), the tree (a,(b,(c,d))) is a supertree (chapter 10).

supervised learning. Artificial intelligence subfield that deals with learning from previously characterized or described examples, especially by learning the relationship between independent attributes and a particular dependent attribute (chapter 8).

support vector machine (SVM). Generalized linear classifier that uses a kernel function to map the original dataset to a very high-dimensional space in which a maximum-margin linear classifier is found (chapter 8).

taxon. Unit of classification (chapter 10).

tertiary structure. Three-dimensional structure of a polypeptide in its normal, folded state (chapter 11).

topological graph. Graph representation that encodes the connectivity information between the vertices (chapter 9).

unsupervised learning. Artificial intelligence subfield that deals with grouping unlabeled data into statistically indistinguishable clusters (chapter 8).

wavelet features. Numerical features calculated from a discrete wavelet transformation of an image (chapter 8).

weighted SSE graph. Graph representation of a protein, where the vertices are the SSEs and the edges denote strength of interaction between the secondary structures (chapter 7).

Zernike moment features. Numerical features that measure the similarity of an image to each of a set of Zernike polynomials, calculated by convolving the image with each polynomial and taking the magnitude (chapter 8).

References

1. G. R. Abecasis, L. R. Cardon, and W. O. Cookson. A general test of association for quantitative traits in nuclear families. *American Journal of Human Genetics*, 66:279–292, 2000.
2. F. Achard, G. Vaysseix, and E. Barillot. XML, bioinformatics and data integration. *Bioinformatics*, 17:115–125, 2001.
3. R. M. Adams, B. Stancampiano, M. McKenna, and D. Small. Case study: a virtual environment for genomic data visualization. In *Proceedings of IEEE Visualization Conference*, pages 513–516, Boston, MA, 2002.
4. D. A. Agard. Optical sectioning microscopy: cellular architecture in three dimensions. *Annu. Rev. Biophys. Bioeng.*, 13:191–219, 1984.
5. R. Agrawal, H. Mannila, R. Srikant, H. T. T. Toivonen, and A. I. Verkamo. Fast discovery of association rules. In U. M. Fayyad, G. Piatetsky-Shapiro, P. Smyth, and R. Uthurusamy (eds.), *Advances in Knowledge Discovery and Data Mining*. AAAI Press, Menlo Park, CA, pages 307–328, 1996.
6. R. Agrawal and R. Srikant. Fast algorithms for mining association rules. In *Proceedings of 1994 Int. Conf. Very Large Data Bases*, pages 487–499, Santiago, Chile, 1994.
7. A. V. Aho, Y. Sagiv, T. G. Szymanski, and J. D. Ullman. Inferring a tree from lowest common ancestors with an application to the optimization of relational expressions. *SIAM Journal of Computing*, 10:405–421, 1981.
8. R. K. Ahuja, T. L. Magnanti, and J. B. Orlin. *Network Flows: Theory, Algorithms, and Applications*. Prentice Hall, Englewood Cliffs, NJ, 1993.
9. T. Akutsu, S. Miyano, and S. Kuhara. Inferring qualitative relations in genetic networks and metabolic pathways. *Bioinformatics*, 16(8):727–734, 2000.
10. B. Alberts, A. Johnson, J. Lewis, M. Raff, K. Roberts, and P. Walter. *Molecular Biology of the Cell*. Garland Science, New York, 2002.
11. D. O. V. Alonso, E. Alm, and V. Daggett. The unfolding pathway of the cell cycle protein p13suc1: implications for domain swapping. *Structure*, 8(1):101–110, 2000.
12. S. F. Altschul, W. Gish, W. Miller, E. W. Myers, and D. J. Lipman. Basic local alignment search tool. *Journal of Molecular Biology*, 215(3):403–410, 1990.
13. S. Altschul, T. Madden, A. Schaffer, J. Zhang, Z. Zhang, W. Miller, and D. Lipman. Gapped BLAST and PSI-BLAST: a new generation of protein database search programs. *Nucleic Acids Research*, 25(17):3389–3402, 1997.
14. A. An and Y. Wang. Comparisons of classification methods for screening potential compounds. In *Proceedings of IEEE International Conference on Data Mining*, 2001.
15. T. A. Andrea and H. Kalayeh. Applications of neural networks in quantitative structure-activity relationships of dihydrofolate reductase inhibitors. *Journal of Medicinal Chemistry*, 34:2824–2836, 1991.

16. C. Anfinsen and H. Scheraga. Experimental and theoretical aspects of protein folding. *Advances in Protein Chemistry*, 29:205–300, 1975.
17. M. Ankerst, M. Breunig, H.-P. Kriegel, and J. Sander. OPTICS: Ordering points to identify the clustering structure. In *Proceedings of ACM SIGMOD Int. Conf. Management of Data*, pages 49–60, Philadelphia, PA, 1999.
18. E. Arjas. Survival models and martingale dynamics. *Scandinavian Journal of Statistics*, 16:177–225, 1989.
19. A. Arkin, J. Ross, and H. A. McAdams. Stochastic kinetic analysis of developmental pathway bifurcation in phage-lambda infected *Escherichia coli* cells. *Genetics*, 149:1633–1648, 1998.
20. K. S. Arun, T. S. Huang, and S. D. Blostein. Least-squares fitting of two 3D point sets. *IEEE Transactions on Pattern Analysis and Machine Intelligence*, 9(5):698–700, 1987.
21. M. M. Astrahan, M. W. Blasgen, D. D. Chamberlin, K. P. Eswaran, J. Gray, P. P. Griffiths, W. F. King III, R. A. Lorie, P. R. McJones, J. W. Mehl, G. R. Putzolu, I. L. Traiger, B. W. Wade, and V. Watson. System R: relational approach to database management. *ACM Transactions on Database Systems*, 1(2):97–137, 1976.
22. J. C. Avise and G. C. Johns. Proposal for a standardized temporal scheme of biological nomenclature. *Proceedings of the National Academy of Sciences of the USA*, 96:7358–7363, 1999.
23. R. Baeza-Yates and B. Ribeiro-Neto. *Modern Information Retrieval*. Addison-Wesley, Reading, MA, 1999.
24. V. Bafna, S. Muthukrishnan, and R. Ravi. Comparing similarity between RNA strings. In *Proceedings of Combinatorial Pattern Matching Conference*, pages 1–14, 1995.
25. S. Bain, J. Todd, and A. Barnett. The British Diabetic Association—Warren Repository. *Autoimmunity*, 7:83–85, 1990.
26. P. Bajcsy. GridLine: automatic grid alignment in DNA microarray scans. *IEEE Transactions on Image Processing*, 13(1):15–25, 2004.
27. D. Baker. A surprising simplicity to protein folding. *Nature*, 405:39–42, 2000.
28. P. Baldi and S. Brunak. *Bioinformatics: The Machine Learning Approach* (2nd ed.). MIT Press, Cambridge, MA, 2001.
29. P. Baldi and G. W. Hatfield. *DNA Microarrays and Gene Expression*. Cambridge University Press, New York, 2002.
30. R. Ballew, T. Duncan, and M. Blasingame. Relational data structures for implementing thesauri. Museum Informatics Project, Information Systems and Technology, University of California, Berkeley, 1999.
31. B. R. Baum. Combining trees as a way of combining data sets for phylogenetic inference, and the desirability of combining gene trees. *Taxon*, 41:3–10, 1992.
32. S. Batzoglou, L. Pachter, J. P. Mesirov, B. Berger, and E. S. Lander. Human and mouse gene structure: comparative analysis and application to exon prediction. *Genome Research*, 10:950–958, 2000.
33. A. Baxevanis and D. Davison, editors. *Current Protocols in Bioinformatics*. John Wiley, New York, 2002.
34. A. Baxevanis and B. F. F. Ouellette. *Bioinformatics: A Practical Guide to the Analysis of Genes and Proteins* (2nd ed.). John Wiley, New York, 2001.
35. N. Beckmann, H.-P. Kriegel, R. Schneider, and B. Seeger. The R*-tree: an efficient and robust access method for points and rectangles. In *Proceedings of ACM SIGMOD International Conference on Management of Data*, pages 322–331, Atlantic City, NJ, 1990.
36. R. Bellman. On the approximation of curves by line segments using dynamic programming. *Communications of the ACM*, 4(6):284, 1961.

37. D. A. Benson, I. Karsch-Mizrachi, D. J. Lipman, J. Ostell, and B. A. Rapp. GenBank. *Nucleic Acids Research*, 28:15–18, 2000.
38. W. G. Berendsohn. The concept of "potential taxa" in databases. *Taxon*, 44:207–212, 1995.
39. H. M. Berman, J. Westbrook, Z. Feng, G. Gilliland, T. N. Bhat, H. Weissig, I. N. Shindyalov, and P. E. Bourne. The Protein Data Bank. *Nucleic Acids Research*, 28(1):235–242, 2000.
40. J. Bernardo and A. Smith. *Bayesian Theory*. John Wiley, New York, 1994.
41. M. R. Berthold and C. Borgelt. Mining molecular fragments: finding relevant substructures of molecules. In *Proceedings of IEEE International Conference on Data Mining*, 2002.
42. O. Bininda-Emonds, J. L. Gittleman, and M. A. Steel. The (super)tree of life. *Annual Review of Ecology and Systematics*, 33:265–289, 2002.
43. O. Bininda-Emonds and M. Sanderson. Assessment of the accuracy of matrix representation with parsimony analysis supertree construction. *Systematic Biology*, 50:565–579, 2001.
44. M. V. Boland, M. K. Markey, and R. F. Murphy. Classification of protein localization patterns obtained via fluorescence light microscopy. In *Proceedings of the 19th Annual International Conference of the IEEE Engineering in Medicine and Biology Society*, pages 594–597, 1997.
45. M. V. Boland, M. K. Markey, and R. F. Murphy. Automated recognition of patterns characteristic of subcellular structures in fluorescence microscopy images. *Cytometry*, 33:366–375, 1998.
46. M. V. Boland and R. F. Murphy. A neural network classifier capable of recognizing the patterns of all major subcellular structures in fluorescence microscope images of hela cells. *Bioinformatics*, 17:1213–1223, 2001.
47. N. B. Booth and A. F. M. Smith. A Bayesian approach to retrospective identification of change-points. *J. Econometr.*, 19:7–22, 1992.
48. M. Borodovsky and J. McIninch. GeneMark: parallel gene recognition for both DNA strands. *Comput. Chem.*, 17:123–133, 1993.
49. J. Bower and H. Bolouri. *Computational Modeling of Genetics and Biochemical Networks*. MIT Press, Cambridge, MA, 2001.
50. N. Bray, I. Dubchak, and L. Pachter. AVID: a global alignment program. *Genome Research*, 13(1):97–102, 2003.
51. A. Brazma, et al. Minimum information about a microarray experiment (miame)—toward standards for microarray data. *Nature Genetics*, 29:365–371, 2001.
52. S. P. Brooks. Markov chain Monte Carlo and its applications. *Statistician*, 47:69–100, 1998.
53. S. P. Brooks and P. Giudici. Diagnosing convergence of reversible jump MCMC algorithms. In J. Bernardo, J. Berger, A. P. Dawid, and A. F. M. Smith (eds.), *Bayesian Statistics* 6. Oxford University Press, Oxford, pages 733–742, 1999.
54. J. W. Brown. The ribonuclease P database. *Nucleic Acids Research*, 27:314, 1999.
55. M. Brudno, C. Do, G. Cooper, M. F. Kim, E. Davydov, E. D. Green, A. Sidow, and S. Batzoglou. Lagan and multi-lagan: efficient tools for large-scale multiple alignment of genomic DNA. *Genome Research*, 13(4):721–731, 2003.
56. S. Bryant. Evaluation of threading specificity and accuracy. *Proteins*, 26(2):172–185, 1996.
57. D. Bryant and M. Steel. Extension operations on sets of leaf-labeled trees. *Advances in Applied Mathematics*, 16:425–453, 1995.
58. C. B. Burge and S. Karlin. Finding the genes in genomic DNA. *Curr. Opin. Struct. Biol.*, 8:346–354, 1998.

59. C. J. C. Burges. A tutorial on support vector machines for pattern recognition. *Data Mining and Knowledge Discovery*, 2:121–168, 1998.

60. S. Burkhardt, A. Crauser, P. Ferragina, H.-P. Lenhof, E. Rivals, and M. Vingron. q-gram based database searching using a suffix array (QUASAR). In *Proceedings of International Conference on Research in Computational Molecular Biology*, pages 77–83, Lyon, 1999.

61. A. Califano and I. Rigoutsos. FLASH: fast look-up algorithm for string homology. In *Proceedings of International Conference on Intelligent Systems for Molecular Biology*, pages 56–64, 1993.

62. O. Camoglu, T. Kahveci, and A. K. Singh. Towards index-based similarity search for protein structure databases. In *Proceedings of IEEE Computer Society Bioinformatics Conference*, pages 148–158, 2003.

63. D. Cantone, G. Cincotti, A. Ferro, and A. Pulvirenti. An efficient algorithm for the 1-median problem. Technical Report, University of Catania, submitted 2003.

64. D. Cantone, A. Ferro, A. Pulvirenti, D. Reforgiato, and D. Shasha. Antipole indexing to support range search and *k*-nearest neighbor metric spaces. Technical Report, University of Catania, submitted 2003.

65. M. J. Carey, D. J. DeWitt, M. J. Franklin, N. E. Hall, M. L. McAuliffe, J. F. Naughton, D. T. Schuh, M. H. Solomon, C. K. Tan, O. G. Tsatalos, S. J. White, and M. J. Zwilling. Shoring up persistent applications. In *Proceedings of ACM SIGMOD International Conference on Management of Data*, Minneapolis, MN, 1994.

66. H. Carrillo and D. Lipmann. The multiple sequence alignment problem in biology. *SIAM Journal on Applied Mathematics*, 48:1073–1082, 1988.

67. K. R. Castleman. *Digital Image Processing*. Prentice Hall, Upper Saddle River, NJ, 1996.

68. T. Cech and B. Bass. Biological catalysis by RNA. *Annual Review of Biochemistry*, 55:599–629, 1988.

69. J. Celko. *SQL for Smarties: Advanced SQL Programming*. Morgan Kaufmann, San Francisco, 1995.

70. E. Chavez, G. Navarro, R. Baeza-Yates, and J. L. Marroquin. Searching in metric spaces. *ACM Computing Surveys*, 33(3):273–321, 2001.

71. D. Chen, O. Eulenstein, D. Fernández-Baca, and M. Sanderson. Supertrees by flipping. Technical Report TR02-01, Department of Computer Science, Iowa State University, 2001.

72. S. Chen, Z. Wang, and K. Zhang. Pattern matching and local alignment for RNA structures. In *Proceedings of International Conference on Mathematics and Engineering Techniques in Medicine and Biological Sciences*, pages 55–61, Las Vegas, Nevada, 2002.

73. X. Chen, M. Velliste, S. Weinstein, J. W. Jarvik, and R. F. Murphy. Location proteomics—building subcellular location trees from high resolution 3D fluorescence microscope images of randomly tagged proteins. In *Proceedings of the SPIE (International Society for Optical Engineering)*, pages 298–306, 2003.

74. Y. Cheng and G. Church. Biclustering of expression data. In *Proceedings of Int. Conf. on Intelligent Systems for Molecular Biology*, La Jolla, CA, 2000.

75. G. Chikenji and M. Kikuchi. What is the role of non-native intermediates of beta-lactoglobulin in protein folding? *Proceedings of the National Academy of Sciences of the USA*, 97:14273–14277, 2000.

76. K. Chou and Y. Cai. Using function domain composition and support vector machines for prediction of protein subcellular location. *Journal of Biological Chemistry*, 277:45765–45769, 2002.

77. J. Clarke, E. Cota, S. B. Fowler, and S. J. Hamill. Folding studies of immunoglobulin-like β-sandwich proteins suggest that they share a common folding pathway. *Structure*, 7:1145–1153, 1999.

78. C. Clementi, P. A. Jennings, and J. N. Onuchic. How native-state topology affects the folding of dihydrofolate reductase and interleukin-1beta. *Proceedings of the National Academy of Sciences of the USA*, 97(11):5871–5876, 2000.

79. M. Cline, G. Liu, A. E. Loraine, J. Cheng, R. Shigeta, G. Mei, D. Kulp, and M. A. Siani-Rose. Structure-based comparison of four eukaryotic genomes. In *Proceedings of Pacific Symposium on Biocomputing*, pages 127–138, 2002.

80. G. Collins, S. Y. Le, and K. Zhang. A new method for computing similarity between RNA structures. In *Proceedings of the 2nd International workshop on Biomolecular Informatics*, pages 761–765, Atlantic City, NJ, 2000.

81. R. Collobert, S. Bengio, and J. Mariéthoz. Torch: a modular machine learning software library. In *IDIAP (Dalle Molle Institute for Perceptual Artificial Intelligence) Research Report*, pages 2–46, 2002.

82. W. Colon and H. Roder. Kinetic intermediates in the formation of the cytochrome c molten globule. *Nature Structural Biology*, 3(12):1019–1025, 1996.

83. L. Conte, S. Brenner, T. Hubbard, C. Chothia, and A. Murzin. SCOP database in 2002: refinements accommodate structural genomics. *Nucleic Acids Research*, 30:264–267, 2002.

84. D. J. Cook and L. B. Holder. Graph-based data mining. *IEEE Intelligent Systems*, 15(2):32–41, 2000.

85. A. Cornish-Bowden. *Fundamentals of Enzyme Kinetics*. Portland Press, London, 1996.

86. F. Corpet and B. Michot. RNAlign program: alignment of RNA sequences using both primary and secondary structures. *Comput. Appl. Biosci.*, 10(4):389–399, 1995.

87. J. Cracraft. The seven great questions of systematic biology: an essential foundation for conservation and the sustainable use of biodiversity. *Annals of the Missouri Botanic Garden*, 89:127–144, 2002.

88. M. Crochemore, G. M. Landau, and M. Ziv-Ukelson. A sub-quadratic sequence alignment algorithm for unrestricted scoring matrices. In *Proceedings of the 13th Annual ACM-SIAM Symposium on Discrete Algorithms*, pages 679–688, 2002.

89. M. J. Daly, J. D. Rioux, S. F. Schaffner, T. J. Hudson, and E. S. Lander. High-resolution haplotype structure in the human genome. *Nature Genetics*, 29:229–232, 2001.

90. A. Danckaert, E. Gonzalez-Couto, L. Bollondi, N. Thompson, and B. Hayes. Automated recognition of intracellular organelles in confocal microscope images. *Traffic*, 3:66–73, 2002.

91. T. Dasu and T. Johnson. *Exploratory Data Mining and Data Cleaning*. John Wiley, New York, 2003.

92. T. Dasu, T. Johnson, S. Muthukrishnan, and V. Shkapenyuk. Mining database structure; or how to build a data quality browser. In *Proceedings of ACM SIGMOD Int. Conf. on Management of Data*, pages 240–251, Madison, WI, 2002.

93. W. H. E. Day. Analysis of quartet dissimilarity measures between undirected phylogenetic trees. *Systematic Zoology*, 35:325–333, 1986.

94. M. L. de Buyser, A. Morvan, S. Aubert, F. Dilasser, and N. El Solh. Evaluation of a ribosomal RNA gene probe for the identification of species and subspecies within the genus *Staphylococcus*. *J. Gen. Microbiol.*, 138:889–899, 1992.

95. L. Dehaspe, H. Toivonen, and R. D. King. Finding frequent substructures in chemical compounds. In *Proceedings of the 4th International Conference on Knowledge Discovery and Data Mining*, pages 30–36, 1998.

96. H. de Jong. Modeling and simulation of genetic regulatory systems: a literature review. *Journal of Computational Biology*, 9(1):67–103, 2002.

97. K. de Queiroz and J. Gauthier. Phylogenetic taxonomy. *Annual Review of Ecology and Systematics*, 23:449–480, 1992.

98. A. L. Delcher, S. Kasif, R. D. Fleischmann, J. Peterson, O. White, and S. L. Salzberg. Alignment of whole genomes. *Nucleic Acids Research*, 27(11):2369–2376, 1999.

99. M. Deshpande and G. Karypis. Automated approaches for classifying structure. In *Proceedings of the 2nd ACM SIGKDD Workshop on Data Mining in Bioinformatics*, 2002.

100. M. Deshpande and G. Karypis. Using conjunction of attribute values for classification. In *Proceedings of the 11th ACM Conference of Information and Knowledge Management*, pages 356–364, 2002.

101. B. Devlin and N. Risch. A comparison of linkage disequilibrium measures for fine-scale mapping. *Genomics*, 29:311–322, 1995.

102. B. Devlin, N. Risch, and K. Roeder. Disequilibrium mapping: composite likelihood for pairwise disequilibrium. *Genomics*, 36:1–16, 1996.

103. P. W. Diaconis and S. P. Holmes. Matchings and phylogenetic trees. *Proceedings of the National Academy of Sciences of the USA*, 95:14600–14602, 1998.

104. T. G. Dietterich. Ensemble methods in machine learning. In *Proceedings of the 1st International Workshop on Multiple Classifier Systems*, pages 1–15, Cagliari, Italy, 2000.

105. J. Ding, D. Berleant, D. Nettleton, and E. Wurtele. Mining MEDLINE: abstracts, sentences, or phrases. In *Proceedings of Pacific Symposium on Biocomputing*, pages 326–337, 2002.

106. A. Drawid and M. Gerstein. A Bayesian system integrating expression data with sequence patterns for localizing proteins: comprehensive application to the yeast genome. *Journal of Molecular Biology*, 301:1059–1075, 2000.

107. Dtp aids antiviral screen dataset. http://dtp.nci.nih.gov.

108. R. O. Duda, P. E. Hart, and D. G. Stork. *Pattern Classification*, 2nd ed. John Wiley, New York, 2000.

109. B. Dunkel and N. Soparkar. Data organization and access for efficient data mining. In *Proceedings of the 15th IEEE International Conference on Data Engineering*, pages 522–529, 1999.

110. R. Durbin, S. Eddy, A. Krogh, and G. Mitchison. *Biological Sequence Analysis: Probability Models of Proteins and Nucleic Acids*. Cambridge University Press, New York, 1998.

111. R. Edwards and L. Glass. Combinatorial explosion in model gene networks. *Chaos*, 10(3):691–704, 2000.

112. M. Eerola, H. Mannila, and M. Salmenkivi. Frailty factors and time-dependent hazards in modeling ear infections in children using Bassist. In *Proceedings of the XIII Symposium on Computational Statistics*, pages 287–292, 1998.

113. I. Eidhammer and I. Jonassen. Protein structure comparison and structure patterns—an algorithmic approach. Tutorial at the 9th International Conference on Intelligent Systems for Molecular Biology, 2001.

114. M. B. Eisen, P. T. Spellman, and P. O. Brown. Cluster analysis and display of genome-wide expression patterns. *Proceedings of the National Academy of Sciences of the USA*, 95:14863, 1998.

115. P. A. Evans. *Algorithms and Complexity for Annotated Sequence Analysis.* PhD thesis, University of Victoria, 1999.

116. W. J. Ewens and G. R. Grant. *Statistical Methods in Bioinformatics: An Introduction.* Springer-Verlag, New York, 2001.

117. R. Fagin. Combining fuzzy information from multiple systems. In *Proceedings of the 15th ACM SIGACT-SIGMOD-SIGART Symposium on Principles of Database Systems*, pages 216–226, Montreal, Canada, 1996.

118. R. Fagin, A. Lotem, and M. Naor. Optimal aggregation algorithms for middleware. In *Proceedings of the 20th ACM SIGACT-SIGMOD-SIGART Symposium on Principles of Database Systems*, Santa Barbara, CA, 2001.

119. C. Faloutsos, M. Ranganathan, and Y. Manolopoulos. Fast subsequence matching in time series databases. In *Proceedings of ACM SIGMOD International Conference on Management of Data*, pages 419–429, Minneapolis, MN, 1994.

120. M. Farach, T. M. Przytycka, and M. Thorup. On the agreement of many trees. *Information Processing Letters*, 55:297–301, 1995.

121. P. L. Farber. *Finding Order in Nature: The Naturalist Tradition from Linnaeus to E. O. Wilson.* Johns Hopkins University Press, Baltimore, MD, 2000.

122. U. Fayyad, G. Grinstein, and A. Wierse. *Information Visualization in Data Mining and Knowledge Discovery.* Morgan Kaufmann, San Francisco, 2001.

123. U. Fayyad, G. Piatetsky-Shapiro, and P. Smyth. From data mining to knowledge discovery: an overview. In *Proceedings of Int. Conf. Knowledge Discovery and Data Mining*, Portland, Oregon, 1996.

124. J. Felsenstein. Phylip— phylogeny inference package (version 3 2). *Cladistics*, 5:164–166, 1989. http://evolution.genetics.washington.edu/phylip.html.

125. J. Felsenstein. Phylogenies from molecular sequences: inferences and reliability. *Annual Reviews of Genetics*, 22:521–565, 1998.

126. D. Feng and R. F. Doolittle. Progressive sequence alignment as a prerequisite to correct phylogenetic trees. *Journal of Molecular Evolution*, 60:351–360, 1987.

127. W. M. Fitch and E. Margoliash. Construction of phylogenetic trees. *Science*, 155:279–284, 1967.

128. S. T. Fitz-Gibbon and C. H. House. Whole genome-based phylogenetic analysis of free-living microorganisms. *Nucleic Acids Research*, 27:4218–4222, 1999.

129. C. Forst and K. Schulten. Evolution of metabolisms: a new method for the comparison of metabolic pathways using genomic information. *Journal of Computational Biology*, 6:343–360, 1999.

130. C. Forst and K. Schulten. Phylogenetic analysis of metabolic pathways. *Journal of Molecular Evolution*, 52:471–489, 2001.

131. I. E. Frank and J. H. Friedman. A statistical view of some chemometrics regression tools. *Technometrics*, 35:109–148, 1993.

132. Y. Freund and R. E. Schapire. A decision-theoretic generalization of online learning and an application to boosting. *Journal of Computer and System Sciences*, 55:119–139, 1997.

133. N. Friedman, M. Linial, I. Nachman, and D. Pe'er. Using Bayesian networks to analyze expression data. *Journal of Computational Biology*, 7(3):601–620, 2000.

134. D. Frishman and P. Argos. Incorporation of non-local interactions in protein secondary structure prediction from amino acid sequence. *Protein Engineering*, 9(2):133–142, 1996.

135. H. N. Gabow. An efficient implementation of Edmonds' algorithm for maximum matching on graphs. *Journal of the ACM*, 23(2):221–234, 1976.

136. V. Ganti, J. Gehrke, and R. Ramakrishnan. Mining very large databases. *Computer*, 32:38–45, 1999.

137. H. Garcia-Molina, J. D. Ullman, and J. Widom. *Database Systems: The Complete Book*. Prentice Hall, Upper Saddle River, NJ, 2002.

138. J. Gasteiger, C. Rudolph, and J. Sadowski. Automatic generation of 3D atomic coordinates for organic molecules. *Tetrahedron Comp. Method*, 3:537–547, 1990.

139. T. A. Geissman. *Principles of Organic Chemistry*. W. H. Freeman and Company, San Francisco, 1968.

140. A. Gelman, J. B. Carlin, H. S. Stern, and D. B. Rubin. *Bayesian Data Analysis*. Chapman & Hall, New York, 1995.

141. M. Gerstein. A structural census of genomes: comparing bacterial, eukaryotic, and archaeal genomes in terms of protein structure. *Journal of Molecular Biology*, 274:562–576, 1997.

142. V. Gewin. All living things, online. *Nature*, 418:362–363, 2002.

143. J.-F. Gibrat, T. Madej, and S. H. Bryant. Surprising similarities in structure comparison. *Current Opinion in Structural Biology*, 6:377–385, 1996.

144. D. T. Gillespie. Exact stochastic simulation of coupled chemical reactions. *Journal of Physical Chemistry*, 81(25):2340–2361, 1977.

145. R. Gilmour. Taxonomic markup language: applying XML to systematic data. *Bioinformatics*, 16:406–407, 2000.

146. W. Gish. WU-blast. http://blast.wustl.edu.

147. H. C. J. Godfray. Challenges for taxonomy. *Nature*, 417:17–19, 2002.

148. P. A. Goloboff and D. Pol. Semi-strict supertrees. *Cladistics*, 18:514–525, 2002.

149. J. Gonzalez, L. Holder, and D. Cook. Application of graph based concept learning to the predictive toxicology domain. In *Proceedings of the Workshop on Predictive Toxicology Challenge at the 5th European Conference on Principles and Practice of Knowledge Discovery in Databases*, 2001.

150. B. Goryachev, P. F. MacGregor, and A. M. Edwards. Unfolding microarray data. *J. Computational Biology*, 8:443–461, 2001.

151. S. Goto, H. Bono, H. Ogata, W. Fujibuchi, T. Nishioka, K. Sato, and M. Kanehisa. Organizing and computing metabolic pathway data in terms of binary relations. In *Proceedings of the 2nd Pacific Symposium on Biocomputing*, pages 175–186, 1996.

152. O. Gotoh. An improved algorithm for matching biological sequences. *Journal of Molecular Biology*, 162:705–708, 1982.

153. J.-L. Gouze. Positive and negative circuits in dynamical systems. *Journal of Biological Systems*, 6(1):11–15, 1998.

154. L. Gravano, P. Ipeirotis, H. Jagadish, N. Koudas, S. Muthukrishnan, and D. Srivastava. Approximate string joins in a database (almost) for free. In *Proceedings of Int. Conf. Very Large Data Bases*, pages 491–500, Rome, Italy, 2001.

155. P. Green. Reversible jump Markov chain Monte Carlo computation and Bayesian model determination. *Biometrika*, 82(4):711–732, 1995.

156. M. Gribskov, R. Luethy, and D. Eisenberg. Profile analysis. *Methods in Enzymology*, 183:146–159, 1989.

157. R. Grossi and J. Vitter. Compressed suffix arrays and suffix trees with applications to text indexing and string matching. In *Proceedings of ACM Symposium on Theory of Computing*, pages 397–406, Crete, Greece, 2001.

158. S. R. Gunn. Support vector machines for classification and regression. Technical Report ISIS-1-98, Department of Electronics and Computer Science, University of Southampton, 1998.

159. S. W. Guo. Linkage disequilibrium measures for fine-scale mapping: a comparison. *Human Heredity*, 47:301–314, 1997.

160. D. Gusfield. *Algorithms on Strings, Trees and Sequences, Computer Science and Computation Biology*. Cambridge University Press, New York, 1997.

161. A. Gut. *An Intermediate Course in Probability*. Springer-Verlag, New York, 1995.

162. S. Guthe, M. Wand, J. Gonser, and W. Straer. Interactive rendering of large volume data sets. In *Proceedings of IEEE Visualization Conference*, pages 53–60, Boston, MA, 2002.

163. P. Guttorp. *Stochastic Modeling of Scientific Data*. Chapman & Hall, London, 1995.

164. L. Hammel and J. M. Patel. Searching on the secondary structure of protein sequences. In *Proceedings of the 28th International Conference on Very Large Data Bases*, pages 634–645, Hong Kong, China, 2002.

165. J. Han and M. Kamber. *Data Mining: Concepts and Techniques*. Morgan Kaufmann, San Francisco, 2001.

166. J. Han, J. Pei, and Y. Yin. Mining frequent patterns without candidate generation. In *Proceedings of ACM SIGMOD Int. Conf. Management of Data*, pages 1–12, Dallas, TX, 2000.

167. C. Hansch, P. P. Maolney, T. Fujita, and R. M. Muir. Correlation of biological activity of phenoxyacetic acids with hammett substituent constants and partition coefficients. *Nature*, 194:178–180, 1962.

168. C. Hansch, R. M. Muir, T. Fujita, C. F. Maloncy, and M. Streich. The correlation of biological activity of plant growth-regulators and chluromycetin derivatives with hammott constants and partition coefficients. *Journal of the American Chemical Society*, 85:2817–2824, 1963.

169. R. M. Haralick. Statistical and structural approaches to texture. *Proceedings of the IEEE*, 67:786–804, 1979.

170. J. Hartigan. Direct clustering of a data matrix. *J. American Stat. Assoc.*, 67:123–129, 1972.

171. T. Hastie, R. Tibshirani, and J. Friedman. *The Elements of Statistical Learning: Data Mining, Inference, and Prediction*. Springer-Verlag, New York, 2001.

172. W. K. Hastings. Monte Carlo sampling methods using Markov chains and their applications. *Biometrika*, 57:97–109, 1970.

173. D. K. Heidary, Jr., J. C. O'Neill, M. Roy, and P. A. Jennings. An essential intermediate in the folding of dihydrofolate reductase. *Proceedings of the National Academy of Sciences of the USA*, 97(11):5866–5870, 2000.

174. I. Herman, G. Melançon, and M. S. Marshall. Graph visualization in information visualization: a survey. *IEEE Transactions on Visualization and Computer Graphics*, 6:24–44, 2000.

175. M. Heymans and A. K. Singh. Deriving phylogenetic trees from the similarity analysis of metabolic pathways. In *Proceedings of International Conference on Intelligent Systems for Molecular Biology*, pages 138–146, Brisbane, Australia, 2003.

176. D. G. Higgins and P. M. Sharp. Clustal: a package for performing multiple sequence alignment on a microcomputer. *Gene*, 73:237–244, 1988.

177. D. G. Higgins, J. T. Thompson, and T. J. Gibson. ClustalW: improving the sensitivity of progressive multiple sequence alignment through sequence weighting, position-specific gap penalties and weight matrix choice. *Nucleic Acid Research*, 22:4673–4680, 1994.

178. D. G. Higgins, J. T. Thompson, and T. J. Gibson. Using Clustal for multiple sequence alignments. *Methods in Enzymology*, 266:383–402, 1996.

179. L. Hirschman, J. Park, J. Tsujii, L. Wong, and C. H. Wu. Accomplishments and challenges in literature data mining for biology. *Bioinformatics*, 18:1553–1561, 2002.

180. L. Holder, D. Cook, and S. Djoko. Substructure discovery in the Subduc system. In *Proceedings of the AAAI Workshop on Knowledge Discovery in Databases*, pages 169–180, 1994.

181. A. Holloway, R. K. van Laar, R. W. Tothill, and D. Bowtell. Options available—from start to finish—for obtaining data from DNA microarrays II. *Nature Genetics Supplement*, 32:481–489, 2002.

182. L. Holm and C. Sander. Protein structure comparison by alignment of distance matrices. *Journal of Molecular Biology*, 233:123–138, 1993.

183. L. Holm and C. Sander. 3D lookup: fast protein structure database searches at 90% reliability. In *Proceedings of the 3rd International Conference on Intelligent Systems for Molecular Biology*, pages 179–187, 1995.

184. S. Holmes. Statistics for phylogenies. *Theoretical Population Biology*, 63:17–32, 2003.

185. S. Hua and Z. Sun. Support vector machine approach for protein subcellular localization prediction. *Bioinformatics*, 17:721–728, 2001.

186. K. Huang and R. F. Murphy. Boosting accuracy of automated classification of fluorescence microscope images for location proteomics. *BMC Bioinformatics*, 5:78, 2004.

187. K. Huang, M. Velliste, and R. F. Murphy. Feature reduction for improved recognition of subcellular location patterns in fluorescence microscope images. In *Proceedings of the SPIE (International Society for Optical Engineering)*, pages 307–318, 2003.

188. X. Huang and A. Madan. CAP3: a DNA sequence assembly program. *Genome Research*, 9:868–877, 1999.

189. M. Hucka et al. The system biology markup language (SBML): a medium for representation and exchange of biochemical network models. *Bioinformatics*, 19:524–531, 2003.

190. J. P. Huelsenbeck and F. Ronquist. MRBAYES: Bayesian inference of phylogenetic trees. *Bioinformatics*, 17:754–755, 2001.

191. T. Ideker, T. Galitski, and L. Hood. A new approach to decoding life: systems biology. *Annu. Rev. Genomics Hum. Genet.*, 2:343–372, 2001.

192. J. R. Iglesias, G. Gupta, E. Pontelli, D. Ranjan, and B. Milligan. Interoperability between bioinformatics tools: a logic programming approach. In *Proceedings of the 3rd International Symposium on Practical Aspects of Declarative Languages*, pages 153–168, 2001.

193. A. Inokuchi, T. Washio, and H. Motoda. An apriori-based algorithm for mining frequent substructures from graph data. In *Proceedings of the 4th European Conference on Principles and Practice of Knowledge Discovery in Databases*, pages 13–23, Lyon, France, 2000.

194. Y. E. Ioannidis. Universality of serial histograms. In *Proceedings of the 19th International Conference on Very Large Data Bases*, Dublin, Ireland, 1993.

195. Y. E. Ioannidis and V. Poosala. Balancing histogram optimality and practicality for query result size estimation. In *Proceedings of ACM SIGMOD International Conference on Management of Data*, pages 233–244, San Jose, CA, 1995.

196. R. M. Jackson and R. B. Russell. The serine protease inhibitor canonical loop conformation: examples found in extracellular hydrolases, toxins, cytokines and viral proteins. *Journal of Molecular Biology*, 296(2), 2000.

197. R. A. Jacobs, M. I. Jordan, S. J. Nowlan, and G. E. Hinton. Adaptive mixtures of local experts. *Neural Computation*, 3:79–87, 1991.

198. H. V. Jagadish, O. Kapitskaia, R. T. Ng, and D. Srivastava. Multi-dimensional substring selectivity estimation. In *Proceedings of the 25th International Conference on Very Large Data Bases*, Edinburgh, Scotland, 1999.

199. H. M. Jamil, G. A. Modica, and M. A. Teran. Querying phylogenies visually. In *Proceedings of the 2nd IEEE International Symposium on Bioinformatics and Bioengineering*, pages 3–10, 2001.

200. J. W. Jarvik, S. A. Adler, C. A. Telmer, V. Subramaniam, and A. J. Lopez. Cd-tagging: a new approach to gene and protein discovery and analysis. *BioTechniques*, 20:896–904, 1996.

201. J. W. Jarvik, G. W. Fisher, C. Shi, L. Hennen, C. Hauser, S. Adler, and P. B. Berget. In vivo functional proteomics: mammalian genome annotation using cd-tagging. *BioTechniques*, 33:852–867, 2002.

202. P. A. Jennings, B. E. Finn, et al. A reexamination of the folding mechanism of dihydrofolate reductase from *Escherichia coli*: verification and refinement of a four-channel model. *Biochemistry*, 32(14):3783–3789, 1993.

203. R. I. Jennrich. Stepwise discriminant analysis. In *Statistical Methods for Digital Computers*, pages 77–95. John Wiley, New York, 1977.

204. T. Jiang, G.-H. Lin, B. Ma, and K. Zhang. The longest common subsequence problem for arc-annotated sequences. In *Proceedings of the 11th Annual Symposium on Combinatorial Pattern Matching*, pages 154–165, 2000.

205. T. Jiang, G. H. Lin, B. Ma, and K. Zhang. A general edit distance between RNA structures. *Journal of Computational Biology*, 9(2):371–388, 2002.

206. T. Joachims. *Advances in Kernel Methods: Support Vector Learning*. MIT Press, Cambridge, MA, 1999.

207. A. K. Joshi. An introduction to tree adjoining grammars. In *Mathematics of Language*, pages 87–115. John Benjamins, Amsterdam, 1987.

208. T. Kahveci and A. Singh. An efficient index structure for string databases. In *Proceedings of International Conference on Very Large Data Bases*, pages 351–360, Rome, Italy, 2001.

209. T. Kahveci and A. Singh. Variable length queries for time series data. In *Proceedings of International Conference on Data Engineering*, pages 273–282, Heidelberg, Germany, 2001.

210. T. Kahveci and A. K. Singh. MAP: searching large genome databases. In *Proceedings of Pacific Symposium on Biocomputing*, pages 303–314, 2003.

211. M. Kanehisa, S. Goto, S. Kawashima, and A. Nakaya. The KEGG databases at GenomeNet. *Nucleic Acids Research*, 30:42–46, 2002.

212. P. Karp, M. Riley, M. Saier, I. Paulsen, J. Collado-Vides, S. Paley, A. Pellegrini-Toole, C. Bonavides, and S. Gama-Castro. The EcoCyc database. *Nucleic Acids Research*, 30:56–58, 2002.

213. K. Karplus, C. Barrett, and R. Hughey. Hidden Markov models for detecting remote protein homologies. *Bioinformatics*, 14(10), 1999.

214. G. Karypis. CLUTO: a clustering toolkit. Technical Report 02-017, Department of Computer Science, University of Minnesota, 2002.

215. G. Karypis, E.-H. Han, and V. Kumar. CHAMELEON: a hierarchical clustering algorithm using dynamic modeling. *Computer*, 32:68–75, 1999.

216. L. Kaufman and P. J. Rousseeuw. *Finding Groups in Data: An Introduction to Cluster Analysis*. John Wiley, New York, 1990.

217. S. L. Kazmirski and V. Daggett. Simulations of the structural and dynamical properties of denatured proteins: the molten coil state of bovine pancreatic trypsin inhibitor. *Journal of Molecular Biology*, 277:487–506, 1998.

218. W. J. Kent. BLAT: The BLAST-like Alignment Tool. *Genome Research*, 12(4):656–664, 2002.

219. E. Keogh and T. Folias. The UCR time series data mining archive. http://www.cs.ucr.edu/~eamonn/TSDMA/index.html, Computer Science and Engineering Department, University of California at Riverside, 2002.

220. A. Khotanzad and Y. H. Hong. Rotation invariant image recognition using features selected via a systematic method. *Pattern Recognition*, 23:1089–1101, 1990.

221. R. D. King, S. Muggleton, R. A. Lewis, and M. J. E. Sternberg. Drug design by machine learning: the use of inductive logic programming to model the structure-activity relationships of trimethoprim analogues binding to dihydrofolate reductase. *Proceedings of the National Academy of Sciences of the USA*, 89:11322–11326, 1992.

222. R. D. King, S. H. Muggleton, A. Srinivasan, and M. J. E. Sternberg. Structure-activity relationships derived by machine learning: the use of atoms and their bond connectivities to predict mutagenecity by inductive logic programming. *Proceedings of the National Academy of Sciences of the USA*, 93:438–442, 1996.

223. R. D. King, A. Srinivasan, and L. Dehaspe. Warmr: a data mining tool for chemical data. *Journal of Computer Aided Molecular Design*, 15:173–181, 2001.

224. H. Kitano. Computational systems biology. *Nature*, 420:206–210, 2002.

225. H. Kitano. Systems biology: a brief overview. *Science*, 295:1662–1664, 2002.

226. J. Kittler and K. Messer. Fusion of multiple experts in multimodal biometric personal identity verification systems. In *Proceedings of IEEE International Workshop on Neural Networks for Signal Processing*, pages 3–12, 2002.

227. D. K. Klimov and D. Thirumalai. Multiple protein folding nuclei and the transition state ensemble in two-state proteins. *Proteins*, 43:465–475, 2001.

228. J. Klingner and N. Amenta. Case study: visualization of evolutionary trees. In *Proceedings of IEEE Information Visualization Conference*, pages 71–74, 2002.

229. S. Kotz, N. L. Johnson, and C. B. Read. *Encyclopedia of Statistical Sciences*. John Wiley, New York, 1981.

230. S. Kramer, L. De Raedt, and C. Helma. Molecular feature mining in HIV data. In *Proceedings of the 7th International Conference on Knowledge Discovery and Data Mining*, 2001.

231. U. Kressel. Pairwise classification and support vector machines. In B. Scholkopf, C. Burges, and A. J. Smola (eds.), *Advances in Kernel Methods - Support Vector Learning*. MIT Press, Cambridge, MA, 1999.

232. L. Kruglyak, M. J. Daly, M. P. Reeve-Daly, and E. S. Lander. Parametric and nonparametric linkage analysis: a unified multipoint approach. *American Journal of Human Genetics*, 58:1347–1363, 1996.

233. A. Kumar, K.-H. Cheung, P. Ross-Macdonald, P. S. R. Coelho, P. Miller, and M. Snyder. Triples: a database of gene function in *Saccharomyces cerevisiae*. *Nucleic Acids Research*, 28:81–84, 2000.

234. M. Kuramochi and G. Karypis. Frequent subgraph discovery. In *Proceedings of IEEE International Conference on Data Mining*, pages 313–320, San Jose, CA, 2001.

235. M. Kuramochi and G. Karypis. Discovering frequent geometric subgraphs. In *Proceedings of IEEE International Conference on Data Mining*, pages 258–265, 2002.

236. M. Kuramochi and G. Karypis. An efficient algorithm for discovering frequent subgraphs. *IEEE Transactions on Knowledge and Data Engineering*, 16(6), 2004.

237. S. Kurtz and C. Schleiermacher. REPuter—fast computation of maximal repeats in complete genomes. *Bioinformatics*, 15(5):426–427, 1999.

238. K. Kuwata, R. Shastry, H. Cheng, M. Hoshino, C. A. Bhatt, Y. Goto, and H. Roder. Structural and kinetic characterization of early folding events of lactoglobulin. *Nature*, 8(2):151–155, 2001.

239. J. C. Lam, K. Roeder, and B. Devlin. Haplotype fine-mapping by evolutionary trees. *American Journal of Human Genetics*, 66:659–673, 2000.

240. J. Lamping, R. Rao, and P. Pirioli. A focus+context technique based on hyperbolic geometry for visualizing large hierarchies. In *Proceedings of International Conference on Human Factors in Computing Systems*, pages 401–408, 1995.

241. C. Lauk. An attempt for a genus-level supertree of birds. BSc(Hons) project, DEEB, IBLS, University of Glasgow, 2002.

242. T. Lazardis and M. Karplus. New view of protein folding reconciled with the old through multiple unfolding simulations. *Science*, 278:1928–1931, 1997.

243. L. C. Lazzeroni. A chronology of fine-scale gene mapping by linkage disequilibrium. *Statistical Methods in Medical Research*, 10:57–76, 2001.

244. S. Y. Le, R. Nussinov, and J. V. Mazel. Tree graphs of RNA secondary structures and their comparisons. *Comput. Biomed. Res.*, 22:461–473, 1989.

245. S. Y. Le, J. Owens, R. Nussinov, J. H. Chen, B. Shapiro, and J. V. Mazel. RNA secondary structures: comparisons and determination of frequently recurring substructures by consensus. *Comput. Appl. Biosci.*, 5:205–210, 1989.

246. S. M. Le Grand and J. K. M. Merz. Rapid approximation to molecular surface area via the use of boolean logic look-up tables. *Journal of Computational Chemistry*, 14:349–352, 1993.

247. A. R. Leach. *Molecular Modeling: Principles and Applications*. Prentice Hall, Upper Saddle River, NJ, 2001.

248. A. M. Lesk. *Introduction to Bioinformatics*. Oxford University Press, New York, 2002.

249. C. Levinthal. Are there pathways for protein folding? *Journal of Chemical Physics*, 65:44–45, 1968.

250. B. Lewin. *Genes VII*. Oxford University Press, New York, 2000.

251. W. Li, J. Han, and J. Pei. CMAR: accurate and efficient classification based on multiple class-association rules. In *Proceedings of IEEE International Conference on Data Mining*, pages 369–376, 2001.

252. S. Liang, S. Fuhrman, and R. Somogyi. REVEAL, a general reverse engineering algorithm for inference of genetic network architectures. In *Proceedings of Pacific Symposium on Biocomputing*, pages 18–29, 1998.

253. L. Liao, S. Kim, and J.-F. Tomb. Genome comparisons based on profiles of metabolic pathways. In *Proceedings of the 6th International Conference on Knowledge-Based Intelligent Information and Engineering Systems*, Crema, Italy, 2002.

254. G.-H. Lin, B. Ma, and K. Zhang. Edit distance between two RNA structures. In *Proceedings of the 5th Annual International Conference on Computational Molecular Biology*, pages 200–209, 2001.

255. B. Liu, W. Hsu, and Y. Ma. Integrating classification and association rule mining. In *Proceedings of the 4th International Conference on Knowledge Discovery and Data Mining*, pages 80–86, 1998.

256. J. S. Liu and C. E. Lawrence. Bayesian inference on biopolymer models. *Bioinformatics*, 15(1):38–52, 1999.

257. V. Lombard, E. B. Cameron, H. E. Parkinson, P. Hingamp, G. Stoesser, and N. Redaschi. EMBL-Align: a new public nucleotide and amino acid multiple sequence alignment database. *Bioinformatics*, 18:763–764, 2002.

258. D. P. Lopresti and A. Tomkins. Block edit models for approximate string matching. *Theoretical Computer Science*, 181(1):159–179, 1997.

259. B. Ma, L. Wang, and K. Zhang. Computing similarity between RNA structures. *Theoretical Computer Science*, 276:111–132, 2002.

260. M. Ma, J. Tromp, and M. Li. PatternHunter: faster and more sensitive homology search. *Bioinformatics*, 18:1–6, 2002.

261. D. R. Maddison, D. L. Swofford, and W. P. Maddison. NEXUS: an extensible file format for systematic information. *Systematic Biology*, 46:590–621, 1997.

262. D. R. Maddison, W. P. Maddison, J. Frumkin, and K.-S. Schulz. The Tree of Life project: a multi-authored, distributed Internet project containing information about phylogeny and biodiversity. In H. Saarenmaa and E. S. Nielsen (eds.), *Towards a Global Biological Information Infrastructure: Challenges, Opportunities, Synergies, and the Role of Entomology*. European Environment Agency, Copenhagen, pages 5–14, 2002.

263. T. Madej, J.-F. Gibrat, and S. H. Bryant. Threading a database of protein cores. *Proteins: Structure, Function, and Genetics*, 23:356–369, 1995.

264. B. L. Maidak, J. R. Cole, T. G. Lilburn, C. T. Parker, P. R. Saxman, R. J. Farris, G. M. Garrity, G. J. Olsen, T. M. Schmidt, and J. M. Tiedje. The RDP-II (Ribosomal Database Project). *Nucleic Acids Research*, 29:173–174, 2001.

265. J. Mallet and K. Willmott. Taxonomy: renaissance or tower of babel. *Trends in Ecology and Evolution*, 18:57–59, 2003.

266. B. S. Manjunath and W. Y. Ma. Texture features for browsing and retrieval of image data. *IEEE Transactions on Pattern Analysis and Machine Intelligence*, 8:837–842, 1996.

267. B. Mann, R. Williams, M. Atkinson, K. Brodlie, A. Storkey, and C. Willimans. Scientific data mining, integration and visualization. In *Report of the Workshop on Scientific Data Mining, Integration and Visualization*, The E-Science Institute, Edinburgh, 2002.

268. H. Mannila and M. Salmenkivi. Finding simple intensity descriptions from event sequence data. In *Proceedings of the 7th ACM SIGKDD International Conference on Knowledge Discovery and Data Mining*, pages 341–346, 2001.

269. R. Mao, D. P. Miranker, J. N. Sarvela, and W. Xu. Clustering sequences in a metric space, the Mobios Project. Technical Report, University of Texas, Austin, 2003.

270. M. K. Markey, M. V. Boland, and R. F. Murphy. Towards objective selection of representative microscope images. *Biophys. J.*, 76:2230–2237, 1999.

271. H. Matsuno, R. Murakani, R. Yamane, N. Yamasaki, S. Fujita, H. Yoshimori, and S. Miyano. Boundary formation by notch signaling in *Drosophila* multicellular systems: experimental observations and gene network modeling by genomic object net. In *Proceedings of Pacific Symposium on Biocomputing*, pages 152–163, 2003.

272. M. S. McPeek and A. Strahs. Assessment of linkage disequilibrium by the decay of haplotype sharing, with applications to fine-scale genetic mapping. *American Journal of Human Genetics*, 65:858–875, 1999.

273. N. Metropolis, A. W. Rosenbluth, M. N. Rosenbluth, A. H. Teller, and E. Teller. Equation of state calculation by fast computing machines. *Journal of Chemical Physics*, 21:1087–1091, 1953.

274. D. P. Minaker. Metric-space indexes as a basis for scalable biological databases. *Omics: A Journal of Integrative Biology*, 7:57–60, 2003.

275. T. M. Mitchell. *Machine Learning*. WCB/McGraw-Hill, New York, 1997.

276. Y. Mok, C. Kay, L. Kay, and J. Forman-Kay. NOE data demonstrating a compact unfolded state for an sh3 domain under non-denaturing conditions. *Journal of Molecular Biology*, 289(3):619–638, 1999.

277. B. Morgenstern, K. Frech, A. Dress, and T. Werner. Dialign: finding local similarities by multiple sequence alignment. *Bioinformatics*, 14:290–294, 1998.

278. K. Morik, P. Brockhausen, and T. Joachims. Combining statistical learning with a knowledge-based approach—a case study in intensive care monitoring. In *Proceedings of International Conference on Machine Learning*, pages 268–277, 1999.

279. A. P. Morris, J. C. Whittaker, and D. J. Balding. Fine-scale mapping of disease loci via shattered coalescent modeling of genealogies. *American Journal of Human Genetics*, 70:686–707, 2002.

280. R. Mott, J. Schultz, P. Bork, and C. P. Ponting. Predicting protein cellular localization using a domain projection method. *Genome Research*, 12:1168–1174, 2002.

281. D. Mount. *Bioinformatics: Sequence and Genome Analysis*. Cold Spring Harbor Laboratory Press, Woodbury, NY, 2001.

282. S. Muggleton. Inverse entailment and Progol. *New Generation Computing*, 13:245–286, 1995.

283. S. Muggleton and L. De Raedt. Inductive logic programming: theory and methods. *Journal of Logic Programming*, 19:629–679, 1994.

284. S. H. Muggleton and C. Feng. Efficient induction of logic programs. In S. Muggleton (ed.), *Inductive Logic Programming*. Academic Press, London, pages 281–298, 1992.

285. T. Munzner. Exploring large graphs in 3D hyperbolic space. *IEEE Computer Graphics and Applications*, 18:18–23, 1998.

286. T. Munzner, F. Guimbretière, S. Tasiran, L. Zhang, and Y. Zhou. TreeJuxtaposer: scalable tree comparison using focus+context with guaranteed visibility. *ACM Transactions on Graphics*, 22(3):453–462, 2003.

287. M Muralikrishna and D. J. DeWitt. Equi-depth histograms for estimating selectivity factors for multi-dimensional queries. In *Proceedings of ACM SIGMOD International Conference on Management of Data*, Chicago, IL, 1994.

288. R. F. Murphy, M. V. Boland, and M. Velliste. Towards a systematics for protein subcellular location: quantitative description of protein localization patterns and automated analysis of fluorescence microscope images. In *Proceedings of the 8th International Conference on Intelligent Systems for Molecular Biology*, pages 251–259, 2000.

289. R. F. Murphy, M. Velliste, and G. Porreca. Robust classification of subcellular location patterns in fluorescence microscope images. In *Proceedings of IEEE International Workshop on Neural Networks for Signal Processing*, pages 67–76, 2002.

290. R. F. Murphy, M. Velliste, and G. Porreca. Robust numerical features for description and classification of subcellular location patterns in fluorescence microscope images. *Journal of VLSI (Very Large Scale Integrated) Signal Processing*, 35:311–321, 2003.

291. S. Muthukrishnan and S. Sahinalp. Approximate nearest neighbors and sequence comparison with block operations. In *Proceedings of ACM Symposium on Theory of Computing*, pages 416–422, Crete, Greece, 2001.

292. E. W. Myers and W. Miller. Optimal alignments in linear space. *Computer Applications in the Biosciences*, 4(1):11–17, 1988.

293. K. Nakai. Protein sorting signals and prediction of subcellular localization. *Adv. Protein Chem.*, 54:277–344, 2000.

294. L. Nakhleh, D. Miranker, F. Barbancon, W. H. Piel, and M. J. Donoghue. Requirements of phylogenetic databases. In *Proceedings of the 3rd IEEE Symposium on Bioinformatics and Bioengineering*, pages 141–148, 2003.

295. A. Natsev, Y.-C. Chang, J. R. Smith, C.-S. Li, and J. S. Vitter. Supporting incremental join queries on ranked inputs. In *Proceedings of the 28th International Conference on Very Large Data Bases*, Rome, Italy, 2001.

296. S. B. Needleman and C. D. Wunsch. A general method applicable to the search for similarities in the amino acid sequence of two proteins. *Journal of Molecular Biology*, 48:443–453, 1970.

297. M. Nei. Phylogenetic analysis in molecular evolutionary genetics. *Annual Review of Genetics*, 30:371–403, 1996.

298. C. Nishimura, S. Prytulla, H. J. Dyson, and P. E. Wright. Conservation of folding pathways in evolutionary distant globin sequences. *Nature Structural Biology*, 7(8):679–686, 2000.

299. K. C. Nixon and J. M. Carpenter. On the other "Phylogenetic Systematics." *Cladistics*, 16:298–318, 2000.

300. B. Nolting, R. Golbik, J. Neira, A. Soler-Gonzalez, G. Schreiber, and A. Fersht. The folding pathway of a protein at high resolution from microseconds to seconds. *Proceedings of the National Academy of Sciences of the USA*, 94(3):826–30, 1997.

301. Nomenclature Committee of the International Union of Biochemistry and Molecular Biology (NC-IUBMB). Enzyme nomenclature recommendations of the Nomenclature Committee of the International Union of Biochemistry and Molecular Biology on the nomenclature and classification of enzyme-catalysed reactions. http://www.chem.qmul.ac.uk/iubmb/enzyme/.

302. C. Notredame, D. G. Higgins, and J. Heringa. T-coffee: a novel method for fast and accurate multiple sequence alignment. *Journal of Molecular Biology*, 302:205–217, 2000.

303. R. Nussinov and H. J. Wolfson. Efficient detection of three-dimensional structural motifs in biological macromolecules by computer vision techniques. *Proceedings of the National Academy of Sciences of the USA*, 88:10495–10499, 1991.

304. H. Ogata, H. Bono, W. Fujibuchi, S. Goto, and M. Kanehisa. Analysis of binary relations and hierarchies of enzymes in the metabolic pathways. *Genome Informatics*, 7:128–136, 1996.

305. V. Ollikainen. Simulation techniques for disease gene localization in isolated populations. Technical Report A-2002-2, University of Helsinki, 2002.

306. P. Onkamo, V. Ollikainen, P. Sevon, H. T. T. Toivonen, H. Mannila, and J. Kere. Association analysis for quantitative traits by data mining: QHPM. *Annals of Human Genetics*, 66:419–429, 2002.

307. C. A. Orengo, A. E. Todd, and J. M. Thornton. From protein structure to function. *Current Opinion in Structural Biology*, 9(3), 1999.

308. R. D. M. Page. TreeView: an application to display phylogenetic trees on personal computers. *Computer Applications in the Biosciences*, 12:357–358, 1996.

309. R. D. M. Page. Modified mincut supertrees. In *Proceedings of the 2nd Workshop on Algorithms in Bioinformatics*, pages 537–551, 2002.

310. R. D. M. Page and E. C. Holmes. *Molecular Evolution: A Phylogenetic Approach*. Blackwell Scientific, Oxford, 1998.

311. C. H. Papadimitriou and M. Yannakakis. Optimization, approximation, and complexity classes. *J. Comput. System Sciences*, 43:425–440, 1991.

312. S. Park, D. Lee, and W. W. Chu. Fast retrieval of similar subsequences in long sequence databases. In *Proceedings of the 3rd IEEE Knowledge and Data Engineering Exchange Workshop*, Chicago, IL, 1999.

313. W. R. Pearson and D. J. Lipman. Improved tools for biological sequence comparison. *Proceedings of the National Academy of Sciences of the USA*, 85:2444–2448, 1988.

314. W. H. Piel, M. J. Donoghue, and M. J. Sanderson. TreeBASE: a database of phylogenetic knowledge. In *To the Interoperable Catalogue of Life with Partners—Species 2000 Asia Oceania—Proceedings of the 2nd International Workshop of Species 2000 (Research Report for the National Institute of Environmental Studies)*, R-171-2002, 2002.

315. W. H. Piel, M. J. Donoghue, and M. J. Sanderson. The small-world dynamics of tree networks and data mining in phyloinformatics. *Bioinformatics*, 19:1162–1168, 2003.

316. P. Pirolli, S. K. Card, and M. M. van Der Wege. The effect of information scent on searching information visualizations of large tree structures. In *Proceedings of the 5th International Working Conference on Advanced Visual Interfaces*, pages 161–172, 2000.

317. C. Plaisant, J. Grosjean, and B. B. Bederson. SpaceTree: supporting exploration in large node link tree, design evolution and empirical evaluation. In *Proceedings of IEEE Symposium on Information Visualization*, pages 57–70, 2002.

318. J. Platt, N. Cristianini, and J. Shawe-Taylor. Large margin dags for multiclass classification. *Adv. Neural Inform. Proc. Systems*, 12:547–553, 2000.

319. F. J. Provost and T. Fawcett. Robust classification for imprecise environments. *Machine Learning*, 42(3):203–231, 2001.

320. M. Purrello, C. Di Pietro, M. Ragusa, A. Pulvirenti, G. Pigola, R. Giugno, E. Modica, V. Zimmitti, V. Di Pietro, T. Maugeri, C. Emmanuele, S. Travali, M. Scalia, D. Shasha, and A. Ferro. In vitro and in silico cloning of *Xenopus laevis* sod2 and its phylogenetic analysis with AntiClustAl, a new algorithm for multiple sequence alignment, demonstrate a very high amino acid sequence conservation during evolution. Submitted, 2003.

321. W. K. Purves, D. E. Sadava, G. H. Orians, and H. C. Heller. *Life, the science of biology*. Sinauer Associates, Sunderland, MA, 2001.

322. R. L. Pyle. Taxonomer: a relational data model for managing information relevant to taxonomic research. *Phyloinformatics*, 1:1–54, 2004.

323. J. Quackenbush. Computational analysis of microarray data. *Natural Review Genetics*, 2:418–427, 2001.

324. J. R. Quinlan. *C4.5: Programs for Machine Learning*. Morgan Kaufmann, San Mateo, CA, 1993.

325. M. A. Ragan. Phylogenetic inference based on matrix representation of trees. *Molecular Phylogenetics and Evolution*, 1:53–58, 1992.

326. C. Raguenaud and J. Kennedy. Multiple overlapping classifications: issues and solutions. In *Proceedings of the 14th International Conference on Scientific and Statistical Database Management*, pages 77–86, 2002.

327. V. Raman and J. M. Hellerstein. Potter's wheel: an interactive data cleaning system. In *Proceedings of Int. Conf. on Very Large Data Bases*, pages 381–390, Rome, Italy, 2001.

328. V. E. Ramensky, V. J. Makeev, M. A. Roytberg, and V. G. Tumanyan. DNA segmentation through the Bayesian approach. *Journal of Computational Biology*, 7(1):215–231, 2000.

329. D. E. Reich, S. F. Schaffner, M. J. Daly, G. McVean, J. C. Mullikin, J. M. Higgins, D. J. Richter, E. S. Lander, and D. Altshuler. Human genome sequence variation, and the influence of gene history, mutation and recombination. *Nature Genetics*, 32:135–142, 2002.

330. G. W. Richards. Virtual screening using grid computing: the screensaver project. *Nature Reviews: Drug Discovery*, 1:551–554, 2002.

331. T. W. Ridler and S. Calvard. Picture thresholding using an iterative selection method. *IEEE Trans. Syst. Man Cybernet*, 8:630–632, 1978.

332. C. J. R. Robertson and G. B. Nunn. Towards a new taxonomy for albatrosses. In G. Robertson and R. Gales (eds.), *Albatross Biology and Conservation*. Surrey Beaty, Chipping Norton, UK, pages 13–19, 1997.

333. D. F. Robinson and L. R. Foulds. Comparison of phylogenetic trees. *Mathematical Biosciences*, 53:131–147, 1981.

334. M. M. Rolls, P. A. Stein, S. S. Taylor, E. Ha, F. McKeon, and T. A. Rapoport. A visual screen of a gfp-fusion library identifies a new type of nuclear envelope membrane protein. *J. Cell Biol*, 146:29–44, 1999.

335. E. J. S. Roques and R. F. Murphy. Objective evaluation of differences in protein subcellular distribution. *Traffic*, 3:61–65, 2002.

336. B. Rost. Review: protein secondary structure prediction continues to rise. *Journal of Structural Biology*, 134(2), 2001.

337. B. Rost. Twilight zone of protein sequence alignments. *Protein Engineering*, 12(2), 2001.

338. U. Rost and E. Bornberg-Bauer. TreeWiz: interactive exploration of huge trees. *Bioinformatics*, 18:109–114, 2002.

339. D. A. Rozwarski, A. M. Groneborn, M. G. Clore, J. F. Bazan, A. Bohm, A. Wlodawer, M. Hatada, and P. A. Karplus. Structural comparisons among the short-chain helical cytokines. *Structure*, 2:159–173, 1994.

340. R. B. Russell, P. D. Sasieni, and M. J. Sternberg. Supersites within superfolds—binding site similarity in the absence of homology. *Journal of Molecular Biology*, 282(4), 1998.

341. D. A. Ruths, E. S. Chen and L. Ellis. Arbor 3D: an interactive environment for examining phylogenetic and taxonomic trees in multiple dimensions. *Bioinformatics*, 16:1003–1009, 2000.

342. N. Saitou and M. Nei. The neighbor-joining method: a new method for reconstructing phylogenetic trees. *Molecular Biology and Evolution*, 4(4):406–425, 1987.

343. S. Salzberg, A. Delcher, S. Kasif, and O. White. Microbial gene identification using interpolated Markov models. *Nucleic Acids Research*, 26:544–548, 1998.

344. R. Sánchez, U. Pieper, N. Mirkovi, P. I. W. de Bakker, E. Wittenstein, and A. Šali. MODBASE, a database of annotated comparative protein structure models. *Nucleic Acids Research*, 28(1):250–253, 2000.

345. M. J. Sanderson, A. Purvis, and C. Henze. Phylogenetic supertrees: assembling the trees of life. *Trends in Ecology and Evolution*, 13:105–109, 1998.

346. S. Sarkar and P. Soundararajan. Supervised learning of large perceptual organization: graph spectral partitioning and learning automata. *IEEE Transactions on Pattern Analysis and Machine Intelligence*, 22:504–525, 2000.

347. M. A. Savageau. Power-law formalism: a canonical nonlinear approach to modeling and analysis. In *Proceedings of the 1st World Congress on Nonlinear Analysis*, pages 3323–3334, 1996.

348. J. Schaff, B. Slepchenko, and L. Loew. Physiological modeling with virtual cell framework. *Methods in Enzymology*, 321:1–23, 2000.

349. R. E. Schapire. The boosting approach to machine learning: an overview. In *Proceedings of the MSRI (Mathematical Sciences Research Institute) Workshop on Nonlinear estimation and Classification*, 2002.

350. R. E. Schapire and Y. Singer. Improved boosting algorithms using confidence-rated predictions. *Machine Learning*, 37:297–336, 1999.

351. C. H. Schilling, D. Letscher, and B. P. Palsson. Theory for the systemic definition of pathways and their use in interpreting metabolic function from a pathway-oriented perspective. *Journal of Theoretical Biology*, 203:229–248, 2000.

352. C. H. Schilling, D. Letscher, and B. P. Palsson. Assessment of the metabolic capabilities of *H. influenzae* Rd through a genome-scale pathway analysis. *Journal of Theoretical Biology*, 203:249–283, 2000.

353. B. Schoelkopf and A. J. Smola. *Learning with Kernels: Support Vector Machines, Regularization, Optimization, and Beyond.* MIT Press, Cambridge, MA, 2002.

354. B. Scholkopf, A. Smola, and K.-R. Muller. Nonlinear component analysis as a kernel eigenvalue problem. *Neural Comput.*, 10:1299–1319, 1998.

355. S. Schwartz, Z. Zhang, K. A. Frazer, A. Smit, C. Riemer, J. Bouck, R. Gibbs, R. Hardison, and W. Miller. PipMaker—a Web server for aligning two genomic DNA sequences. *Genome Research*, 10(4):577–586, 2000.

356. P. G. Selinger, M. M. Astrahan, D. D. Chamberlin, R. A. Lorie, and T. G. Price. Access path selection in a relational database management system. In *Proceedings of ACM SIGMOD International Conference on Management of Data*, Boston, 1979.

357. C. Semple and M. Steel. A supertree method for rooted trees. *Discrete Applied Mathematics*, 105:147–158, 2000.

358. S. K. Service, D. W. T. Lang, N. B. Freimer, and L. A. Sandkuijl. Linkage-disequilibrium mapping of disease genes by reconstruction of ancestral haplotypes in founder populations. *American Journal of Human Genetics*, 64:1728–1738, 1999.

359. P. Sevon, P. Onkamo, V. Ollikainen, H. T. T. Toivonen, H. Mannila, and J. Kere. Mining the associations between phenotype, genotype, and covariates. Genetic Analysis Workshop 12, *Genetic Epidemiology*, 21(Suppl. 1):S588–S593, 2001.

360. P. Sevon, H. T. T. Toivonen, and V. Ollikainen. TreeDT: gene mapping by tree disequilibrium test. In *Proceedings of the 7th ACM SIGKDD International Conference on Knowledge Discovery and Data Mining*, pages 365–370, 2001 (extended version available at http://www.cs.helsinki.fi/TR/C.html).

361. H. Shan, K. G. Herbert, W. H. Piel, D. Shasha, and J. T. L. Wang. A structure-based search engine for phylogenetic databases. In *Proceedings of the 14th International Conference on Scientific and Statistical Database Management*, pages 7–10, 2002.

362. B. A. Shapiro. An algorithm for comparing multiple RNA secondary structures. *Comput. Appl. Biosci.*, 4(3):387–393, 1988.

363. B. A. Shapiro and K. Zhang. Comparing multiple RNA secondary structures using tree comparisons. *Comput. Appl. Biosci.*, 6(4):309–318, 1990.

364. D. Shasha, J. T. L. Wang, H. Shan, and K. Zhang. ATreeGrep: approximate searching in unordered trees. In *Proceedings of the 14th International Conference on Scientific and Statistical Database Management*, pages 89–98, 2002.

365. P. Shenoy, J. R. Haritsa, S. Sundarshan, G. Bhalotia, M. Bawa, and D. Shah. Turbo-charging vertical mining of large databases. In *Proceedings of ACM SIGMOD International Conference on Management of Data*, pages 22–33, 2000.

366. J. Shi and J. Malik. Normalized cuts and image segmentation. In *Proceedings of IEEE Conference on Computer Vision and Pattern Recognition*, pages 731–737, 1997.

367. I. N. Shindyalov and P. E. Bourne. Protein structure alignment by incremental combinatorial extension (CE) of the optimal path. *Protein Engineering*, 11(9):739–747, 1998.

368. A. P. Singh and D. L. Brutlag. Hierarchical protein structure superposition using both secondary structure and atomic representations. In *Proceedings of the 5th International Conference on Intelligent Systems for Molecular Biology*, pages 284–293, 1997.

369. K. T. Simons, C. Kooperberg, E. Huang, and D. Baker. Assembly of protein tertiary structures from fragments with similar local sequences using simulated annealing and Bayesian scoring functions. *Journal of Molecular Biology*, 268(1):209–225, 1997.

370. M. Sippl. Helmholtz free energy of peptide hydrogen bonds in proteins. *Journal of Molecular Biology*, 260(5):644–648, 1996.

371. M. Sipser. *Introduction to the Theory of Computation*. PWS, Boston, 1997.

372. J. Skolnick, A. Kolinski, and A. Ortiz. Derivation of protein-specific pair potentials based on weak sequence fragment similarity. *Proteins*, 38(1):3–16, 2000.

373. T. F. Smith and M. S. Waterman. Comparison of biosequences. *Adv. Appl. Math.*, 2:482–489, 1981.

374. T. F. Smith and M. S. Waterman. Identification of common molecular subsequences. *Journal of Molecular Biology*, 147(1):195–197, 1981.

375. P. H. A. Sneath and R. R. Sokal. *Numerical Taxonomy*, W. H. Freeman and Company, San Francisco, pages 230–234, 1973.

376. M. Sofer. Genealogical representation of trees in databases. Unpublished manuscript (http://www.utdt.edu/~mig/sql-trees/).

377. R. Sole, R. Ferrer-Cancho, J. Montoya, and S. Valverde. Selection, tinkering, and emergence in complex networks. *Complexity*, 8:20–33, 2003.

378. R. Somogyi, S. Fuhrman, and X. Wen. *Genetic network inference in computational models and applications to large-scale gene expression data*. MIT Press, Cambridge, MA, 2001.

379. R. Somogyi and C. A. Sniegoski. Modeling the complexity of genetic networks: understanding multigenic and pleiotropic regulation. *Journal of Computational Biology*, 6(1):45–63, 1996.

380. K. Sparck-Jones and J. Galliers. *Evaluating Natural Language Processing Systems, an analysis and review*. Springer-Verlag, New York, 1996.

381. P. T. Spellman et al. Design and implementation of microarray gene expression markup language (MAGE-ML). *Genome Biology*, 3:0046.1–9, 2002.

382. R. S. Spielman, R. E. McGinnis, and W. J. Ewens. Transmission test for linkage disequilibrium: the insulin gene region and insulin-dependent diabetes mellitus (IDDM). *American Journal of Human Genetics*, 52:506–516, 1993.

383. A. Srinivasan, R. D. King, S. H. Muggleton, and M. Sternberg. The predictive toxicology evaluation challenge. In *Proceedings of the 15th International Joint Conference on Artificial Intelligence*, pages 1–6, 1997.

384. A. Sriniviasan and R. D. King. Feature construction with inductive logic programming: a study of quantitative predictions of biological activity aided by structural attributes. *Knowledge Discovery and Data Mining*, 3:37–57, 1999.

385. N. Stahl and G. D. Yancopoulos. The alphas, betas, and kinases of cytokine receptor complexes. *Cell*, 74:587–590, 1993.

386. B. Stapley and G. Benoit. Biobibliometrics: information retrieval and visualization from co-occurrences of gene names in MEDLINE abstracts. In *Proceedings of Pacific Symp. Biocomputing*, pages 529–540, 2000.

387. D. J. States and P. Agarwal. Compact encoding strategies for DNA sequence similarity search. In *Proceedings of International Conference on Intelligent Systems for Molecular Biology*, pages 211–217, 1996.

388. D. J. Stephens and V. J. Allan. Light microscopy techniques for live cell imaging. *Science*, 300:82–86, 2003.

389. M. J. E. Sternberg and J. M. Thornton. On the conformation of proteins: the handedness of the connection between parallel beta strands. *Journal of Molecular Biology*, 110:269–283, 1977.

390. M. Stoer and F. Wagner. A simple min-cut algorithm. *Journal of the ACM*, 44(4):585–591, 1997.

391. A. M. Sugden, B. R. Jasny, E. Culotta, and E. Pennisi. Charting the evolutionary history of life. *Science*, 300:1691, 2003.

392. K. C. Tai. The tree to tree correction problem. *Journal of the ACM*, 26(3):422–433, 1979.

393. T. A. Tatusova and T. L. Madden. BLAST 2 sequences, a new tool for comparing protein and nucleotide sequences. *FEMS Microbiology Letters*, pages 247–250, 1999.

394. W. R. Taylor. Protein structure comparison using iterated double dynamic programming. *Protein Science*, 8:654–665, 1999.

395. W. R. Taylor and C. O. Orengo. Protein structure alignment. *Journal of Molecular Biology*, 208:1–22, 1989.

396. C. A. Telmer, P. B. Berget, B. Ballou, R. F. Murphy, and J. W. Jarvik. Epitope tagging genomic DNA using a cd-tagging tn10 minitransposon. *BioTechniques*, 32:422–430, 2002.

397. J. D. Terwilliger. A powerful likelihood method for the analysis of linkage disequilibrium between trait loci and one or more polymorphic marker loci. *American Journal of Human Genetics*, 56:777–787, 1995.

398. R. Thomas and R. D'Ari. *Biological Feedback*. CRC Press, Boca Raton, FL, 1990.

399. R. Thomas, D. Thieffry, and M. Kaufman. Dynamical behavior of biological regulatory networks: I. Biological role of feedback loops and practical use of the concept of the loop-characteristic state. *Bulletin of Mathematical Biology*, 57(2):247–276, 1995.

400. J. D. Thompson, F. Plewniak, and O. Poch. A comprehensive comparison of multiple sequence alignment programs. *Nucleic Acids Research*, 27(13):2682–2690, 1999.

401. J. L. Thorley and R. D. M. Page. RadCon: phylogenetic tree comparison and consensus. *Bioinformatics*, 16:486–487, 2000.

402. L. Tierney. Markov chains for exploring posterior distributions. *Annals of Statistics*, 22(4):1701–1728, 1994.

403. H. T. T. Toivonen, P. Onkamo, K. Vasko, V. Ollikainen, P. Sevon, H. Mannila, M. Herr, and J. Kere. Data mining applied to linkage disequilibrium mapping. *American Journal of Human Genetics*, 67:133–145, 2000.

404. H. T. T. Toivonen, P. Onkamo, K. Vasko, V. Ollikainen, P. Sevon, H. Mannila, and J. Kere. Gene mapping by haplotype pattern mining. In *Proceedings of IEEE International Symposium on Bio-Informatics and Biomedical Engineering*, pages 99–108, 2000.

405. M. Tomita et al. E-cell: software environment for while-call simulation. *Bioinformatics*, 15:72–84, 1999.

406. B. Tower. Docking topical hierarchies: a comparison of two algorithms for reconciling keyword structures. Technical Report CS2001-0669, Department of Computer Science and Engineering, University of California at San Diego, 2001.

407. C. Traina, A. Traina, L. Wu, and C. Faloutsos. Fast feature selection using the fractal dimension. In *Proceedings of the XV Brazilian Symposium on Databases*, 2000.

408. E. C. Uberbacher and R. J. Mural. Locating protein-coding regions in human DNA sequences by a multiple sensor-neural network approach. *Proceedings of the National Academy of Sciences of the USA*, 88:11261–11265, 1991.

409. G. Valiente. Constrained tree inclusion. In *Proceedings of the 14th Annual Symposium on Combinatorial Pattern Matching*, pages 361–371, 2003.

410. V. Vapnik. *Nature of Statistical Learning Theory*. Springer-Verlag, New York, 1995.

411. V. Vapnik. *Statistical Learning Theory*. John Wiley, New York, 1998.

412. E. O. Voit. *Computational Analysis of Biochemical Systems. A Practical Guide for Biochemists and Molecular Biologists*. Cambridge University Press, Cambridge, UK, 2000.

413. M. Velliste. Image interpretation methods for a systematic of protein subcellular location. Technical Report, Carnegie Mellon University, Pittsburgh, PA, 2002.

414. M. Velliste and R. F. Murphy. Automated determination of protein subcellular locations from 3D fluorescence microscope images. In *Proceedings of IEEE International Symposium on Biomedical Imaging*, pages 867–870, 2002.

415. M. Vendruscolo, E. Kussell, and E. Domany. Recovery of protein structure from contact maps. *Folding and Design*, 2(5):295–306, 1997.

416. M. Vendruscolo, E. Paci, C. M. Dobson, and M. Karplus. Three key residues form a critical contact network in a protein folding transition state. *Nature*, 409:641–645, 2001.

417. V. Villegas, J. C. Martinez, F. X. Aviles, and L. Serrano. Structure of the transition state in the folding process of human procarboxypeptidase A2 activation domain. *Journal of Molecular Biology*, 283:1027–1036, 1998.

418. G. von Heijne, H. Nielsen, J. Engelbrecht, and S. Brunak. Identification of prokaryotic and eukaryotic signal peptides and prediction of their cleavage sites. *Protein Engineering*, 10:1–6, 1997.

419. R. Waagepetersen and D. Sorensen. A tutorial on Reversible Jump MCMC with a view toward applications in QTL-mapping. *International Statistical Review*, 69:49–62, 2001.

420. H. M. Wain, M. Lush, F. Ducluzeau, and S. Povey. Genew: the human nomenclature database. *Nucleic Acids Research*, 30:169–171, 2002.

421. H. Wang, W. Wang, J. Yang, and P. S. Yu. Clustering by pattern similarity in large data sets. In *Proceedings of ACM SIGMOD Int. Conf. on Management of Data*, pages 418–427, Madison, WI, 2002.

422. J. T. L. Wang, H. Shan, D. Shasha, and W. H. Piel. TreeRank: a similarity measure for nearest neighbor searching in phylogenetic databases. In *Proceedings of the 15th International Conference on Scientific and Statistical Database Management*, pages 71–180, 2003.

423. Z. Wang and K. Zhang. Alignment between RNA structures. In *Proceedings of the 26th International Symposium on Mathematical Foundations of Computer Science*, pages 690–702, 2001.

424. S. R. Waterhouse. Classification and regression using mixtures of experts. Technical Report, Cambridge, UK, 1997.

425. D. Weininger. SMILES: a chemical language and information system. 1. Introduction to methodology and encoding rules. *Journal of Chemical Information and Computer Sciences*, 28:31–36, 1988.

426. O. S. Weislow, R. Kiser, D. L. Fine, J. Bader, R. H. Shoemaker, and M. R. Boyd. New soluble formazan assay for HIV-1 cytopathic effects: application to high flux screening of synthetic and natural products for AIDS antiviral activity. *Journal of the National Cancer Institute*, 81:577–586, 1989.

427. D. R. Westhead, T. W. F. Slidel, T. P. J. Flores, and J. M. Thornton. Protein structural topology: automated analysis, diagrammatic representation and database searching. *Protein Science*, 8:897–904, 1999.

428. D. L. Wheeler, C. Chappey, A. E. Lash, D. D. Leipe, T. L. Madden, G. D. Schulter, T. A. Tatusova, and B. A. Rapp. Database resources of the National Center for Biotechnology Information. *Nucleic Acids Research*, 28:10–14, 2000.

429. H. E. Williams and J. Zobel. Indexing and retrieval for genomic databases. *IEEE Transactions on Knowledge and Data Engineering*, 14(1):63–78, 2002.

430. WIT2. http://www-unix.mcs.anl.gov/compbio/.

431. I. H. Witten and E. Frank. *Data Mining: Practical Machine Learning Tools and Techniques with Java Implementations*. Morgan Kaufmann, San Mateo, CA, 2000.

432. Y. I. Wolf, I. B. Rogozin, N. V. Grishin, and E. V. Koonin. Genome trees and the Tree of Life. *Trends in Genetics*, 18:472–479, 2002.

433. H. J. Wolfson and I. Rigoutsos. Geometric hashing: an overview. *IEEE Computational Science and Engineering*, 4(4):10–21, 1997.

434. C. H. Wu, T. S. Yeh, H. Huang, L. Arminski, J. Castro-Alvear, Y. Chen, Z. Hu, P. Kourtesis, R. S. Ledley, B. E. Suzek, C. R. Vinayaka, J. Zhang, and W. C. Barker. The protein information resource. *Nucleic Acids Research*, 31(1):390–392, 2003.

435. Z. Wu and R. M. Leahy. An optimal graph theoretic approach to data clustering: theory and its application to image segmentation. *IEEE Transactions on Pattern Analysis and Machine Intelligence*, 15(11):1101–1113, 1993.

436. X. Yan and J. Han. gSpan: graph-based substructure pattern mining. In *Proceedings of Int. Conf. on Data Mining*, pages 721–724, Maebashi, Japan, 2002.

437. X. Yan and J. Han. CloseGraph: mining closed frequent graph patterns. In *Proceedings of ACM SIGKDD Int. Conf. Knowledge Discovery and Data Mining*, Washington, DC, 2003.

438. X. Yan, J. Han, and R. Afshar. CloSpan: mining closed sequential patterns in large datasets. In *Proceedings of SIAM Int. Conf. Data Mining*, pages 166–177, San Francisco, 2003.

439. M. D. Yandell and W. H. Majoros. Genomics and natural language processing. *Nature Review, Genetics*, 3:601–610, 2002.

440. J. Yang and V. Honavar. Feature subset selection using a genetic algorithm. *IEEE Intell. Systems*, 13:44–49, 1998.

441. J. Yang, W. Wang, H. Wang, and P. S. Yu. δ-cluster: capturing subspace correlation in a large data set. In *Proceedings of Int. Conf. Data Engineering*, pages 517–528, San Francisco, 2002.

442. J. Yang, W. Wang, and P. S. Yu. Mining asynchronous periodic patterns in time series data. In *Proceedings of ACM SIGKDD Conf. Knowledge Discovery and Data Mining*, pages 275–279, Boston, 2000.

443. J. Yang, W. Wang, P. S. Yu, and J. Han. Mining long sequential patterns in a noisy environment. In *Proceedings of ACM SIGMOD Int. Conf. on Management of Data*, pages 406–417, Madison, WI, 2002.

444. H. Yu, J. Yang, and J. Han. Classifying large data sets using SVM with hierarchical clusters. In *Proceedings of ACM SIGKDD Conf. Knowledge Discovery and Data Mining*, Washington, DC, 2003.

445. M. J. Zaki. Scalable algorithms for association mining. *IEEE Transactions on Knowledge and Data Engineering*, 12(2):372–390, 2000.

446. M. J. Zaki and K. Gouda. Fast vertical mining using diffsets. In *Proceedings of ACM SIGKDD Conference on Knowledge Discovery and Data Mining*, pages 326–335, 2003.

447. K. Zhang. Computing similarity between RNA secondary structures. In *Proceedings of IEEE International Joint Symposia on Intelligence and Systems*, pages 126–132, Rockville, MD, 1998.

448. K. Zhang, L. Wang, and B. Ma. Computing similarity between RNA structures. In *Proceedings of the 10th Symposium on Combinatorial Pattern Matching*, pages 281–293, 1999.

449. K. Zhang and D. Shasha. Simple fast algorithms for the editing distance between trees and related problems. *SIAM J. Computing*, 18(6):1245–1262, 1989.

450. K. Zhang, J. T. L. Wang, and D. Shasha. On the editing distance between undirected acyclic graphs. *International Journal of Foundations of Computer Science*, 7(1):43–57, 1996.

451. S. Zhang and H. Zhao. Linkage disequilibrium mapping with genotype data. *Genetic Epidemiology*, 22:66–77, 2002.

452. S. Zhang, K. Zhang, J. Li, and H. Zhao. On a family-based haplotype pattern mining method for linkage disequilibrium mapping. In *Proceedings of the 7th Pacific Symposium on Biocomputing*, pages 100–111, 2002.

453. T. Zhang, R. Ramakrishnan, and M. Livny. BIRCH: an efficient data clustering method for very large databases. In *Proceedings of ACM SIGMOD Int. Conf. Management of Data*, pages 103–114, Montreal, Canada, 1996.

454. Z. Zhang, A. A. Schaffer, W. Miller, T. L. Madden, D. J. Lipman, E. V. Koonin, and S. F. Altschul. Protein sequence similarity searches using patterns as seeds. *Nucleic Acids Research*, 26(17):3986–3990, 1998.

455. Z. Zhang, S. Schwartz, L. Wagner, and W. Miller. A greedy algorithm for aligning DNA sequences. *Journal of Computational Biology*, 7:203–214, 2000.

456. Y. Zhong, S. Jung, S. Pramanik, and J. H. Beaman. Data model and comparison and query methods for interacting classifications in a taxonomic database. *Taxon*, 45:223–241, 1996.

457. Y. Zhong, C. A. Meacham, and S. Pramanik. A general method for tree-comparison based on subtree similarity and its use in a taxonomic database. *BioSystems*, 42:1–8, 1997.

458. Y. Zhong, Y. Luo, S. Pramanik, and J. H. Beaman. HICLAS: a taxonomic database system for displaying and comparing biological classification and phylogenetic trees. *Bioinformatics*, 15:149–156, 1999.

Biographies

Peter Bajcsy earned his Ph.D. degree from the Electrical and Computer Engineering Department, University of Illinois at Urbana-Champaign, IL, 1997; M.S. degree from the Electrical Engineering Department, University of Pennsylvania, Philadelphia, PA, 1994; and Diploma Engineer degree from the Electrical Engineering Department, Slovak Technical University, Bratislava, Slovakia, 1987. He is currently with the Automated Learning Group at the National Center for Supercomputing Applications at the University of Illinois at Urbana-Champaign, Illinois, working as a research scientist on problems related to automatic transfer of image content to knowledge. In the past, he worked on real-time machine vision problems for semiconductor industry and synthetic aperture radar (SAR) technology for government contracting industry. He developed several software systems for automatic feature extraction, feature selection, segmentation, classification, tracking and statistical modeling from medical microscopy, electro-optical, SAR, laser and hyperspectral datasets. Dr. Bajcsy's scientific interests include image and signal processing, data mining, statistical data analysis, pattern recognition, novel sensor technology, and computer and machine vision.

Deb Bardhan is an M.S. student in the Computer Science Department at Rensselaer Polytechnic Institute.

Chris Bystroff is an assistant professor of biology at Rensselaer Polytechnic Institute. He received his Ph.D. from the University of California, San Diego, in 1988. Before joining Rensselaer in 1999, he worked with Joseph Kraut, Robert Fletterick, and David Baker and taught as a Fulbright fellow in Nicaragua. He has published numerous articles on protein crystallography and bioinformatics, especially regarding protein folding.

Mukund Deshpande received a Ph.D. from the Department of Computer Science at the University of Minnesota in 2004 and is currently working at Oracle Corporation. He received an M.E. in system science and automation from the Indian Institute of Science, Bangalore, India, in 1997.

Cinzia Di Pietro obtained her B.S. degree in biology from the University
of Catania (Italy) in November 1984 and her Ph.D. from the University of
Bari (Italy) in June 1992. In July 1995 she obtained a Specialty Degree in
medical genetics. She is now a research associate at the School of Medicine of
the University of Catania and teaches biology and genetics at the School of
Medicine of the same university. She works at the Department of Biomedical
Science in the group of M. Purrello on the genomic and transcriptional
analysis of general transcription factors and their involvement in oncogenesis
and the characterization of novel genes by computational biology.

Alfredo Ferro received the B.S. degree in mathematics from Catania
University, Italy, in 1973 and a Ph.D. in computer science from New
York University in 1981 (received the Jay Krakauer Award for the best
dissertation in the field of sciences at NYU). He is currently a professor
of computer science at Catania University and has been the director of
graduate studies in computer science for several years. Since 1989 he has been
the director of the International School for Computer Science Researchers
(Lipari School http://lipari.cs.unict.it). Together with Raffaele Giancarlo
and Michele Purrello he is the director of the Lipari International School
in BioMedicine and BioInformatics (http://lipari.cs.unict.it/bio-info/). His
research interests include bioinformatics, algorithms for large data set
management, data mining, computational logic and networking.

Laurie Jane Hammel grew up in the mid-Michigan area and did her
undergraduate work at the University of Michigan in Ann Arbor, earning
a Bachelor of Arts in mathematics and a Bachelor of Music in French
horn performance in 2000. She then continued her University of Michigan
education in the Electrical Engineering and Computer Science Department,
earning a Master of Science in computer science and engineering in 2002.
While in the EECS department, Hammel worked with Professor Jignesh M.
Patel on database research, specializing in bioinformatics and the secondary
structure of proteins. She currently lives in Annapolis, Maryland, and is a
computer scientist for the Department of Defense.

Jiawei Han received his Ph.D. in computer science in the University
of Wisconsin in 1985. He is a professor in the Department of Computer
Science at the University of Illinois at Urbana-Champaign. Previously, he
was an endowed university professor at Simon Fraser University, Canada.

He has been working on research in data mining, data warehousing, spatial and multimedia databases, deductive and object-oriented databases, and biomedical databases and has produced over 250 journal and conference publications. He has chaired or served in many program committees of international conferences and workshops, including ACM SIGKDD Conferences (2001 best paper award chair, 2002 student award chair, 1996 PC cochair), SIAM-Data Mining Conferences (2001 and 2002 PC cochair), ACM SIGMOD Conferences (2000 exhibit program chair), and International Conferences on Data Engineering (2004 and 2002 PC vice chair). He also served or is serving on the editorial boards for *Data Mining and Knowledge Discovery: An International Journal*, *IEEE Transactions on Knowledge and Data Engineering*, and *Journal of Intelligent Information Systems*. He is currently serving on the board of directors for the executive committee of ACM Special Interest Group on Knowledge Discovery and Data Mining (SIGKDD). Dr. Han has received an IBM Faculty Award, the Outstanding Contribution Award at the 2002 International Conference on Data Mining, and an ACM Service Award. He is the first author of the textbook *Data Mining: Concepts and Techniques* (Morgan Kaufmann, 2001). He has been an ACM Fellow since 2003.

Kai Huang was born in Yueyang, Hunan Province, China in 1979. He received his S.B. in biological sciences and biotechnology from Tsinghua University in 2000 and a Master's degree in computational and statistical learning from Carnegie Mellon University in 2003. He is currently a Ph.D. candidate in the Department of Biological Sciences at Carnegie Mellon University, where he is a Merck Fellow. He was a lecturer at the workshop "New Directions in Data Mining and Machine Learning" hosted by the Center for Automated Learning and Discovery of the School of Computer Science at Carnegie Mellon. His research focuses on statistical data mining from fluorescence microscope images including classification, feature reduction, segmentation, and multidimensional image database retrieval.

Donald Huddler is an assistant research scientist at the University of Michigan. He earned a Ph.D. from Princeton University in 1999. His graduate thesis research focused on the structural biology of plant cytoskeletal proteins involved in pollen tube elongation. His postdoctoral research at the University of Michigan Medical School examined proteins from the Yersinia type III pathogenesis system. As an assistant research scientist at the University of Michigan, he continues to structurally characterize enzymes that perform large-scale domain rearrangements. Understanding the mechanism of rearrangements and the key elements of protein structures that facilitate these motions is a focus of current research. He is a member of the American

Crystallographic Association and the Biophysical Society.

George Karypis is an assistant professor in the Computer Science and Engineering Department at the University of Minnesota, Twin Cities. His research interests span the areas of parallel algorithm design, data mining, bioinformatics, information retrieval, applications of parallel processing in scientific computing and optimization, sparse matrix computations, parallel preconditioners, and parallel programming languages and libraries. His research has resulted in the development of software libraries for serial and parallel graph partitioning (METIS and ParMETIS), hypergraph partitioning (hMETIS), parallel Cholesky factorization (PSPASES), collaborative filtering-based recommendation algorithms (SUGGEST), clustering high-dimensional datasets (CLUTO), and finding frequent patterns in diverse datasets (PAFI). He has cowritten more than 90 journal and conference papers on these topics and a book entitled *Introduction to Parallel Computing* (second edition, Addison Wesley, 2003). He is serving on the program committees of many conferences and workshops on these topics and is an associate editor of the *IEEE Transactions on Parallel and Distributed Systems*.

Michihiro Kuramochi received the B.Eng. and M.Eng. degrees from the University of Tokyo and the M.S. degree from Yale University. He is currently a Ph.D. candidate in the Department of Computer Science and Engineering at the University of Minnesota, Twin Cities.

Lei Liu received his Ph.D. in cell biology from the University of Connecticut in 1997. He then worked as a postdoctoral fellow for two years at the Department of Computer Science and Engineering at the University of Connecticut. In 1999, Dr. Liu joined the W. M. Keck Center for Comparative and Functional Genomics at the University of Illinois as the founding director of the bioinformatics unit. His expertise is in the areas of comparative genomics, biological databases, and data mining. He was the NCSA faculty fellow for the year 2000–2001. He is currently a co-PI in several projects funded by NSF, NIH, and USDA.

Heikki Mannila is the research director of the Basic Research Unit of Helsinki Institute for Information Technology, a joint research unit of the University of Helsinki and Helsinki University of Technology. He is also a professor of computer science at Helsinki University of Technology. He received his Ph.D. in 1985 and has been a professor at University of Helsinki, senior researcher in Microsoft Research, Redmond, Washington, research fellow at Nokia Research Center, and a visiting researcher at the Max Planck Institute for Computer Science and at the Technical University of Vienna. His research areas are data mining, algorithms, and databases. He is the author of two books and over 120 scientific publications. He is a member of the Finnish Academy of Science and Letters and editor-in-chief of the journal *Data Mining and Knowledge Discovery*. Dr. Mannila is the recipient of an ACM SIGKDD Innovation Award in 2003.

Robert F. Murphy was born in Brooklyn, New York, in 1953. He earned an A.B. in biochemistry from Columbia College in 1974 and a Ph.D. in biochemistry from the California Institute of Technology in 1980. He was a Damon Runyon-Walter Winchell Cancer Foundation postdoctoral fellow with Dr. Charles R. Cantor at Columbia University from 1979 through 1983, after which he became an assistant professor of biological sciences at Carnegie Mellon University in Pittsburgh, Pennsylvania. He received a Presidential Young Investigator Award from the National Science Foundation shortly after joining the faculty at Carnegie Mellon in 1983 and has received research grants from the National Institutes of Health, the National Science Foundation, the American Cancer Society, the American Heart Association, the Arthritis Foundation, and the Rockefeller Brothers Fund. He has coedited two books and published over 90 research papers. His research group at Carnegie Mellon focuses primarily on the application of fluorescence methods to problems in cell biology, with particular emphasis on the automated interpretation of fluorescence microscope images. He has a long-standing interest in computer applications in biology and developed the first formal undergraduate degree program in computational biology in 1987. He also founded and directs the Merck Computational Biology and Chemistry Program at Carnegie Mellon. In 1984, he codeveloped the Flow Cytometry Standard data file format used throughout the cytometry industry, and he is chair of the Cytometry Development Workshop held each year in Asilomar, California. He is currently a professor of biological sciences and biomedical engineering and voting faculty member at the Center for Automated Learning and Discovery in the School of Computer Science at Carnegie Mellon.

Vinay Nadimpally is an M.S. student in the Computer Science Department at Rensselaer Polytechnic Institute.

Päivi Onkamo is a postdoctoral researcher at the Helsinki Institute for Information Technology, University of Helsinki, Finland. She received her M.Sc. on the topic of molecular evolution of Artiodactyls in 1995. Later on,

Data Mining in Bioinformatics

she combined genetics with biometry, concentrating in the field of genetic epidemiology of complex human diseases. She received her Ph.D. in 2002 on genetic epidemiology of type 1 diabetes.

Onkamo has published 15 original articles on various aspects of genetic epidemiology. She holds two patent applications. As a coauthor of a presentation on applying data mining methods to gene mapping, she received an award for the best presentation by a graduate student at the annual meeting of the International Genetic Epidemiology Society in 2000. Currently, she continues her work with application of various computer scientific methods to genetic problems in the group of Hannu Toivonen and Heikki Mannila.

Roderic Page is a professor of taxonomy at the University of Glasgow. A New Zealander, he did his undergraduate and Ph.D. studies at the University of Auckland. After postdoctoral research at the American Museum of Natural History, New York, and the Natural History Museum, London, Dr. Page took up a lectureship at the University of Oxford in 1993. Since 1995 he has been at the University of Glasgow. He cowrote the book *Molecular Evolution: A Phylogenetic Approach* and edited *Tangled Trees: Phylogeny, Cospeciation, and Coevolution*. He is currently the editor of *Systematic Biology*. Dr. Page has written several user-friendly programs for phylogenetic analysis, including TreeView and GeneTree. Current research interests include phylogenetic analysis, tree comparison, taxonomy, and databases.

Jignesh M. Patel is an assistant professor at the University of Michigan. He received a Ph.D. from the University of Wisconsin in 1998. As a graduate student, he led the efforts to develop the Paradise database system, a parallel object-relational database system, which is currently being commercialized at NCR Corp. After graduating from the University of Wisconsin, he joined NCR as a consultant and software engineer for the Paradise system. Since 1999, he has been a faculty member in the EECS department at the University of Michigan, where his research has focused on bioinformatics, spatial query processing, XML query processing, and interactions between DBMSs and processor architectures. He is the recipient of a 2001 NSF Career Award and IBM Faculty Awards in the years 2001 and 2003. He has served on a number of program committees including ACM SIGMOD and VLDB, and is currently associate editor for the systems and prototype section of *ACM SIGMOD Record*, and a vice chair of IEEE International Conference on Data Engineering, 2005.

Giuseppe Pigola received a B.S. degree in computer science from Catania University, Italy, in 2002. He is currently a Ph.D. student in the Department of Computer Science at Catania University. His research interests include computational geometry, data structure, approximate algorithms, bioinformatics, and networking.

Alfredo Pulvirenti received a B.S. degree in computer science from Catania University, Italy, in 1999 and a Ph.D. in computer science from Catania University in 2003. He currently has a postdoctoral position in the Department of Computer Science at Catania University. His research interests include bioinformatics, data structure, approximate algorithms, structured databases, information retrieval, graph theory, and networking.

Michele Purrello obtained his M.D. degree at the University of Catania (Italy) in November 1976 and his Ph.D. at the University of Bari (Italy) in June 1987. In October 1986 he obtained a Specialty Degree in medical genetics. He was a research associate scientist in the Department of Cell and Molecular Biology, Memorial Sloan-Kettering Cancer Center, New York, from December 1980 to June 1987. He is currently a professor of cell biology and molecular genetics at the School of Medicine of the University of Catania and director of the Specialty School in Human Genetics at the same University. He is the director of graduate studies in biology, human genetics and bioinformatics at the University of Catania. Together with Alfredo Ferro and Raffaele Giancarlo, he shares the directorship of the Lipari International School in BioMedicine and BioInformatics. His research interests include genomics, molecular oncogenesis, and bioinformatics.

Marco Ragusa obtained his B.S. degree in biology at the University of Catania in June 2002 with a thesis on bioinformatics, under the tutorship of Michele Purrello. He is now a Ph.D. student working in collaboration with Purrello and Dr. A. Ferro on many aspects of genomics and bioinformatics.

Marko Salmenkivi is a postdoctoral researcher in the Basic Research Unit of Helsinki Institute for Information Technology, a joint research unit of the University of Helsinki and Helsinki University of Technology. He received his Ph.D. in 2001. His research areas are data mining, computer-intensive data analysis, and bioinformatics.

Petteri Sevon received his M.Sc. degree in computer science at the University of Helsinki, Finland, in 2000. He is currently a Ph.D. student under Hannu Toivonen. His research interests include data mining and statistical genetics. He has three years of experience in practical genetic analyses with Juha Kere's research groups at the Finnish Genome Center, Helsinki, and Karolinska Institute, Huddinge, Sweden.

Sevon has published five refereed papers on methods for genetic analysis and their applications. He holds four patent applications.

Dennis Shasha is a professor of computer science at the Courant Institute of New York University where he does research on biological pattern discovery for microarrays, combinatorial design, network inference, database tuning, and algorithms and databases for time series. He spends most of his time these days working with biologists and physicists creating and implementing algorithms that may be useful.

Ambuj K. Singh is a professor in the Department of Computer Science at the University of California at Santa Barbara. He received his B.Tech. (Hons) in computer science and engineering from the Indian Institute of Technology, Kharagpur, in 1982, an M.S. in computer science from Iowa State University in 1984, and a Ph.D. in computer science from the University of Texas at Austin in 1989. His research interests are bioinformatics, distributed systems, and databases.

Hannu Toivonen is a professor of computer science at the University of Helsinki, Finland. He received his M.Sc. and Ph.D. degrees in computer science from the University of Helsinki in 1991 and 1996, respectively. Toivonen's research interests include data mining and computational methods for data analysis, with applications in genetics, ecology, and mobile communications. Prior to his current position, he worked for six years at Nokia Research Center.

Dr. Toivonen has published over 50 refereed papers on data mining and analysis and holds over 10 patent applications. He cowrote the Best Applied Research Award paper in KDD-98, and he is ranked among the 1000 most cited computer scientists by CiteSeer. He regularly serves on the program committees of all major data mining conferences. He was a program committee cochair for the ECML/PKDD conferences in 2002, and he is a founding cochair of the KDD workshop series Data Mining in Bioinformatics.

Jason T. L. Wang received a B.S. degree in mathematics from National Taiwan University, Taipei, Taiwan, and a Ph.D. degree in computer science from the Courant Institute of Mathematical Sciences, New York University, in 1991. He is currently a professor of computer science in the College of Computing Sciences at New Jersey Institute of Technology and director of the university's Data and Knowledge Engineering Laboratory. His research interests include data mining and databases, pattern recognition, bioinformatics, and Web information retrieval. He has published over 100 refereed papers and presented 3 SIGMOD software demos in these areas.

Dr. Wang is a coauthor of the book *Mining the World Wide Web: An Information Search Approach* (2001, Kluwer Academic), and an editor and author of two books, *Pattern Discovery in Biomolecular Data: Tools, Techniques and Applications* (1999, Oxford University Press) and *Computational Biology and Genome Informatics* (2003, World Scientific). He is on the editorial boards of four journals, has served on the program committees of 50 national and international conferences, is program cochair of the 2001 Atlantic Symposium on Computational Biology, Genome Information Systems and Technology, held at Duke University, program cochair of the 1998 IEEE International Joint Symposia on Intelligence and Systems held at Rockville, Maryland, and a founding chair of the ACM SIGKDD Workshop on Data Mining in Bioinformatics.

Jiong Yang earned his B.S. degree from the Electrical Engineering and Computer Science Department at the University of California at Berkeley in 1994. He received his M.S. and Ph.D. degrees from the Computer Science Department at the University of California at Los Angeles in 1996 and 1999, respectively. Dr. Yang is currently with the Computer Science Department at the University of Illinois at Urbana-Champaign as a visiting assistant professor. His current research interests include data mining, bioinformatics, and database systems. He is the author or coauthor of over 40 journal or conference publications. He has served on many program committees of international conferences and workshops. He is also the guest editor of the *IEEE Transaction on Knowledge and Data Engineering* special issue on mining biological data.

Mohammed J. Zaki is an associate professor of computer science at Rensselaer Polytechnic Institute. He received his Ph.D. degree in computer science from the University of Rochester in 1998. His research interests include the design of efficient, scalable, and parallel algorithms for various data mining techniques, and he is especially interested in developing novel data mining techniques for bioinformatics. He has written over 90 publications, has coedited eight books, and has served as guest editor for

Information Systems, *SIGKDD Explorations*, and *Distributed and Parallel Databases: An International Journal*. He is a founding cochair of the ACM SIGKDD Workshops on Data Mining in Bioinformatics (BIOKDD) and has cochaired several workshops on high-performance data mining. He is currently an associate editor for *IEEE Transactions on Knowledge and Data Engineering*. He received the NSF CAREER Award in 2001 and the DOE Early Career Principal Investigator Award in 2002. He also received an ACM Recognition of Service Award in 2003.

Kaizhong Zhang   received an M.S. degree in mathematics from Peking University, Beijing, People's Republic of China, in 1981, and the M.S. and Ph.D. degrees in computer science from the Courant Institute of Mathematical Sciences, New York University, in 1986 and 1989, respectively. He is a professor in the Department of Computer Science, University of Western Ontario, London, Ontario, Canada. His research interests include computational biology, pattern recognition, image processing, and sequential and parallel algorithms.

Index